# W Juliet

## Volume 10

Story & Art by Emura

# W Juliet
## Volume 10

## Story and Art by Emura

Translation & English Adaptation/Naomi Kokubo & Jeff Carlson
Touch-up Art & Lettering/Krysta Lau, Jmaginary Friends Studios
Graphic Design/Hidemi Sahara
Editor/Carrie Shepherd

Managing Editor/Annette Roman
Director of Production/Noboru Watanabe
Vice President of Publishing/Alvin Lu
Sr. Director of Acquisitions/Rika Jnouye
Vice President of Sales & Marketing/Liza Coppola
Publisher/Hyoe Narita

W Juliet by Emura © Emura 2001. All rights reserved.
First published in Japan in 2002 by HAKUSENSHA, Inc., Tokyo. English language translation
rights in America and Canada arranged with HAKUSENSHA, Inc., Tokyo.
The W JULIET logo is a trademark of VIZ Media, LLC.
The stories, characters and incidents mentioned in this publication are entirely fictional.

Printed in the U.S.A.

Published by VIZ Media, LLC
P.O. Box 77010
San Francisco, CA 94107

10 9 8 7 6 5 4 3 2 1
First printing, May 2006

www.viz.com
store.viz.com

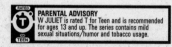

**PARENTAL ADVISORY**
W JULIET is rated T for Teen and is recommended
for ages 13 and up. The series contains mild
sexual situations/humor and tobacco usage.

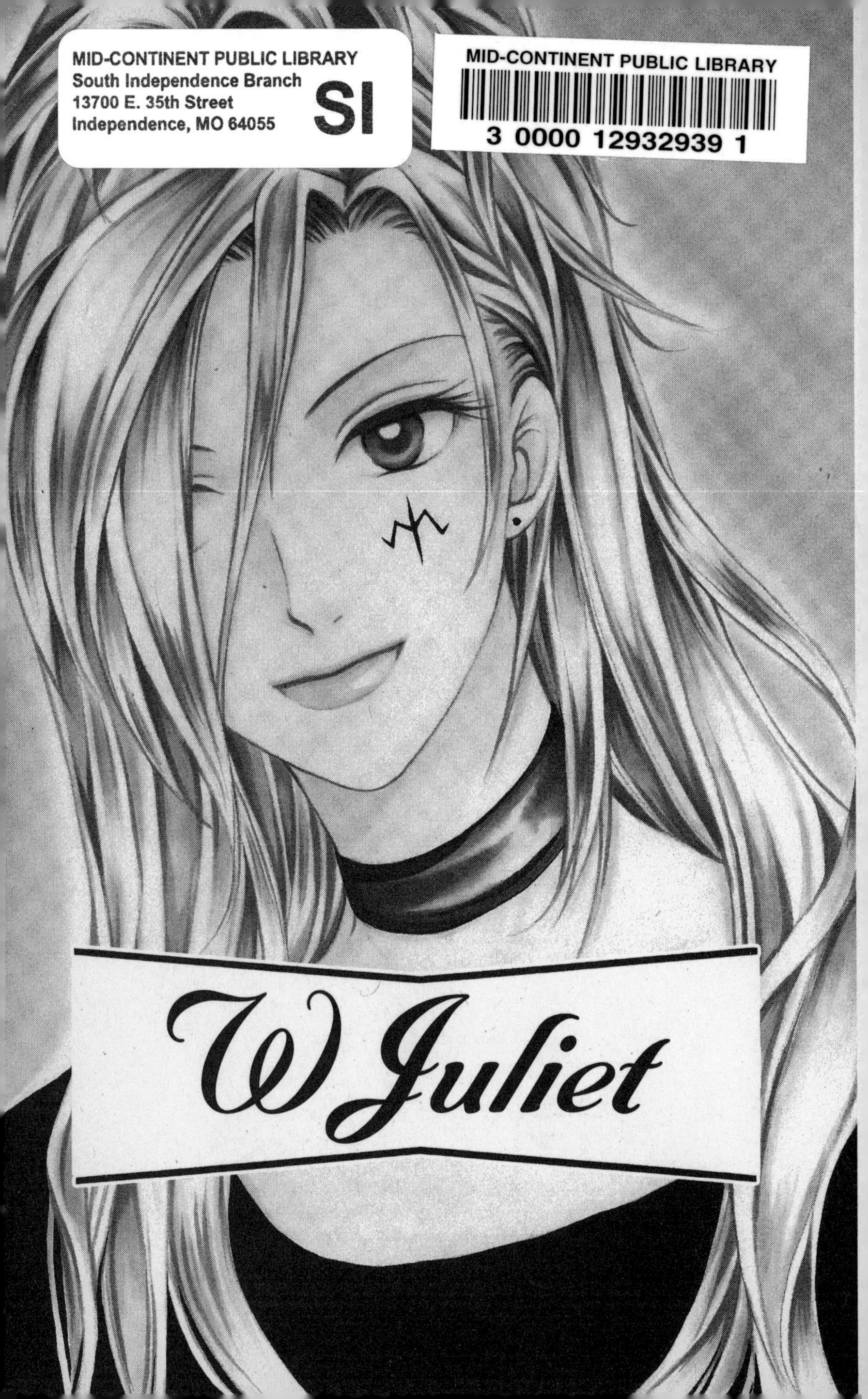
W Juliet

2001 Hana to Yume
No. 15 →
draft cover art
(B4 size)

2001. 5.28

2002 Hana to Yume
No. 1 gift calendar draft
for May (B4 size)
↓

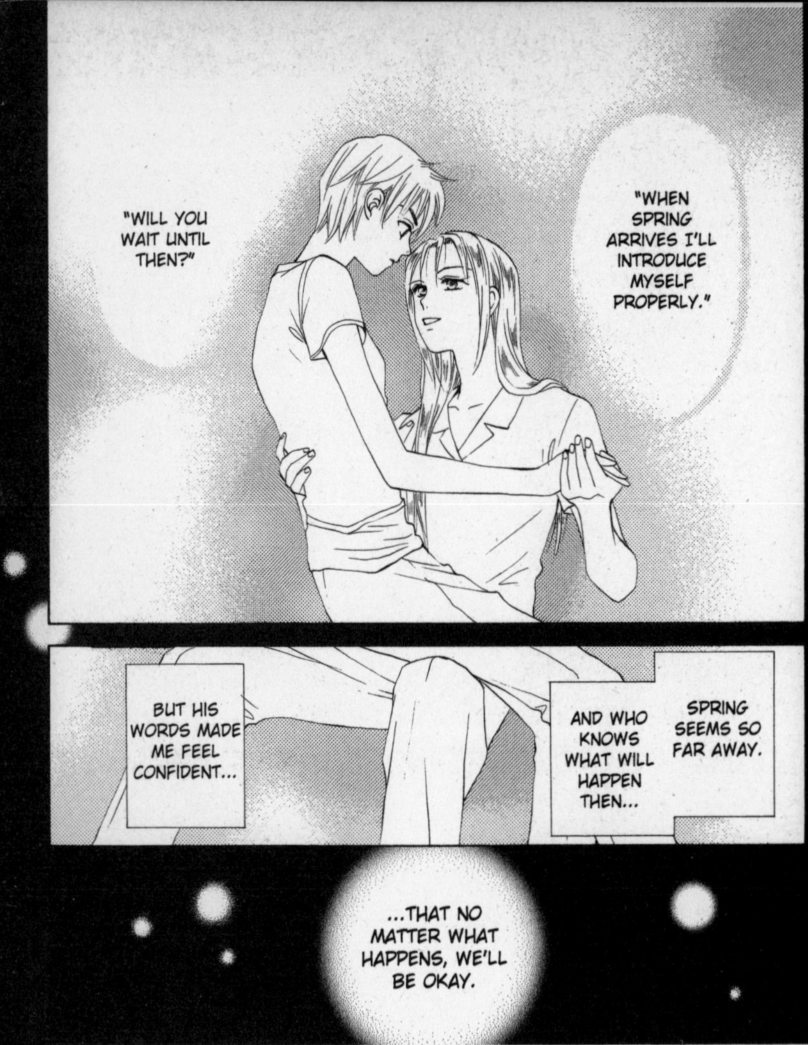
"WHEN SPRING ARRIVES I'LL INTRODUCE MYSELF PROPERLY."
"WILL YOU WAIT UNTIL THEN?"
SPRING SEEMS SO FAR AWAY.
AND WHO KNOWS WHAT WILL HAPPEN THEN...
BUT HIS WORDS MADE ME FEEL CONFIDENT...
...THAT NO MATTER WHAT HAPPENS, WE'LL BE OKAY.

—Behind the Scenes Story ①—

The school dormitory that appears in this story is where I actually lived when I was in high school. I mean, I modeled it after it. ♥ It was so run-down ♪♪ But I guess it doesn't look that way in the picture. When we lived in the dormitory, there were many girls who were homesick—but for me, the place was a paradise. ♥ My parents were a bit too strict, you see. (Laugh) I suppose my personality was adjusted there. (So what was I like before then..?) From what I hear, the dormitory is built the same way as reform schools. ♪ My old high school no longer lets students live in a dormitory, and iron lattices are placed on all the first floor windows now—turning it into a scary building. (Laugh) Apparently, it gets vandalized otherwise. ♪

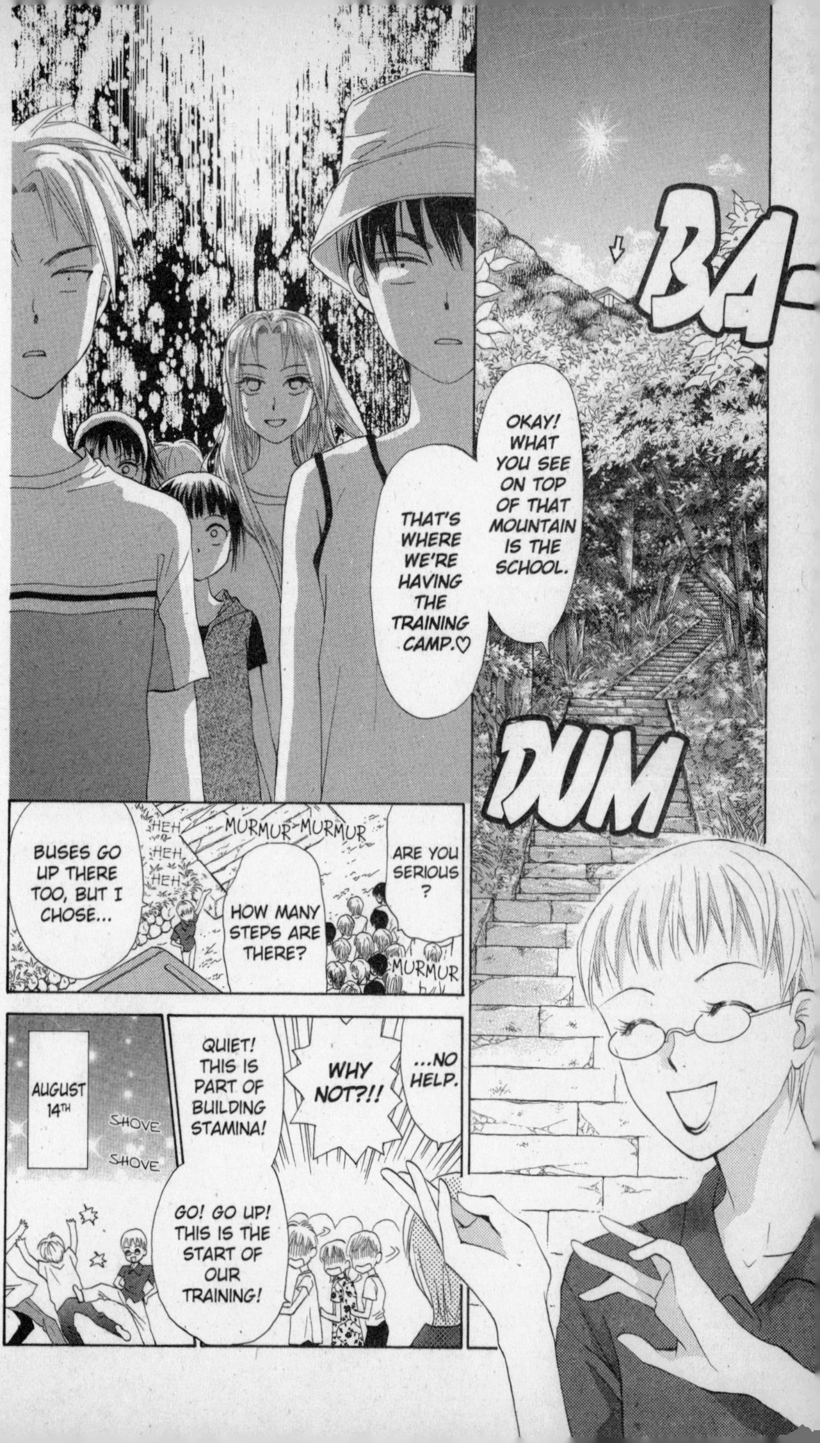
BA-
DUM
OKAY! WHAT YOU SEE ON TOP OF THAT MOUNTAIN IS THE SCHOOL.
THAT'S WHERE WE'RE HAVING THE TRAINING CAMP.♡
ARE YOU SERIOUS?
MURMUR MURMUR
HOW MANY STEPS ARE THERE?
MURMUR
HEH HEH HEH
BUSES GO UP THERE TOO, BUT I CHOSE...
...NO HELP.
WHY NOT?!!
QUIET! THIS IS PART OF BUILDING STAMINA!
GO! GO UP! THIS IS THE START OF OUR TRAINING!
SHOVE
SHOVE
AUGUST 14TH

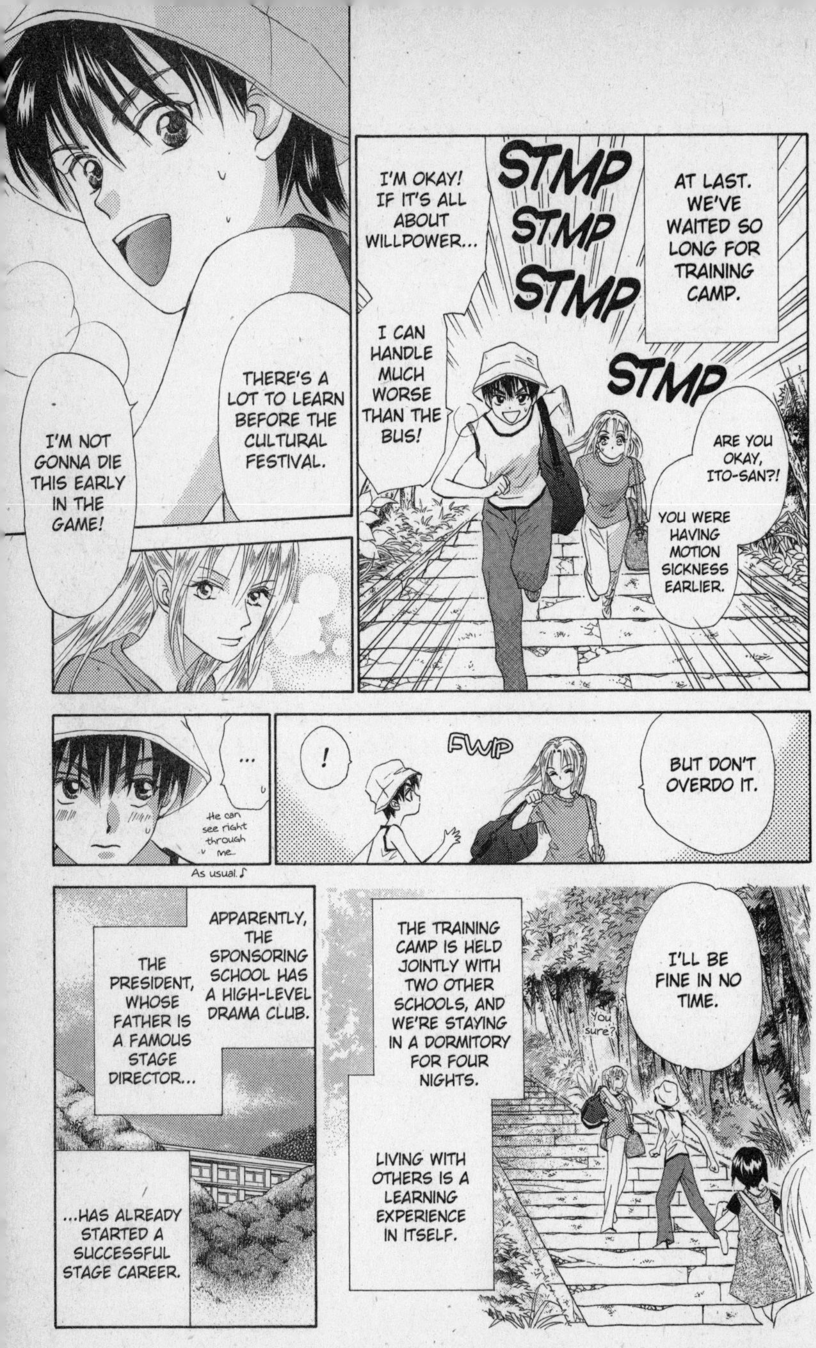
AT LAST. WE'VE WAITED SO LONG FOR TRAINING CAMP.
STMP STMP STMP
STMP
ARE YOU OKAY, ITO-SAN?!
YOU WERE HAVING MOTION SICKNESS EARLIER.
I'M OKAY! IF IT'S ALL ABOUT WILLPOWER...
I CAN HANDLE MUCH WORSE THAN THE BUS!
THERE'S A LOT TO LEARN BEFORE THE CULTURAL FESTIVAL.
I'M NOT GONNA DIE THIS EARLY IN THE GAME!
BUT DON'T OVERDO IT.
FWIP
!
...
He can see right through me.
As usual.♪
I'LL BE FINE IN NO TIME.
You sure?
THE TRAINING CAMP IS HELD JOINTLY WITH TWO OTHER SCHOOLS, AND WE'RE STAYING IN A DORMITORY FOR FOUR NIGHTS.
LIVING WITH OTHERS IS A LEARNING EXPERIENCE IN ITSELF.
APPARENTLY, THE SPONSORING SCHOOL HAS A HIGH-LEVEL DRAMA CLUB.
THE PRESIDENT, WHOSE FATHER IS A FAMOUS STAGE DIRECTOR...
...HAS ALREADY STARTED A SUCCESSFUL STAGE CAREER.

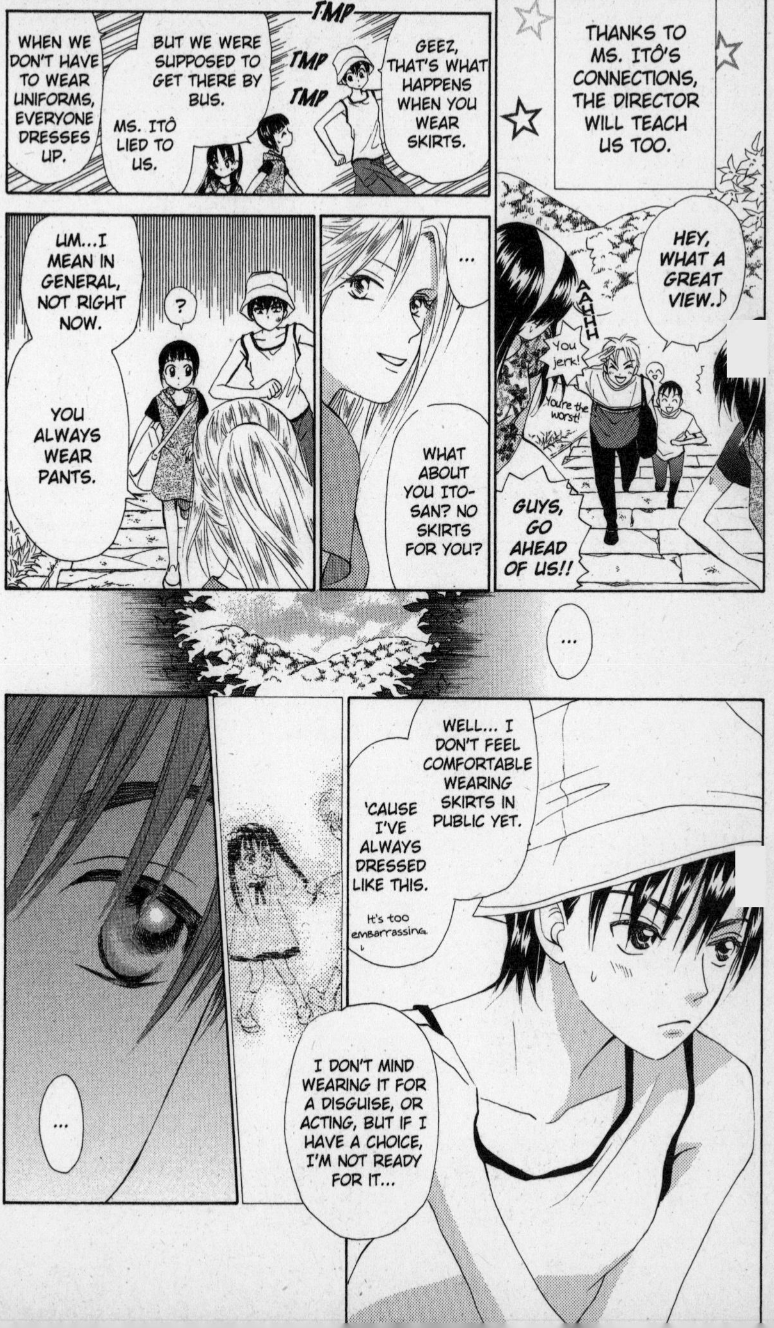
THANKS TO MS. ITÔ'S CONNECTIONS, THE DIRECTOR WILL TEACH US TOO.
HEY, WHAT A GREAT VIEW.♪
AAHHH
You jerk!
You're the worst!
GUYS, GO AHEAD OF US!!
TMP
TMP
TMP
GEEZ, THAT'S WHAT HAPPENS WHEN YOU WEAR SKIRTS.
BUT WE WERE SUPPOSED TO GET THERE BY BUS.
MS. ITÔ LIED TO US.
WHEN WE DON'T HAVE TO WEAR UNIFORMS, EVERYONE DRESSES UP.
...
WHAT ABOUT YOU ITO-SAN? NO SKIRTS FOR YOU?
?
UM...I MEAN IN GENERAL, NOT RIGHT NOW.
YOU ALWAYS WEAR PANTS.
...
WELL... I DON'T FEEL COMFORTABLE WEARING SKIRTS IN PUBLIC YET.
'CAUSE I'VE ALWAYS DRESSED LIKE THIS.
It's too embarrassing.
I DON'T MIND WEARING IT FOR A DISGUISE, OR ACTING, BUT IF I HAVE A CHOICE, I'M NOT READY FOR IT...
...

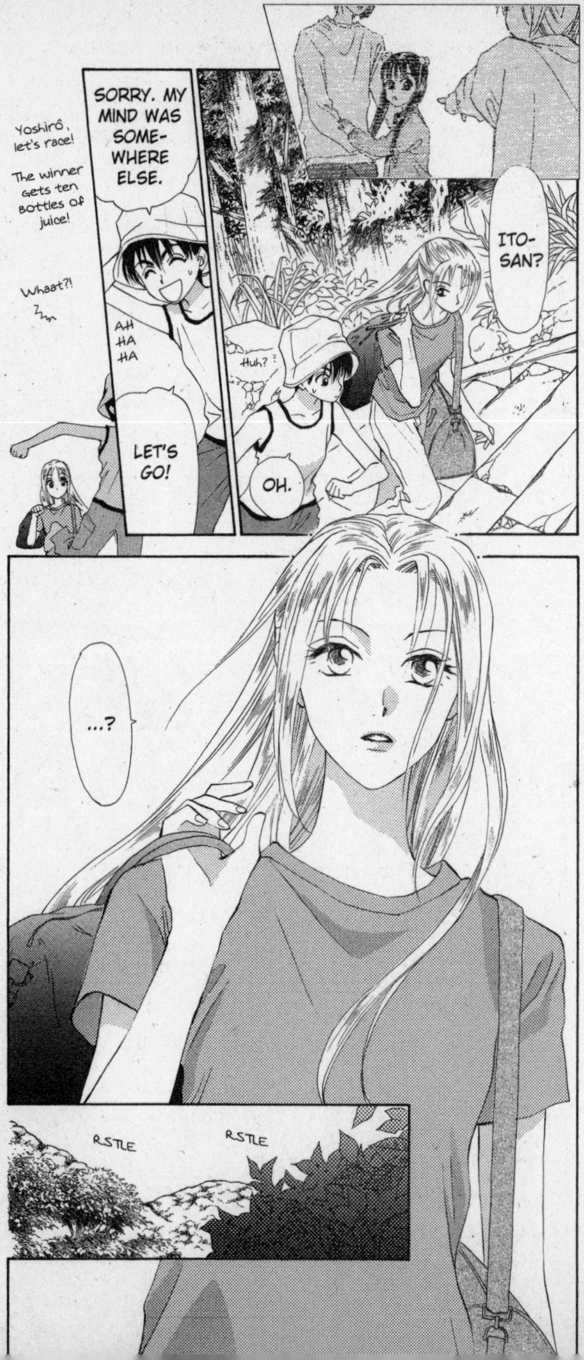
ITO-SAN?
Huh?
OH.
SORRY. MY MIND WAS SOMEWHERE ELSE.
AH HA HA
LET'S GO!
Yoshirô, let's race!
The winner gets ten bottles of juice!
Whaat?!
...?
RSTLE
RSTLE

## GREETINGS

Hello. This is Emura. It's volume 10 at last! I made it to double-digits. ♪ But my "Nana-iro no Shinwa" (Rainbow Myth) became the tenth comic for me to commemorate. This volume 10 turned out to be my 11th comic. (Laugh)

I'd be delighted if you'd check out "Nana-iro no Shinwa" (Rainbow Myth) too. ♥ You'll find Tatsuyoshi, Misaki, Nobuko, and Yoshirô in there, playing different roles. ♪

Okay, as promised in the previous volume, I'd like to write about my sister.

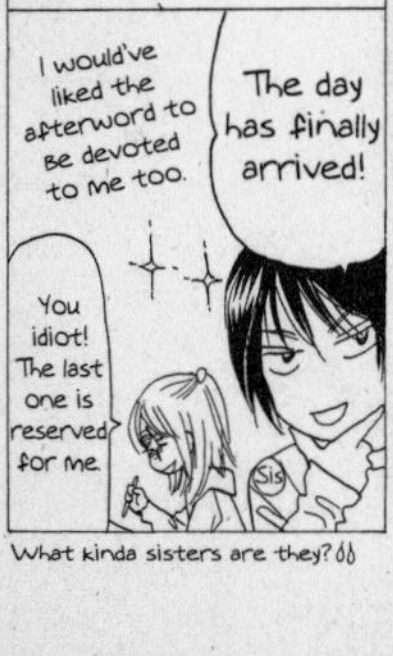
The day has finally arrived!
I would've liked the afterword to be devoted to me too.
You idiot! The last one is reserved for me.
Sis

What kinda sisters are they?

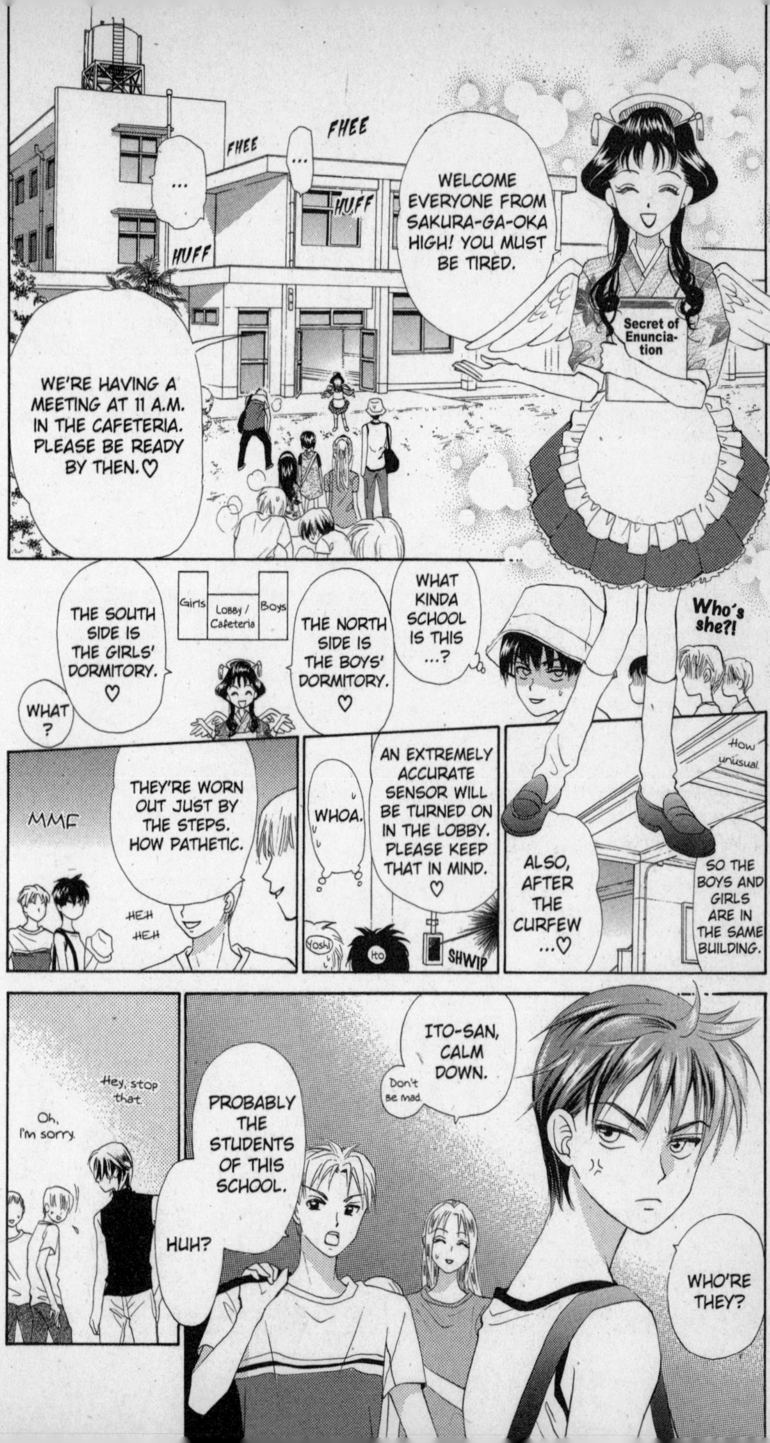
WELCOME EVERYONE FROM SAKURA-GA-OKA HIGH! YOU MUST BE TIRED.
Secret of Enunciation
FHEE
...
HUFF
FHEE
...
HUFF
WE'RE HAVING A MEETING AT 11 A.M. IN THE CAFETERIA. PLEASE BE READY BY THEN. ♡
...
Who's she?!
WHAT KINDA SCHOOL IS THIS ...?
THE NORTH SIDE IS THE BOYS' DORMITORY. ♡
Boys
Lobby / Cafeteria
Girls
THE SOUTH SIDE IS THE GIRLS' DORMITORY. ♡
WHAT ?
How unusual.
SO THE BOYS AND GIRLS ARE IN THE SAME BUILDING.
ALSO, AFTER THE CURFEW ...♡
AN EXTREMELY ACCURATE SENSOR WILL BE TURNED ON IN THE LOBBY. PLEASE KEEP THAT IN MIND. ♡
WHOA.
SHWIP
Ito
Yoshi
THEY'RE WORN OUT JUST BY THE STEPS. HOW PATHETIC.
MMF
HEH HEH
ITO-SAN, CALM DOWN.
Don't be mad.
WHO'RE THEY?
PROBABLY THE STUDENTS OF THIS SCHOOL.
HUH?
Hey, stop that.
Oh, I'm sorry.

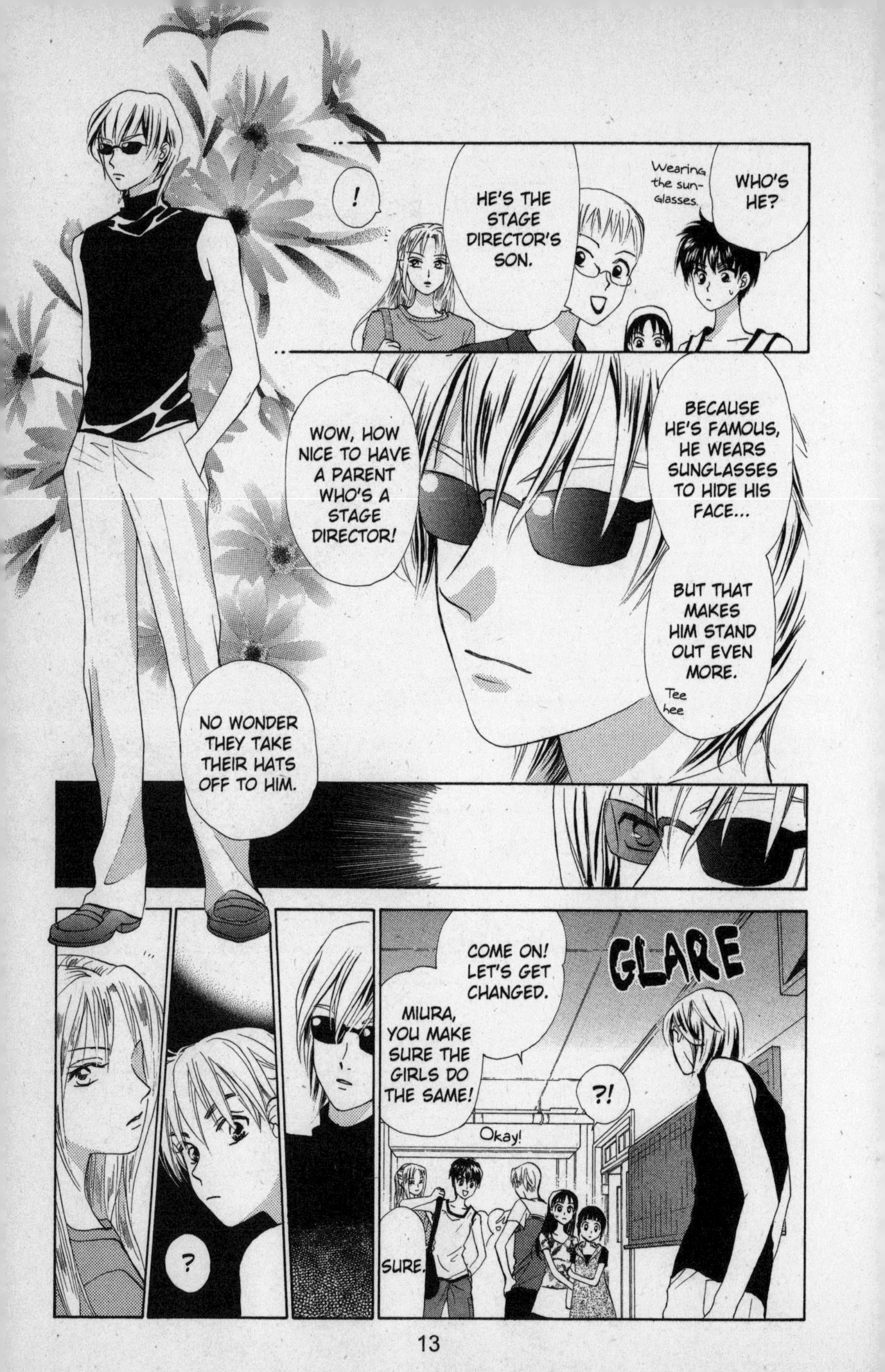
WHO'S HE?
Wearing the sun-glasses.
HE'S THE STAGE DIRECTOR'S SON.
!
BECAUSE HE'S FAMOUS, HE WEARS SUNGLASSES TO HIDE HIS FACE...
BUT THAT MAKES HIM STAND OUT EVEN MORE.
Tee hee
WOW, HOW NICE TO HAVE A PARENT WHO'S A STAGE DIRECTOR!
NO WONDER THEY TAKE THEIR HATS OFF TO HIM.
GLARE
COME ON! LET'S GET CHANGED.
MIURA, YOU MAKE SURE THE GIRLS DO THE SAME!
?!
Okay!
SURE.
?

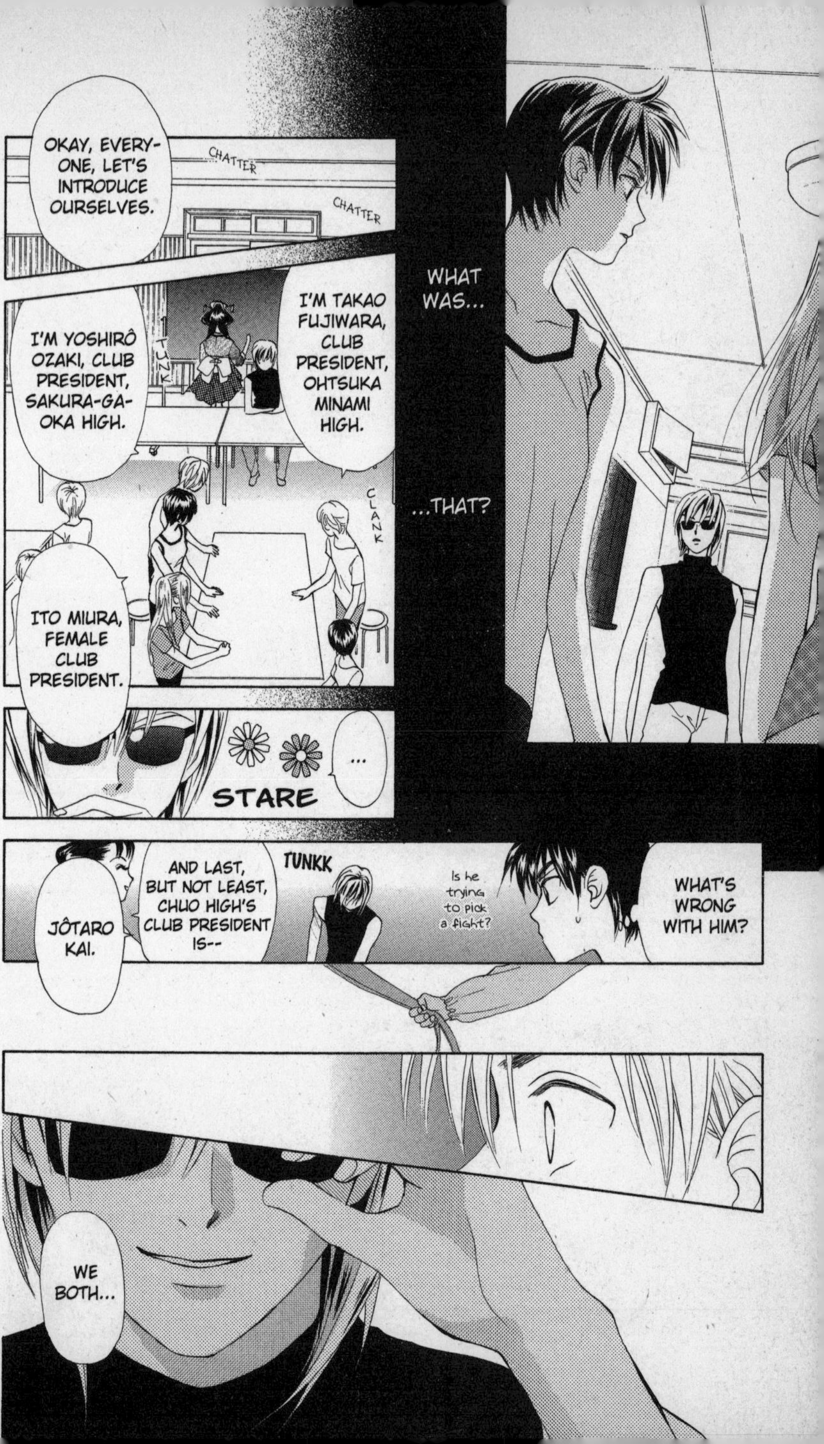
WHAT WAS...
...THAT?
OKAY, EVERYONE, LET'S INTRODUCE OURSELVES.
CHATTER
CHATTER
I'M TAKAO FUJIWARA, CLUB PRESIDENT, OHTSUKA MINAMI HIGH.
TUNK
I'M YOSHIRÔ OZAKI, CLUB PRESIDENT, SAKURA-GA-OKA HIGH.
CLANK
ITO MIURA, FEMALE CLUB PRESIDENT.
...
STARE
WHAT'S WRONG WITH HIM?
Is he trying to pick a fight?
TUNKK
AND LAST, BUT NOT LEAST, CHUO HIGH'S CLUB PRESIDENT IS--
JÔTARO KAI.
WE BOTH...

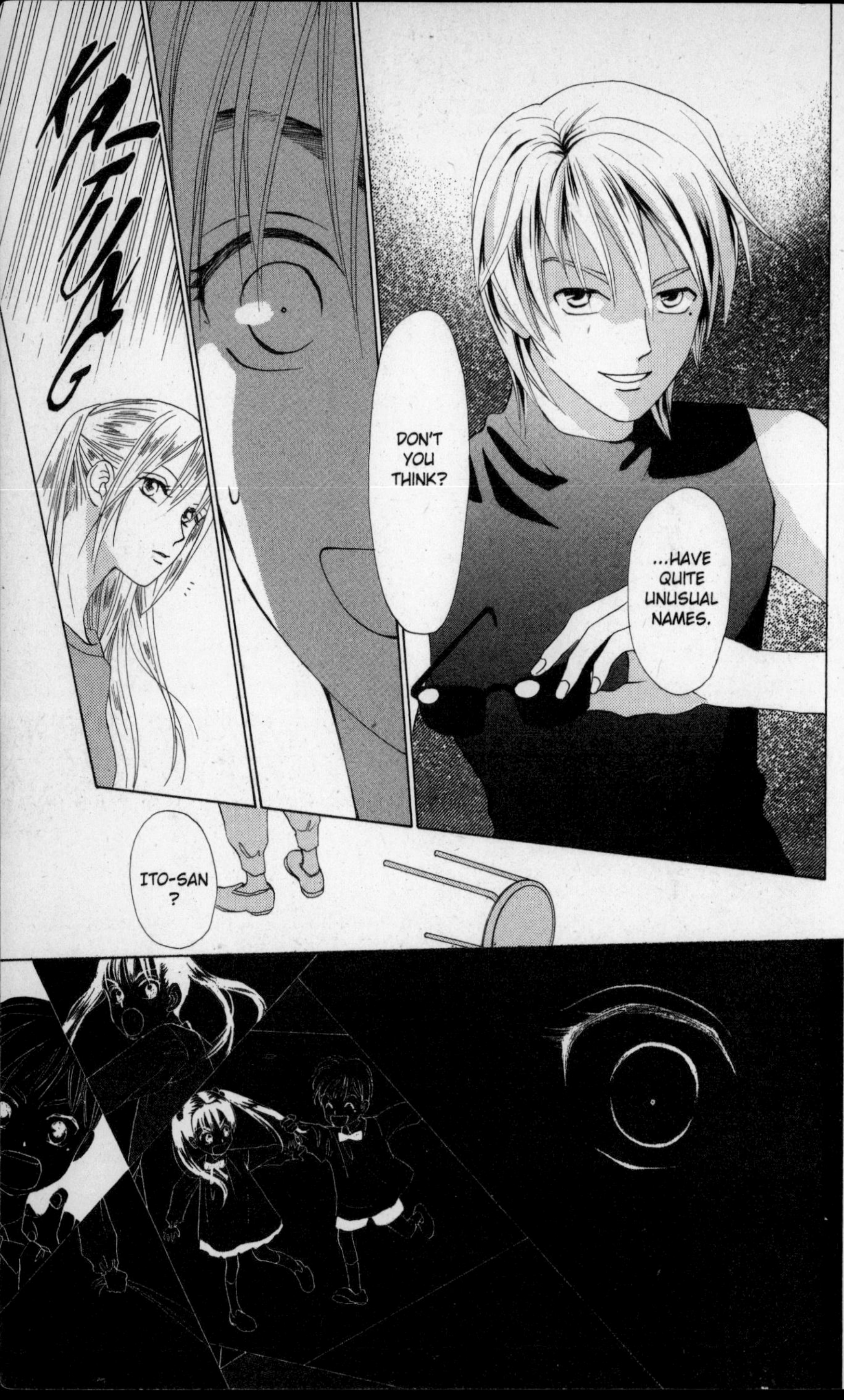
...HAVE QUITE UNUSUAL NAMES.
DON'T YOU THINK?
KA-TUNG
ITO-SAN ?

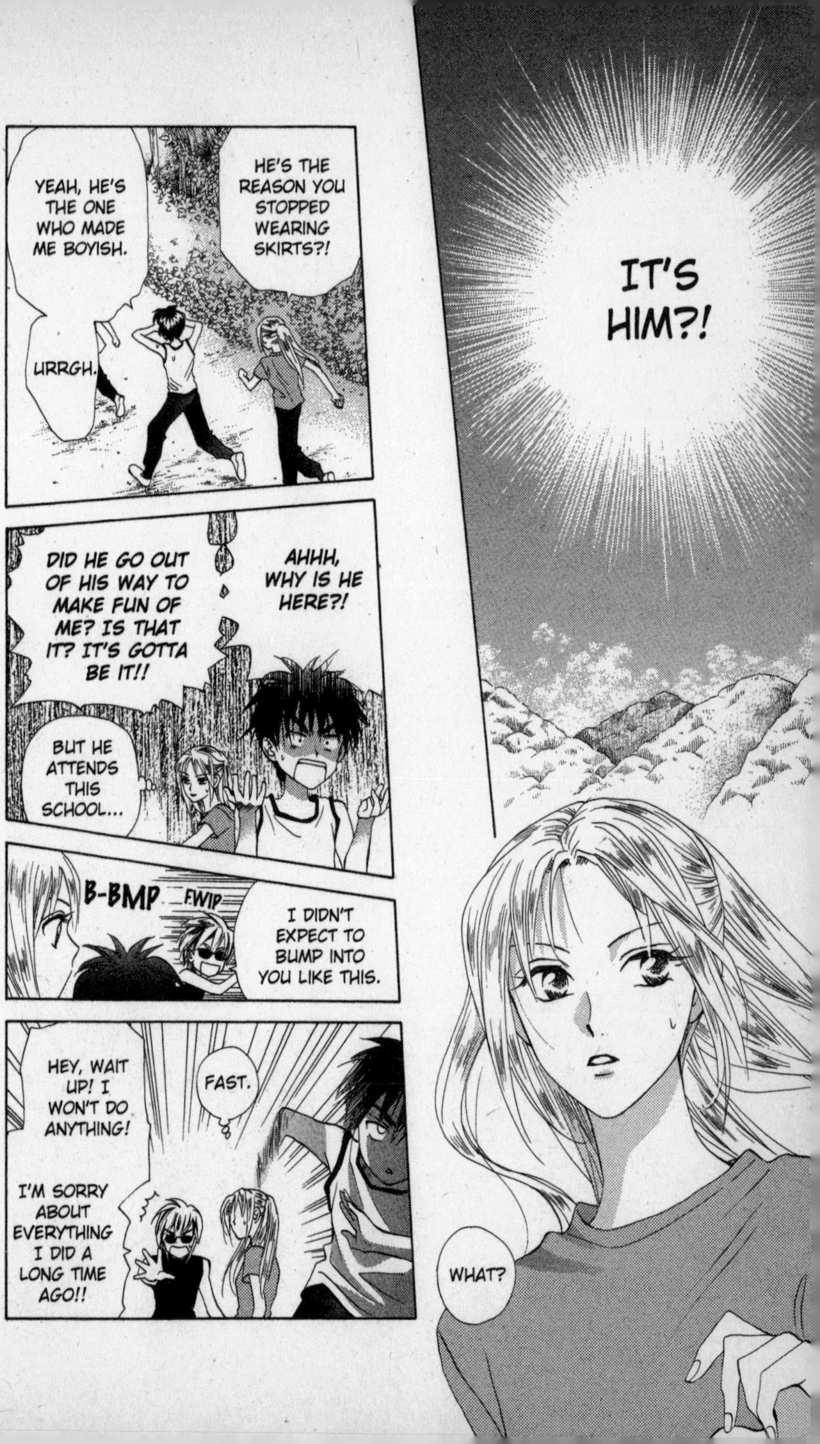
IT'S HIM?!
WHAT?
HE'S THE REASON YOU STOPPED WEARING SKIRTS?!
YEAH, HE'S THE ONE WHO MADE ME BOYISH.
URRGH.
AHHH, WHY IS HE HERE?!
DID HE GO OUT OF HIS WAY TO MAKE FUN OF ME? IS THAT IT? IT'S GOTTA BE IT!!
BUT HE ATTENDS THIS SCHOOL...
I DIDN'T EXPECT TO BUMP INTO YOU LIKE THIS.
FWIP
B-BMP
FAST.
HEY, WAIT UP! I WON'T DO ANYTHING!
I'M SORRY ABOUT EVERYTHING I DID A LONG TIME AGO!!

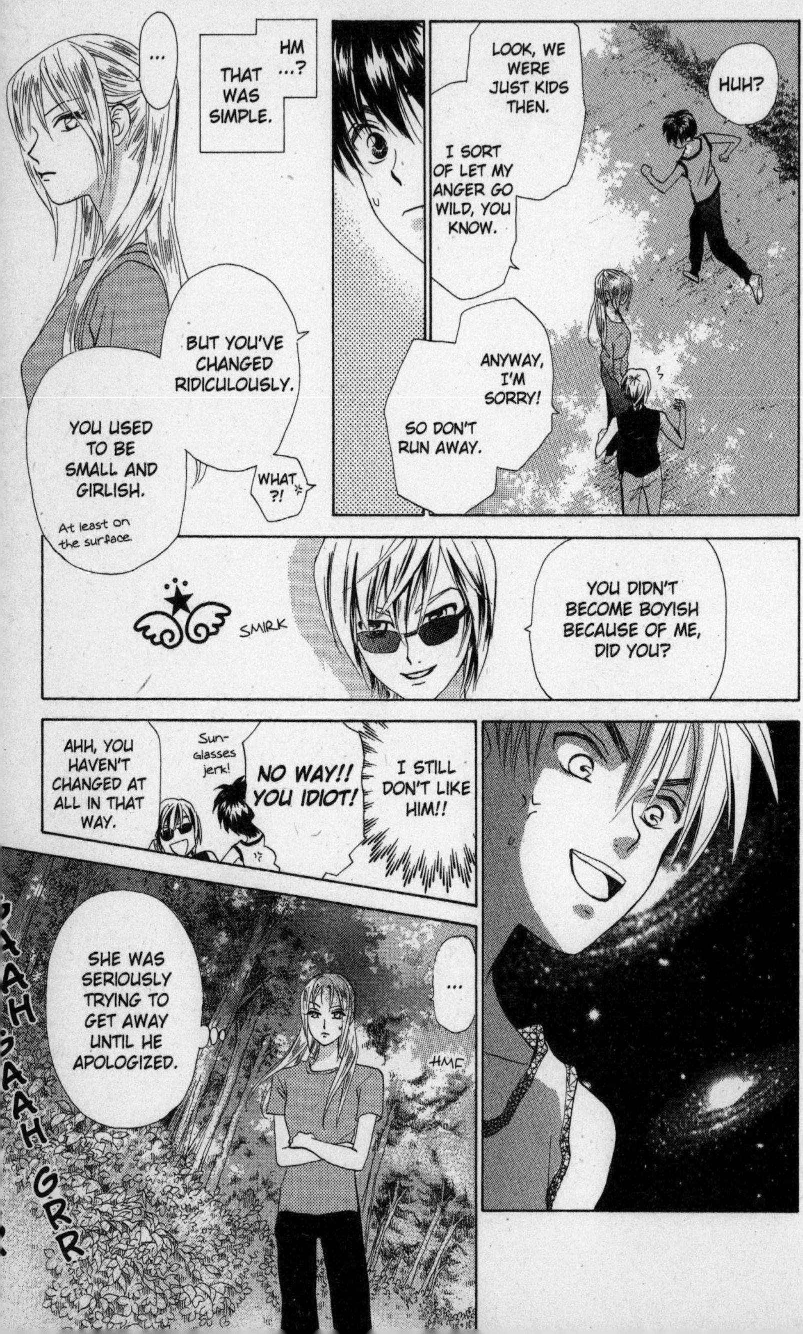
HUH?
LOOK, WE WERE JUST KIDS THEN.
I SORT OF LET MY ANGER GO WILD, YOU KNOW.
ANYWAY, I'M SORRY!
SO DON'T RUN AWAY.
HM ...?
THAT WAS SIMPLE.
...
BUT YOU'VE CHANGED RIDICULOUSLY.
WHAT ?!
YOU USED TO BE SMALL AND GIRLISH.
At least on the surface
YOU DIDN'T BECOME BOYISH BECAUSE OF ME, DID YOU?
SMIRK
I STILL DON'T LIKE HIM!!
NO WAY!! YOU IDIOT!
Sun-Glasses jerk!
AHH, YOU HAVEN'T CHANGED AT ALL IN THAT WAY.
...
SHE WAS SERIOUSLY TRYING TO GET AWAY UNTIL HE APOLOGIZED.
HMF
GRR

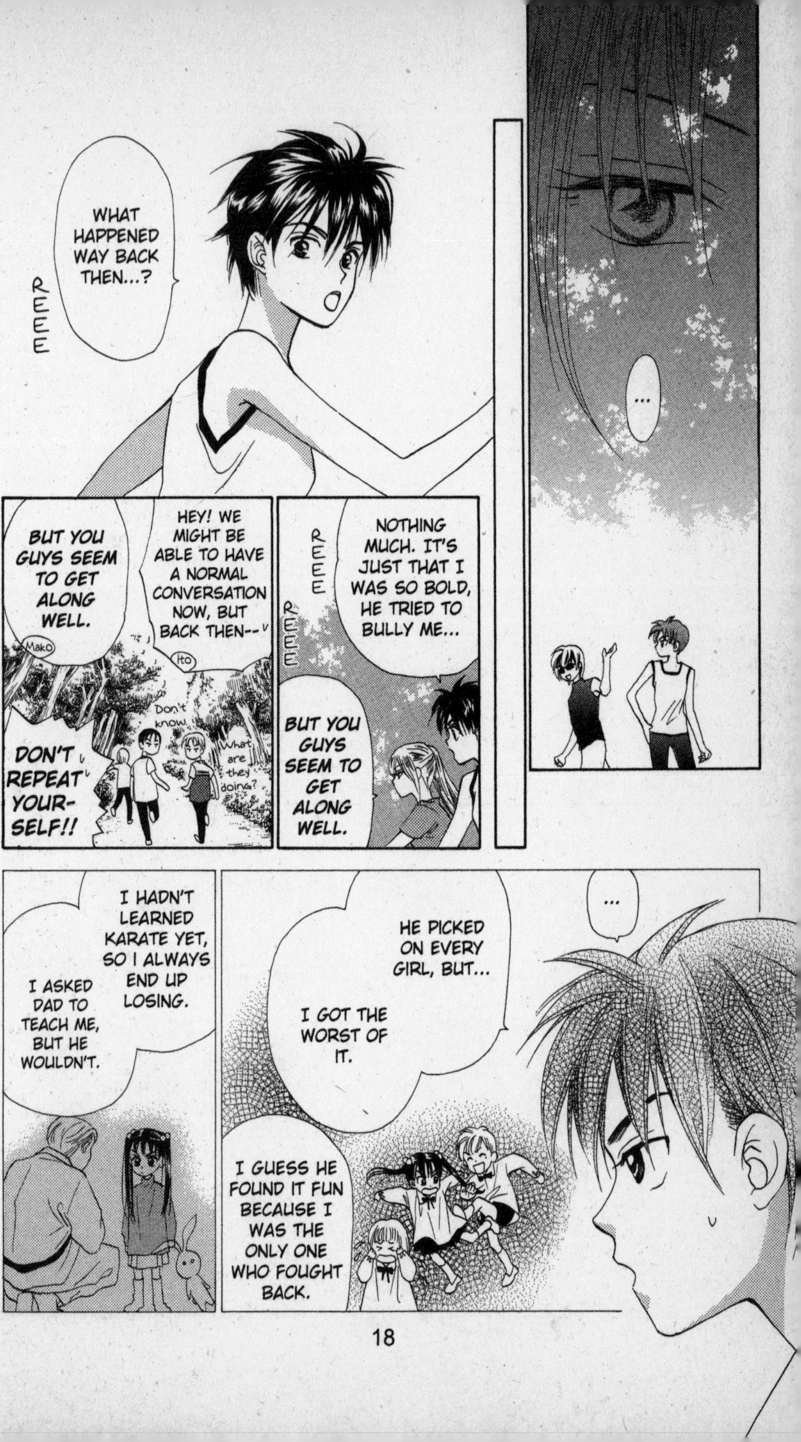
...
WHAT HAPPENED WAY BACK THEN...?
REEE
REEE
NOTHING MUCH. IT'S JUST THAT I WAS SO BOLD, HE TRIED TO BULLY ME...
REEE
BUT YOU GUYS SEEM TO GET ALONG WELL.
HEY! WE MIGHT BE ABLE TO HAVE A NORMAL CONVERSATION NOW, BUT BACK THEN--
BUT YOU GUYS SEEM TO GET ALONG WELL.
Ito
Mako
What are they doing?
Don't know.
DON'T REPEAT YOURSELF!!
...
HE PICKED ON EVERY GIRL, BUT...
I GOT THE WORST OF IT.
I GUESS HE FOUND IT FUN BECAUSE I WAS THE ONLY ONE WHO FOUGHT BACK.
I HADN'T LEARNED KARATE YET, SO I ALWAYS END UP LOSING.
I ASKED DAD TO TEACH ME, BUT HE WOULDN'T.

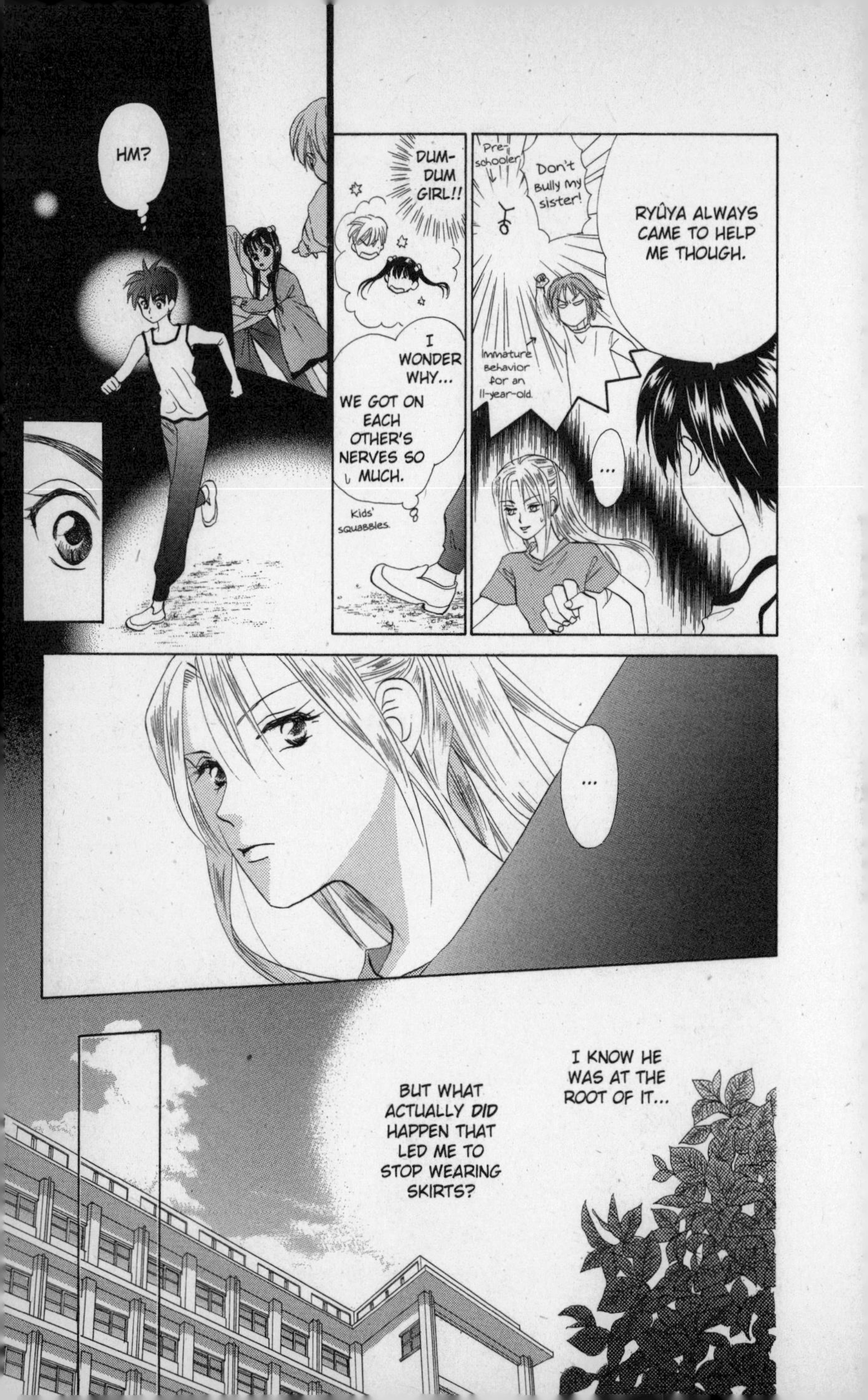
RYÛYA ALWAYS CAME TO HELP ME THOUGH.
Don't bully my sister!
Pre-schooler
Immature behavior for an 11-year-old.
...
DUM-DUM GIRL!!
I WONDER WHY...
WE GOT ON EACH OTHER'S NERVES SO MUCH.
Kids' squabbles.
HM?
...
I KNOW HE WAS AT THE ROOT OF IT...
BUT WHAT ACTUALLY *DID* HAPPEN THAT LED ME TO STOP WEARING SKIRTS?

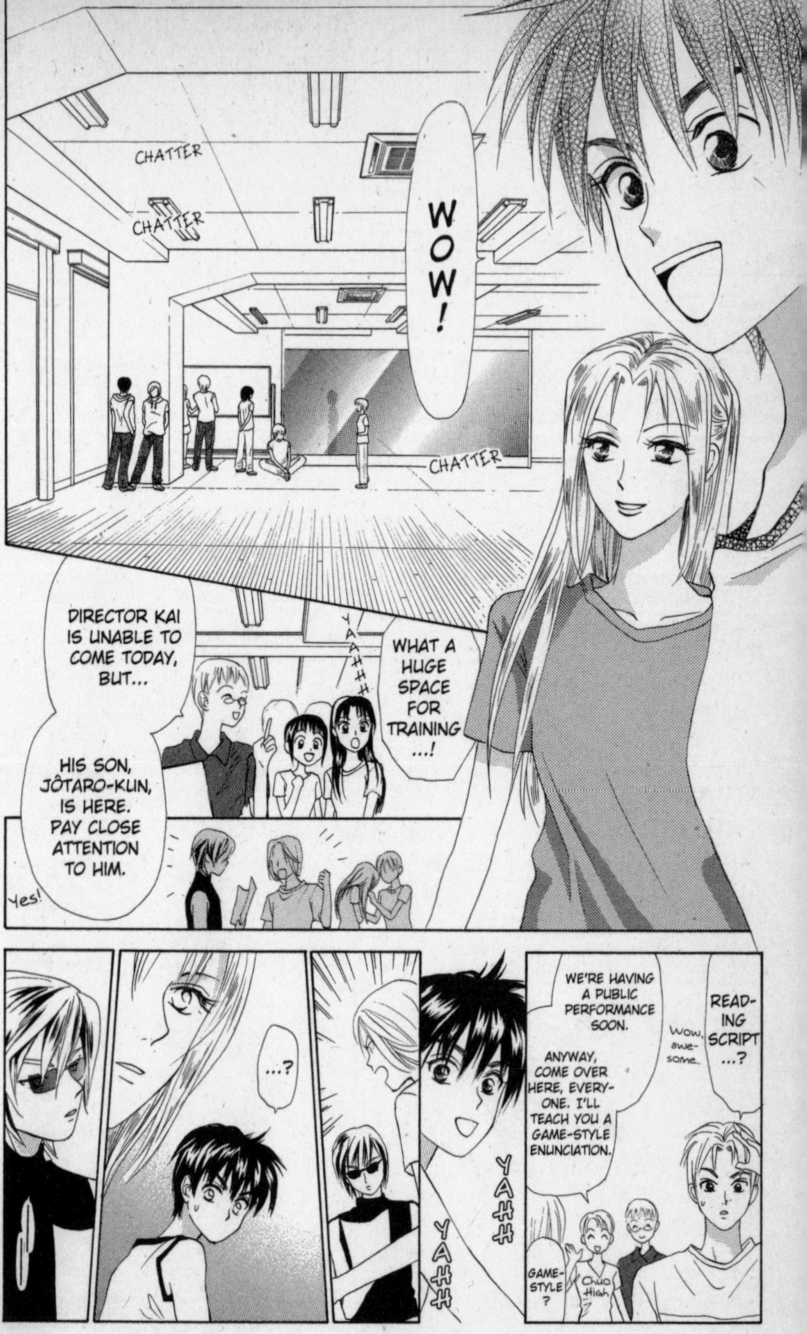
WOW!
CHATTER
CHATTER
CHATTER
WHAT A HUGE SPACE FOR TRAINING ...!
YAAHHH
DIRECTOR KAI IS UNABLE TO COME TODAY, BUT...
HIS SON, JÔTARO-KUN, IS HERE. PAY CLOSE ATTENTION TO HIM.
Yes!
READING SCRIPT ...?
Wow, awesome
WE'RE HAVING A PUBLIC PERFORMANCE SOON.
ANYWAY, COME OVER HERE, EVERYONE. I'LL TEACH YOU A GAME-STYLE ENUNCIATION.
YAHH
Chuo High
GAME-STYLE ?
YAHH
...?

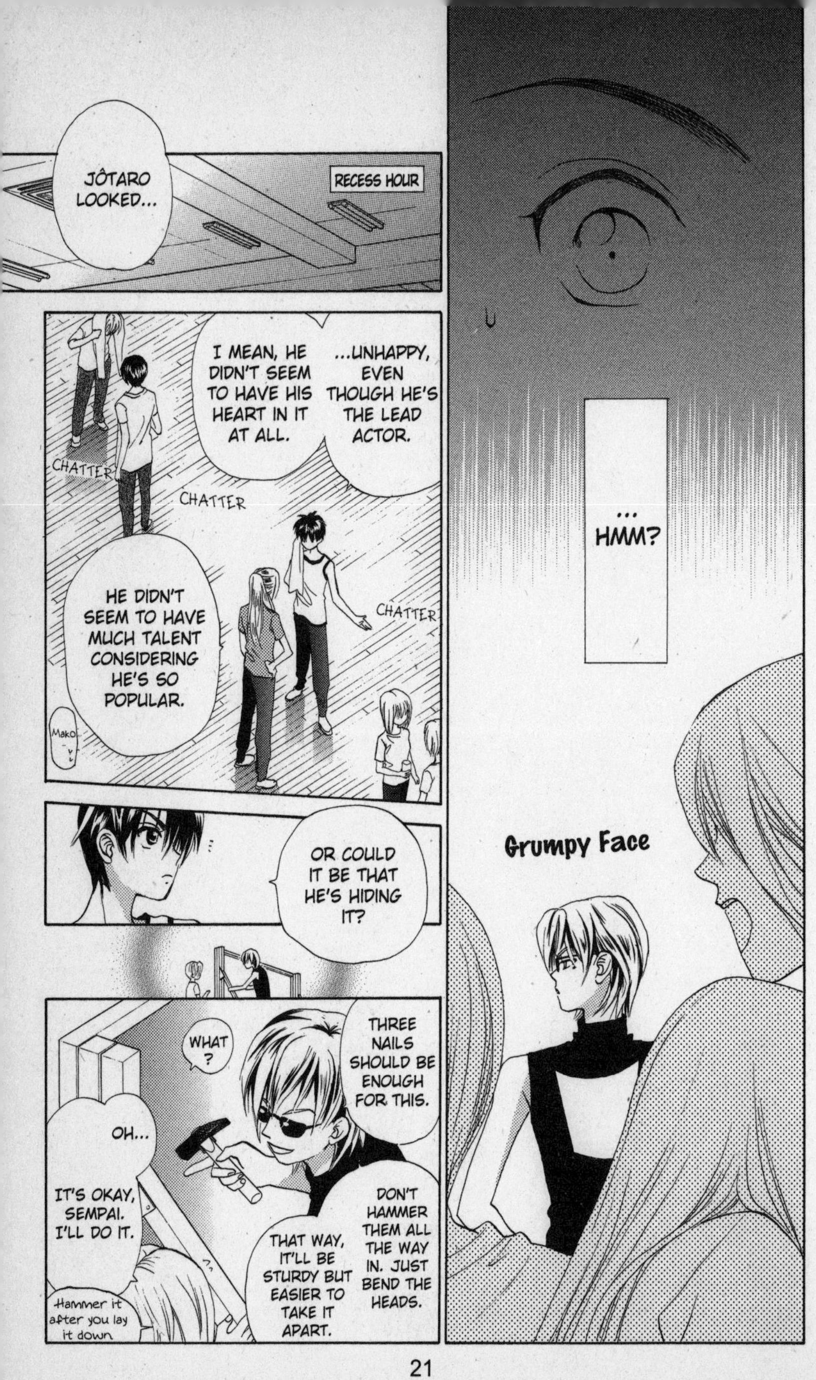
...
HMM?
Grumpy Face
JÔTARO LOOKED...
RECESS HOUR
...UNHAPPY, EVEN THOUGH HE'S THE LEAD ACTOR.
I MEAN, HE DIDN'T SEEM TO HAVE HIS HEART IN IT AT ALL.
CHATTER
CHATTER
CHATTER
HE DIDN'T SEEM TO HAVE MUCH TALENT CONSIDERING HE'S SO POPULAR.
OR COULD IT BE THAT HE'S HIDING IT?
THREE NAILS SHOULD BE ENOUGH FOR THIS.
WHAT?
OH...
DON'T HAMMER THEM ALL THE WAY IN. JUST BEND THE HEADS.
THAT WAY, IT'LL BE STURDY BUT EASIER TO TAKE IT APART.
IT'S OKAY, SEMPAI. I'LL DO IT.
Hammer it after you lay it down

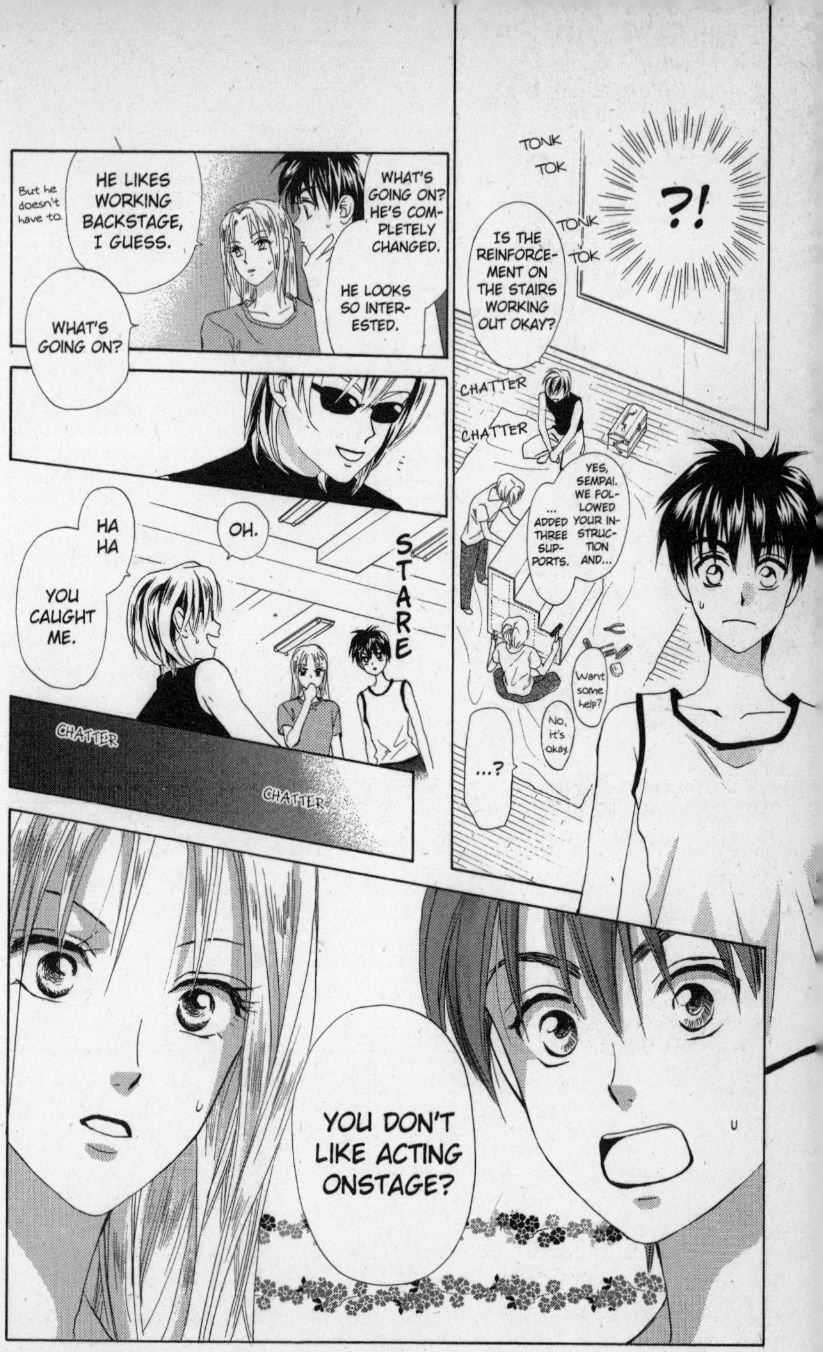
TONK
TOK
?!
IS THE REINFORCEMENT ON THE STAIRS WORKING OUT OKAY?
TONK
TOK
CHATTER
CHATTER
YES, SEMPAI. WE FOLLOWED YOUR INSTRUCTION AND...
... ADDED THREE SUPPORTS.
Want some help?
No, it's okay.
...?
WHAT'S GOING ON? HE'S COMPLETELY CHANGED.
HE LOOKS SO INTERESTED.
HE LIKES WORKING BACKSTAGE, I GUESS.
But he doesn't have to.
WHAT'S GOING ON?
OH.
STARE
HA HA
YOU CAUGHT ME.
CHATTER
CHATTER
YOU DON'T LIKE ACTING ONSTAGE?

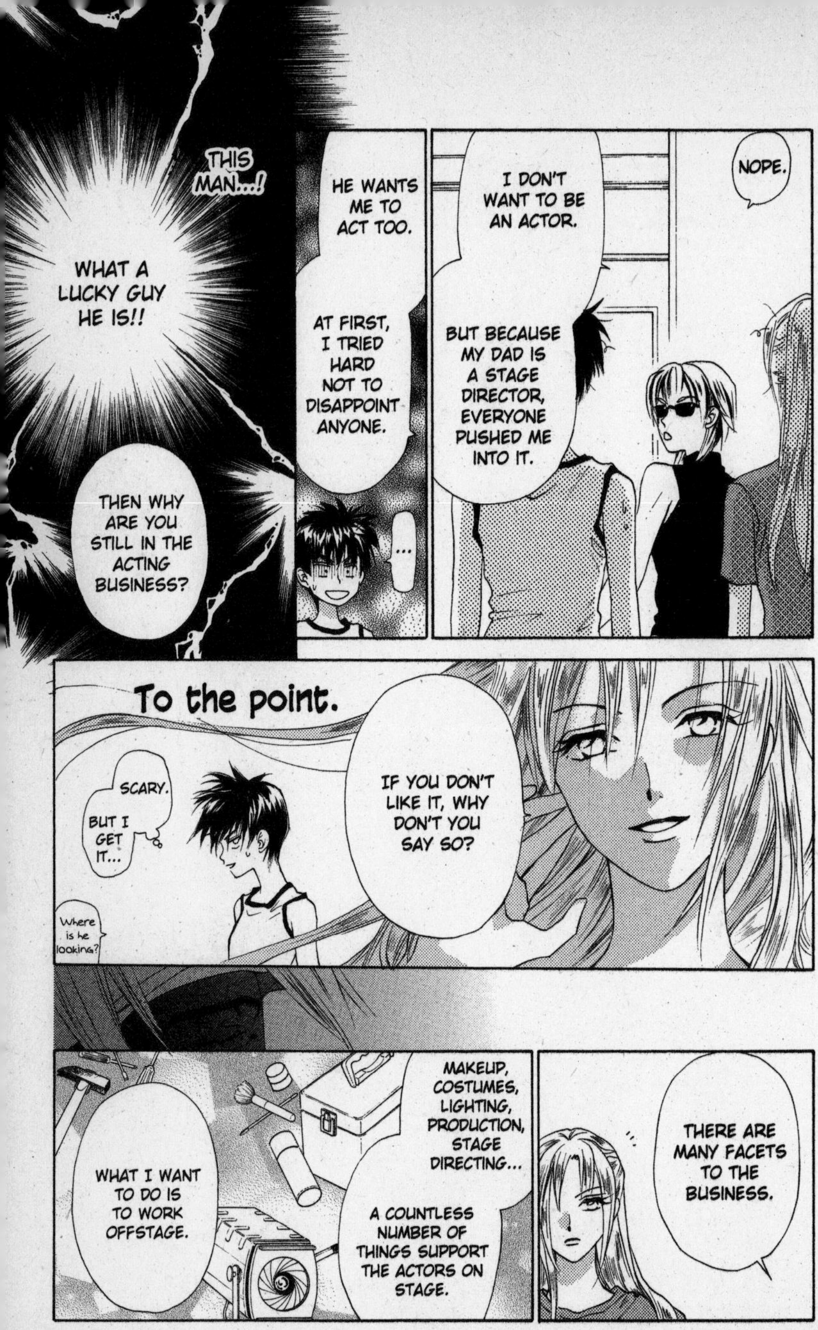
NOPE.
I DON'T WANT TO BE AN ACTOR.
BUT BECAUSE MY DAD IS A STAGE DIRECTOR, EVERYONE PUSHED ME INTO IT.
HE WANTS ME TO ACT TOO.
AT FIRST, I TRIED HARD NOT TO DISAPPOINT ANYONE.
...
THIS MAN...!
WHAT A LUCKY GUY HE IS!!
THEN WHY ARE YOU STILL IN THE ACTING BUSINESS?
IF YOU DON'T LIKE IT, WHY DON'T YOU SAY SO?
To the point.
SCARY.
BUT I GET IT...
Where is he looking?
THERE ARE MANY FACETS TO THE BUSINESS.
MAKEUP, COSTUMES, LIGHTING, PRODUCTION, STAGE DIRECTING...
A COUNTLESS NUMBER OF THINGS SUPPORT THE ACTORS ON STAGE.
WHAT I WANT TO DO IS TO WORK OFFSTAGE.

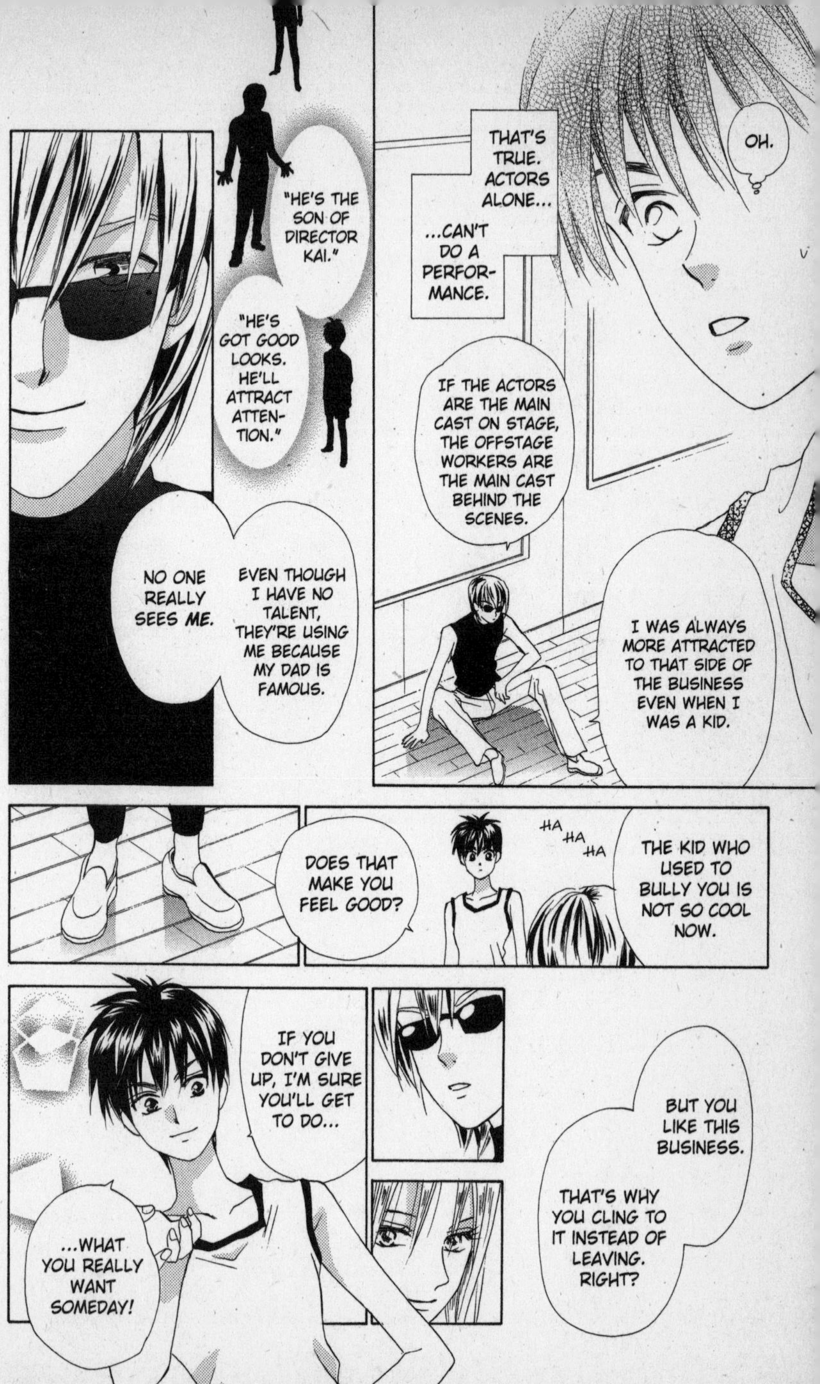
OH.
THAT'S TRUE. ACTORS ALONE...
...CAN'T DO A PERFORMANCE.
IF THE ACTORS ARE THE MAIN CAST ON STAGE, THE OFFSTAGE WORKERS ARE THE MAIN CAST BEHIND THE SCENES.
I WAS ALWAYS MORE ATTRACTED TO THAT SIDE OF THE BUSINESS EVEN WHEN I WAS A KID.
"HE'S THE SON OF DIRECTOR KAI."
"HE'S GOT GOOD LOOKS. HE'LL ATTRACT ATTENTION."
EVEN THOUGH I HAVE NO TALENT, THEY'RE USING ME BECAUSE MY DAD IS FAMOUS.
NO ONE REALLY SEES *ME*.
HA HA HA
THE KID WHO USED TO BULLY YOU IS NOT SO COOL NOW.
DOES THAT MAKE YOU FEEL GOOD?
BUT YOU LIKE THIS BUSINESS.
THAT'S WHY YOU CLING TO IT INSTEAD OF LEAVING. RIGHT?
IF YOU DON'T GIVE UP, I'M SURE YOU'LL GET TO DO...
...WHAT YOU REALLY WANT SOMEDAY!

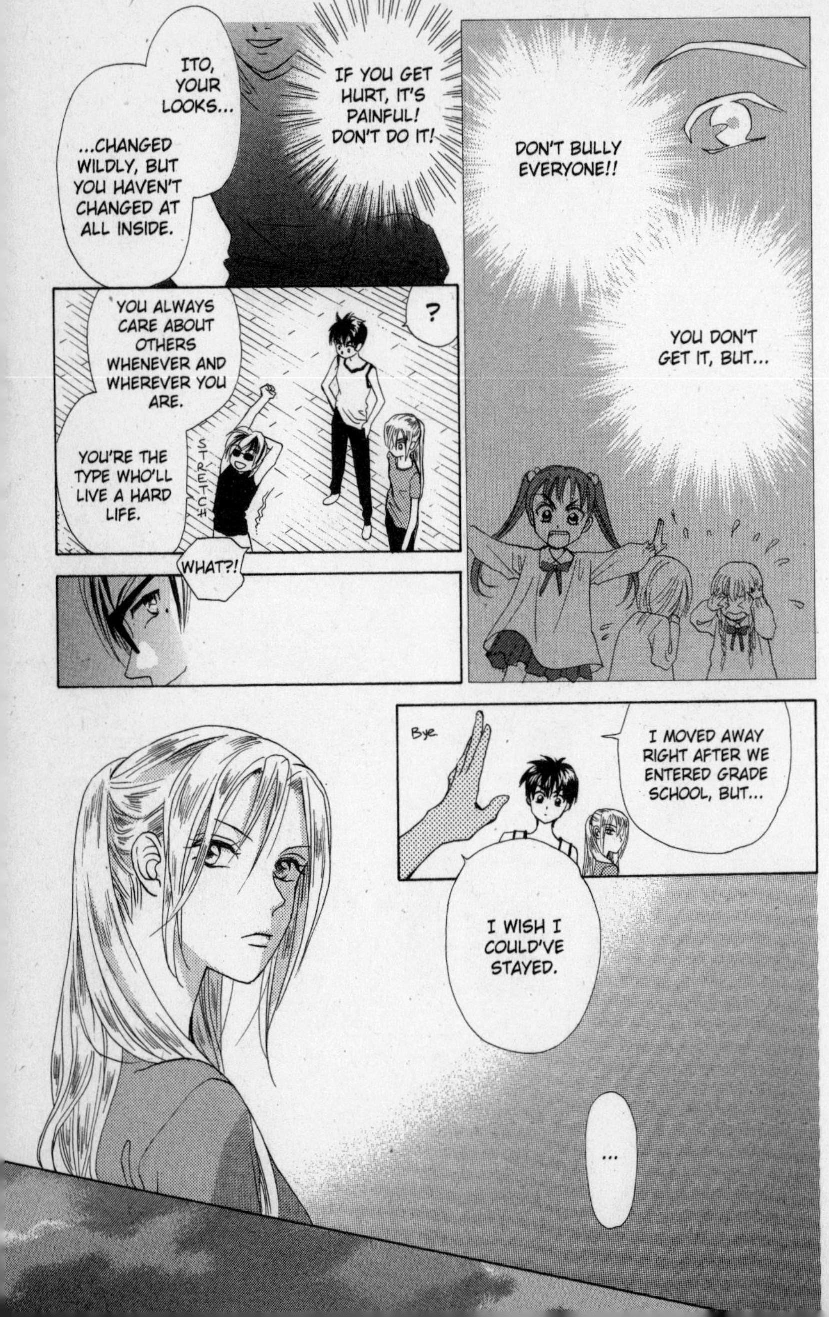
DON'T BULLY EVERYONE!!
YOU DON'T GET IT, BUT...
IF YOU GET HURT, IT'S PAINFUL! DON'T DO IT!
ITO, YOUR LOOKS...
...CHANGED WILDLY, BUT YOU HAVEN'T CHANGED AT ALL INSIDE.
?
YOU ALWAYS CARE ABOUT OTHERS WHENEVER AND WHEREVER YOU ARE.
YOU'RE THE TYPE WHO'LL LIVE A HARD LIFE.
STRETCH
WHAT?!
I MOVED AWAY RIGHT AFTER WE ENTERED GRADE SCHOOL, BUT...
Bye
I WISH I COULD'VE STAYED.
...

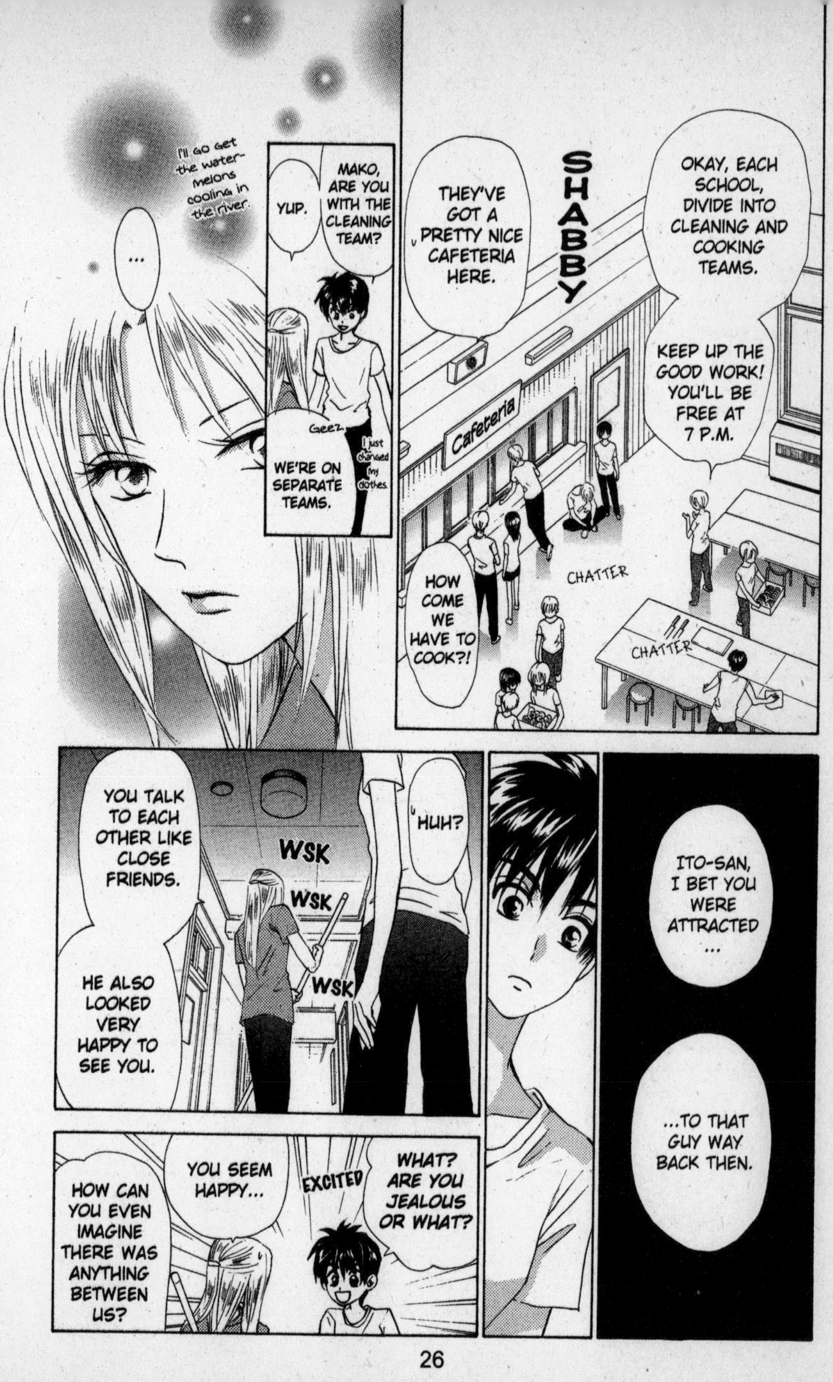
OKAY, EACH SCHOOL, DIVIDE INTO CLEANING AND COOKING TEAMS.
KEEP UP THE GOOD WORK! YOU'LL BE FREE AT 7 P.M.
SHABBY
THEY'VE GOT A PRETTY NICE CAFETERIA HERE.
Cafeteria
CHATTER
CHATTER
HOW COME WE HAVE TO COOK?!
MAKO, ARE YOU WITH THE CLEANING TEAM?
YUP.
Geez.
I just changed my clothes.
WE'RE ON SEPARATE TEAMS.
I'll go get the water-melons cooling in the river.
...
ITO-SAN, I BET YOU WERE ATTRACTED ...
...TO THAT GUY WAY BACK THEN.
HUH?
YOU TALK TO EACH OTHER LIKE CLOSE FRIENDS.
WSK
WSK
WSK
HE ALSO LOOKED VERY HAPPY TO SEE YOU.
WHAT? ARE YOU JEALOUS OR WHAT?
EXCITED
YOU SEEM HAPPY...
HOW CAN YOU EVEN IMAGINE THERE WAS ANYTHING BETWEEN US?

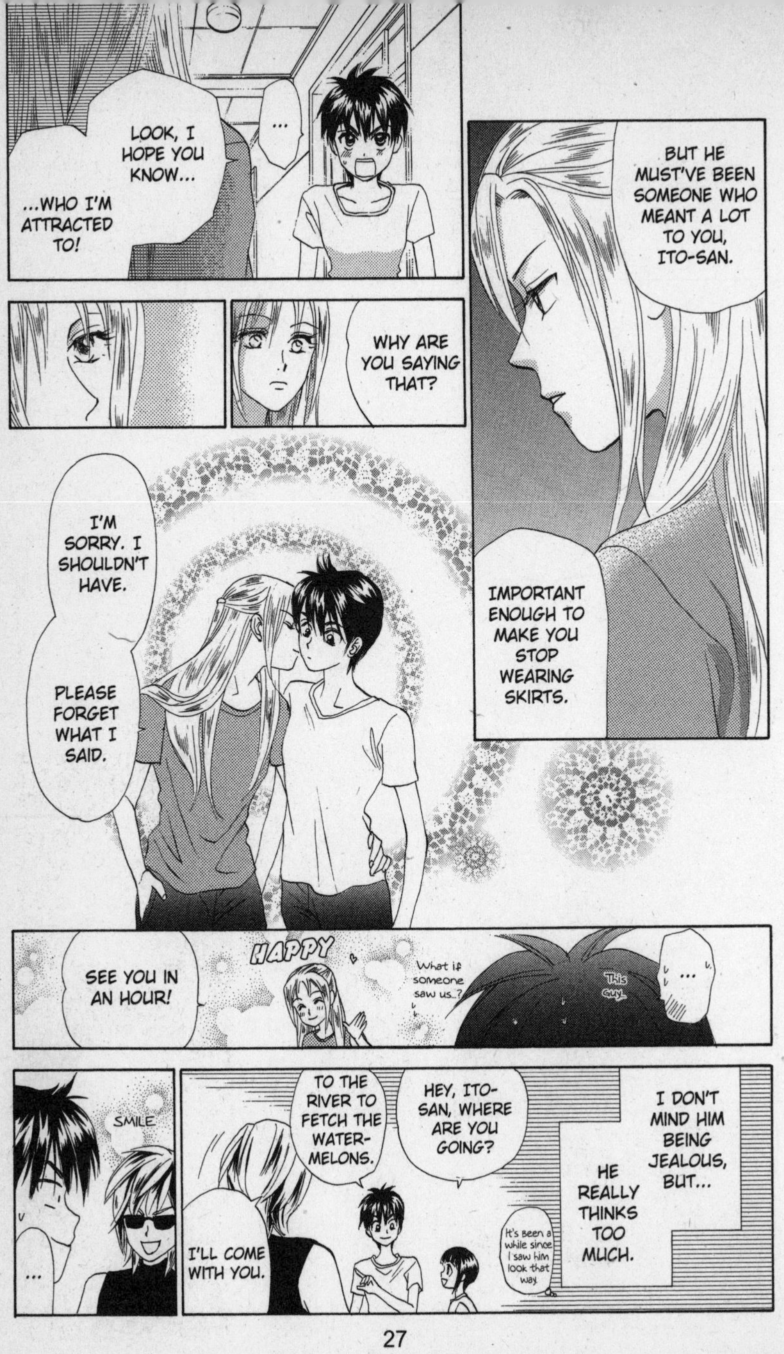
LOOK, I HOPE YOU KNOW...
...
...WHO I'M ATTRACTED TO!
BUT HE MUST'VE BEEN SOMEONE WHO MEANT A LOT TO YOU, ITO-SAN.
IMPORTANT ENOUGH TO MAKE YOU STOP WEARING SKIRTS.
WHY ARE YOU SAYING THAT?
I'M SORRY. I SHOULDN'T HAVE.
PLEASE FORGET WHAT I SAID.
...
This guy...
What if someone saw us...?
HAPPY
SEE YOU IN AN HOUR!
I DON'T MIND HIM BEING JEALOUS, BUT...
HE REALLY THINKS TOO MUCH.
HEY, ITO-SAN, WHERE ARE YOU GOING?
TO THE RIVER TO FETCH THE WATER-MELONS.
It's been a while since I saw him look that way.
I'LL COME WITH YOU.
SMILE
...

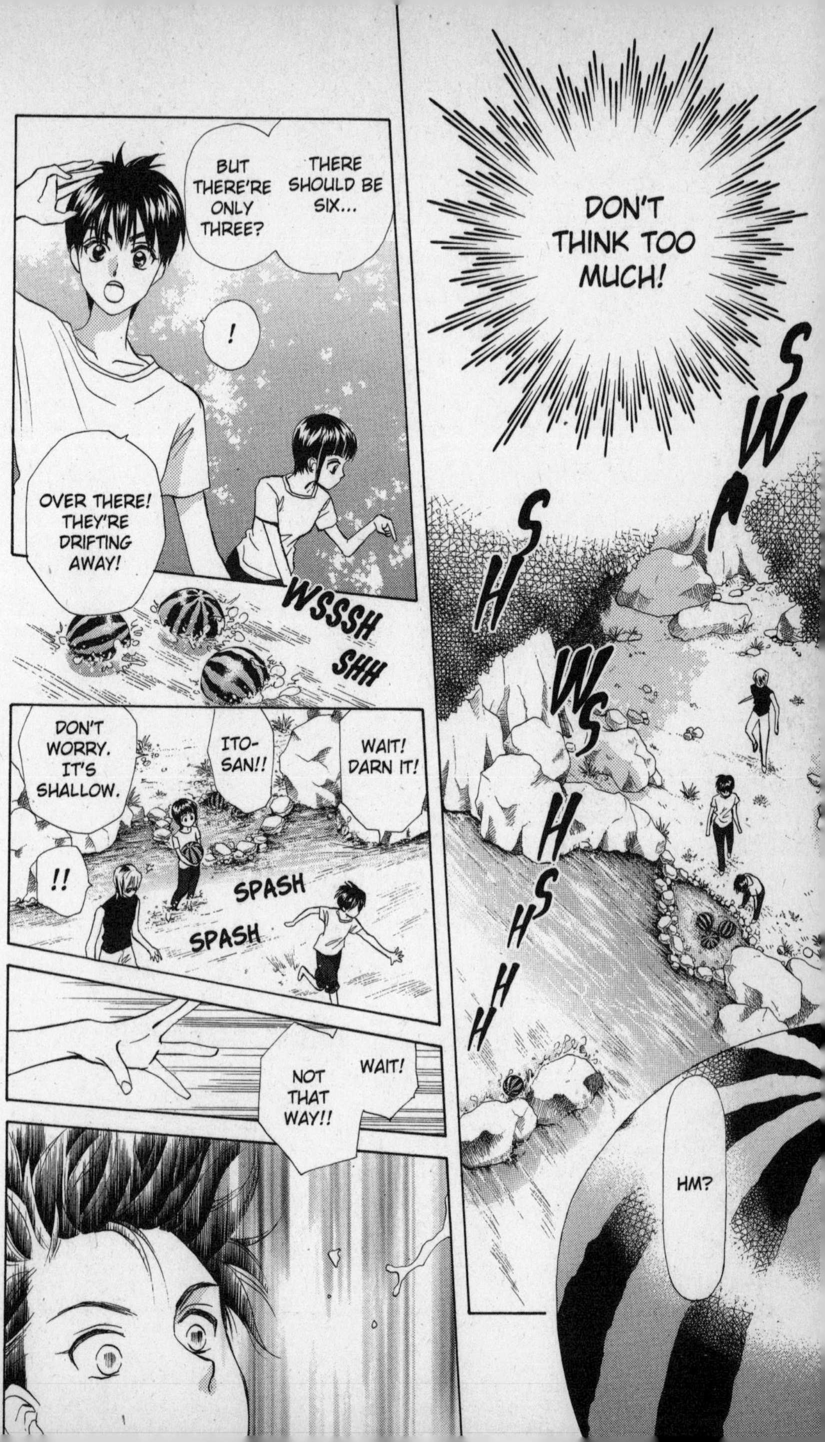
DON'T THINK TOO MUCH!
HM?
THERE SHOULD BE SIX...
BUT THERE'RE ONLY THREE?
!
OVER THERE! THEY'RE DRIFTING AWAY!
WSSSH
SHH
WAIT! DARN IT!
ITO-SAN!!
DON'T WORRY. IT'S SHALLOW.
!!
SPASH
SPASH
WAIT!
NOT THAT WAY!!

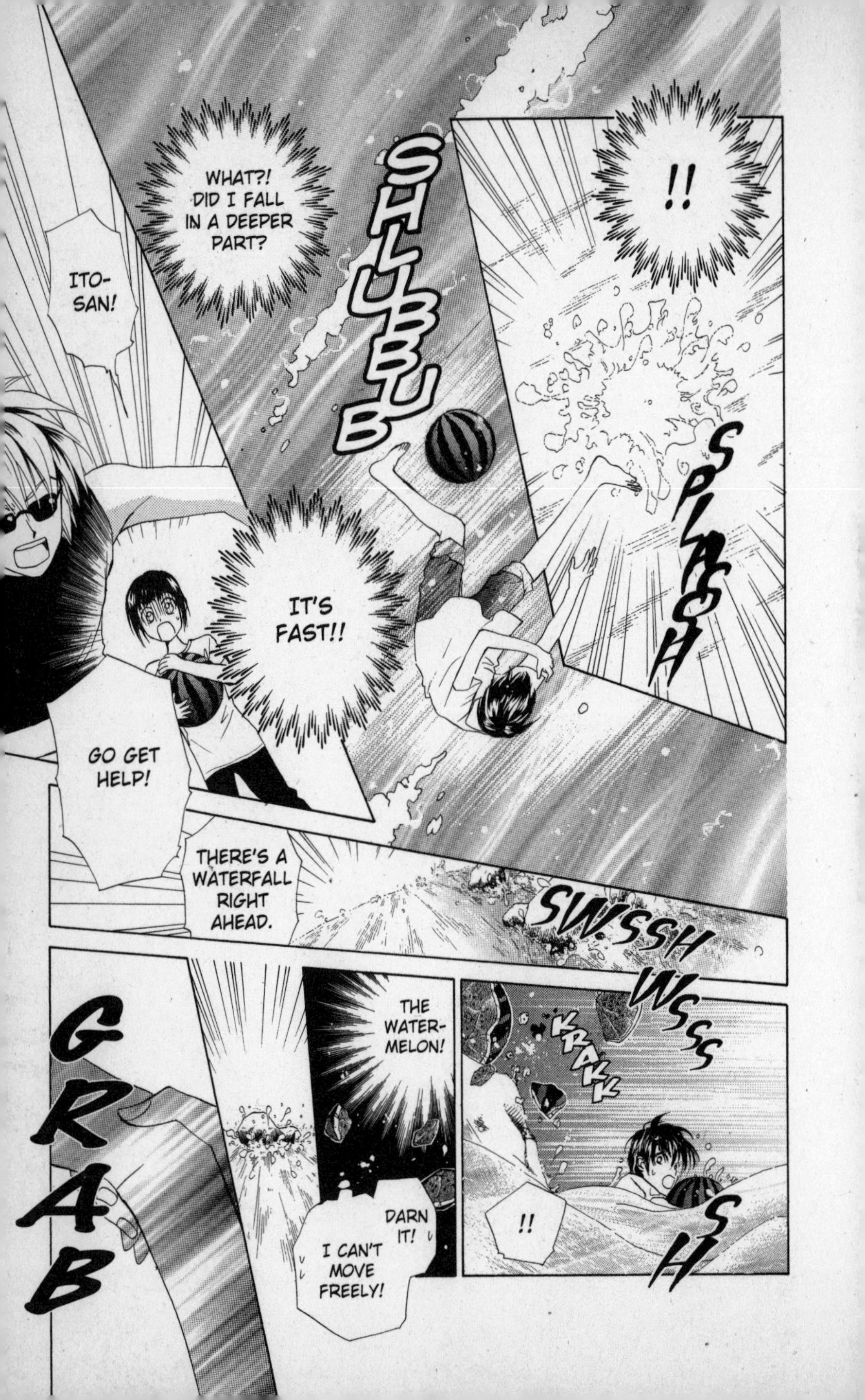
!!
SPLASH
SHLUBBUB
WHAT?! DID I FALL IN A DEEPER PART?
IT'S FAST!!
ITO-SAN!
GO GET HELP!
THERE'S A WATERFALL RIGHT AHEAD.
SWSSH
WSSS
KRAKK
SH
!!
THE WATER-MELON!
DARN IT!
I CAN'T MOVE FREELY!
GRAB

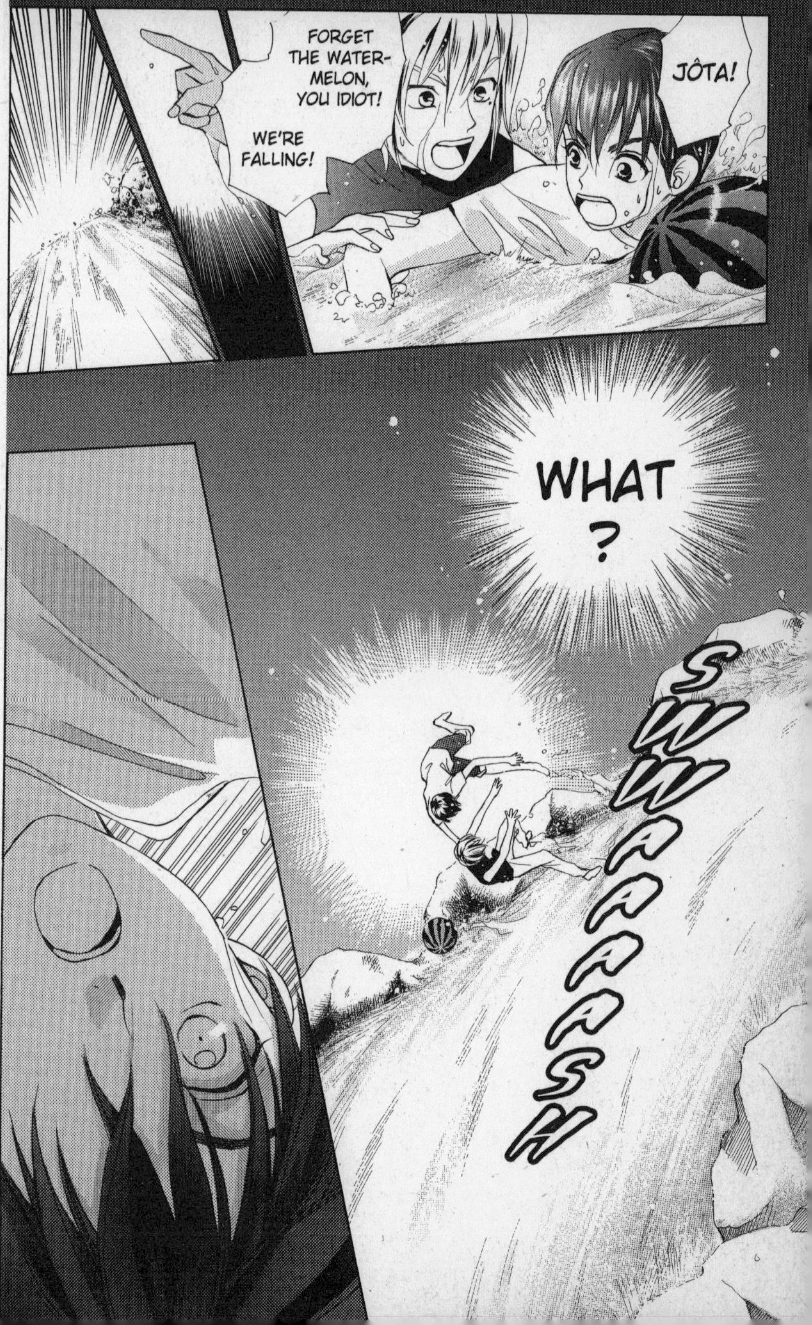
JÔTA!
FORGET THE WATER-MELON, YOU IDIOT!
WE'RE FALLING!
WHAT?
SWWAAAAASH

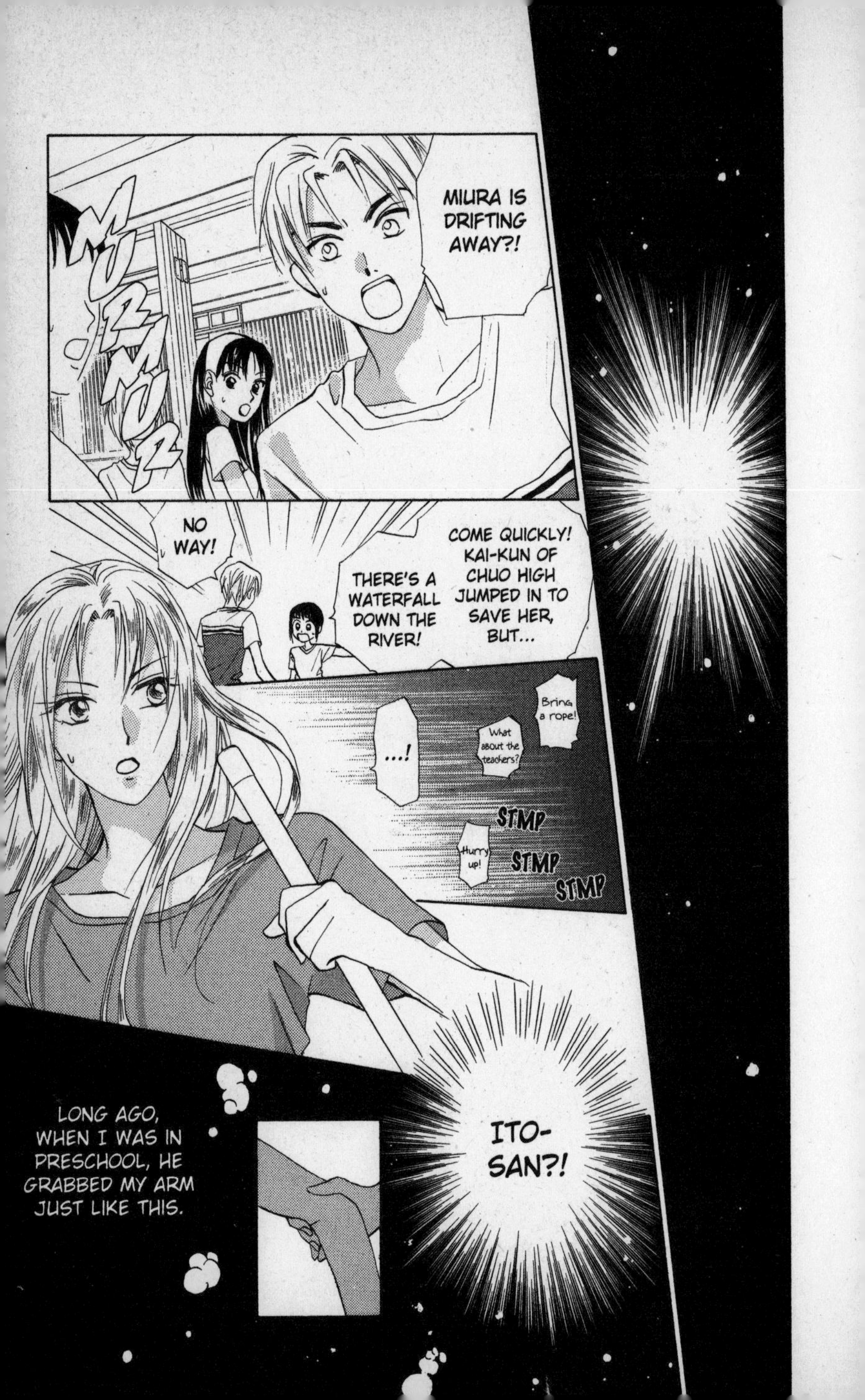
MIURA IS DRIFTING AWAY?!
MURMUR
COME QUICKLY! KAI-KUN OF CHUO HIGH JUMPED IN TO SAVE HER, BUT...
THERE'S A WATERFALL DOWN THE RIVER!
NO WAY!
Bring a rope!
What about the teachers?
...!
STMP
Hurry up!
STMP
STMP
ITO-SAN?!
LONG AGO, WHEN I WAS IN PRESCHOOL, HE GRABBED MY ARM JUST LIKE THIS.

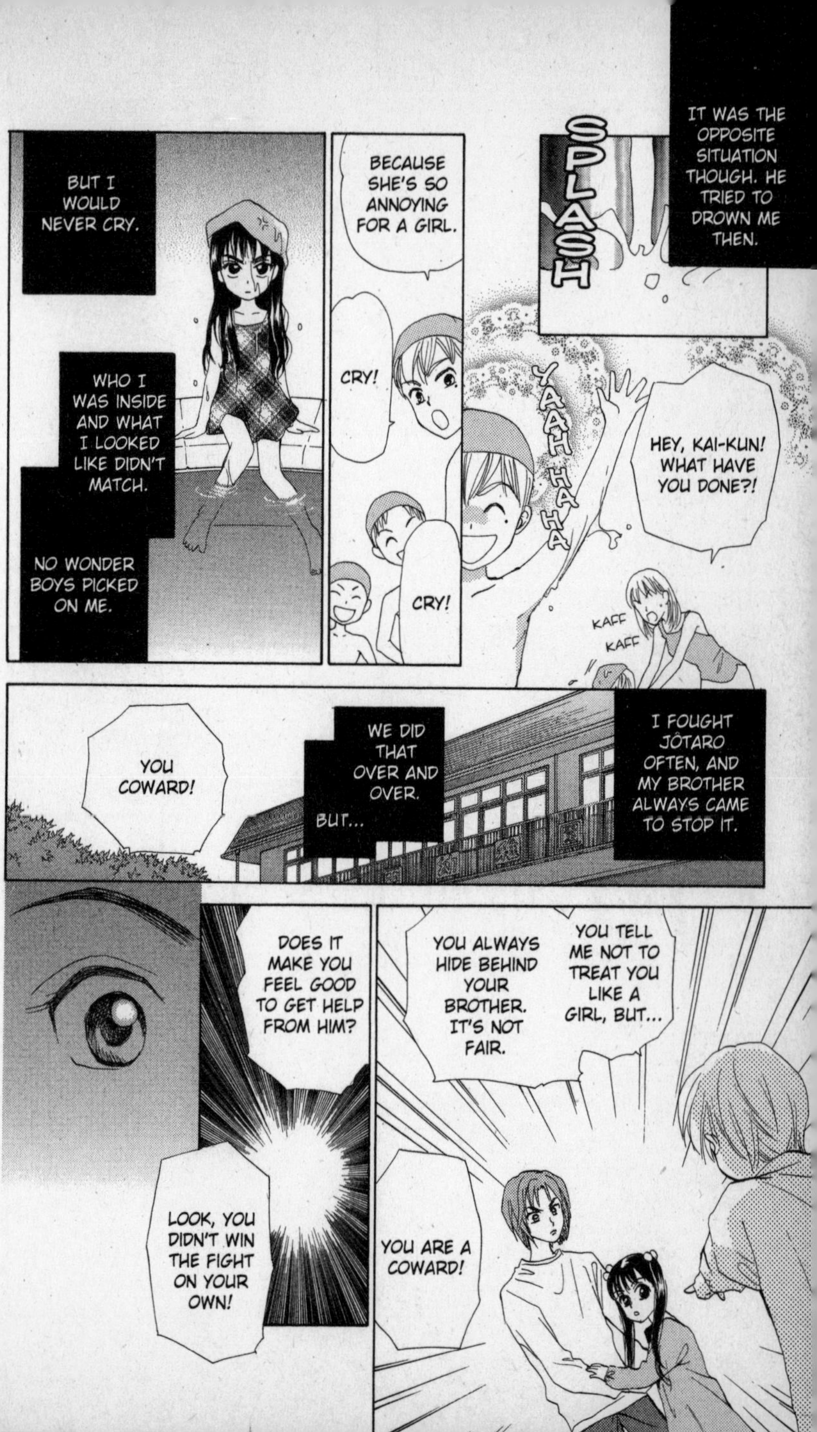
IT WAS THE OPPOSITE SITUATION THOUGH. HE TRIED TO DROWN ME THEN.
SPLASH
YAAH HA HA
HEY, KAI-KUN! WHAT HAVE YOU DONE?!
KAFF KAFF
BECAUSE SHE'S SO ANNOYING FOR A GIRL.
CRY!
CRY!
BUT I WOULD NEVER CRY.
WHO I WAS INSIDE AND WHAT I LOOKED LIKE DIDN'T MATCH.
NO WONDER BOYS PICKED ON ME.
I FOUGHT JŌTARO OFTEN, AND MY BROTHER ALWAYS CAME TO STOP IT.
WE DID THAT OVER AND OVER.
BUT...
YOU COWARD!
YOU TELL ME NOT TO TREAT YOU LIKE A GIRL, BUT...
YOU ALWAYS HIDE BEHIND YOUR BROTHER. IT'S NOT FAIR.
YOU ARE A COWARD!
DOES IT MAKE YOU FEEL GOOD TO GET HELP FROM HIM?
LOOK, YOU DIDN'T WIN THE FIGHT ON YOUR OWN!

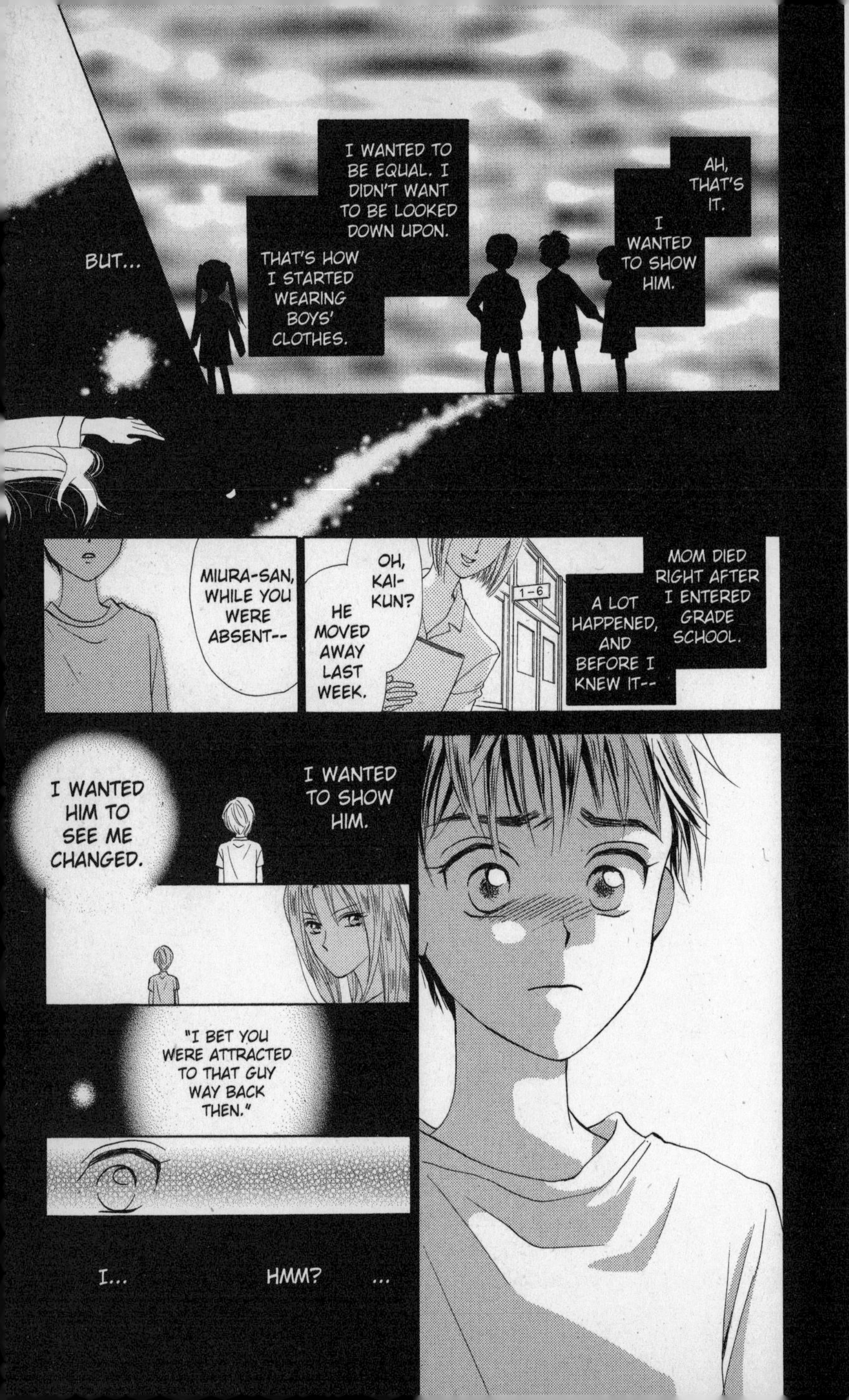
AH, THAT'S IT.
I WANTED TO SHOW HIM.
I WANTED TO BE EQUAL. I DIDN'T WANT TO BE LOOKED DOWN UPON.
THAT'S HOW I STARTED WEARING BOYS' CLOTHES.
BUT...
MOM DIED RIGHT AFTER I ENTERED GRADE SCHOOL.
A LOT HAPPENED, AND BEFORE I KNEW IT--
1-6
OH, KAI-KUN?
HE MOVED AWAY LAST WEEK.
MIURA-SAN, WHILE YOU WERE ABSENT--
I WANTED TO SHOW HIM.
I WANTED HIM TO SEE ME CHANGED.
"I BET YOU WERE ATTRACTED TO THAT GUY WAY BACK THEN."
...
HMM?
I...

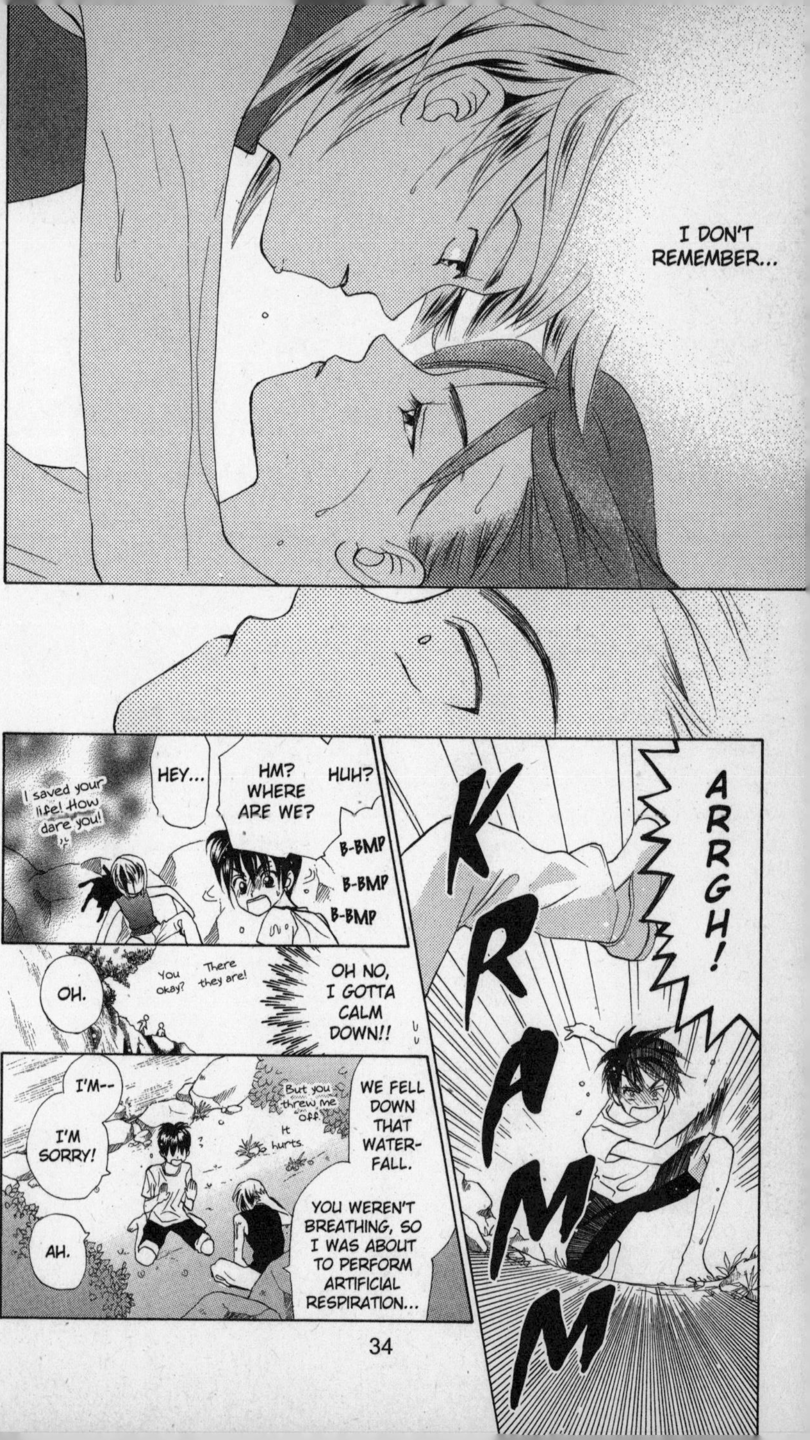
I DON'T REMEMBER...
ARRGH!
KRAMMM
HUH?
HM? WHERE ARE WE?
B-BMP
B-BMP
B-BMP
HEY...
I saved your life! How dare you!
OH NO, I GOTTA CALM DOWN!!
There they are!
You okay?
OH.
WE FELL DOWN THAT WATER-FALL.
YOU WEREN'T BREATHING, SO I WAS ABOUT TO PERFORM ARTIFICIAL RESPIRATION...
But you threw me off.
It hurts.
I'M--
I'M SORRY!
AH.

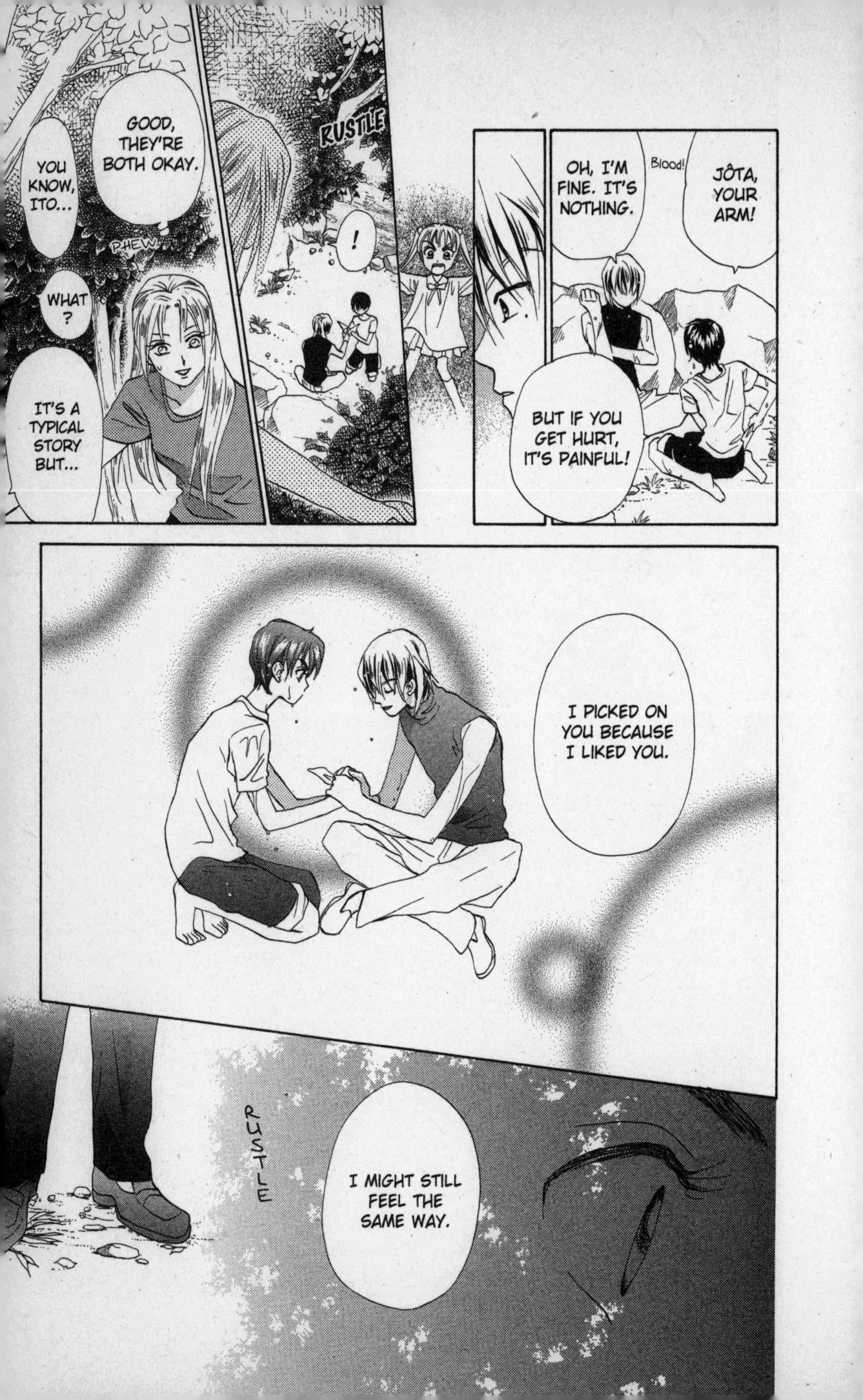
JÔTA, YOUR ARM!
Blood!
OH, I'M FINE. IT'S NOTHING.
BUT IF YOU GET HURT, IT'S PAINFUL!
RUSTLE
!
GOOD, THEY'RE BOTH OKAY.
PHEW
YOU KNOW, ITO...
WHAT?
IT'S A TYPICAL STORY BUT...
I PICKED ON YOU BECAUSE I LIKED YOU.
I MIGHT STILL FEEL THE SAME WAY.
RUSTLE

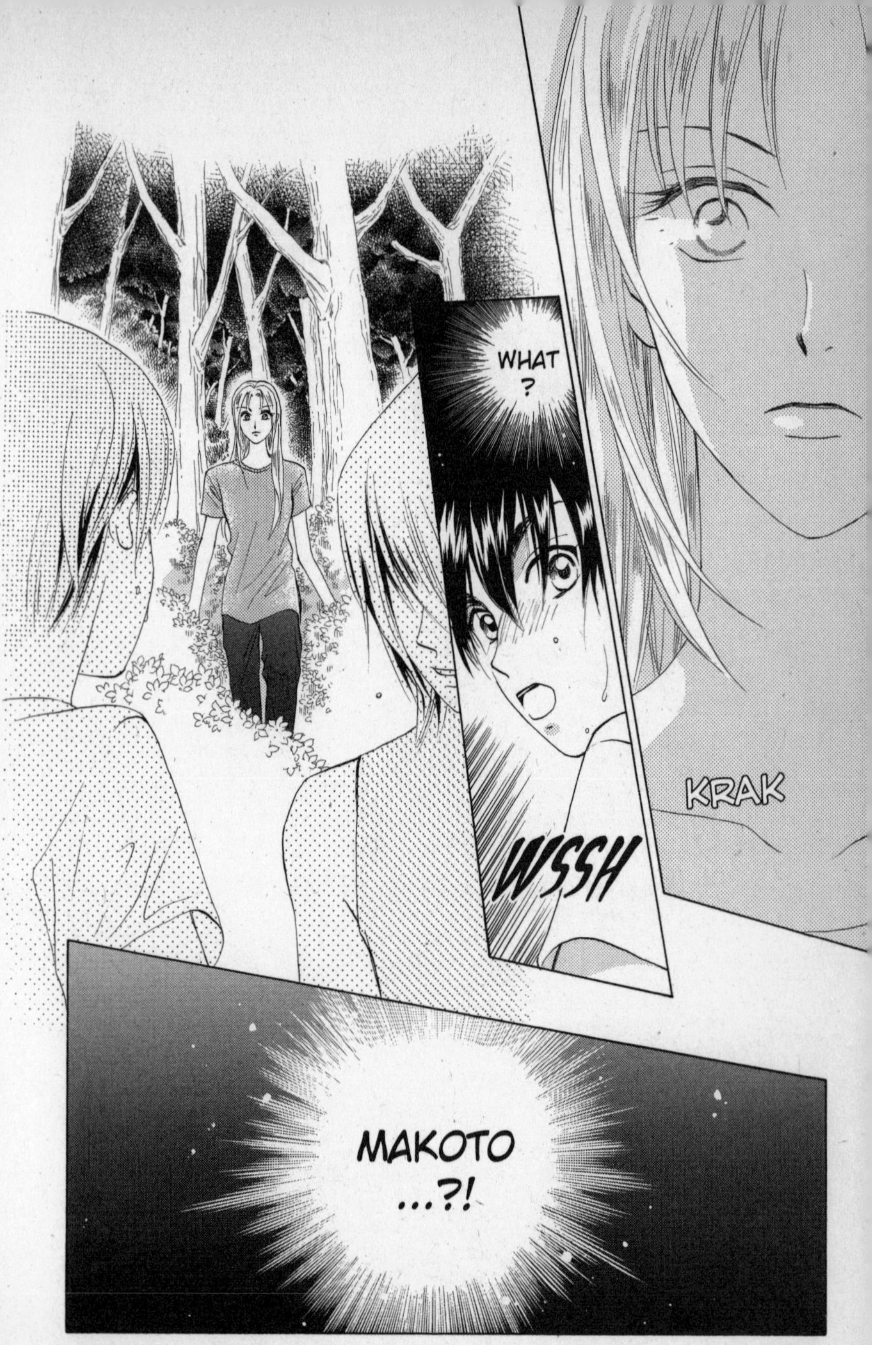
KRAK
WHAT?
WSSH
MAKOTO ...?!

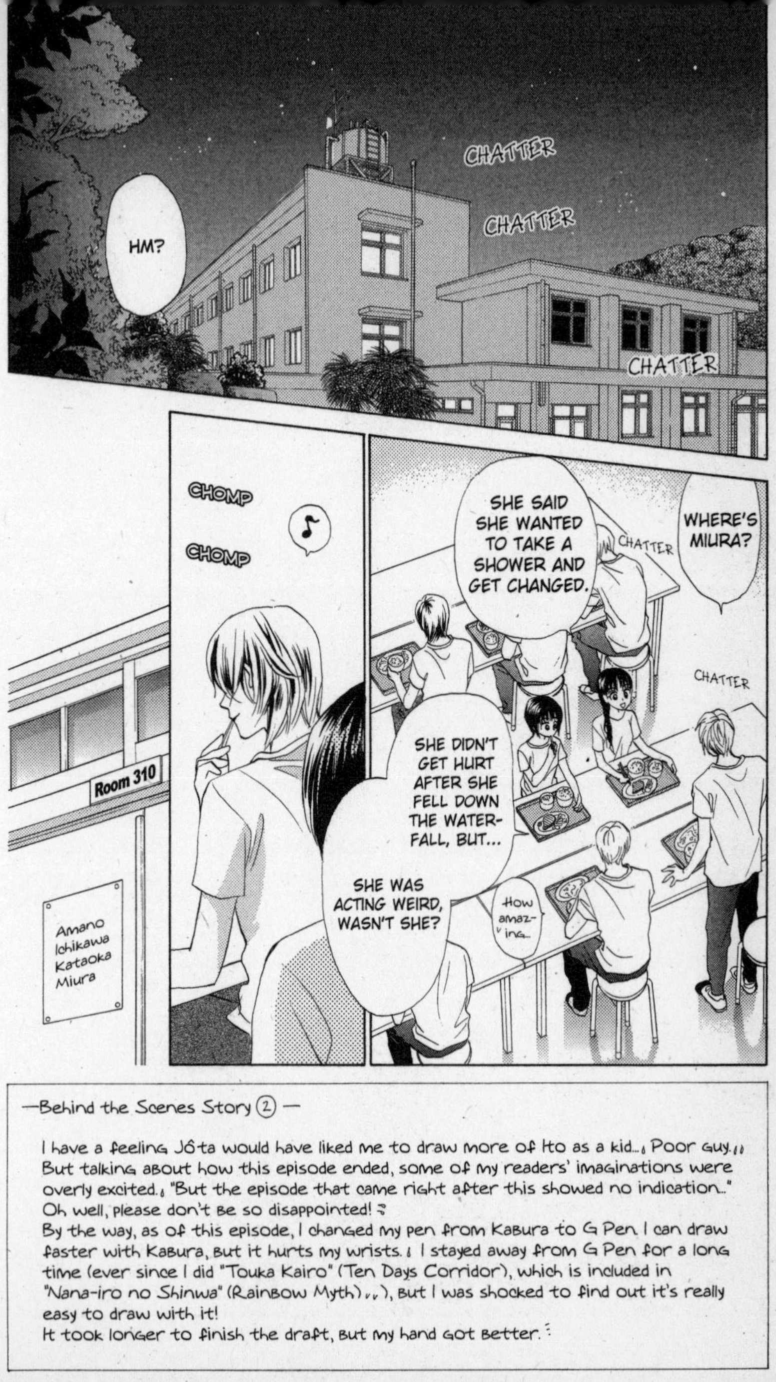
CHATTER
CHATTER
HM?
CHATTER
WHERE'S MIURA?
CHATTER
SHE SAID SHE WANTED TO TAKE A SHOWER AND GET CHANGED.
CHATTER
SHE DIDN'T GET HURT AFTER SHE FELL DOWN THE WATER-FALL, BUT...
How amaz-ing...
SHE WAS ACTING WEIRD, WASN'T SHE?
CHOMP
CHOMP
Room 310
Amano
Ichikawa
Kataoka
Miura

—Behind the Scenes Story ② —

I have a feeling Jôta would have liked me to draw more of Ito as a kid... Poor guy. But talking about how this episode ended, some of my readers' imaginations were overly excited. "But the episode that came right after this showed no indication..." Oh well, please don't be so disappointed!
By the way, as of this episode, I changed my pen from Kabura to G Pen. I can draw faster with Kabura, but it hurts my wrists. I stayed away from G Pen for a long time (ever since I did "Touka Kairo" (Ten Days Corridor), which is included in "Nana-iro no Shinwa" (Rainbow Myth)), but I was shocked to find out it's really easy to draw with it!
It took longer to finish the draft, but my hand got better.

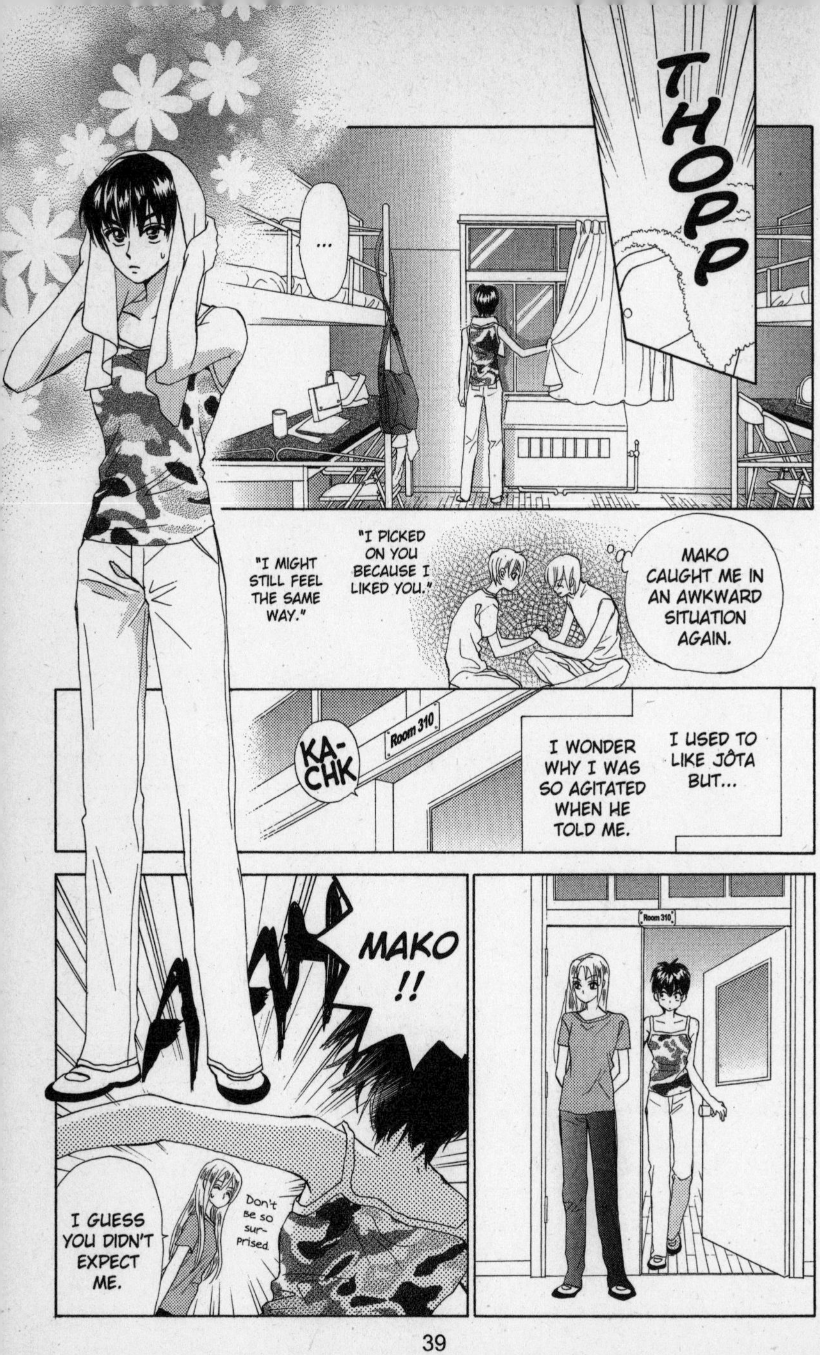
THOPP
...
MAKO CAUGHT ME IN AN AWKWARD SITUATION AGAIN.
"I PICKED ON YOU BECAUSE I LIKED YOU."
"I MIGHT STILL FEEL THE SAME WAY."
I USED TO LIKE JÔTA BUT...
I WONDER WHY I WAS SO AGITATED WHEN HE TOLD ME.
Room 310
KA-CHK
Room 310
MAKO !!
Don't be so sur-prised.
I GUESS YOU DIDN'T EXPECT ME.

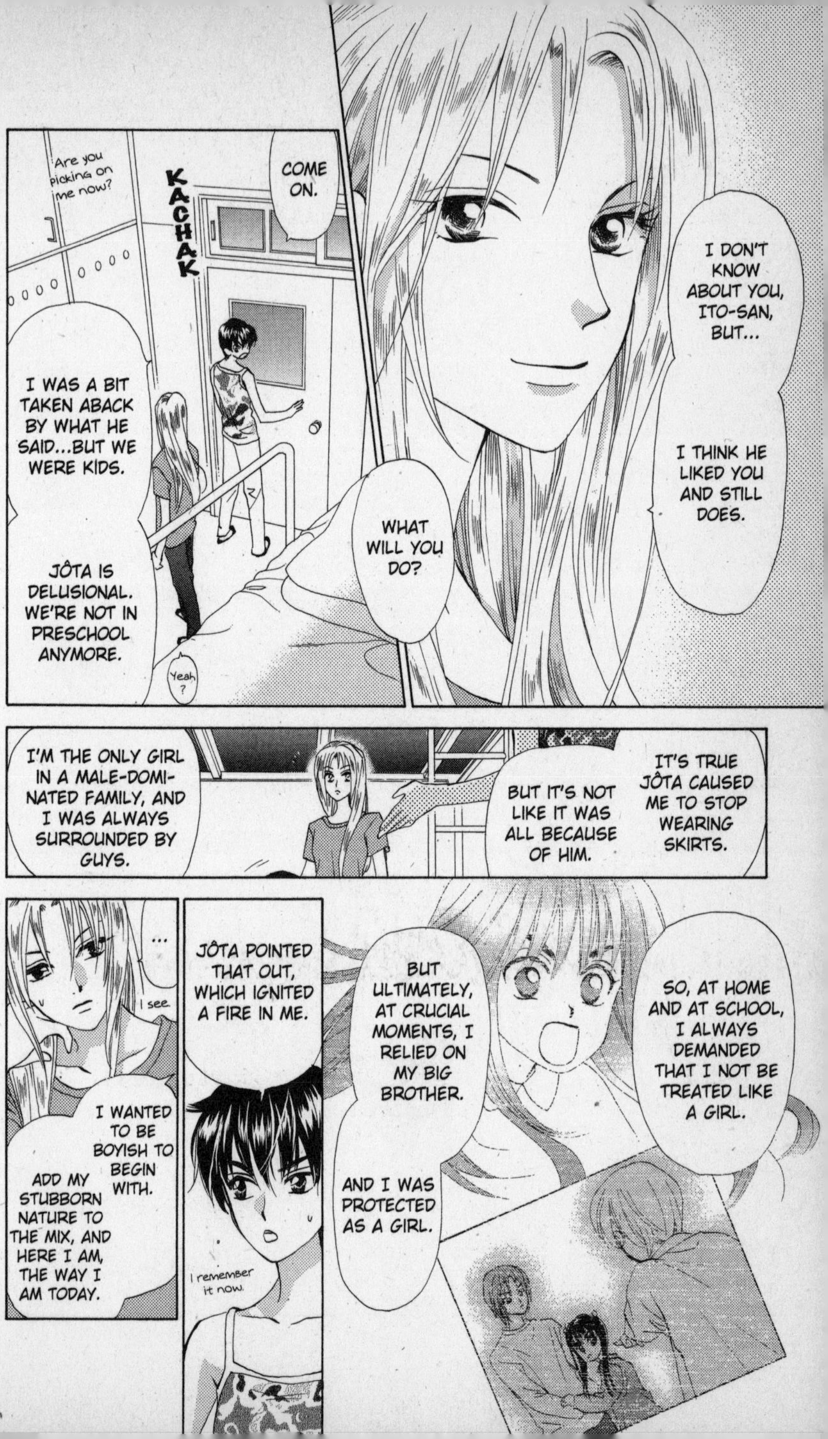
I DON'T KNOW ABOUT YOU, ITO-SAN, BUT...
I THINK HE LIKED YOU AND STILL DOES.
WHAT WILL YOU DO?
COME ON.
KACHAK
Are you picking on me now?
I WAS A BIT TAKEN ABACK BY WHAT HE SAID...BUT WE WERE KIDS.
JÔTA IS DELUSIONAL. WE'RE NOT IN PRESCHOOL ANYMORE.
Yeah?
IT'S TRUE JÔTA CAUSED ME TO STOP WEARING SKIRTS.
BUT IT'S NOT LIKE IT WAS ALL BECAUSE OF HIM.
I'M THE ONLY GIRL IN A MALE-DOMI-NATED FAMILY, AND I WAS ALWAYS SURROUNDED BY GUYS.
SO, AT HOME AND AT SCHOOL, I ALWAYS DEMANDED THAT I NOT BE TREATED LIKE A GIRL.
BUT ULTIMATELY, AT CRUCIAL MOMENTS, I RELIED ON MY BIG BROTHER.
AND I WAS PROTECTED AS A GIRL.
JÔTA POINTED THAT OUT, WHICH IGNITED A FIRE IN ME.
I remember it now.
...
I see.
I WANTED TO BE BOYISH TO BEGIN WITH.
ADD MY STUBBORN NATURE TO THE MIX, AND HERE I AM, THE WAY I AM TODAY.

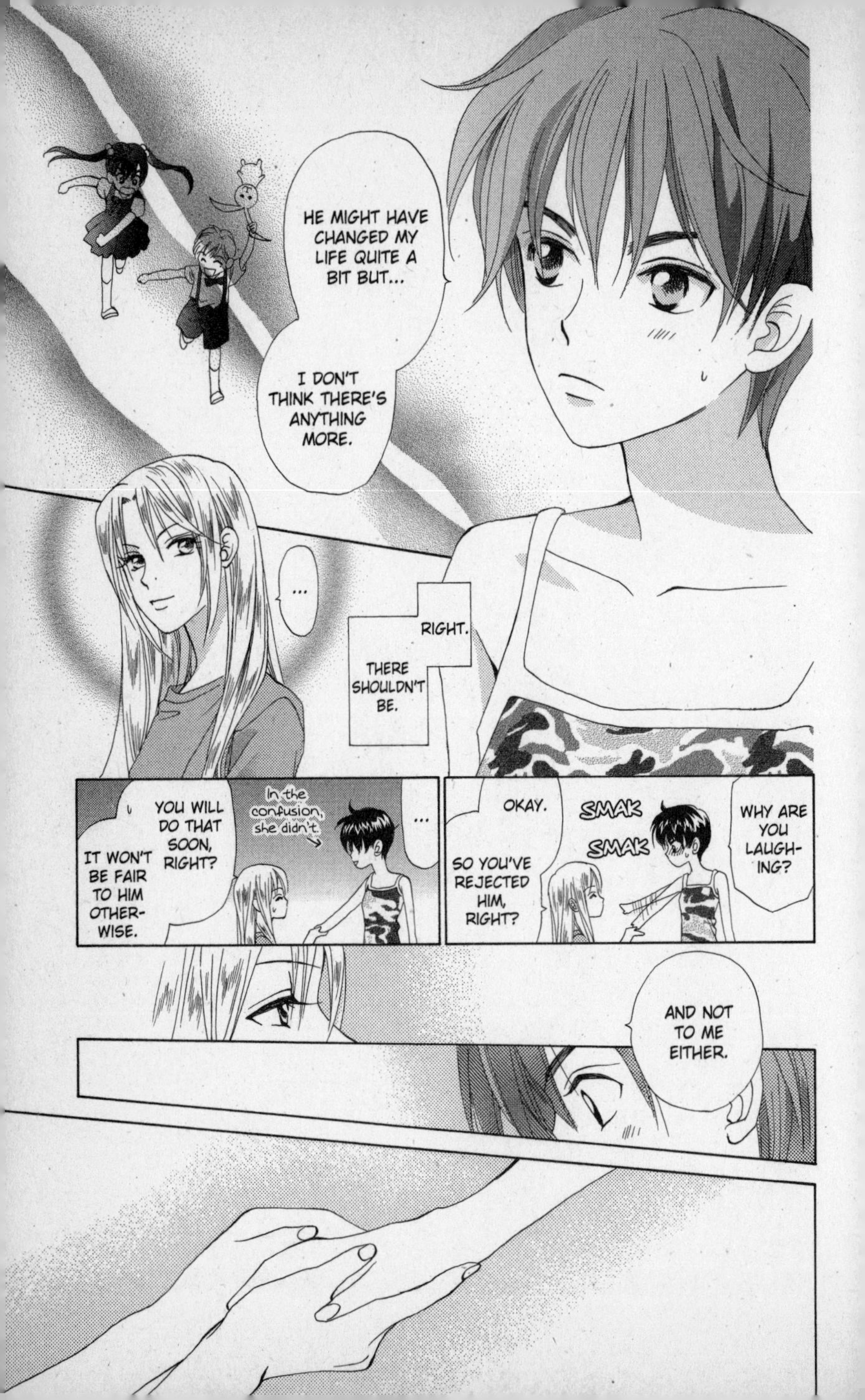
HE MIGHT HAVE CHANGED MY LIFE QUITE A BIT BUT...
I DON'T THINK THERE'S ANYTHING MORE.
RIGHT.
THERE SHOULDN'T BE.
...
WHY ARE YOU LAUGHING?
SMAK
SMAK
OKAY.
SO YOU'VE REJECTED HIM, RIGHT?
...
In the confusion, she didn't.
YOU WILL DO THAT SOON, RIGHT?
IT WON'T BE FAIR TO HIM OTHERWISE.
AND NOT TO ME EITHER.

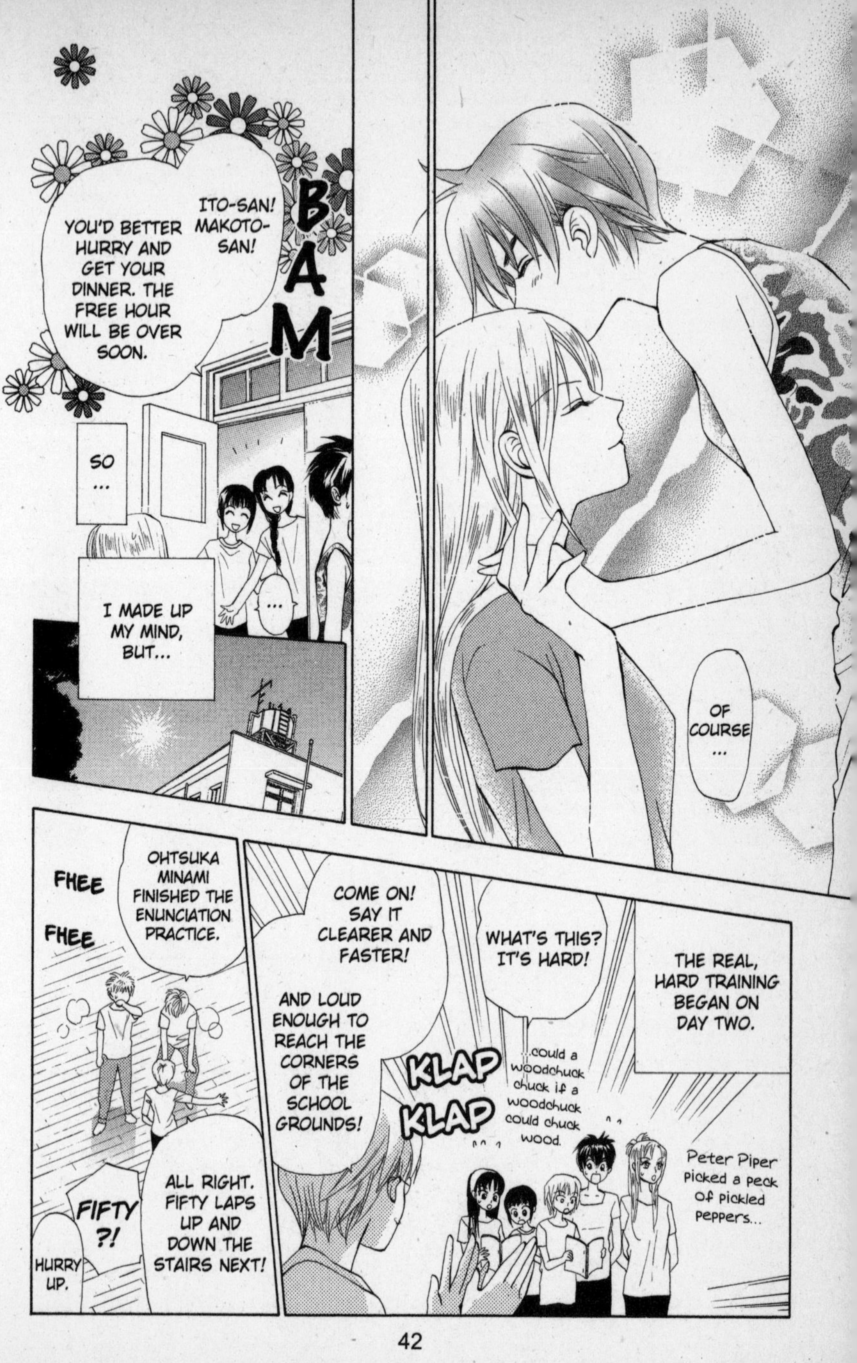
OF COURSE ...
ITO-SAN! MAKOTO-SAN!
YOU'D BETTER HURRY AND GET YOUR DINNER. THE FREE HOUR WILL BE OVER SOON.
BAM
SO ...
...
I MADE UP MY MIND, BUT...
THE REAL, HARD TRAINING BEGAN ON DAY TWO.
WHAT'S THIS? IT'S HARD!
COME ON! SAY IT CLEARER AND FASTER!
AND LOUD ENOUGH TO REACH THE CORNERS OF THE SCHOOL GROUNDS!
Peter Piper picked a peck of pickled peppers...
...could a woodchuck chuck if a woodchuck could chuck wood.
KLAP
KLAP
OHTSUKA MINAMI FINISHED THE ENUNCIATION PRACTICE.
FHEE
FHEE
ALL RIGHT. FIFTY LAPS UP AND DOWN THE STAIRS NEXT!
FIFTY ?!
HURRY UP.

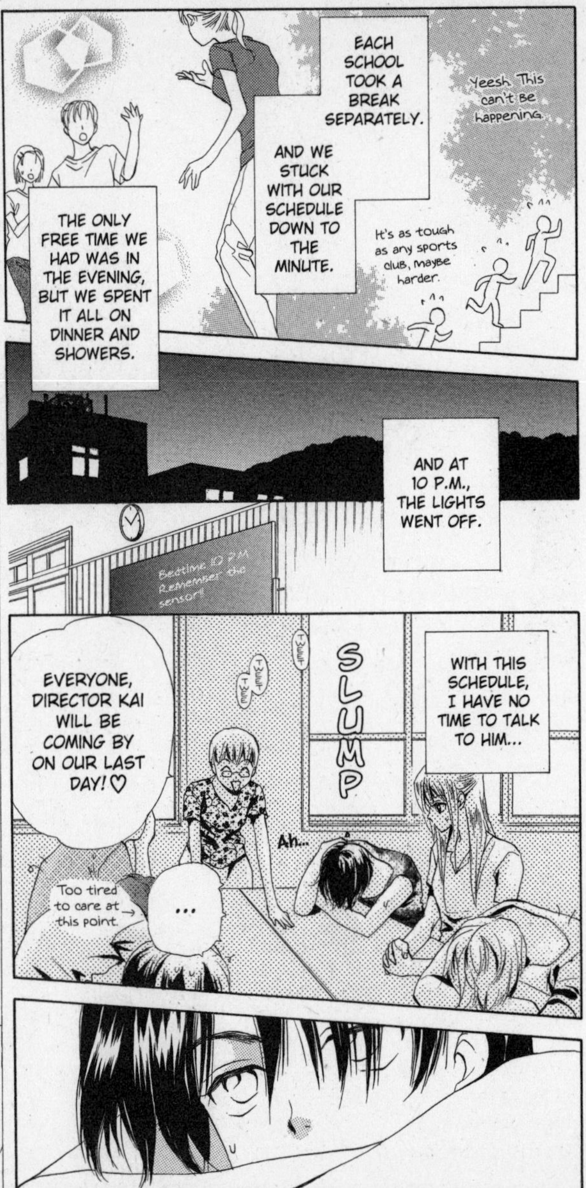
Yeesh. This can't be happening.
EACH SCHOOL TOOK A BREAK SEPARATELY.
AND WE STUCK WITH OUR SCHEDULE DOWN TO THE MINUTE.
It's as tough as any sports club, maybe harder.
THE ONLY FREE TIME WE HAD WAS IN THE EVENING, BUT WE SPENT IT ALL ON DINNER AND SHOWERS.
AND AT 10 P.M., THE LIGHTS WENT OFF.
Bedtime 10 P.M. Remember the sensor!
WITH THIS SCHEDULE, I HAVE NO TIME TO TALK TO HIM...
SLUMP
Thump
Thump
Thump
EVERYONE, DIRECTOR KAI WILL BE COMING BY ON OUR LAST DAY! ♡
Ah...
...
Too tired to care at this point. →

# PROFILE

My Sister - Sayaka

Born on June 23rd
Blood type B
Astrological sign: Cancer
Former sprinter for the Field & Track Club.
She believes that's what made her legs get fat.

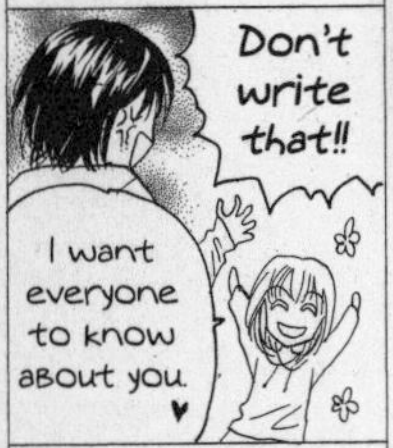
Don't write that!!
I want everyone to know about you. ♥

Her hobby is baking sweets. She's a pretty good cook. I take my hat off to her. (I can't bake or cook).

She's been my assistant the longest, and she now works for me exclusively, but I don't remember when she became my "official assistant."

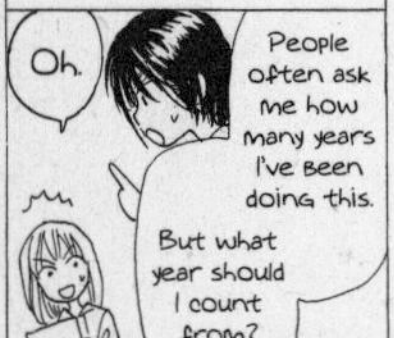
Oh.
People often ask me how many years I've been doing this.
But what year should I count from?

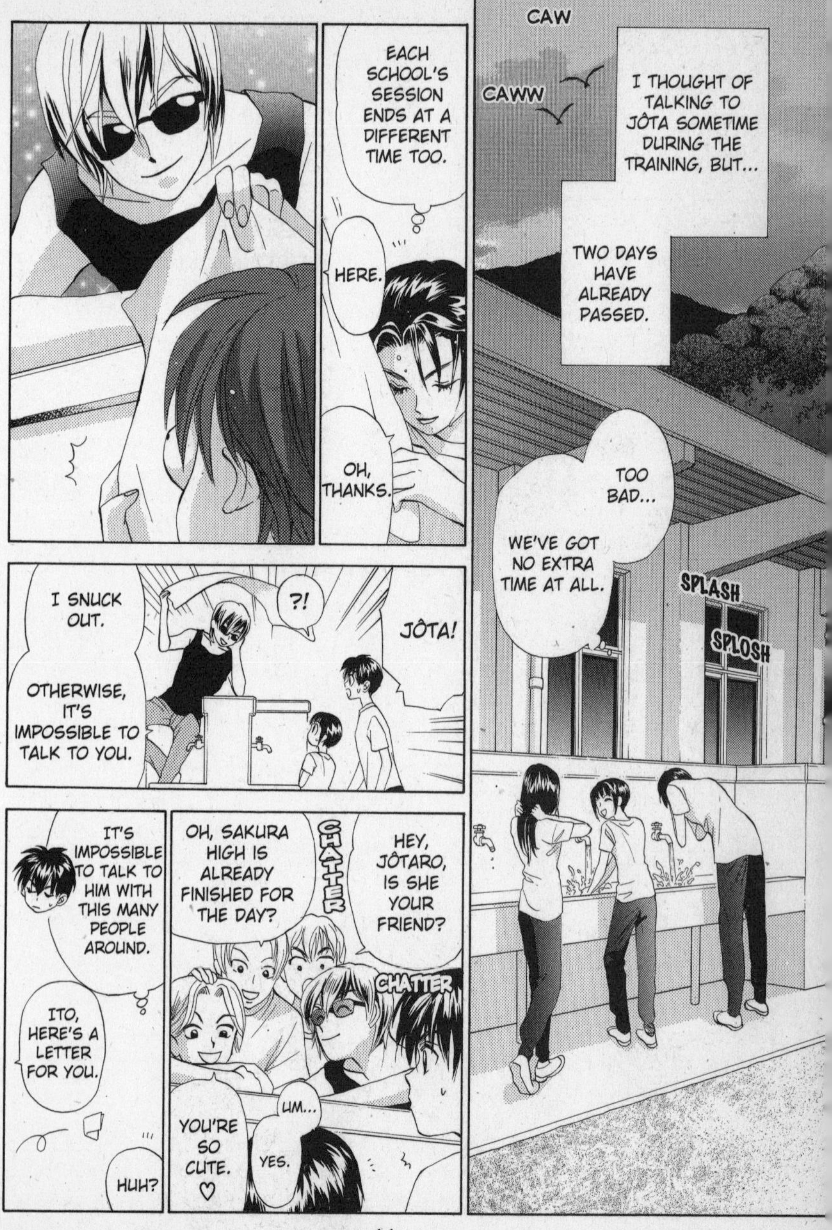
CAW
CAWW
I THOUGHT OF TALKING TO JÔTA SOMETIME DURING THE TRAINING, BUT...
TWO DAYS HAVE ALREADY PASSED.
TOO BAD...
WE'VE GOT NO EXTRA TIME AT ALL.
SPLASH
SPLOSH
EACH SCHOOL'S SESSION ENDS AT A DIFFERENT TIME TOO.
HERE.
OH, THANKS.
JÔTA!
?!
I SNUCK OUT.
OTHERWISE, IT'S IMPOSSIBLE TO TALK TO YOU.
HEY, JÔTARO, IS SHE YOUR FRIEND?
CHATTER
OH, SAKURA HIGH IS ALREADY FINISHED FOR THE DAY?
CHATTER
UM...
YES.
YOU'RE SO CUTE. ♡
IT'S IMPOSSIBLE TO TALK TO HIM WITH THIS MANY PEOPLE AROUND.
ITO, HERE'S A LETTER FOR YOU.
HUH?

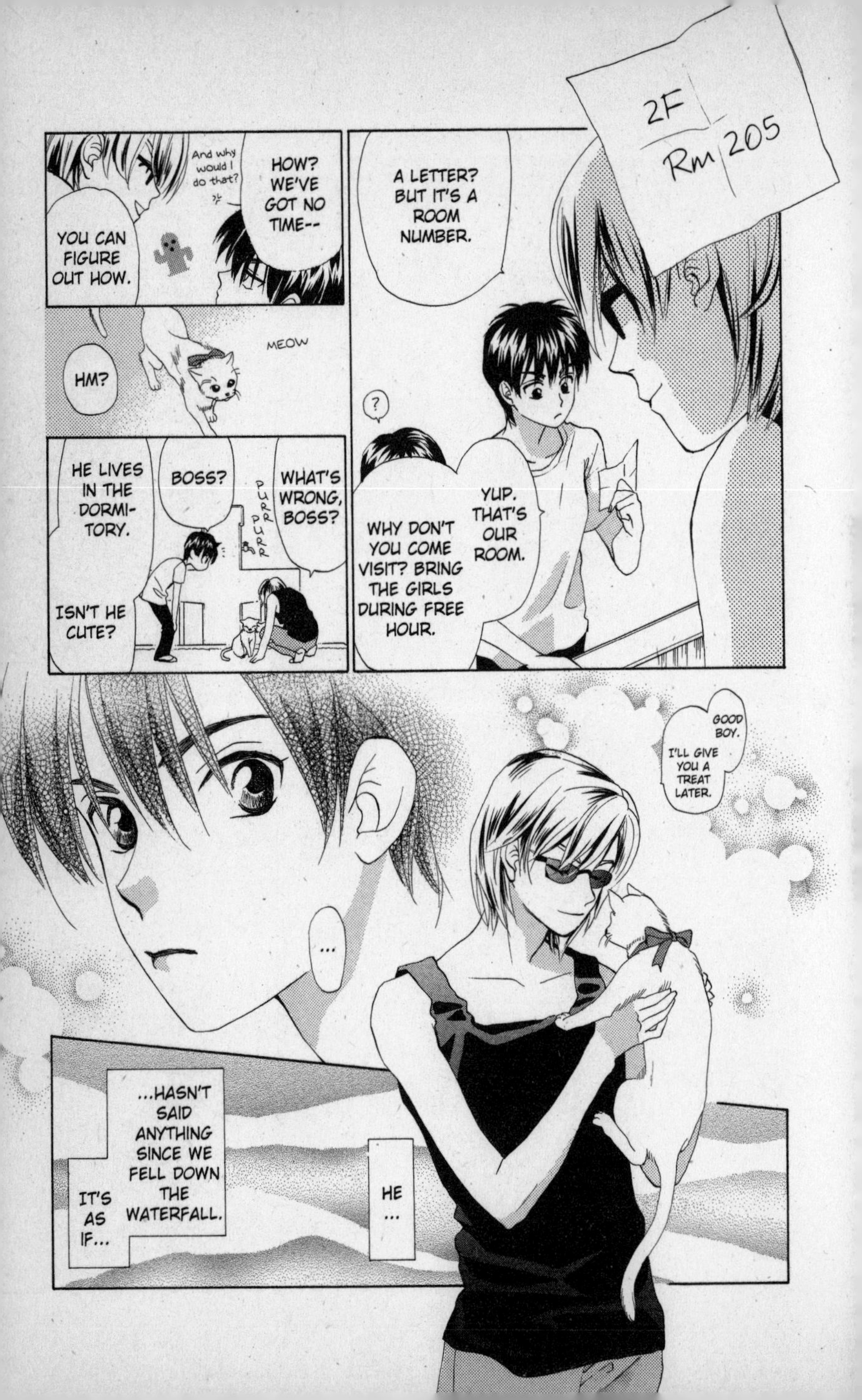
2F
Rm 205
A LETTER? BUT IT'S A ROOM NUMBER.
?
YUP. THAT'S OUR ROOM.
WHY DON'T YOU COME VISIT? BRING THE GIRLS DURING FREE HOUR.
HOW? WE'VE GOT NO TIME--
And why would I do that?
YOU CAN FIGURE OUT HOW.
MEOW
HM?
WHAT'S WRONG, BOSS?
PURR PURR
BOSS?
HE LIVES IN THE DORMITORY.
ISN'T HE CUTE?
GOOD BOY. I'LL GIVE YOU A TREAT LATER.
...
HE ...
...HASN'T SAID ANYTHING SINCE WE FELL DOWN THE WATERFALL.
IT'S AS IF...

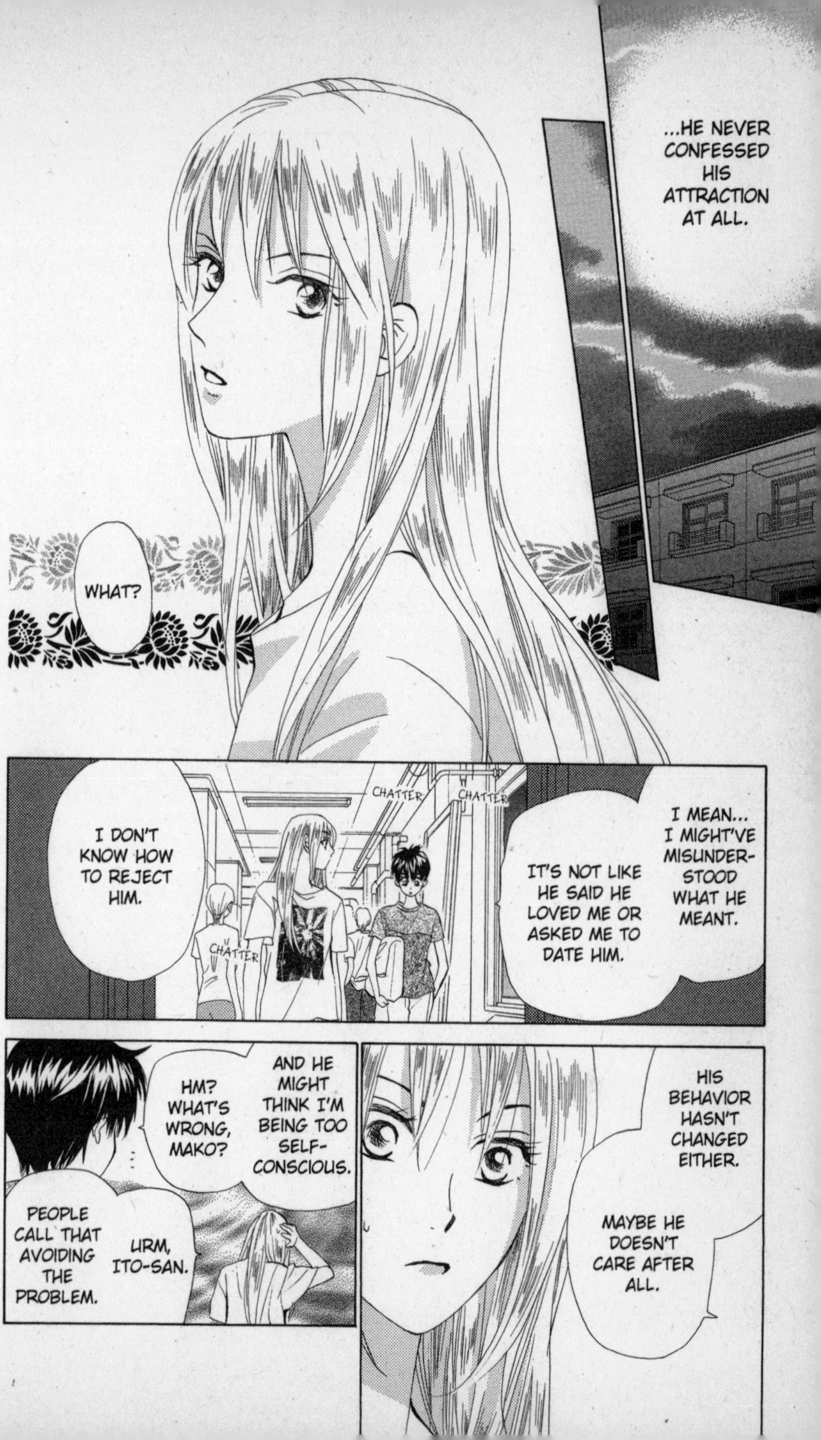
...HE NEVER CONFESSED HIS ATTRACTION AT ALL.
WHAT?
I MEAN... I MIGHT'VE MISUNDER-STOOD WHAT HE MEANT.
IT'S NOT LIKE HE SAID HE LOVED ME OR ASKED ME TO DATE HIM.
CHATTER
CHATTER
CHATTER
I DON'T KNOW HOW TO REJECT HIM.
HIS BEHAVIOR HASN'T CHANGED EITHER.
MAYBE HE DOESN'T CARE AFTER ALL.
AND HE MIGHT THINK I'M BEING TOO SELF-CONSCIOUS.
HM? WHAT'S WRONG, MAKO?
URM, ITO-SAN.
PEOPLE CALL THAT AVOIDING THE PROBLEM.

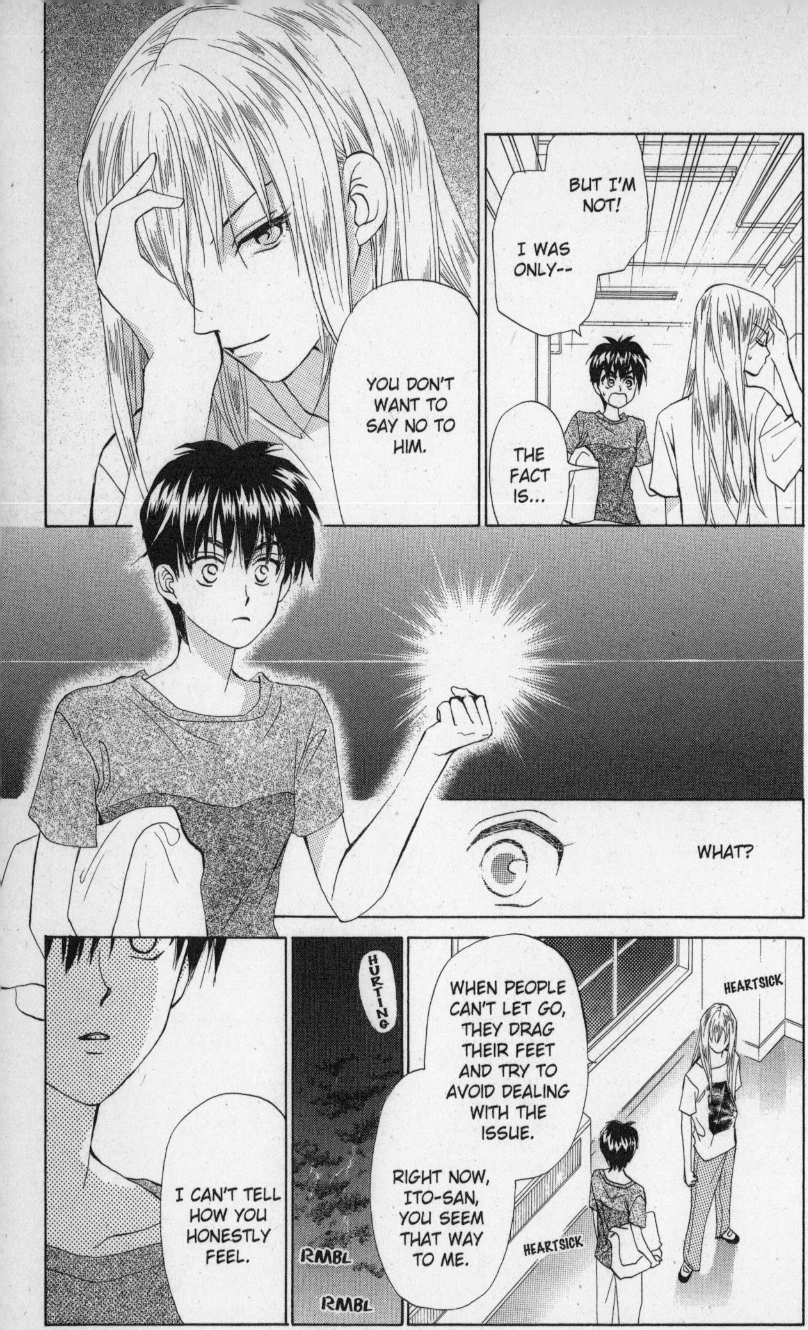
BUT I'M NOT!
I WAS ONLY--
THE FACT IS...
YOU DON'T WANT TO SAY NO TO HIM.
WHAT?
HEARTSICK
WHEN PEOPLE CAN'T LET GO, THEY DRAG THEIR FEET AND TRY TO AVOID DEALING WITH THE ISSUE.
RIGHT NOW, ITO-SAN, YOU SEEM THAT WAY TO ME.
HEARTSICK
HURTING
RMBL
RMBL
I CAN'T TELL HOW YOU HONESTLY FEEL.

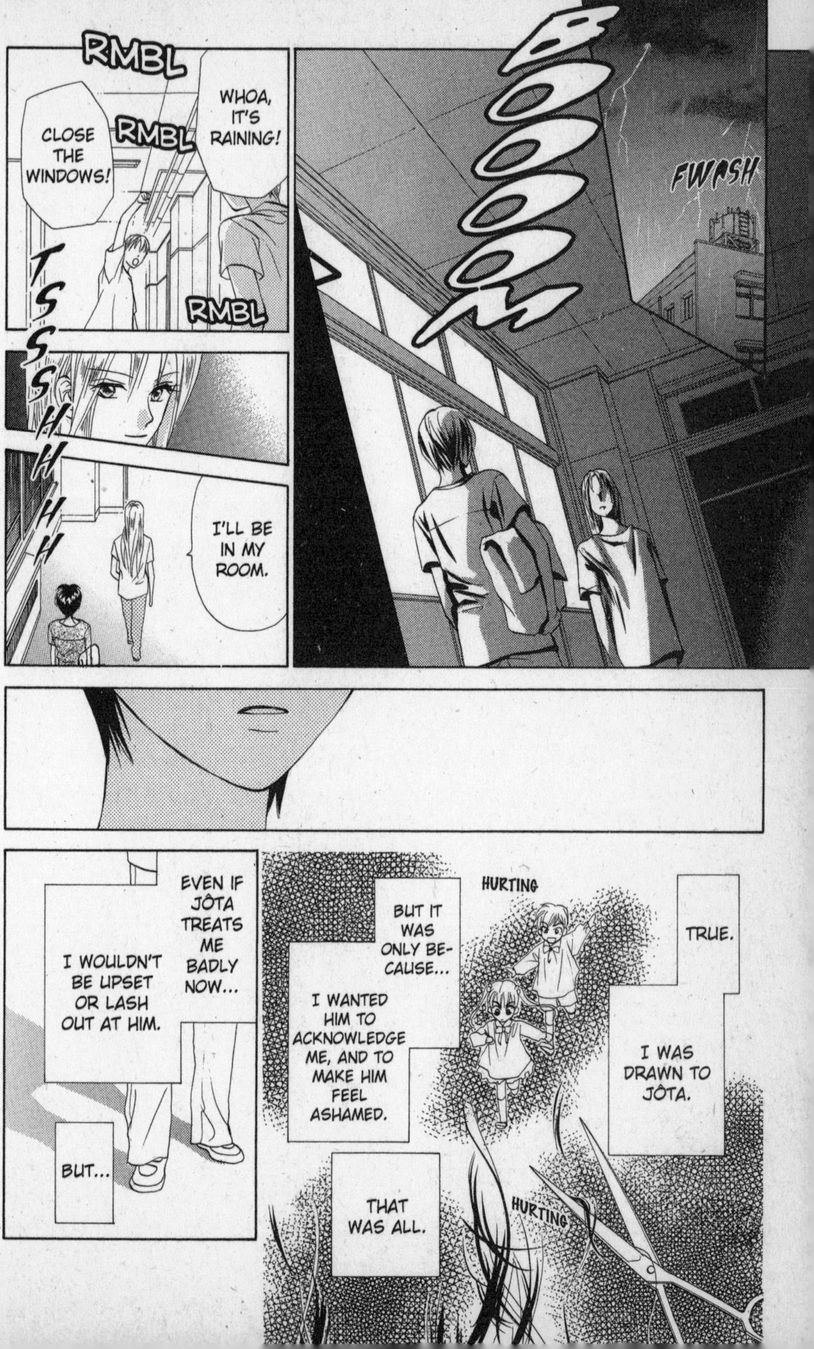
BOOOOOM
FWASH
RMBL
WHOA, IT'S RAINING!
CLOSE THE WINDOWS!
RMBL
RMBL
TSSSHHHHH
I'LL BE IN MY ROOM.
TRUE.
I WAS DRAWN TO JÔTA.
HURTING
BUT IT WAS ONLY BE-CAUSE...
I WANTED HIM TO ACKNOWLEDGE ME, AND TO MAKE HIM FEEL ASHAMED.
THAT WAS ALL.
HURTING
EVEN IF JÔTA TREATS ME BADLY NOW...
I WOULDN'T BE UPSET OR LASH OUT AT HIM.
BUT...

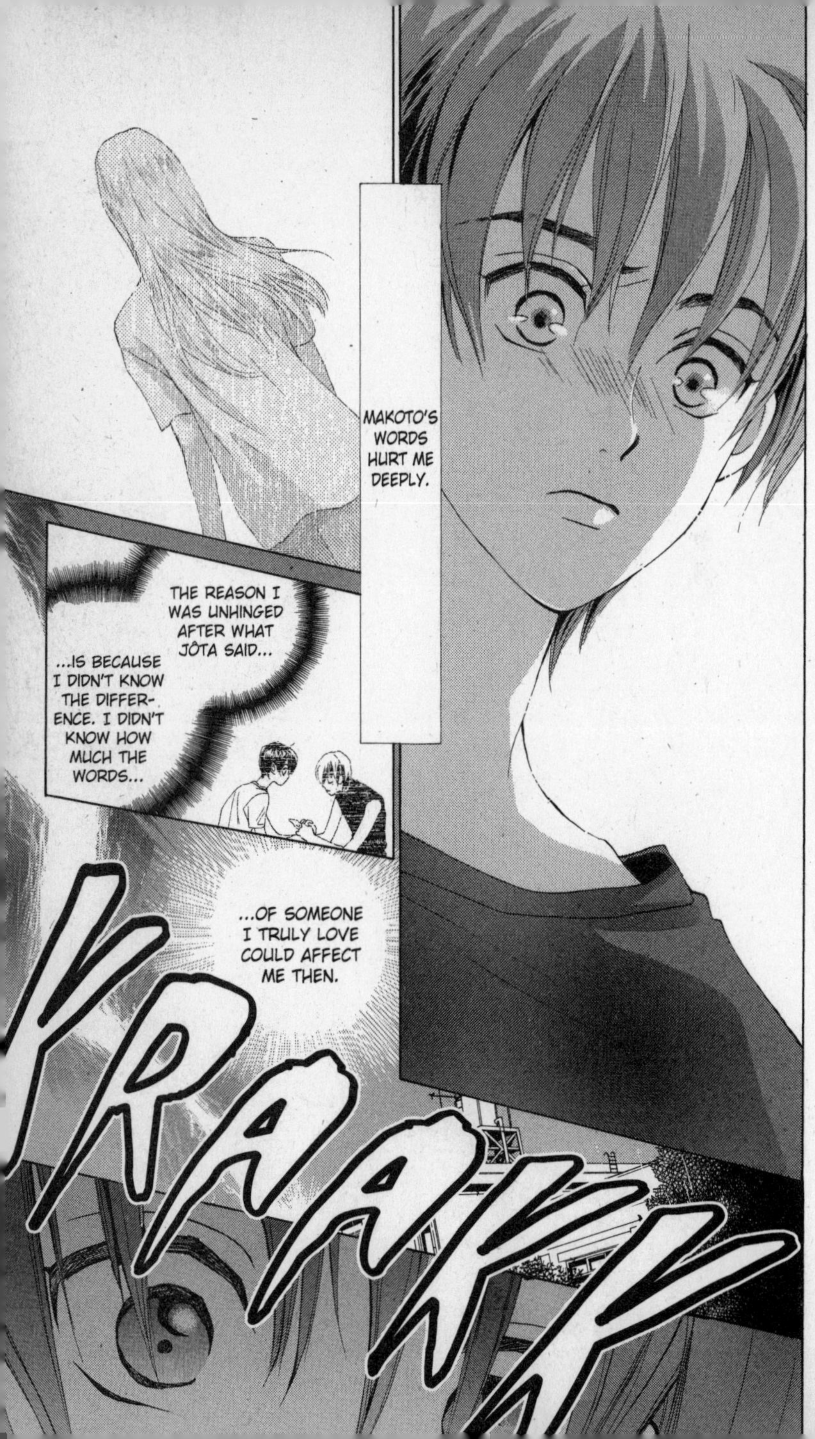
MAKOTO'S WORDS HURT ME DEEPLY.
THE REASON I WAS UNHINGED AFTER WHAT JÔTA SAID...
...IS BECAUSE I DIDN'T KNOW THE DIFFER-ENCE. I DIDN'T KNOW HOW MUCH THE WORDS...
...OF SOMEONE I TRULY LOVE COULD AFFECT ME THEN.
KRAAKK

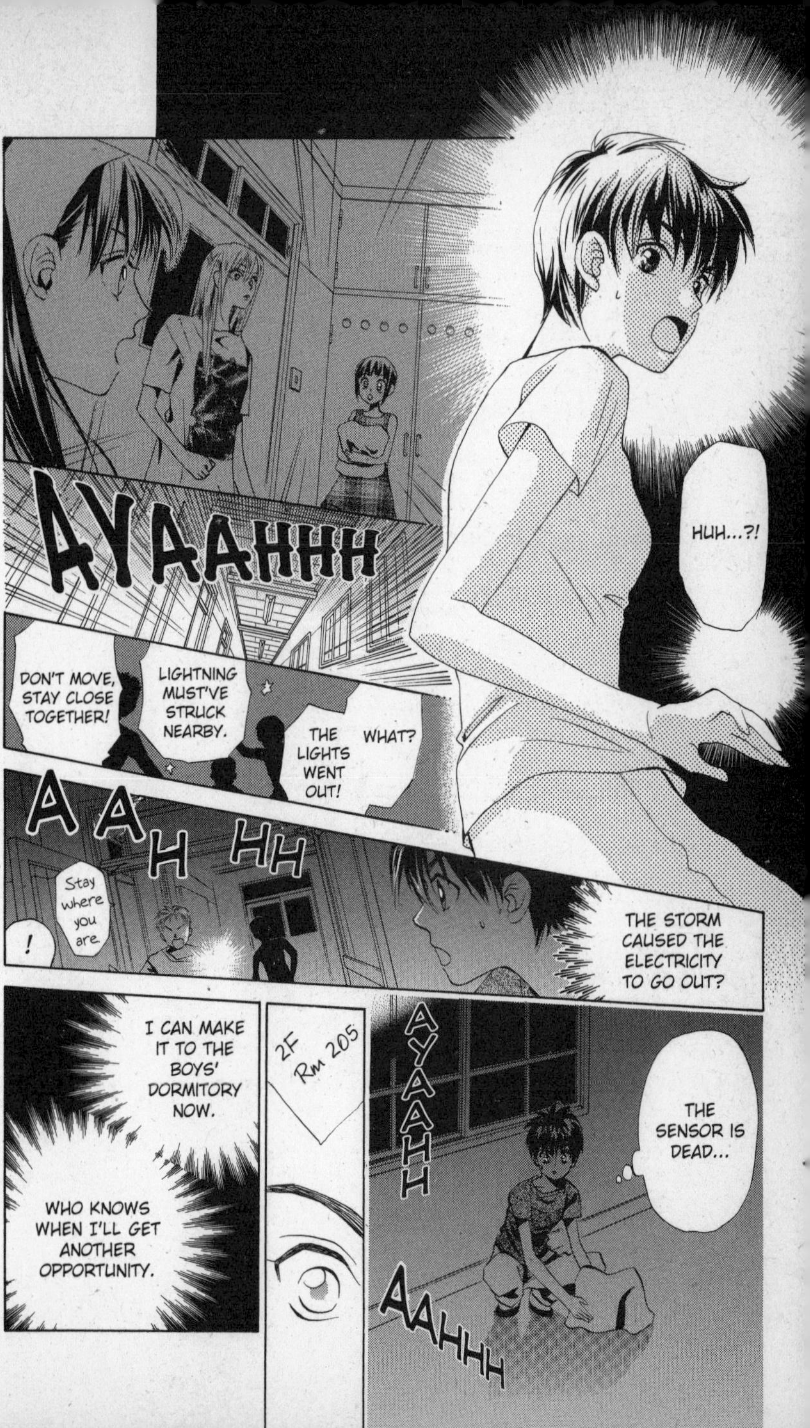
HUH...?!
AYAAHHH
WHAT?
THE LIGHTS WENT OUT!
LIGHTNING MUST'VE STRUCK NEARBY.
DON'T MOVE, STAY CLOSE TOGETHER!
AAHHH
THE STORM CAUSED THE ELECTRICITY TO GO OUT?
Stay where you are.
!
AYAAAHH
THE SENSOR IS DEAD...
AAHHH
2F Rm 205
I CAN MAKE IT TO THE BOYS' DORMITORY NOW.
WHO KNOWS WHEN I'LL GET ANOTHER OPPORTUNITY.

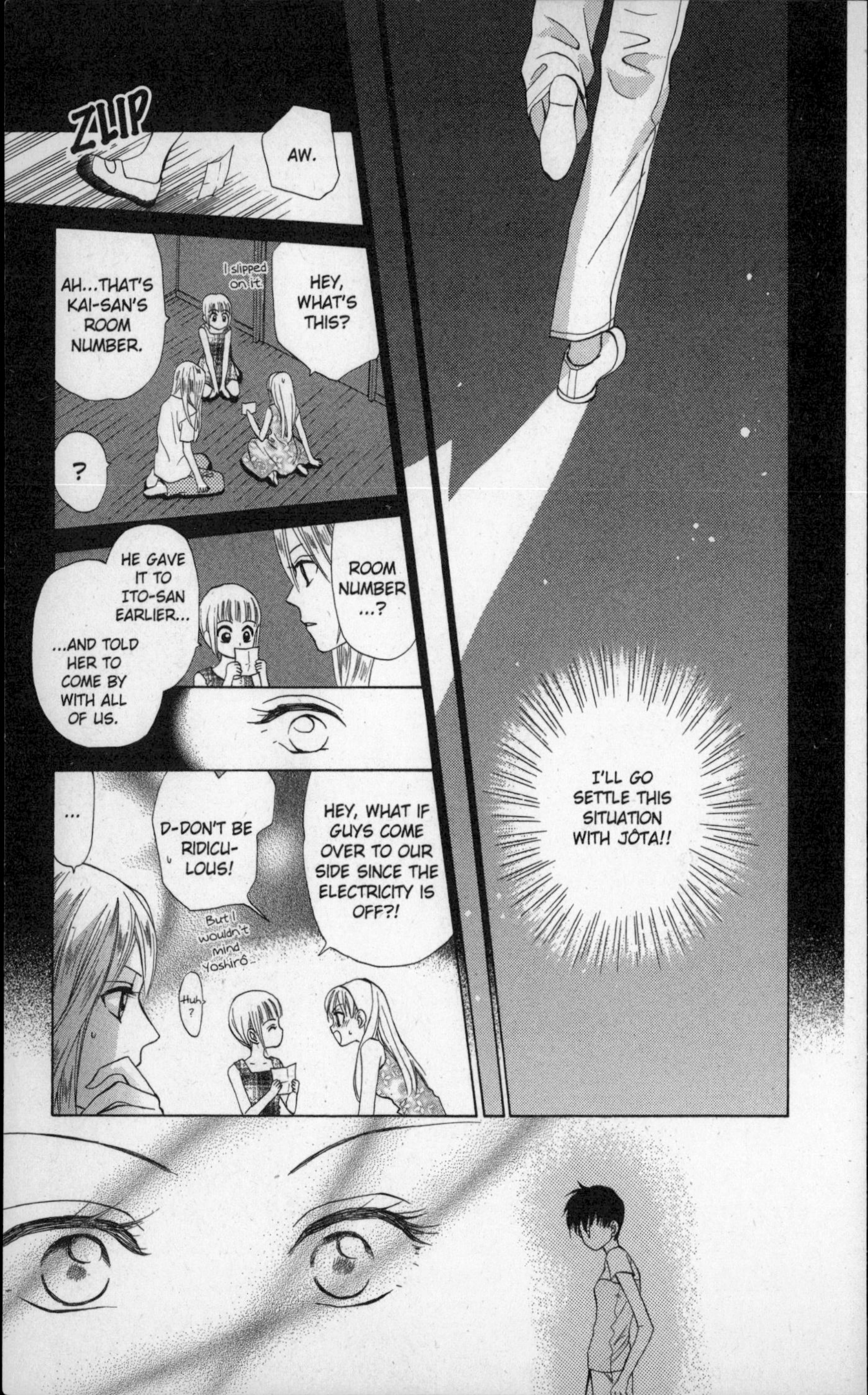
I'LL GO SETTLE THIS SITUATION WITH JÔTA!!
ZLIP
AW.
HEY, WHAT'S THIS?
I slipped on it.
AH...THAT'S KAI-SAN'S ROOM NUMBER.
?
ROOM NUMBER ...?
HE GAVE IT TO ITO-SAN EARLIER...
...AND TOLD HER TO COME BY WITH ALL OF US.
HEY, WHAT IF GUYS COME OVER TO OUR SIDE SINCE THE ELECTRICITY IS OFF?!
D-DON'T BE RIDICULOUS!
But I wouldn't mind Yoshirô...
...
Huh?

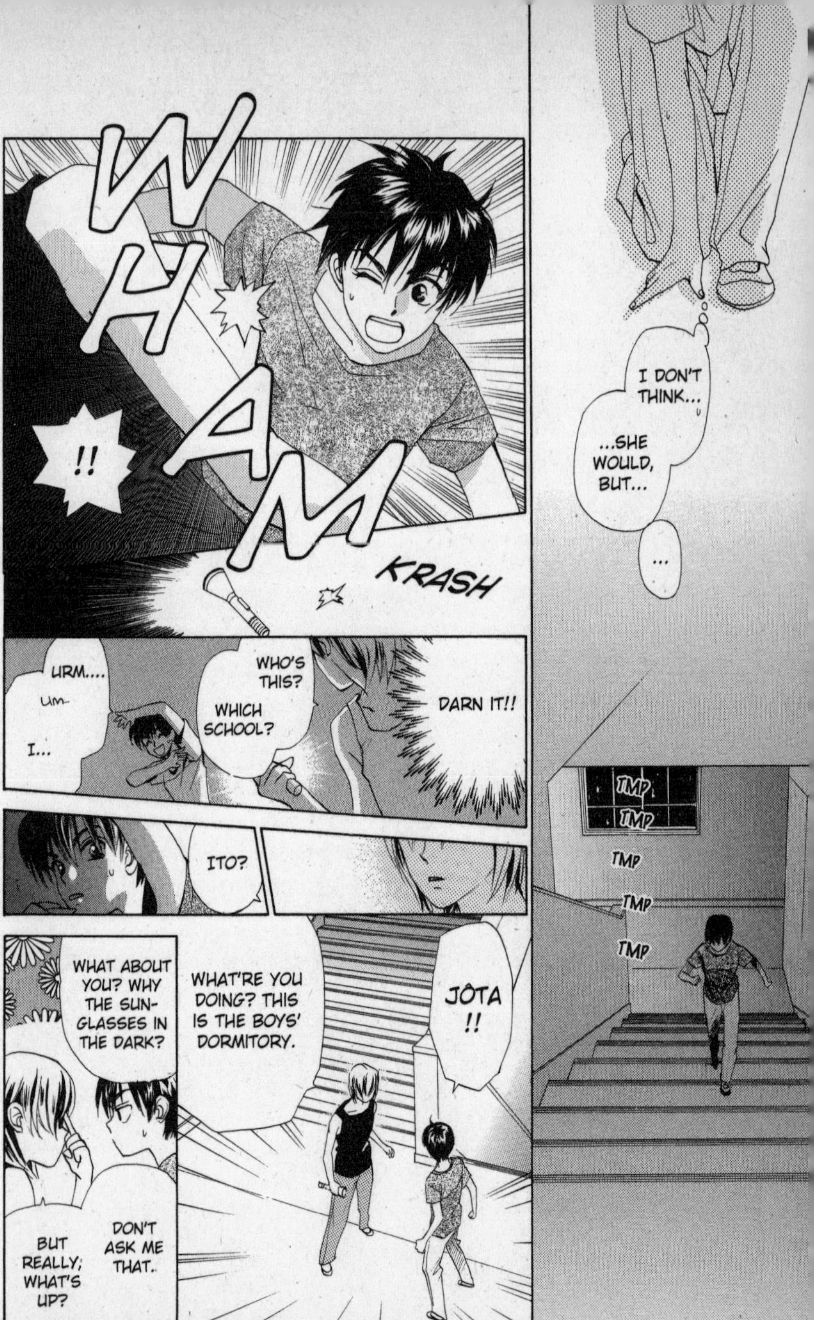
I DON'T THINK...
...SHE WOULD, BUT...
...
TMP
TMP
TMP
TMP
TMP
WHAM
!!
KRASH
DARN IT!!
WHO'S THIS? WHICH SCHOOL?
URM.... Um... I...
ITO?
JÔTA !!
WHAT'RE YOU DOING? THIS IS THE BOYS' DORMITORY.
WHAT ABOUT YOU? WHY THE SUN-GLASSES IN THE DARK?
DON'T ASK ME THAT.
BUT REALLY; WHAT'S UP?

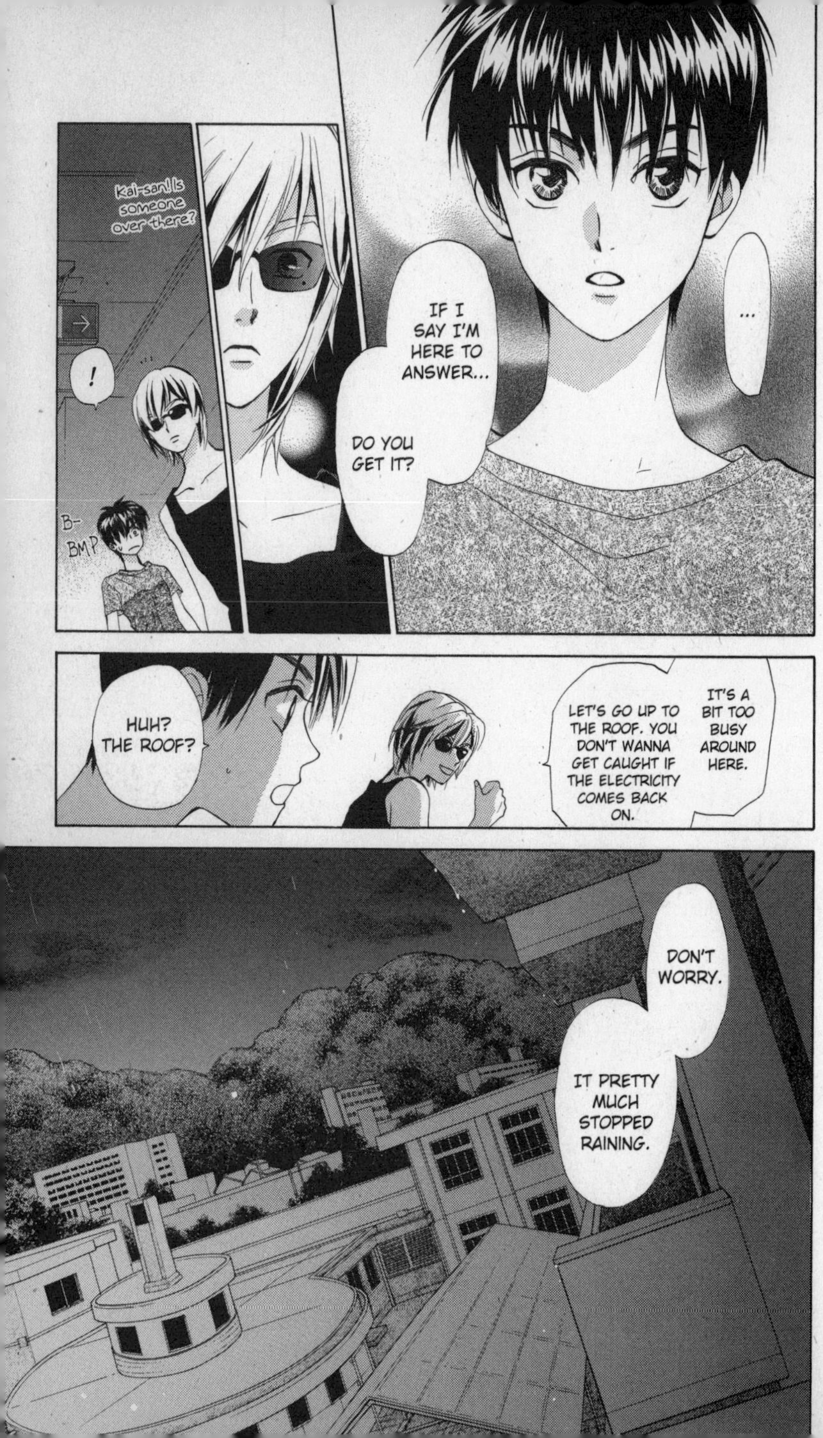
...
IF I SAY I'M HERE TO ANSWER...
DO YOU GET IT?
Kai-san! Is someone over there?
!
...
B-BMP
IT'S A BIT TOO BUSY AROUND HERE.
LET'S GO UP TO THE ROOF. YOU DON'T WANNA GET CAUGHT IF THE ELECTRICITY COMES BACK ON.
HUH? THE ROOF?
DON'T WORRY.
IT PRETTY MUCH STOPPED RAINING.

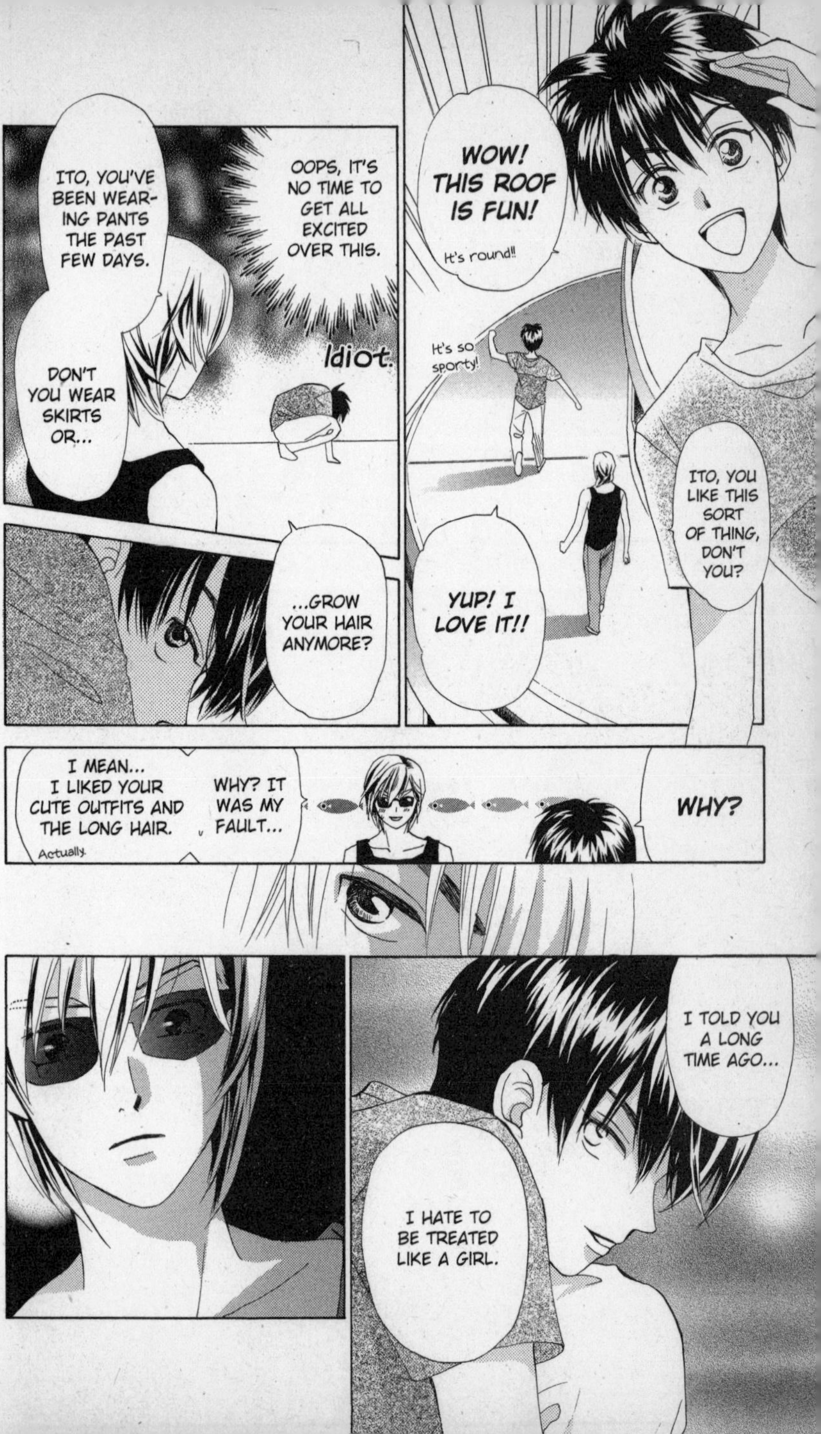
WOW! THIS ROOF IS FUN!
It's round!!
It's so sporty!
ITO, YOU LIKE THIS SORT OF THING, DON'T YOU?
YUP! I LOVE IT!!
OOPS, IT'S NO TIME TO GET ALL EXCITED OVER THIS.
Idiot.
ITO, YOU'VE BEEN WEAR-ING PANTS THE PAST FEW DAYS.
DON'T YOU WEAR SKIRTS OR...
...GROW YOUR HAIR ANYMORE?
WHY?
WHY? IT WAS MY FAULT...
I MEAN... I LIKED YOUR CUTE OUTFITS AND THE LONG HAIR.
Actually.
I TOLD YOU A LONG TIME AGO...
I HATE TO BE TREATED LIKE A GIRL.

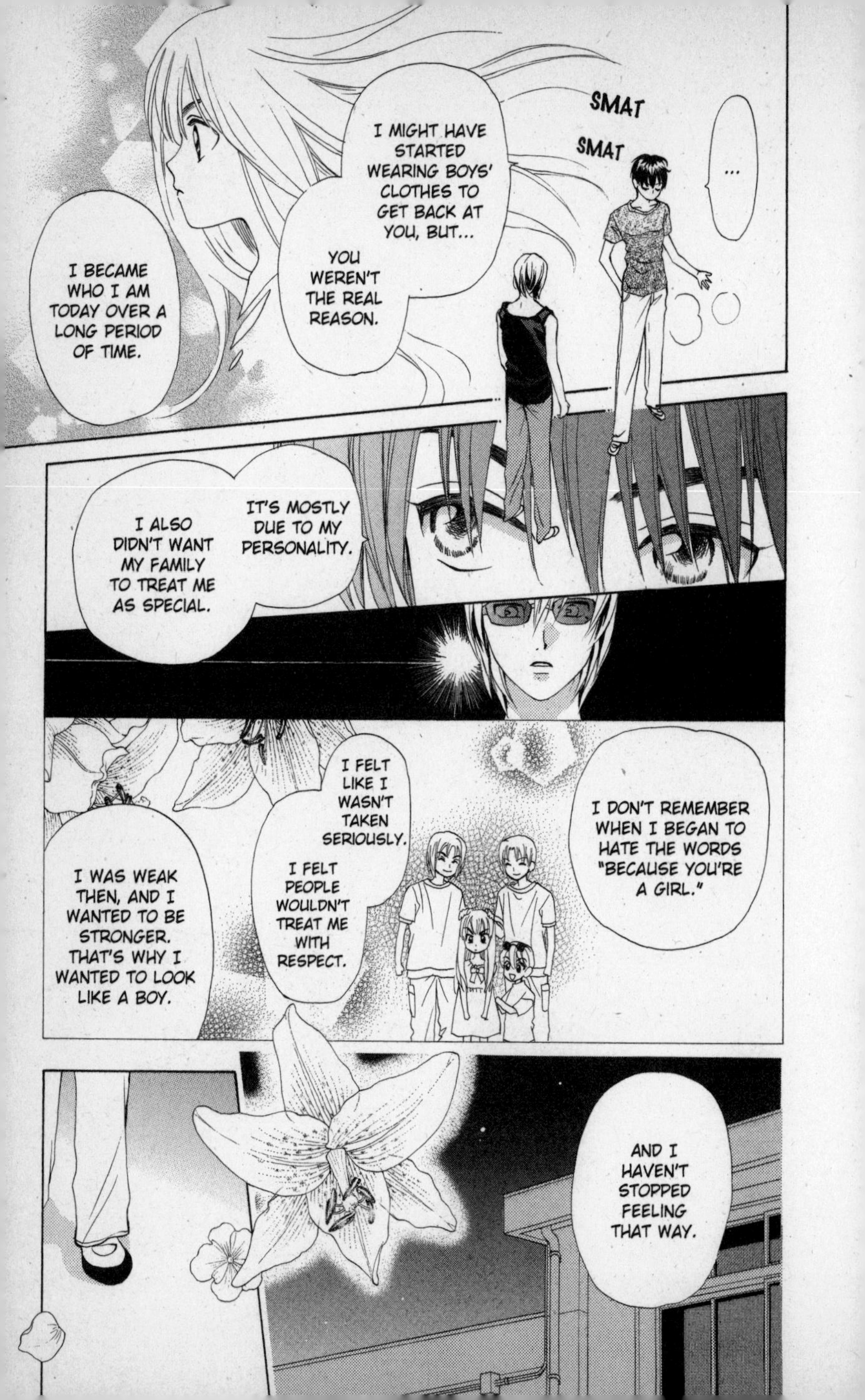
...
SMAT
SMAT
I MIGHT HAVE STARTED WEARING BOYS' CLOTHES TO GET BACK AT YOU, BUT...
YOU WEREN'T THE REAL REASON.
I BECAME WHO I AM TODAY OVER A LONG PERIOD OF TIME.
IT'S MOSTLY DUE TO MY PERSONALITY.
I ALSO DIDN'T WANT MY FAMILY TO TREAT ME AS SPECIAL.
I DON'T REMEMBER WHEN I BEGAN TO HATE THE WORDS "BECAUSE YOU'RE A GIRL."
I FELT LIKE I WASN'T TAKEN SERIOUSLY.
I FELT PEOPLE WOULDN'T TREAT ME WITH RESPECT.
I WAS WEAK THEN, AND I WANTED TO BE STRONGER. THAT'S WHY I WANTED TO LOOK LIKE A BOY.
AND I HAVEN'T STOPPED FEELING THAT WAY.

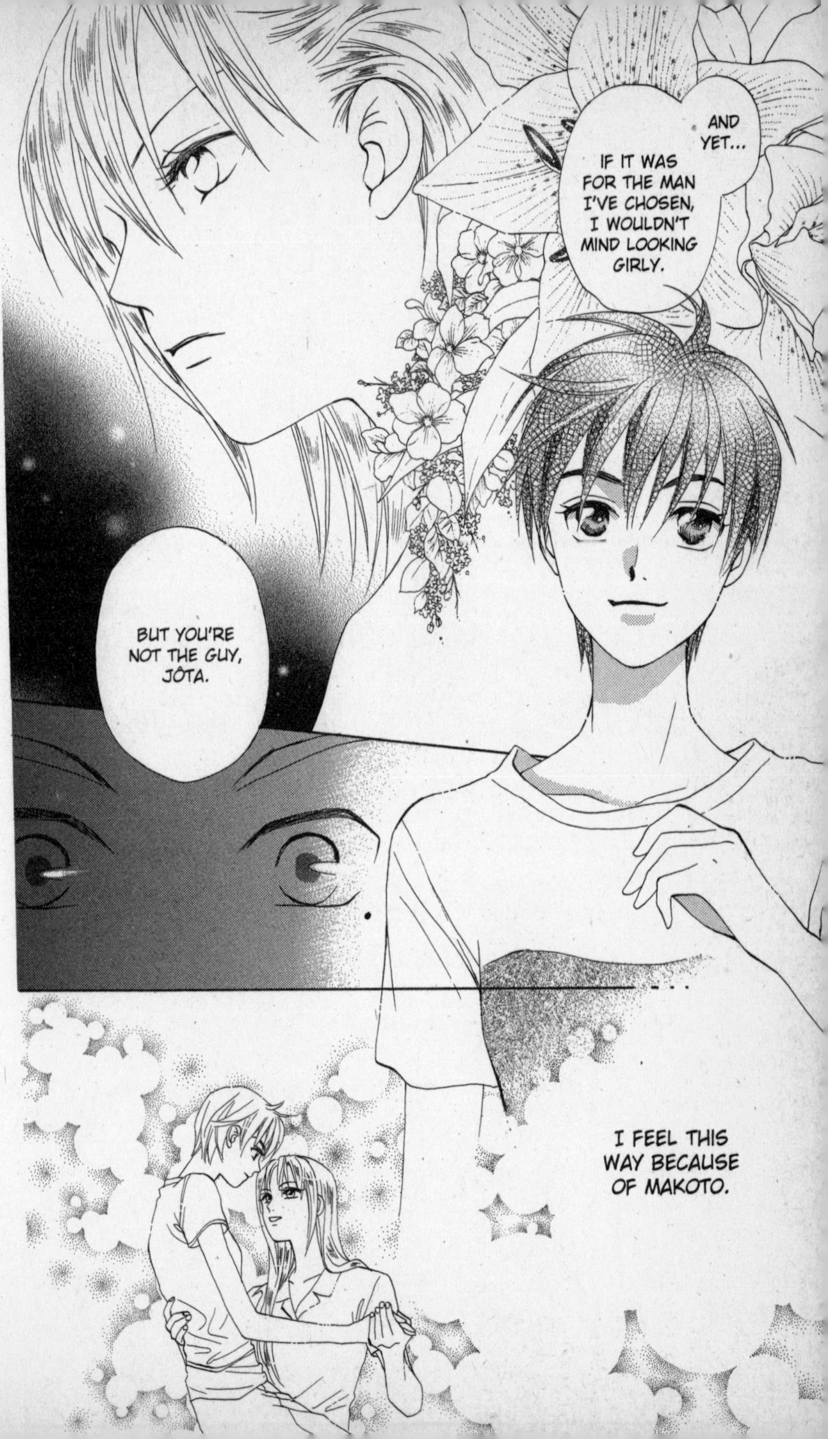
AND YET...
IF IT WAS FOR THE MAN I'VE CHOSEN, I WOULDN'T MIND LOOKING GIRLY.
BUT YOU'RE NOT THE GUY, JÔTA.
I FEEL THIS WAY BECAUSE OF MAKOTO.

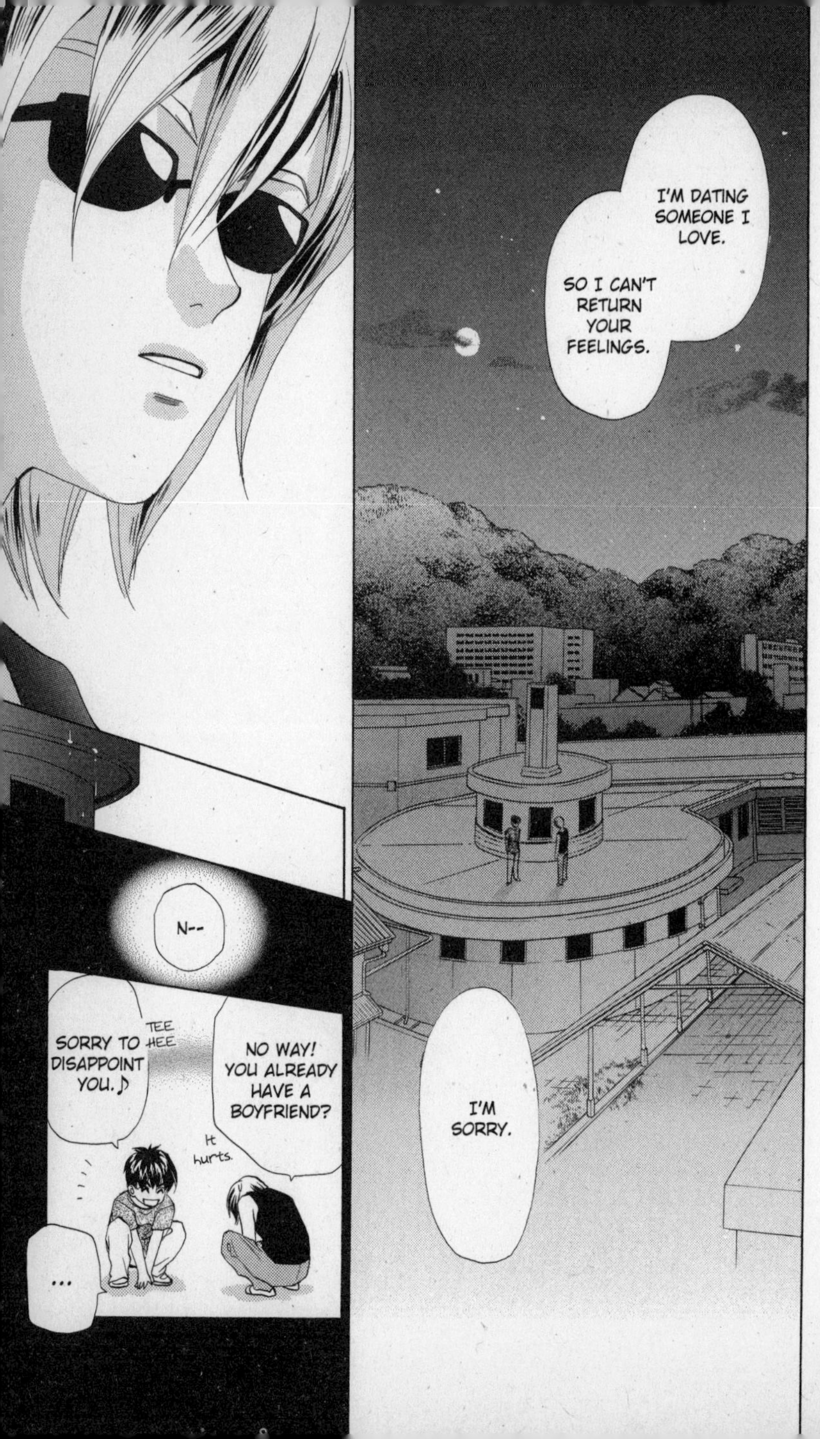
I'M DATING SOMEONE I LOVE.
SO I CAN'T RETURN YOUR FEELINGS.
I'M SORRY.
N--
NO WAY! YOU ALREADY HAVE A BOYFRIEND?
It hurts.
TEE HEE
SORRY TO DISAPPOINT YOU.♪
...

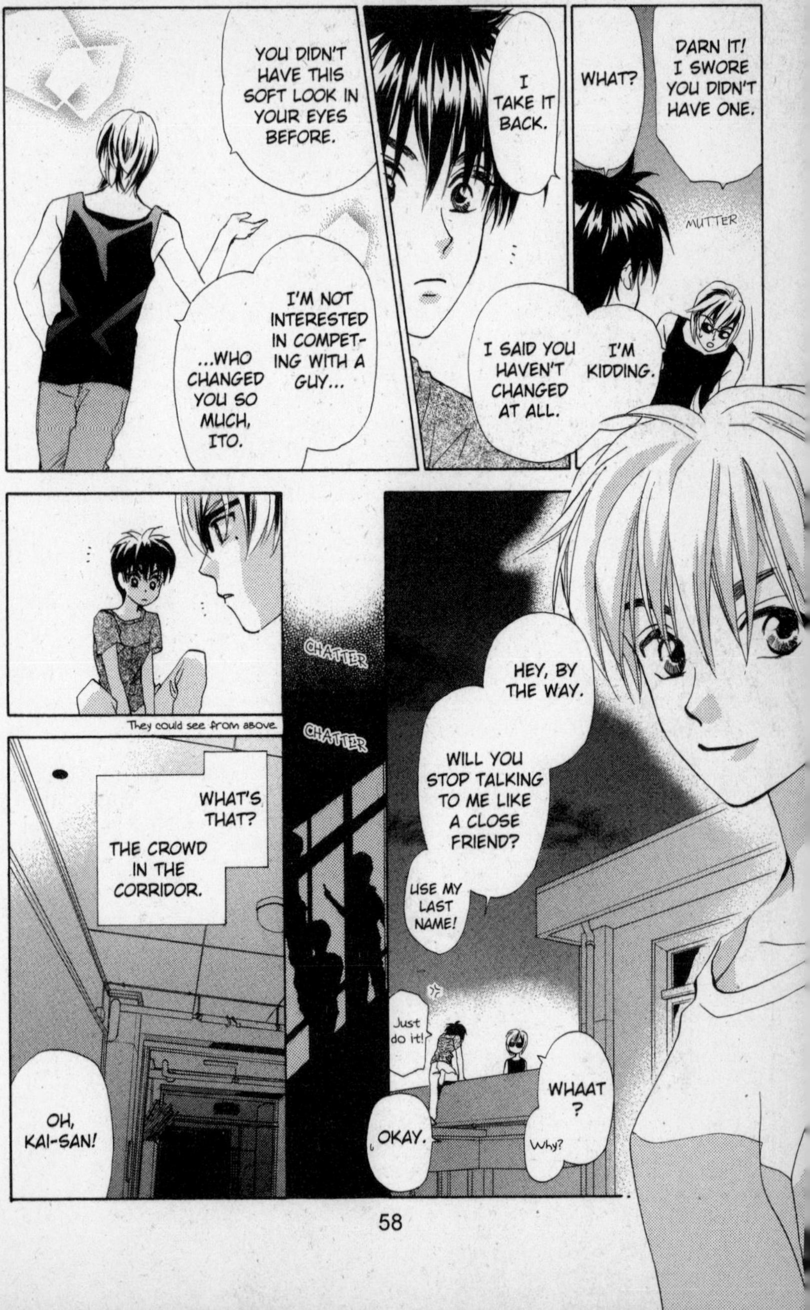
DARN IT! I SWORE YOU DIDN'T HAVE ONE.
WHAT?
MUTTER
I'M KIDDING.
I SAID YOU HAVEN'T CHANGED AT ALL.
I TAKE IT BACK.
YOU DIDN'T HAVE THIS SOFT LOOK IN YOUR EYES BEFORE.
I'M NOT INTERESTED IN COMPETING WITH A GUY...
...WHO CHANGED YOU SO MUCH, ITO.
HEY, BY THE WAY.
WILL YOU STOP TALKING TO ME LIKE A CLOSE FRIEND?
USE MY LAST NAME!
WHAAT?
Why?
Just do it!
OKAY.
CHATTER
CHATTER
They could see from above.
WHAT'S THAT?
THE CROWD IN THE CORRIDOR.
OH, KAI-SAN!

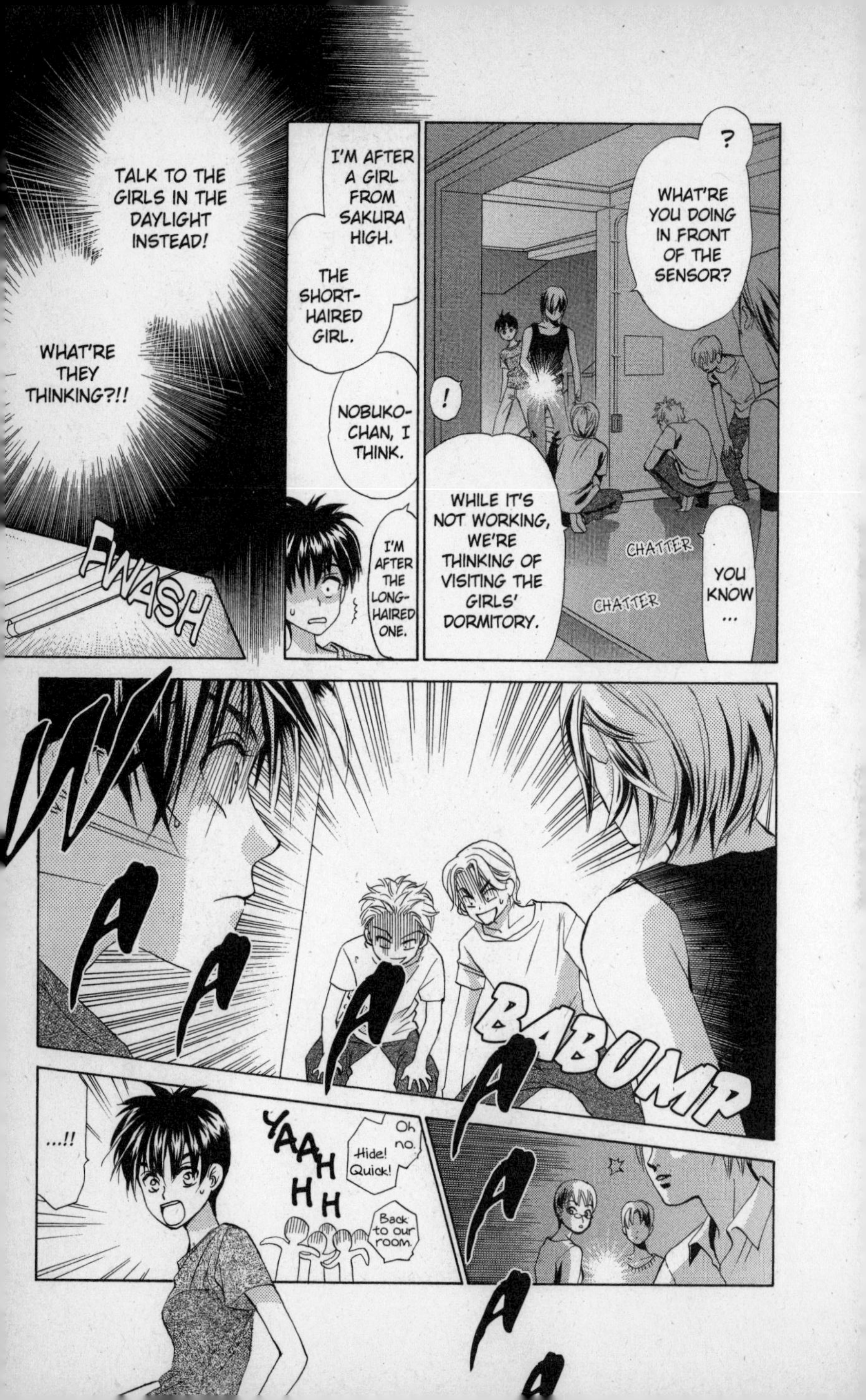
?
WHAT'RE YOU DOING IN FRONT OF THE SENSOR?
!
YOU KNOW...
CHATTER
CHATTER
WHILE IT'S NOT WORKING, WE'RE THINKING OF VISITING THE GIRLS' DORMITORY.
I'M AFTER A GIRL FROM SAKURA HIGH.
THE SHORT-HAIRED GIRL.
NOBUKO-CHAN, I THINK.
I'M AFTER THE LONG-HAIRED ONE.
TALK TO THE GIRLS IN THE DAYLIGHT INSTEAD!
WHAT'RE THEY THINKING?!!
FWASH
WAAAAAAAA
BABUMP
Oh no.
Hide! Quick!
Back to our room.
YAAAHHH
...!!

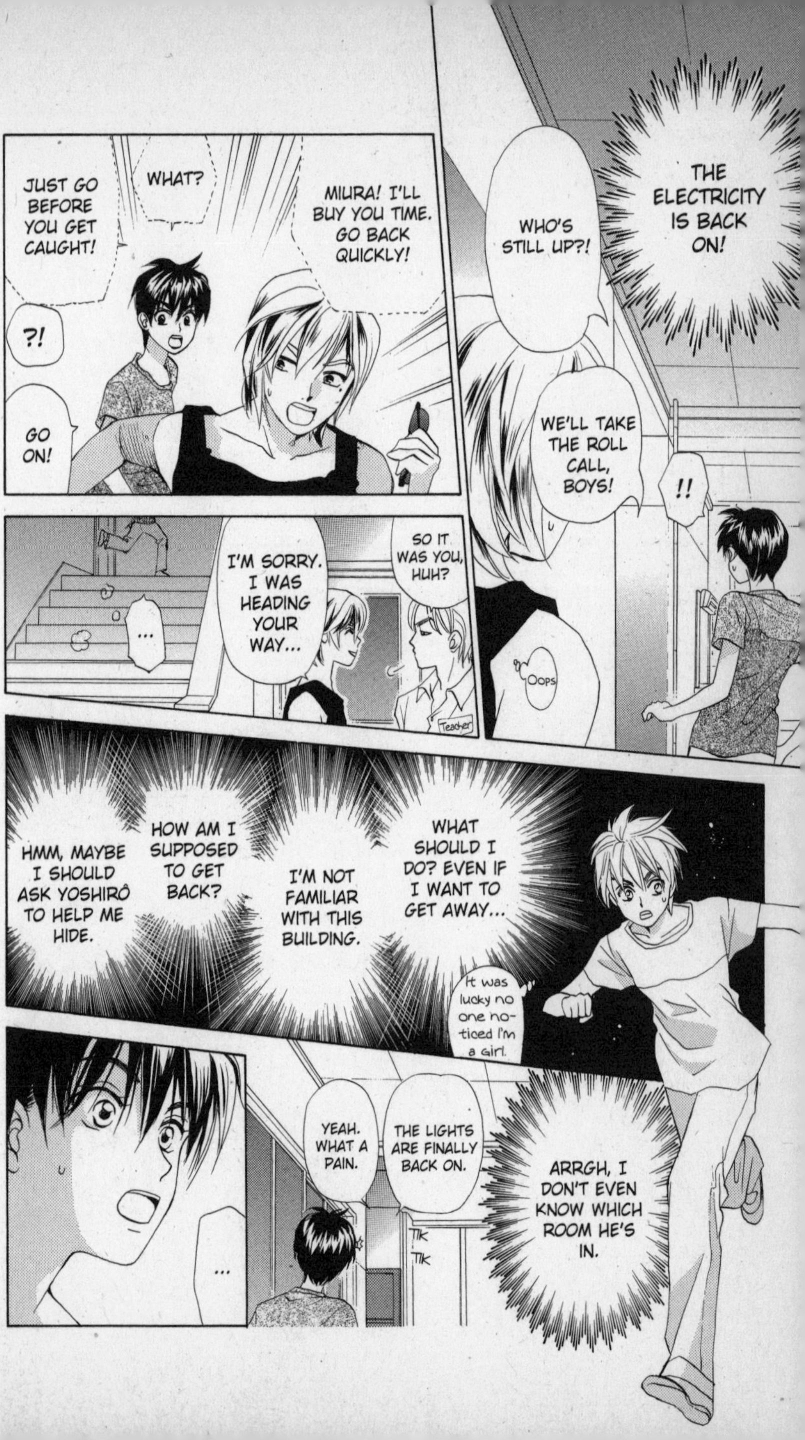
THE ELECTRICITY IS BACK ON!
WHO'S STILL UP?!
WE'LL TAKE THE ROLL CALL, BOYS!
!!
Oops
MIURA! I'LL BUY YOU TIME. GO BACK QUICKLY!
WHAT?
JUST GO BEFORE YOU GET CAUGHT!
?!
GO ON!
SO IT WAS YOU, HUH?
I'M SORRY. I WAS HEADING YOUR WAY...
...
Teacher
WHAT SHOULD I DO? EVEN IF I WANT TO GET AWAY...
I'M NOT FAMILIAR WITH THIS BUILDING.
HOW AM I SUPPOSED TO GET BACK?
HMM, MAYBE I SHOULD ASK YOSHIRÔ TO HELP ME HIDE.
It was lucky no one noticed I'm a girl.
ARRGH, I DON'T EVEN KNOW WHICH ROOM HE'S IN.
THE LIGHTS ARE FINALLY BACK ON.
YEAH. WHAT A PAIN.
TIK TIK
...

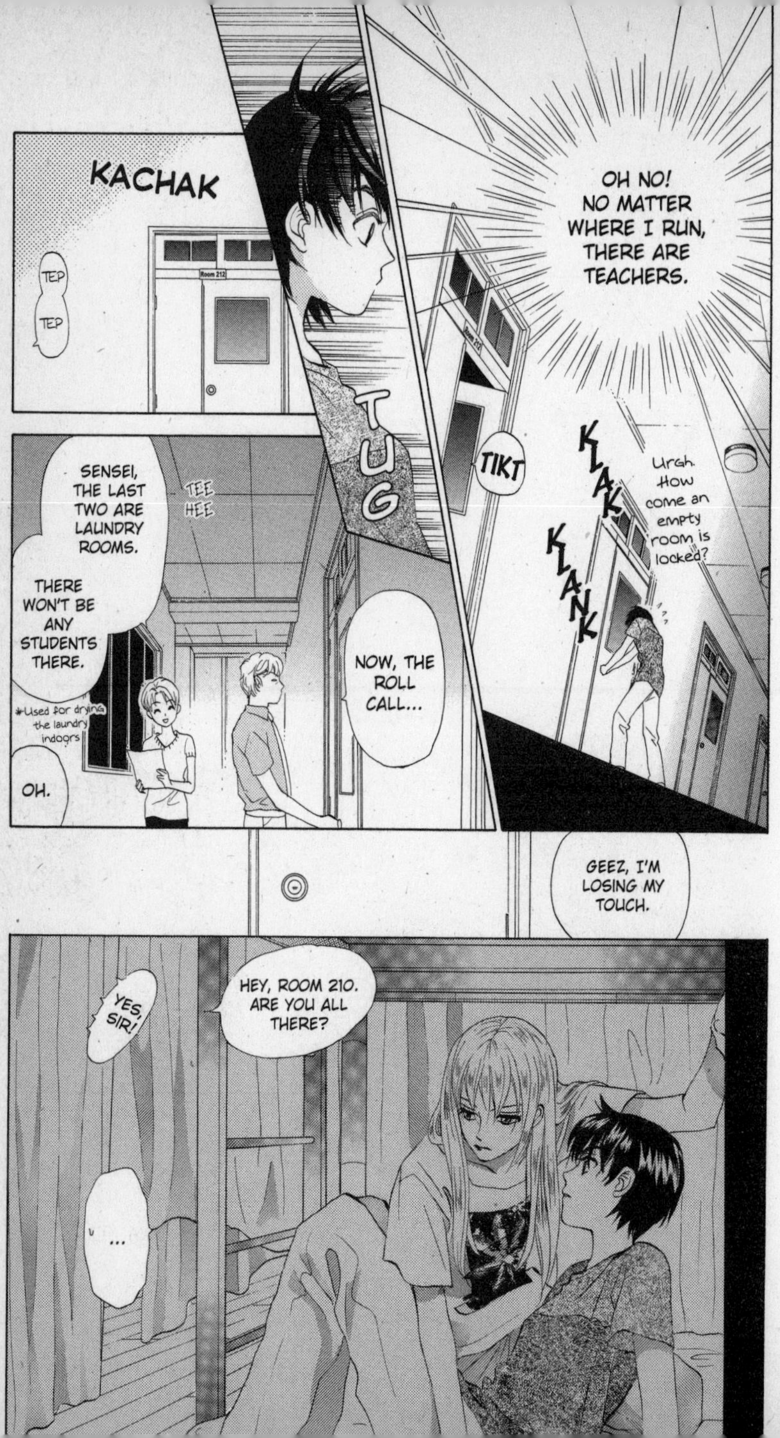
OH NO! NO MATTER WHERE I RUN, THERE ARE TEACHERS.
TIKT
KLAK KLANK
Urgh. How come an empty room is locked?
TUG
KACHAK
TEP TEP
NOW, THE ROLL CALL...
SENSEI, THE LAST TWO ARE LAUNDRY ROOMS.
THERE WON'T BE ANY STUDENTS THERE.
TEE HEE
*Used for drying the laundry indoors
OH.
GEEZ, I'M LOSING MY TOUCH.
HEY, ROOM 210. ARE YOU ALL THERE?
YES, SIR!
...

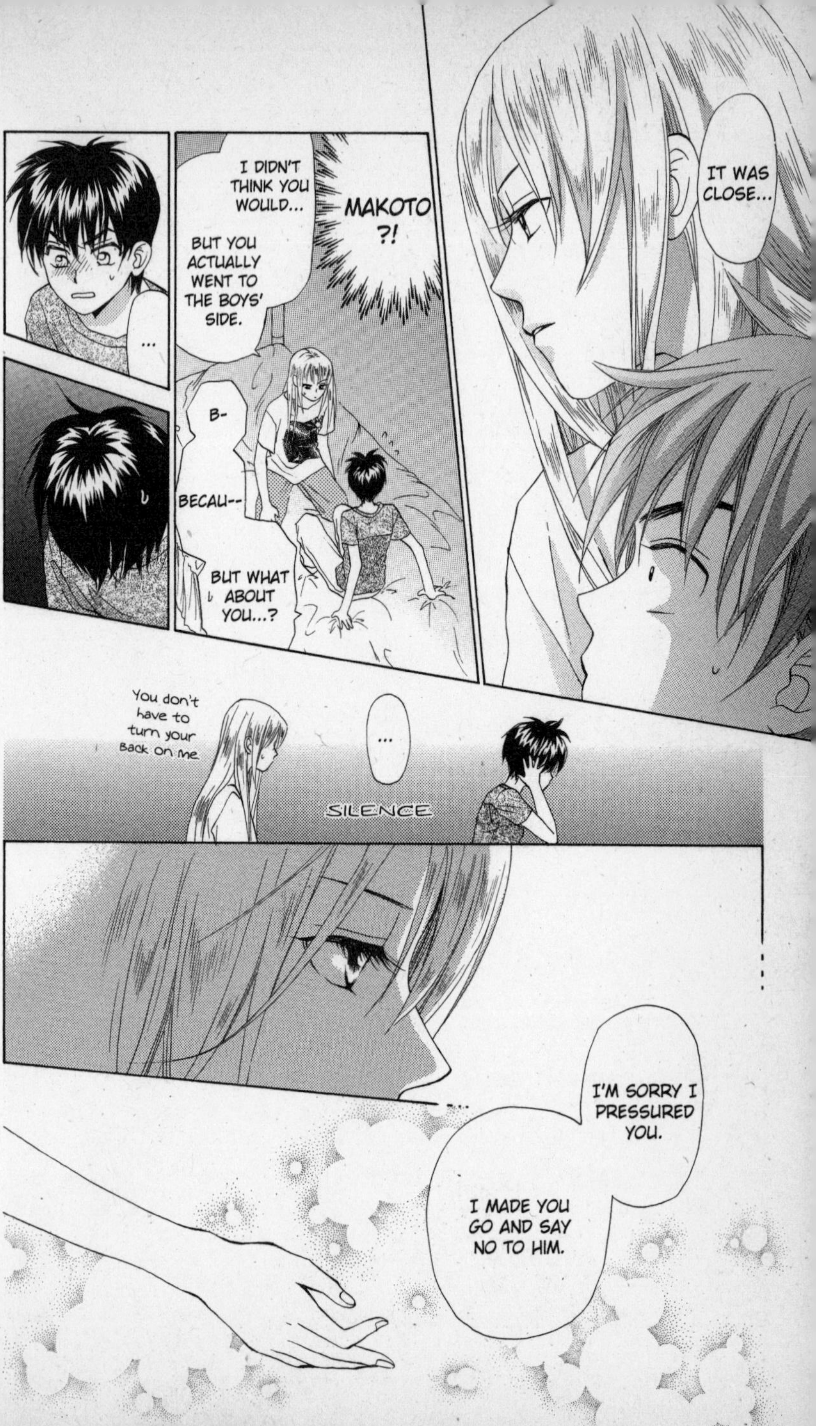
IT WAS CLOSE...
MAKOTO ?!
I DIDN'T THINK YOU WOULD...
BUT YOU ACTUALLY WENT TO THE BOYS' SIDE.
B-
BECAU--
BUT WHAT ABOUT YOU...?
...
...
SILENCE
You don't have to turn your Back on me
...
I'M SORRY I PRESSURED YOU.
I MADE YOU GO AND SAY NO TO HIM.

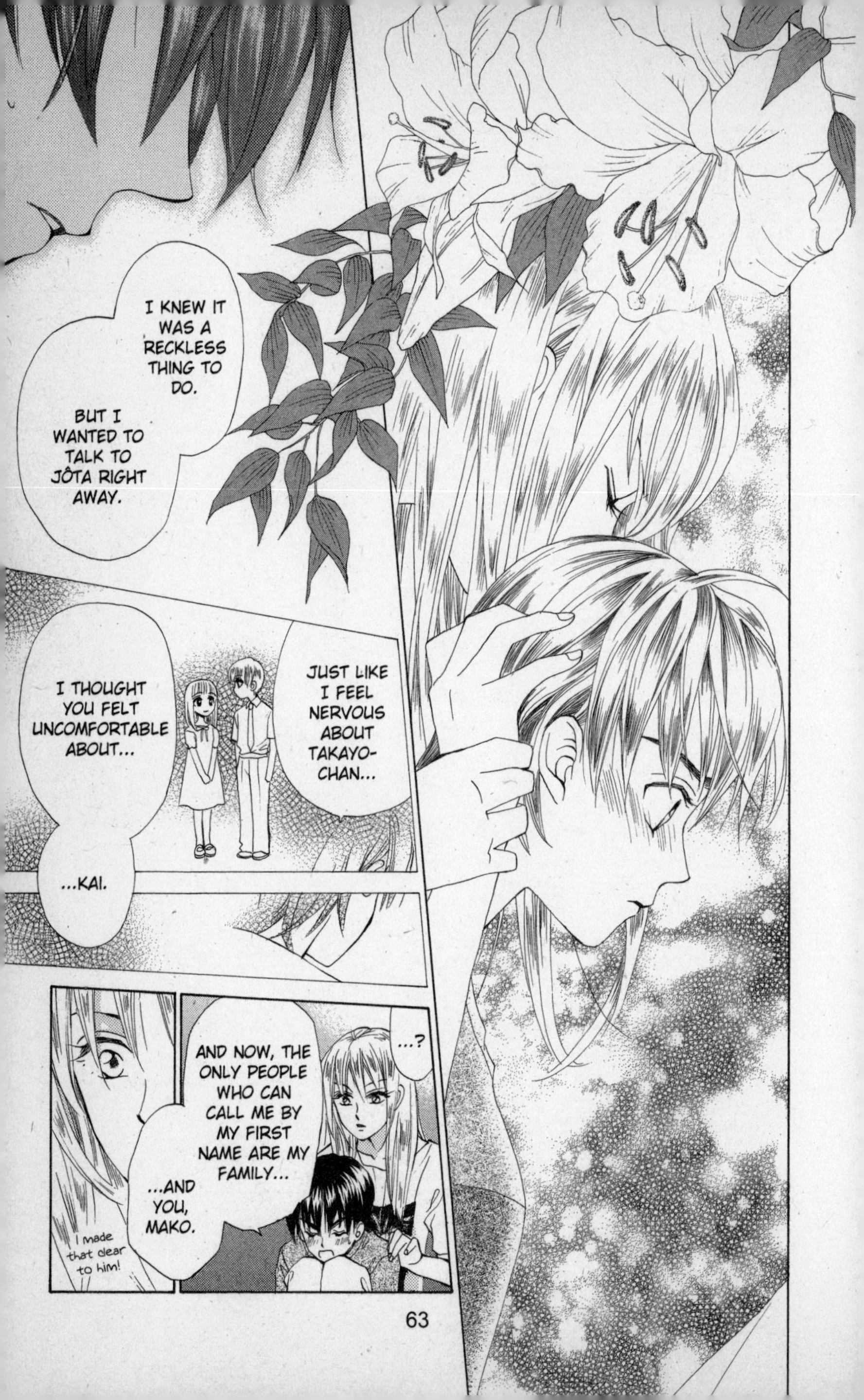
I KNEW IT WAS A RECKLESS THING TO DO.
BUT I WANTED TO TALK TO JÔTA RIGHT AWAY.
JUST LIKE I FEEL NERVOUS ABOUT TAKAYO-CHAN...
I THOUGHT YOU FELT UNCOMFORTABLE ABOUT...
...KAI.
...?
AND NOW, THE ONLY PEOPLE WHO CAN CALL ME BY MY FIRST NAME ARE MY FAMILY...
...AND YOU, MAKO.
I made that clear to him!

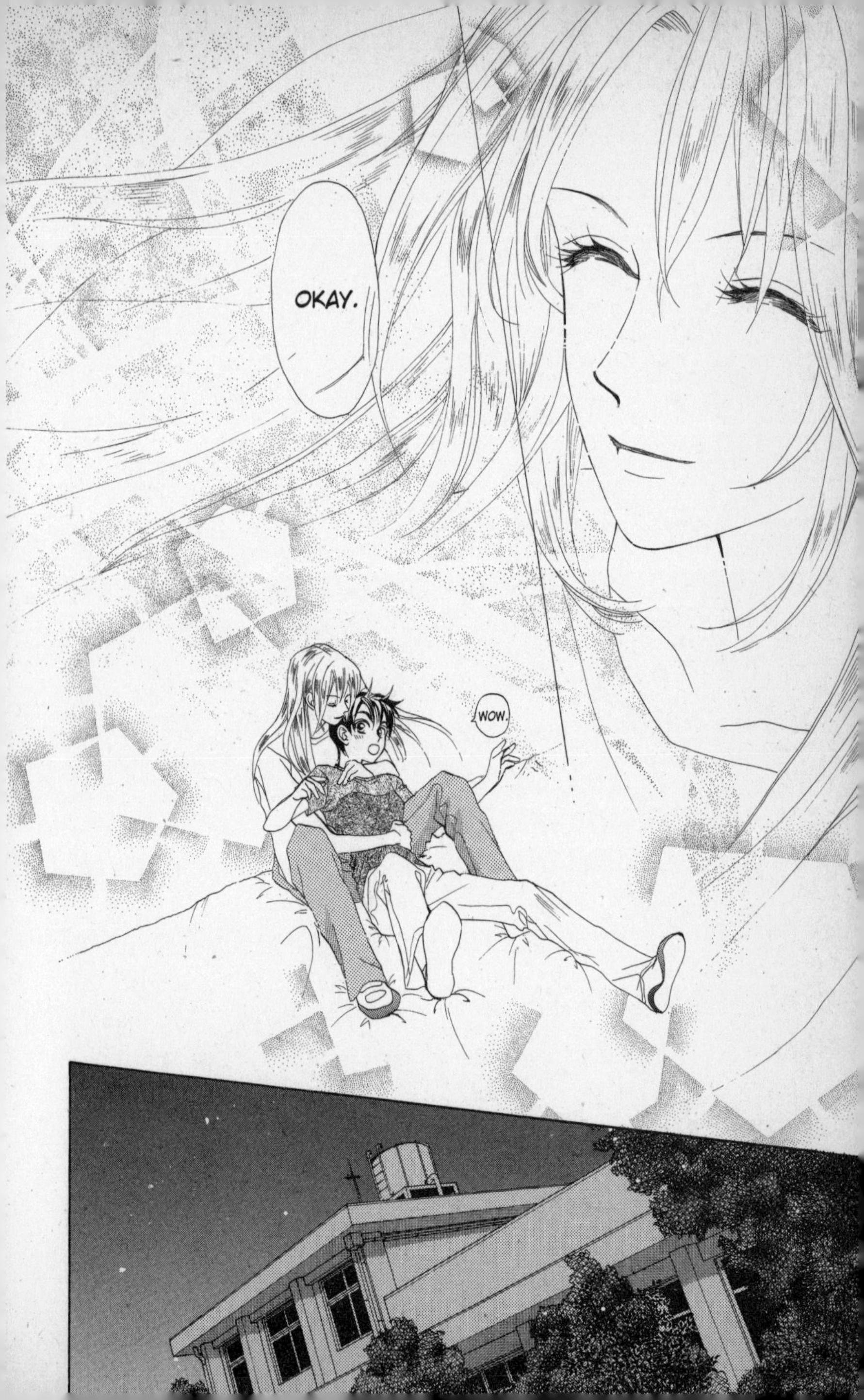
OKAY.
WOW.

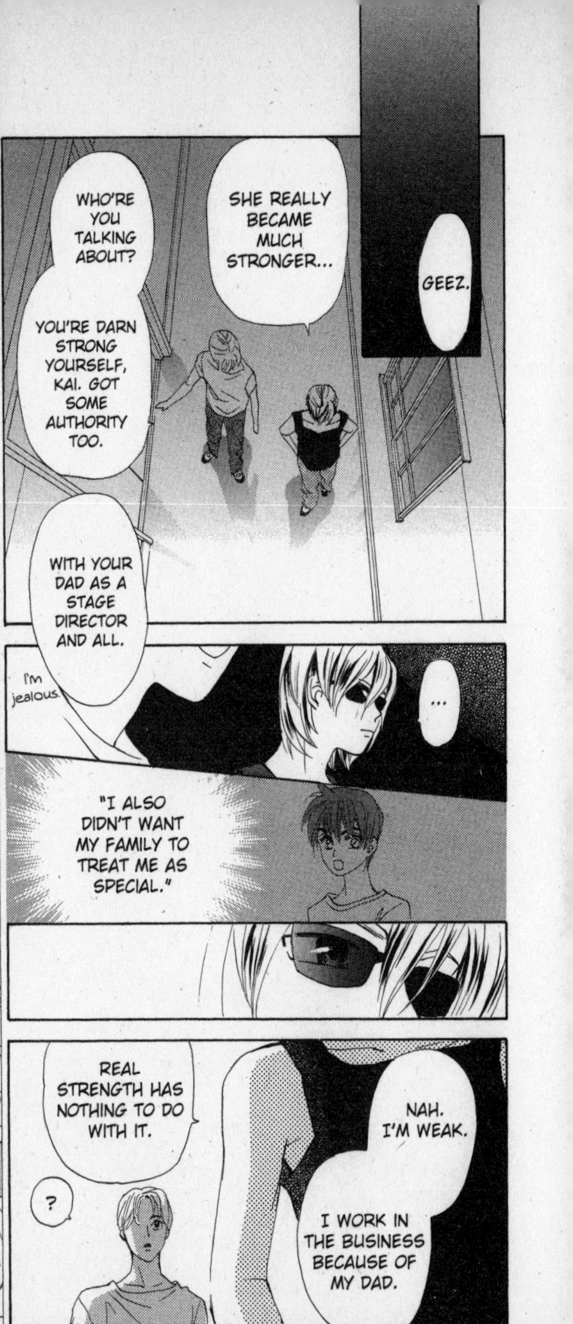
GEEZ.
SHE REALLY BECAME MUCH STRONGER...
WHO'RE YOU TALKING ABOUT?
YOU'RE DARN STRONG YOURSELF, KAI. GOT SOME AUTHORITY TOO.
WITH YOUR DAD AS A STAGE DIRECTOR AND ALL.
I'm jealous.
...
"I ALSO DIDN'T WANT MY FAMILY TO TREAT ME AS SPECIAL."
NAH. I'M WEAK.
I WORK IN THE BUSINESS BECAUSE OF MY DAD.
REAL STRENGTH HAS NOTHING TO DO WITH IT.
?

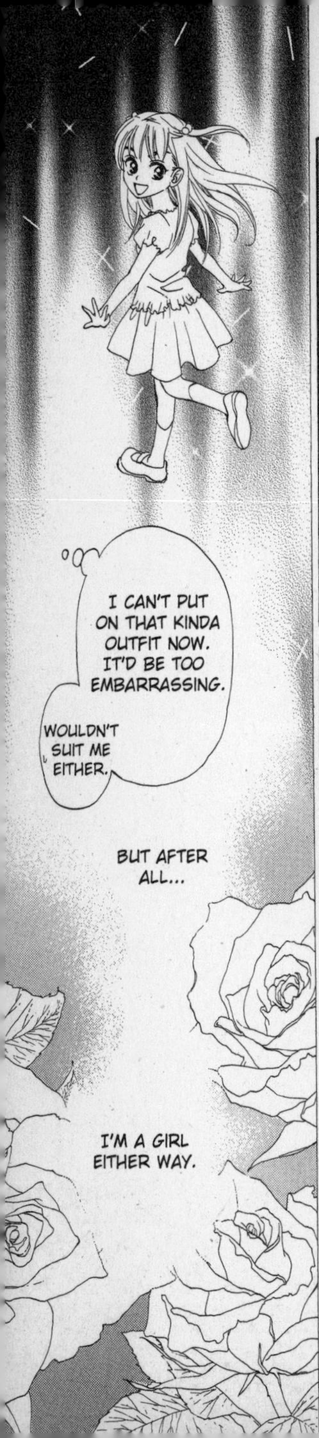
I CAN'T PUT ON THAT KINDA OUTFIT NOW. IT'D BE TOO EMBARRASSING.
WOULDN'T SUIT ME EITHER.
BUT AFTER ALL...
I'M A GIRL EITHER WAY.

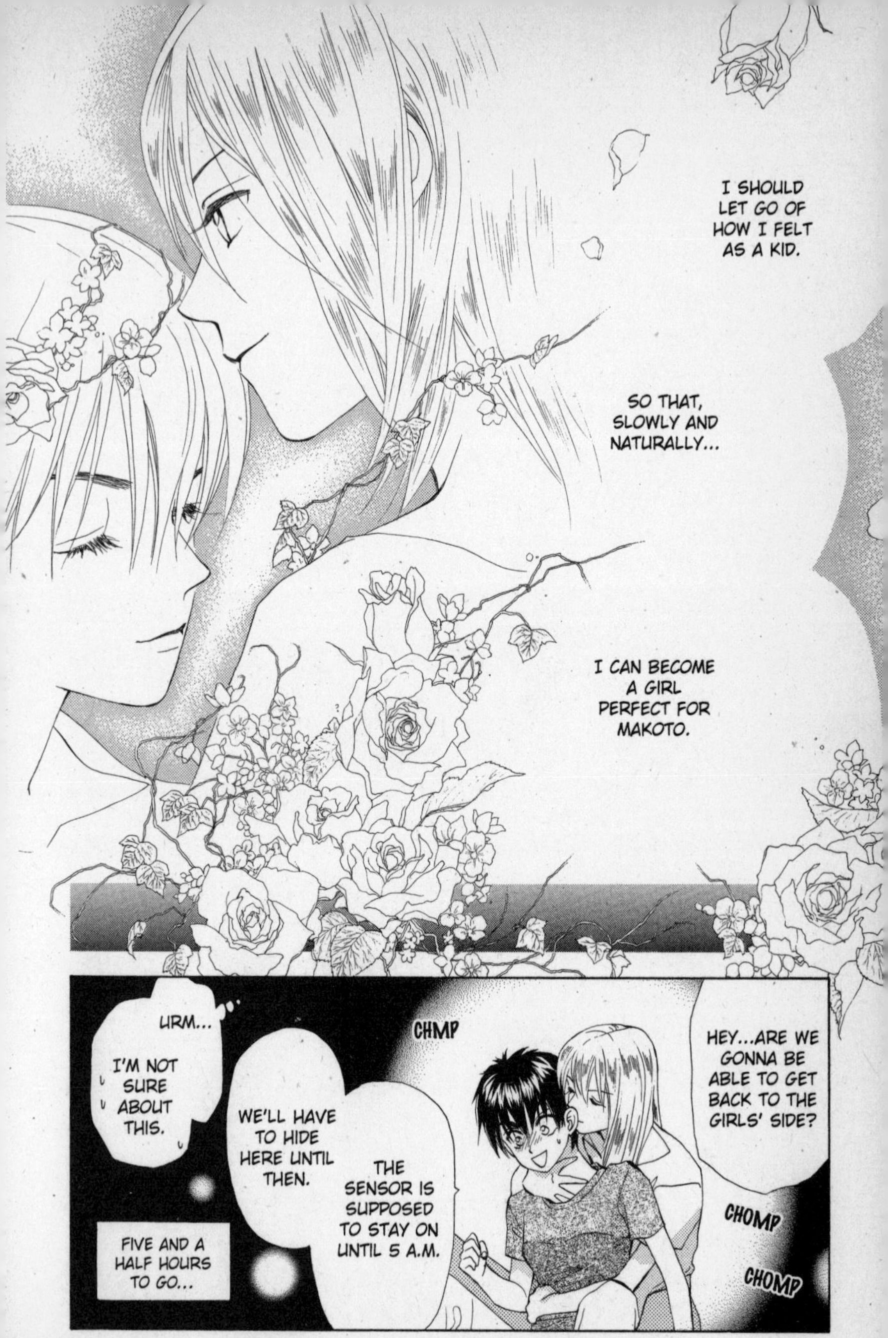
I SHOULD LET GO OF HOW I FELT AS A KID.
SO THAT, SLOWLY AND NATURALLY...
I CAN BECOME A GIRL PERFECT FOR MAKOTO.
HEY...ARE WE GONNA BE ABLE TO GET BACK TO THE GIRLS' SIDE?
CHMP
CHOMP
CHOMP
THE SENSOR IS SUPPOSED TO STAY ON UNTIL 5 A.M.
WE'LL HAVE TO HIDE HERE UNTIL THEN.
URM...
I'M NOT SURE ABOUT THIS.
FIVE AND A HALF HOURS TO GO...

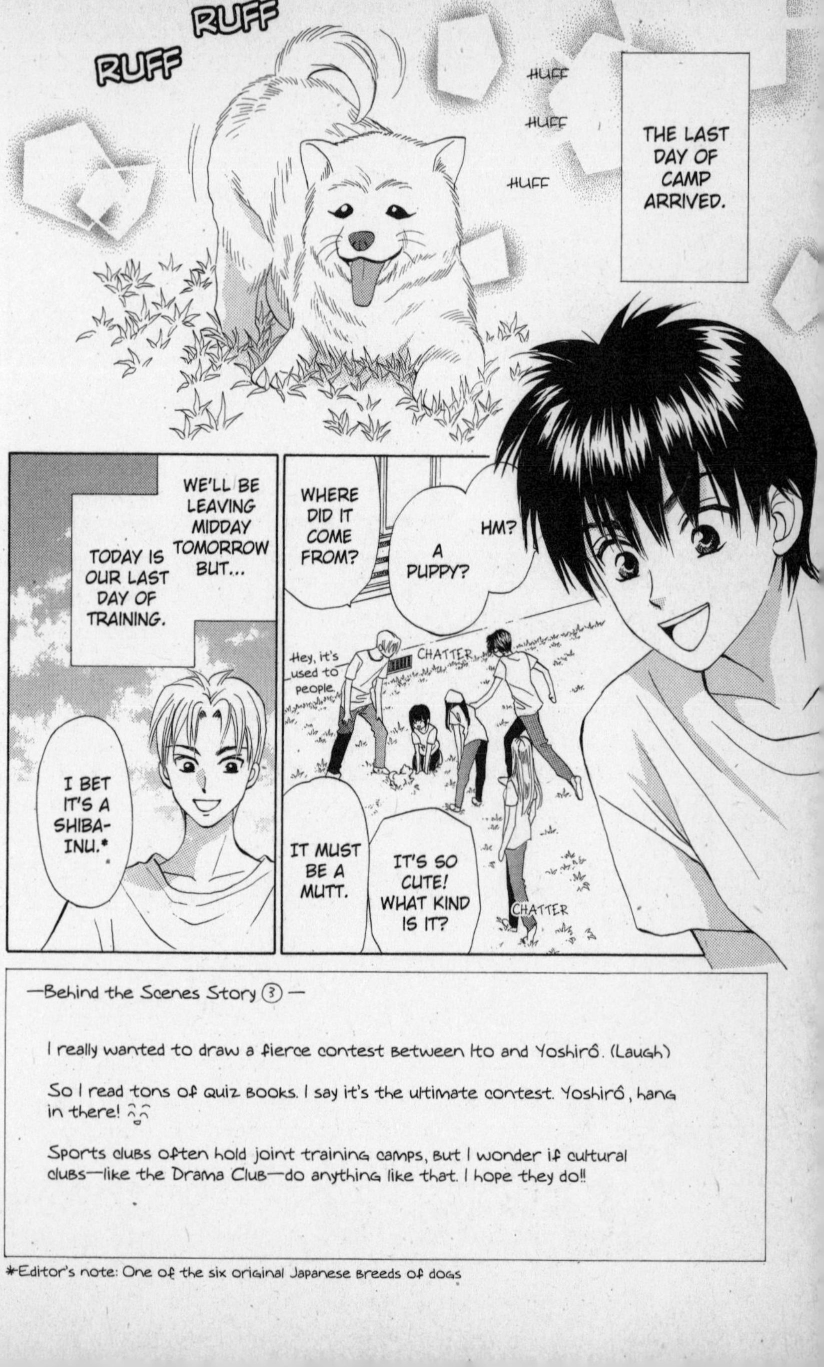
THE LAST DAY OF CAMP ARRIVED.
HUFF
HUFF
HUFF
RUFF
RUFF
HM?
A PUPPY?
WHERE DID IT COME FROM?
Hey, it's used to people.
CHATTER
IT'S SO CUTE! WHAT KIND IS IT?
IT MUST BE A MUTT.
CHATTER
WE'LL BE LEAVING MIDDAY TOMORROW BUT...
TODAY IS OUR LAST DAY OF TRAINING.
I BET IT'S A SHIBA-INU.*

—Behind the Scenes Story ③—

I really wanted to draw a fierce contest between Ito and Yoshirô. (Laugh)

So I read tons of quiz books. I say it's the ultimate contest. Yoshirô, hang in there!

Sports clubs often hold joint training camps, but I wonder if cultural clubs—like the Drama Club—do anything like that. I hope they do!!

*Editor's note: One of the six original Japanese breeds of dogs

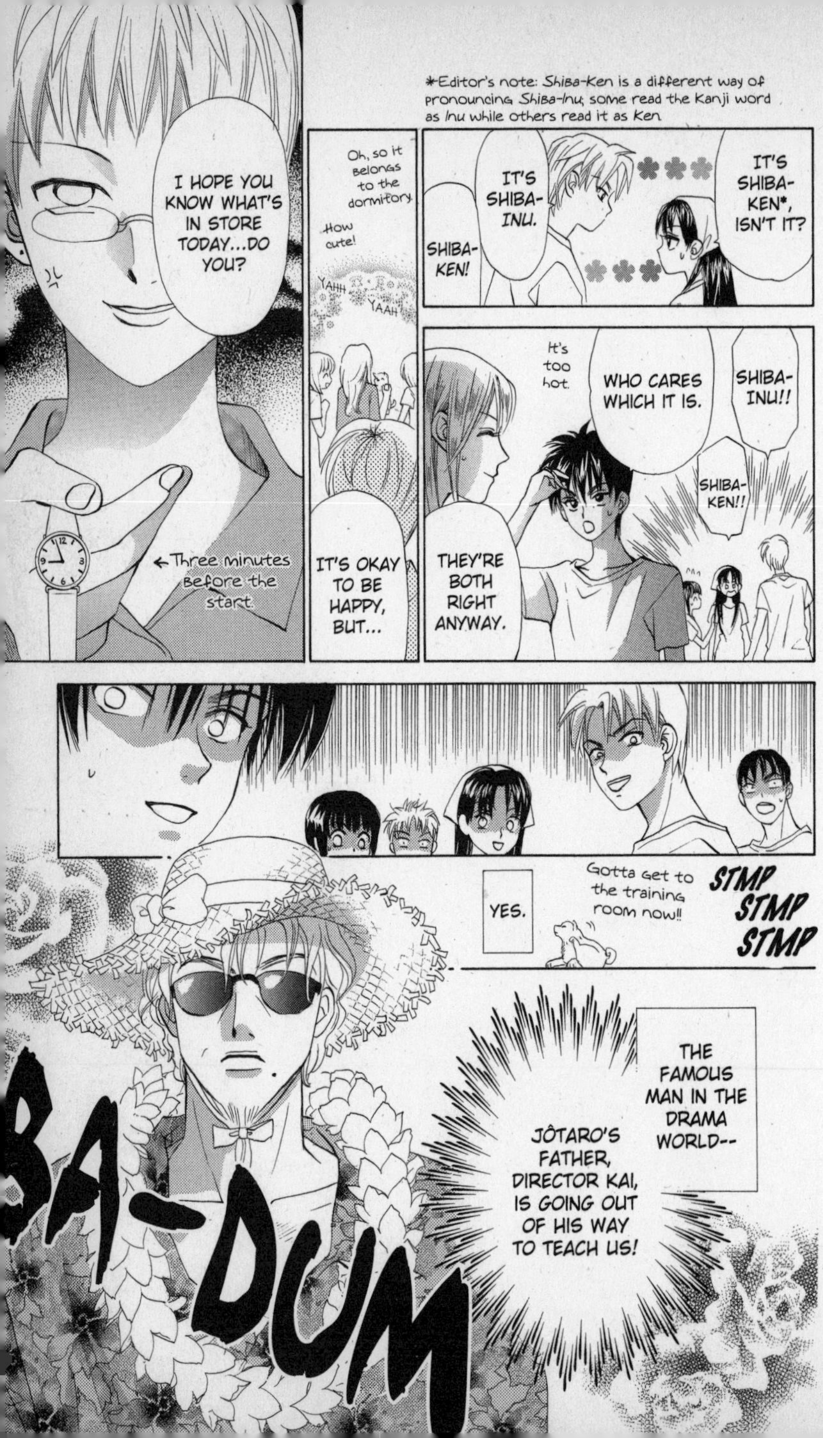
IT'S SHIBA-KEN*, ISN'T IT?
IT'S SHIBA-INU.
SHIBA-KEN!
SHIBA-INU!!
WHO CARES WHICH IT IS.
SHIBA-KEN!!
It's too hot.
THEY'RE BOTH RIGHT ANYWAY.
Oh, so it belongs to the dormitory.
How cute!
YAHH
YAAH
IT'S OKAY TO BE HAPPY, BUT...
I HOPE YOU KNOW WHAT'S IN STORE TODAY...DO YOU?
←Three minutes before the start.
STMP STMP STMP
Gotta get to the training room now!!
YES.
THE FAMOUS MAN IN THE DRAMA WORLD--
JÔTARO'S FATHER, DIRECTOR KAI, IS GOING OUT OF HIS WAY TO TEACH US!
BA-DUM
*Editor's note: Shiba-Ken is a different way of pronouncing Shiba-Inu; some read the Kanji word as Inu while others read it as Ken.

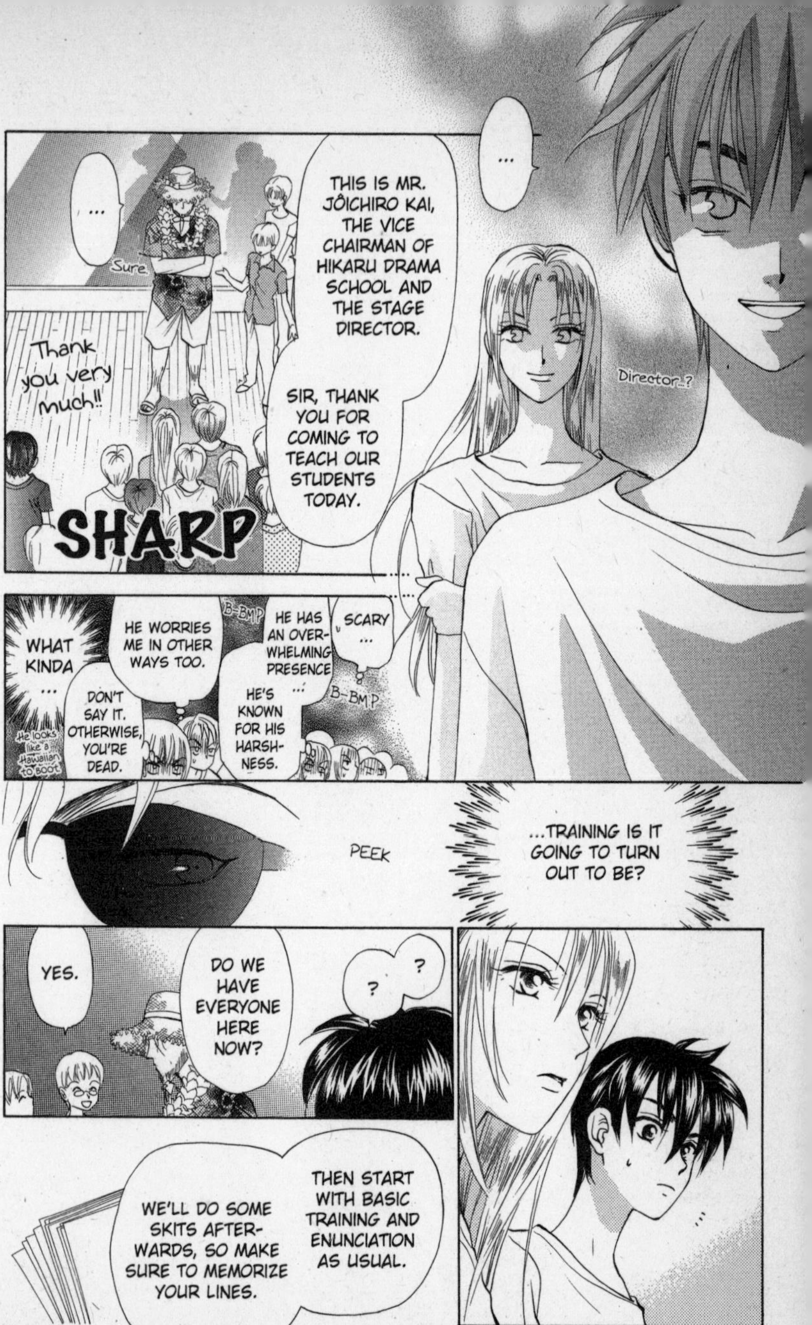
...
Director...?
.....
.....
...
THIS IS MR. JÔICHIRO KAI, THE VICE CHAIRMAN OF HIKARU DRAMA SCHOOL AND THE STAGE DIRECTOR.
Sure.
SIR, THANK YOU FOR COMING TO TEACH OUR STUDENTS TODAY.
Thank you very much!!
SHARP
SCARY ...
B-BMP
HE HAS AN OVER-WHELMING PRESENCE ...
B-BMP
HE'S KNOWN FOR HIS HARSH-NESS.
HE WORRIES ME IN OTHER WAYS TOO.
DON'T SAY IT. OTHERWISE, YOU'RE DEAD.
WHAT KINDA ...
He looks like a Hawaiian to boot
...TRAINING IS IT GOING TO TURN OUT TO BE?
PEEK
...
? ?
DO WE HAVE EVERYONE HERE NOW?
YES.
THEN START WITH BASIC TRAINING AND ENUNCIATION AS USUAL.
WE'LL DO SOME SKITS AFTER-WARDS, SO MAKE SURE TO MEMORIZE YOUR LINES.

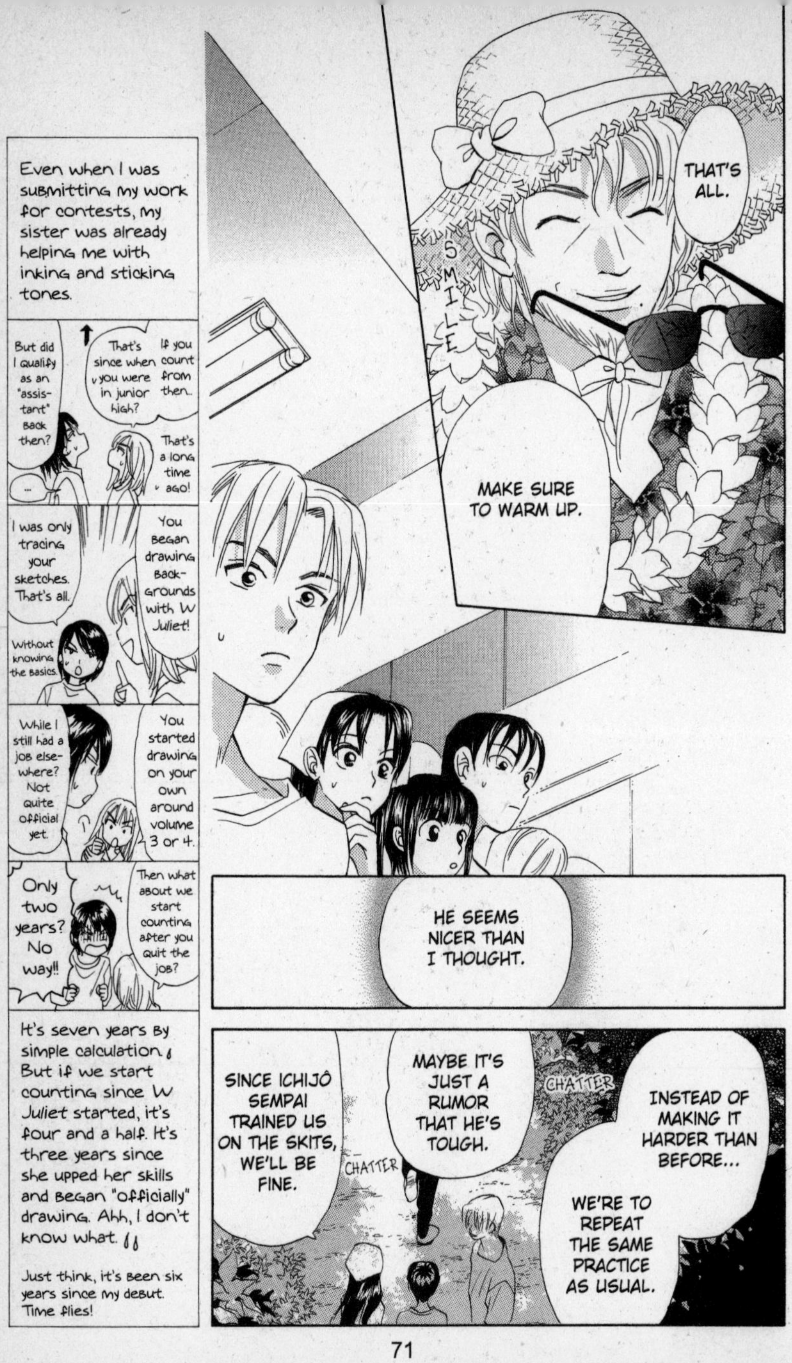
THAT'S ALL.
SMILE
MAKE SURE TO WARM UP.
HE SEEMS NICER THAN I THOUGHT.
INSTEAD OF MAKING IT HARDER THAN BEFORE...
WE'RE TO REPEAT THE SAME PRACTICE AS USUAL.
CHATTER
MAYBE IT'S JUST A RUMOR THAT HE'S TOUGH.
CHATTER
SINCE ICHIJÔ SEMPAI TRAINED US ON THE SKITS, WE'LL BE FINE.
Even when I was submitting my work for contests, my sister was already helping me with inking and sticking tones.
If you count from then...
That's since when you were in junior high?
That's a long time ago!
But did I qualify as an "assistant" back then?
...
You began drawing backgrounds with W Juliet!
I was only tracing your sketches. That's all.
Without knowing the basics.
You started drawing on your own around volume 3 or 4.
While I still had a job elsewhere? Not quite official yet.
Then what about we start counting after you quit the job?
Only two years? No way!!
It's seven years by simple calculation. But if we start counting since W Juliet started, it's four and a half. It's three years since she upped her skills and began "officially" drawing. Ahh, I don't know what.
Just think, it's been six years since my debut. Time flies!

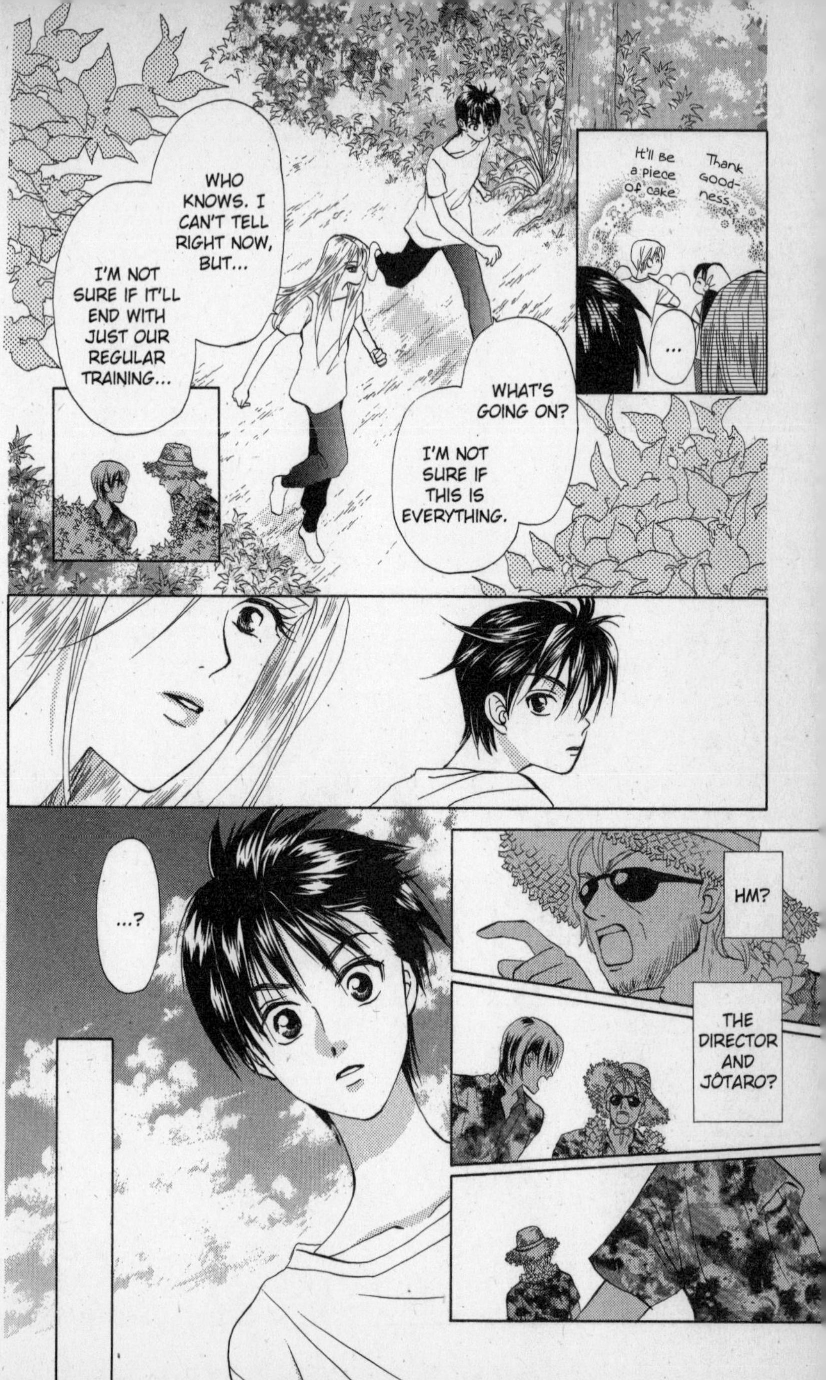
Thank goodness.
It'll be a piece of cake
...
WHAT'S GOING ON?
I'M NOT SURE IF THIS IS EVERYTHING.
WHO KNOWS. I CAN'T TELL RIGHT NOW, BUT...
I'M NOT SURE IF IT'LL END WITH JUST OUR REGULAR TRAINING...
HM?
THE DIRECTOR AND JÔTARO?
...?

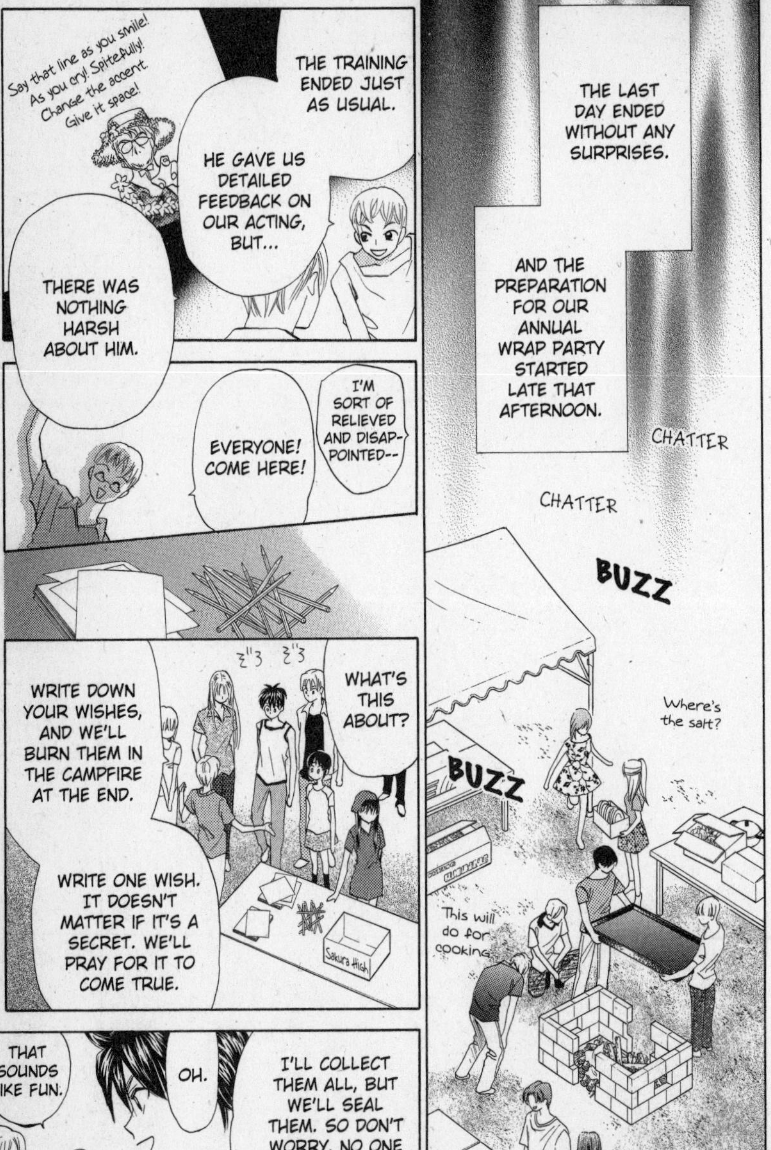
THE LAST DAY ENDED WITHOUT ANY SURPRISES.
AND THE PREPARATION FOR OUR ANNUAL WRAP PARTY STARTED LATE THAT AFTERNOON.
CHATTER
CHATTER
BUZZ
Where's the salt?
BUZZ
This will do for cooking.
THE TRAINING ENDED JUST AS USUAL.
HE GAVE US DETAILED FEEDBACK ON OUR ACTING, BUT...
Say that line as you smile! As you cry! Spitefully! Change the accent. Give it space!
THERE WAS NOTHING HARSH ABOUT HIM.
I'M SORT OF RELIEVED AND DISAPPOINTED--
EVERYONE! COME HERE!
WHAT'S THIS ABOUT?
WRITE DOWN YOUR WISHES, AND WE'LL BURN THEM IN THE CAMPFIRE AT THE END.
WRITE ONE WISH. IT DOESN'T MATTER IF IT'S A SECRET. WE'LL PRAY FOR IT TO COME TRUE.
Sakura High
I'LL COLLECT THEM ALL, BUT WE'LL SEAL THEM. SO DON'T WORRY, NO ONE WILL SEE IT.
OH.
THAT SOUNDS LIKE FUN.

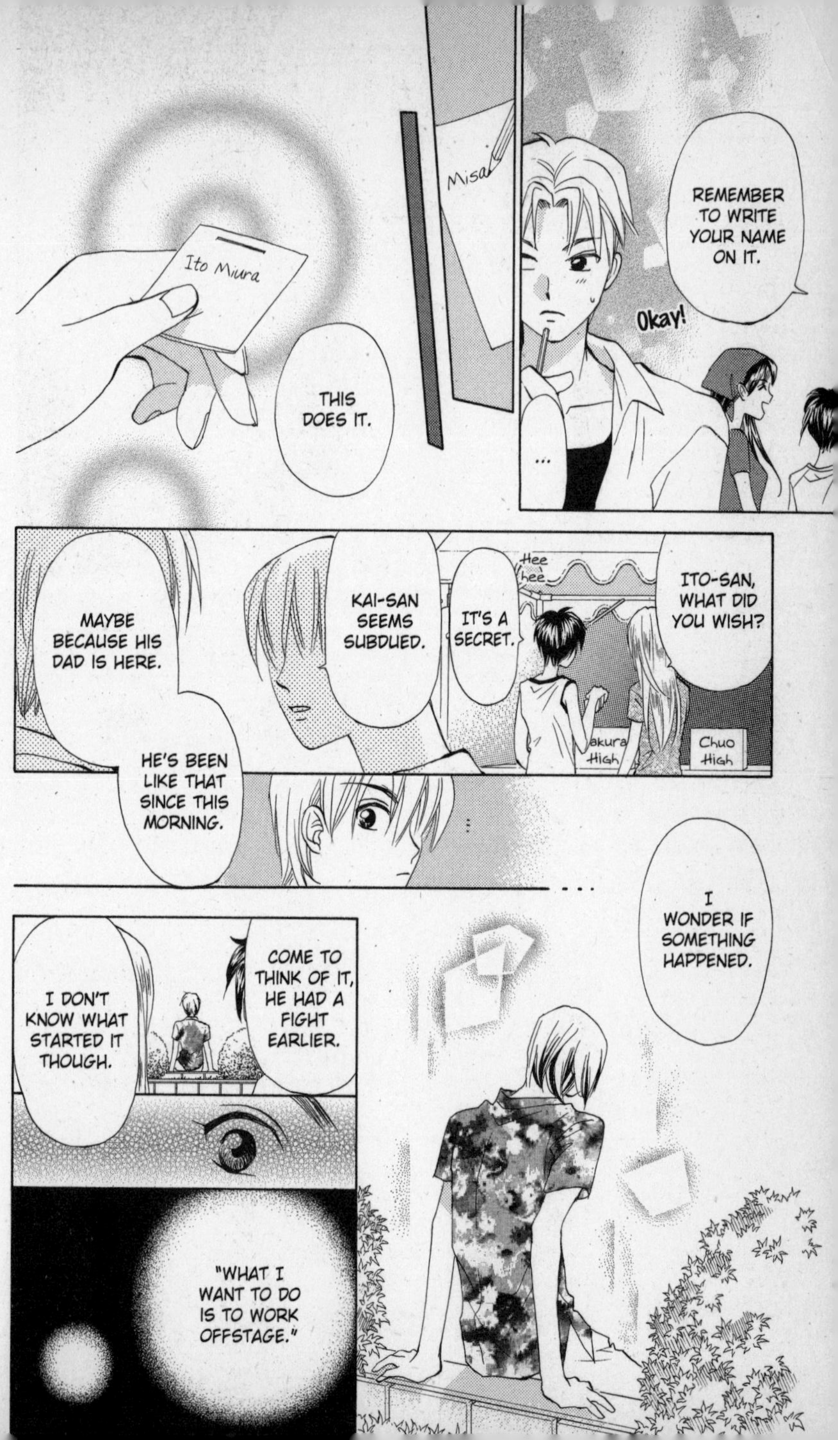
REMEMBER TO WRITE YOUR NAME ON IT.
Okay!
Misa
...
Ito Miura
THIS DOES IT.
ITO-SAN, WHAT DID YOU WISH?
Hee hee
IT'S A SECRET.
akura High
Chuo High
KAI-SAN SEEMS SUBDUED.
MAYBE BECAUSE HIS DAD IS HERE.
HE'S BEEN LIKE THAT SINCE THIS MORNING.
...
I WONDER IF SOMETHING HAPPENED.
COME TO THINK OF IT, HE HAD A FIGHT EARLIER.
I DON'T KNOW WHAT STARTED IT THOUGH.
"WHAT I WANT TO DO IS TO WORK OFFSTAGE."

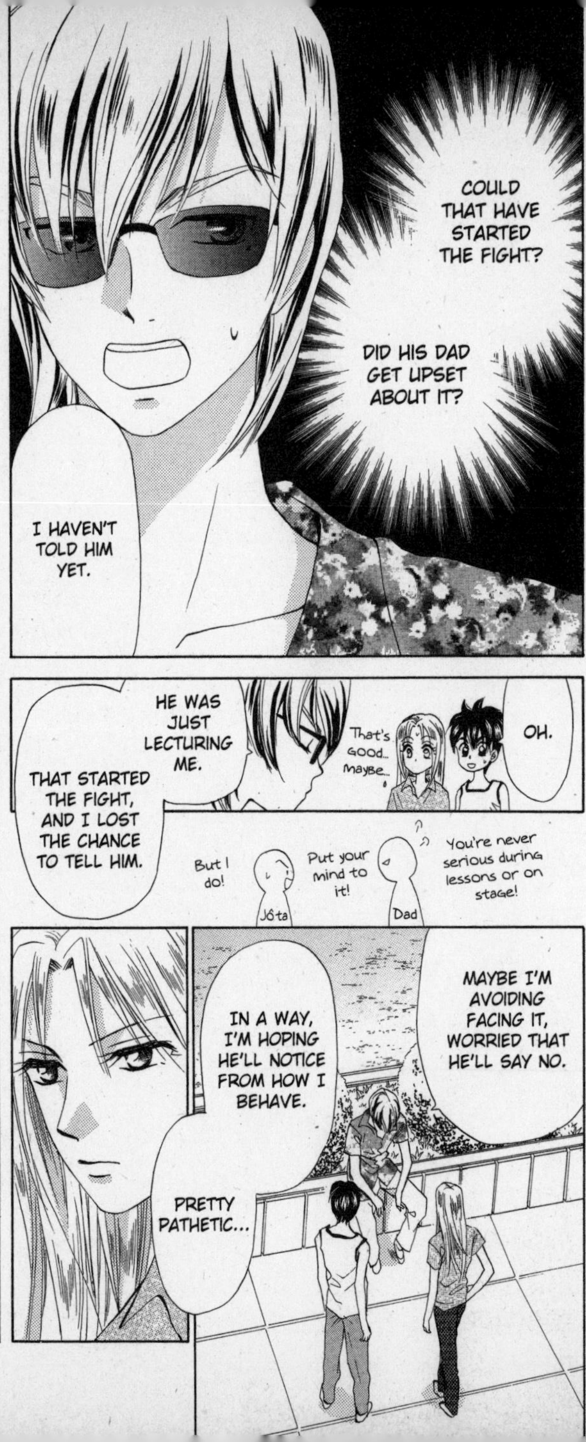
COULD THAT HAVE STARTED THE FIGHT?
DID HIS DAD GET UPSET ABOUT IT?
I HAVEN'T TOLD HIM YET.
OH.
That's good... maybe...
HE WAS JUST LECTURING ME.
THAT STARTED THE FIGHT, AND I LOST THE CHANCE TO TELL HIM.
You're never serious during lessons or on stage!
Dad
Put your mind to it!
But I do!
Jôta
MAYBE I'M AVOIDING FACING IT, WORRIED THAT HE'LL SAY NO.
IN A WAY, I'M HOPING HE'LL NOTICE FROM HOW I BEHAVE.
PRETTY PATHETIC...

Once W Juliet became a series, other assistants started to come and help. That's when my sister began upping her skills too. (I mean, I taught her what style of drawing I preferred). Thus she became one of my strongest warriors—but by that time, she was working for a company, and it was her official career.

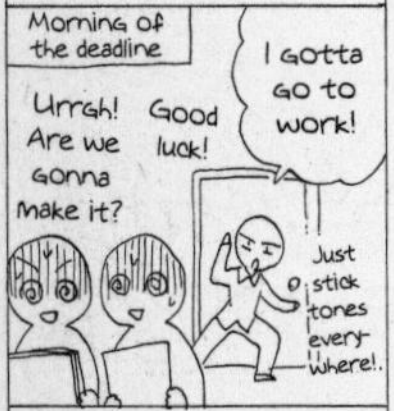
Morning of the deadline
I gotta go to work!
Good luck!
Urrgh! Are we gonna make it?
Just stick tones everywhere!.

↑Shirômaru-san and me

When we were finishing the draft, my sister would pull an all-nighter, and then she'd go to work during the day, and then she'd pull another all-nighter. It was too crazy. (It was right around this time when she had that paralyzed feeling I described in volume 3.)

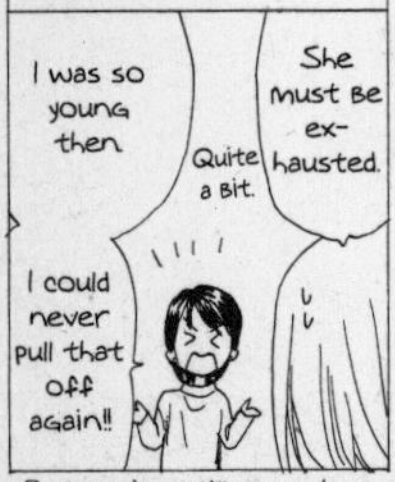
She must be exhausted.
I was so young then
Quite a bit.
I could never pull that off again!!

But you're still young!

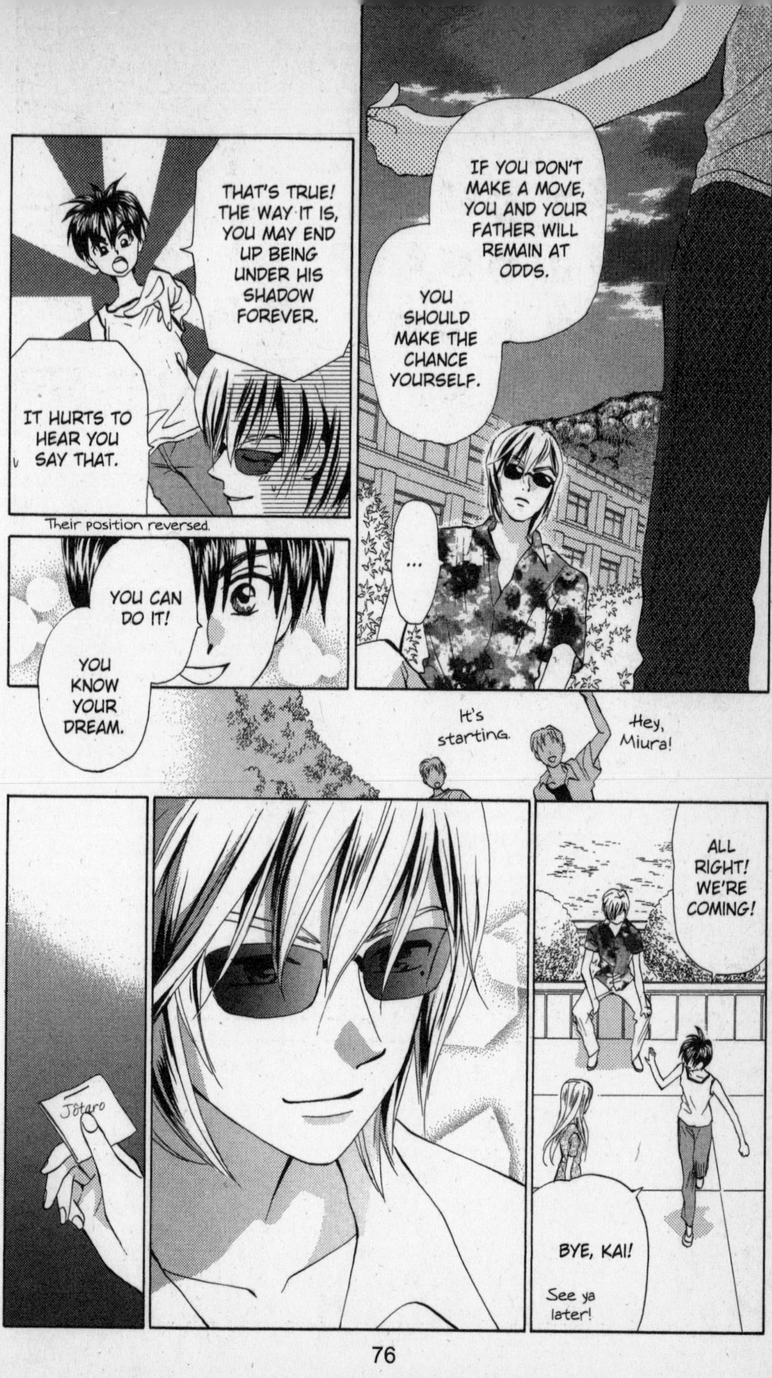
IF YOU DON'T MAKE A MOVE, YOU AND YOUR FATHER WILL REMAIN AT ODDS.
YOU SHOULD MAKE THE CHANCE YOURSELF.
...
THAT'S TRUE! THE WAY IT IS, YOU MAY END UP BEING UNDER HIS SHADOW FOREVER.
IT HURTS TO HEAR YOU SAY THAT.
Their position reversed.
YOU CAN DO IT!
YOU KNOW YOUR DREAM.
Hey, Miura!
It's starting.
ALL RIGHT! WE'RE COMING!
BYE, KAI!
See ya later!
Jōtaro

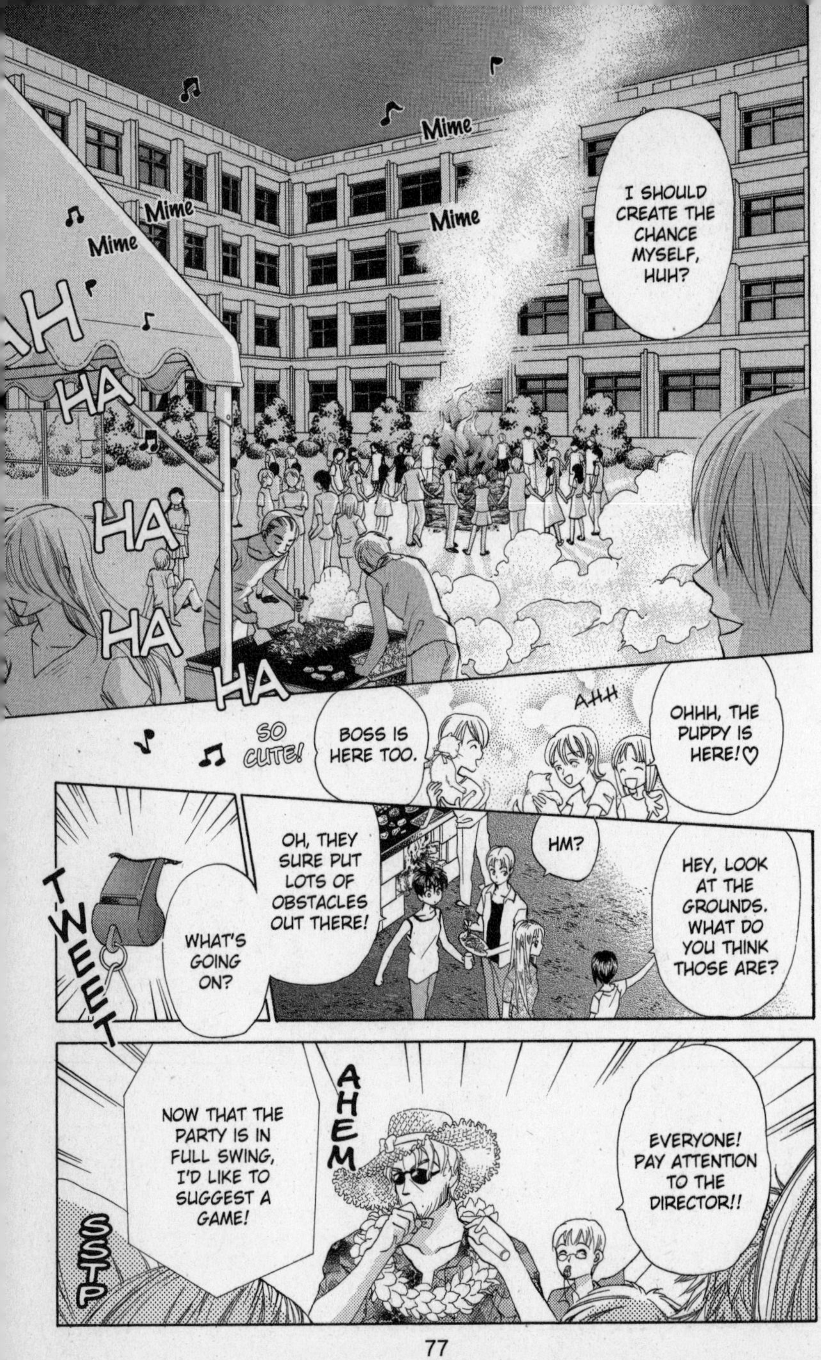
I SHOULD CREATE THE CHANCE MYSELF, HUH?
Mime
Mime
Mime
Mime
AH HA HA HA HA
OHHH, THE PUPPY IS HERE!♡
AHH
BOSS IS HERE TOO.
SO CUTE!
HEY, LOOK AT THE GROUNDS. WHAT DO YOU THINK THOSE ARE?
HM?
OH, THEY SURE PUT LOTS OF OBSTACLES OUT THERE!
WHAT'S GOING ON?
TWEET
EVERYONE! PAY ATTENTION TO THE DIRECTOR!!
AHEM
NOW THAT THE PARTY IS IN FULL SWING, I'D LIKE TO SUGGEST A GAME!
SSTP

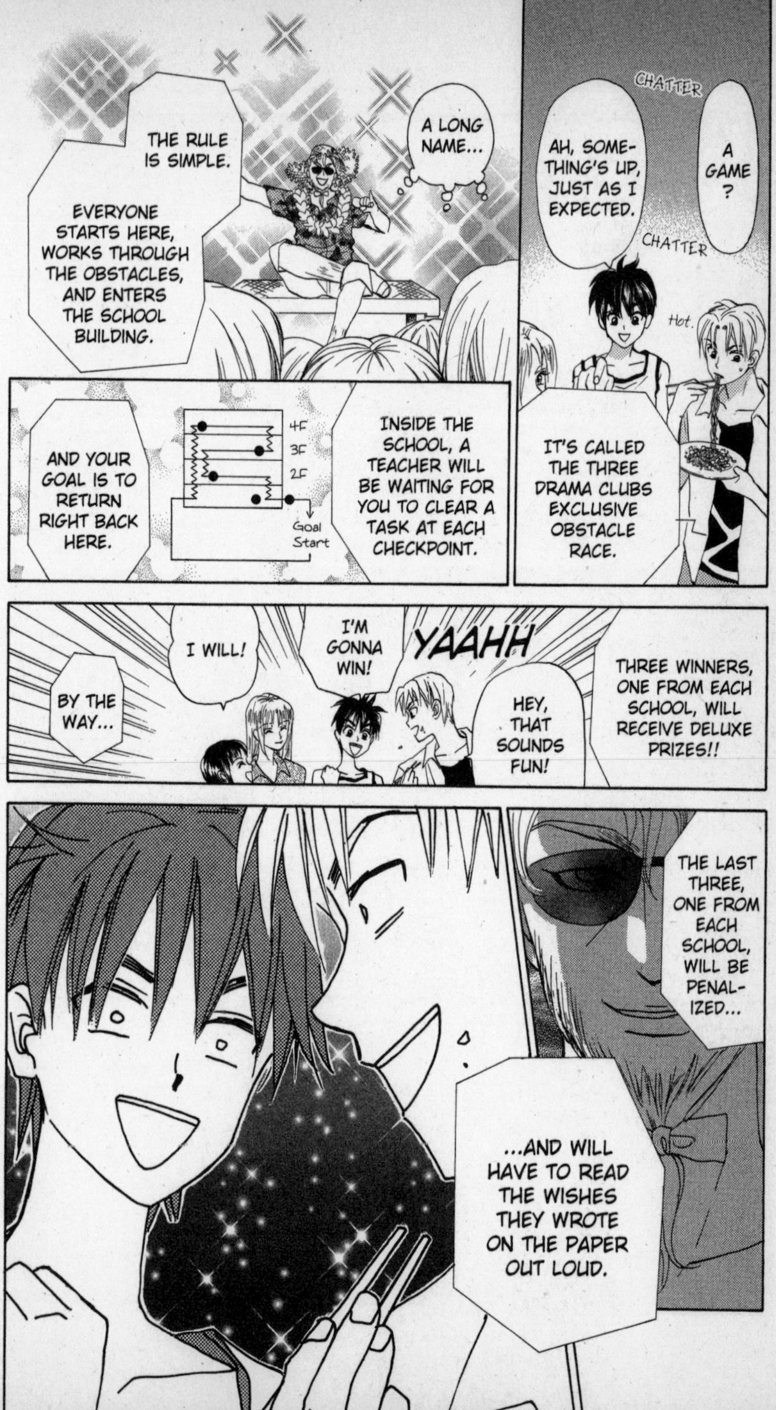
CHATTER
A GAME?
AH, SOME-THING'S UP, JUST AS I EXPECTED.
CHATTER
Hot.
IT'S CALLED THE THREE DRAMA CLUBS EXCLUSIVE OBSTACLE RACE.
A LONG NAME...
THE RULE IS SIMPLE.
EVERYONE STARTS HERE, WORKS THROUGH THE OBSTACLES, AND ENTERS THE SCHOOL BUILDING.
INSIDE THE SCHOOL, A TEACHER WILL BE WAITING FOR YOU TO CLEAR A TASK AT EACH CHECKPOINT.
4F
3F
2F
Goal
Start
AND YOUR GOAL IS TO RETURN RIGHT BACK HERE.
THREE WINNERS, ONE FROM EACH SCHOOL, WILL RECEIVE DELUXE PRIZES!!
HEY, THAT SOUNDS FUN!
YAAHH
I'M GONNA WIN!
I WILL!
BY THE WAY...
THE LAST THREE, ONE FROM EACH SCHOOL, WILL BE PENAL-IZED...
...AND WILL HAVE TO READ THE WISHES THEY WROTE ON THE PAPER OUT LOUD.

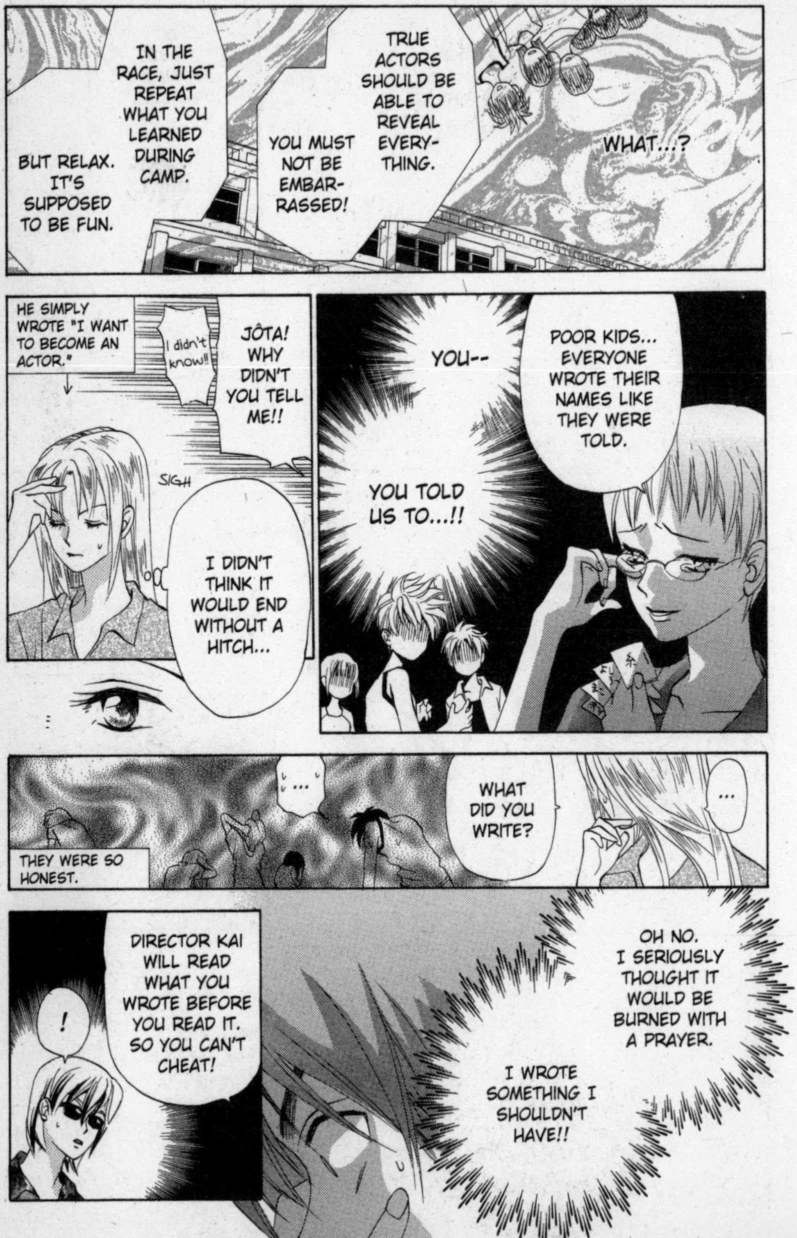
WHAT...?
TRUE ACTORS SHOULD BE ABLE TO REVEAL EVERYTHING.
YOU MUST NOT BE EMBARRASSED!
IN THE RACE, JUST REPEAT WHAT YOU LEARNED DURING CAMP.
BUT RELAX. IT'S SUPPOSED TO BE FUN.
POOR KIDS... EVERYONE WROTE THEIR NAMES LIKE THEY WERE TOLD.
YOU--
YOU TOLD US TO...!!
JÔTA! WHY DIDN'T YOU TELL ME!!
I didn't know!!
HE SIMPLY WROTE "I WANT TO BECOME AN ACTOR."
SIGH
I DIDN'T THINK IT WOULD END WITHOUT A HITCH...
...
...
WHAT DID YOU WRITE?
...
THEY WERE SO HONEST.
OH NO. I SERIOUSLY THOUGHT IT WOULD BE BURNED WITH A PRAYER.
I WROTE SOMETHING I SHOULDN'T HAVE!!
DIRECTOR KAI WILL READ WHAT YOU WROTE BEFORE YOU READ IT. SO YOU CAN'T CHEAT!
!

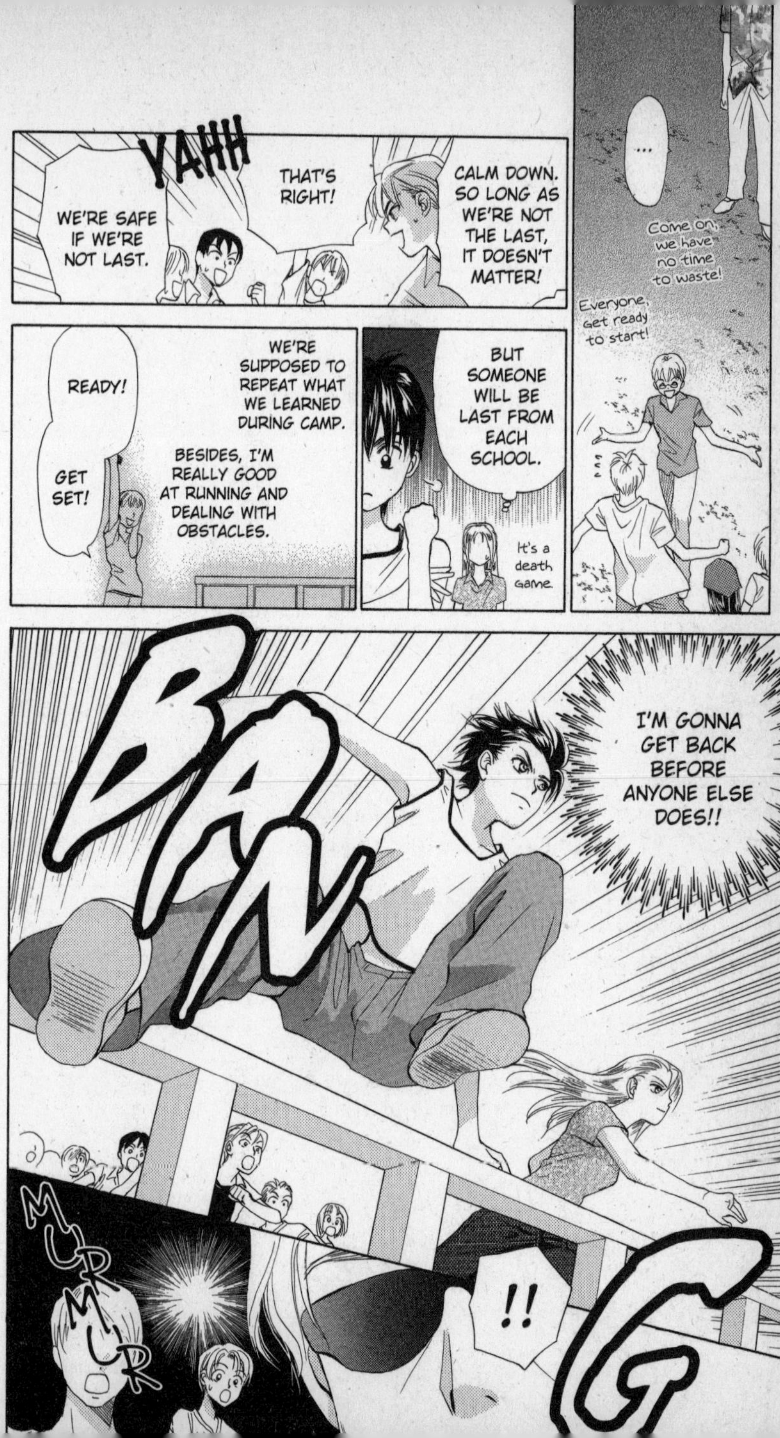
...
Come on, we have no time to waste!
Everyone, get ready to start!
CALM DOWN. SO LONG AS WE'RE NOT THE LAST, IT DOESN'T MATTER!
THAT'S RIGHT!
YAHH
WE'RE SAFE IF WE'RE NOT LAST.
BUT SOMEONE WILL BE LAST FROM EACH SCHOOL.
It's a death game.
WE'RE SUPPOSED TO REPEAT WHAT WE LEARNED DURING CAMP.
READY!
BESIDES, I'M REALLY GOOD AT RUNNING AND DEALING WITH OBSTACLES.
GET SET!
I'M GONNA GET BACK BEFORE ANYONE ELSE DOES!!
BANG
!!
MURMUR

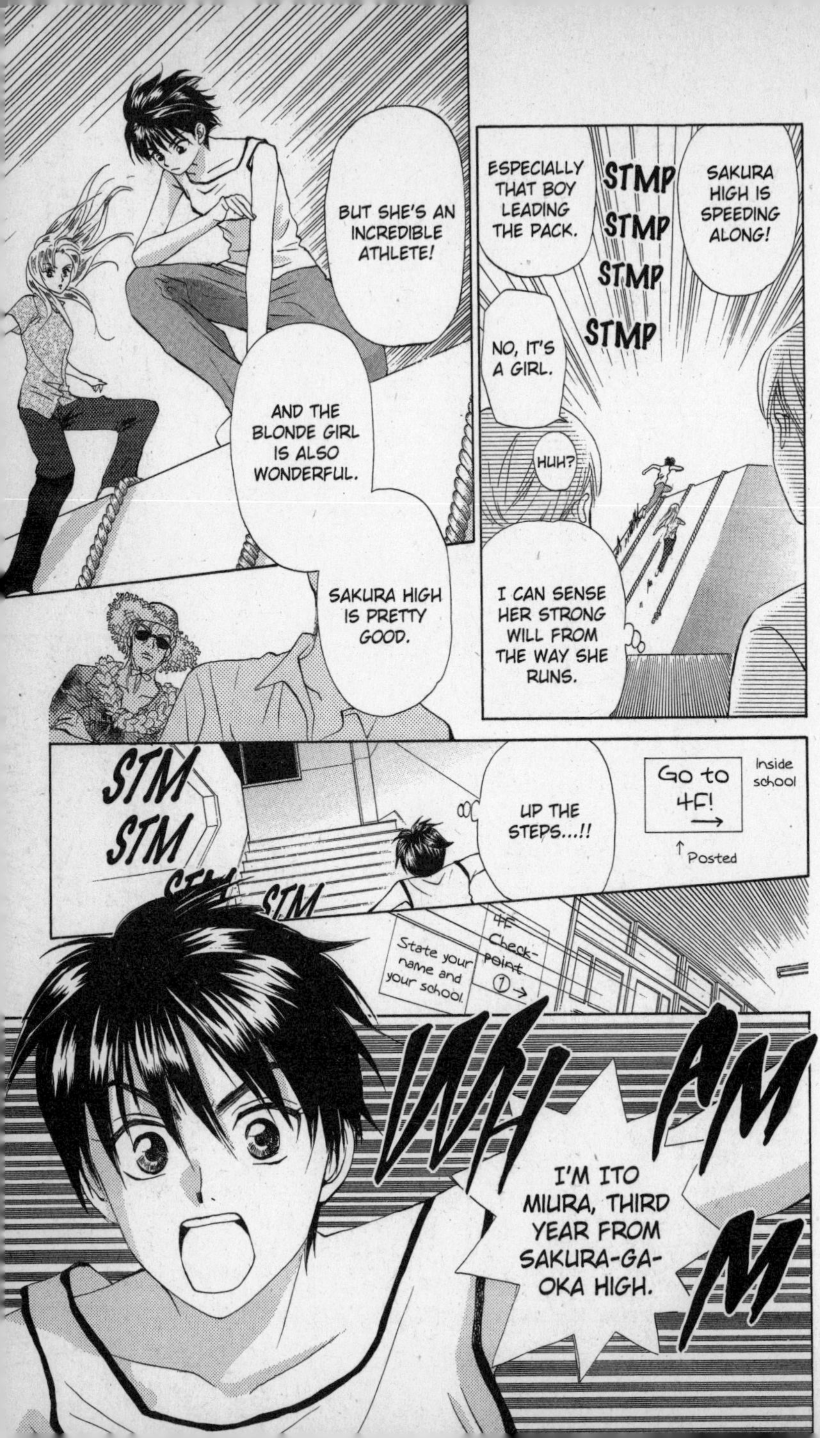
SAKURA HIGH IS SPEEDING ALONG!
STMP STMP STMP STMP
ESPECIALLY THAT BOY LEADING THE PACK.
NO, IT'S A GIRL.
HUH?
I CAN SENSE HER STRONG WILL FROM THE WAY SHE RUNS.
BUT SHE'S AN INCREDIBLE ATHLETE!
AND THE BLONDE GIRL IS ALSO WONDERFUL.
SAKURA HIGH IS PRETTY GOOD.
Inside school
Go to 4F! →
↑ Posted
UP THE STEPS...!!
STM STM
STM
4F Check-point ① →
State your name and your school.
WHAM
I'M ITO MIURA, THIRD YEAR FROM SAKURA-GA-OKA HIGH.

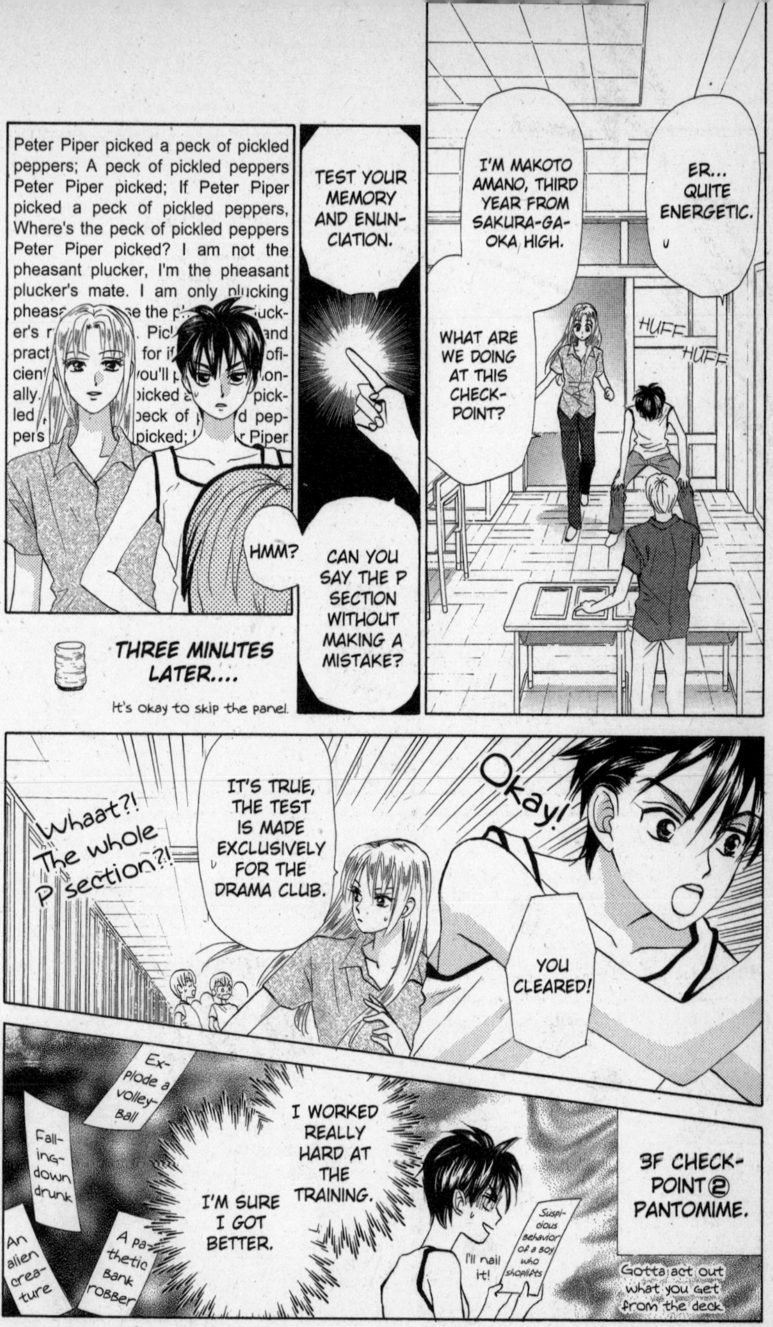
HUFF HUFF
I'M MAKOTO AMANO, THIRD YEAR FROM SAKURA-GA-OKA HIGH.
ER... QUITE ENERGETIC.
WHAT ARE WE DOING AT THIS CHECKPOINT?
TEST YOUR MEMORY AND ENUNCIATION.
CAN YOU SAY THE P SECTION WITHOUT MAKING A MISTAKE?
HMM?
Peter Piper picked a peck of pickled peppers; A peck of pickled peppers Peter Piper picked; If Peter Piper picked a peck of pickled peppers, Where's the peck of pickled peppers Peter Piper picked? I am not the pheasant plucker, I'm the pheasant plucker's mate. I am only plucking
pheasa se the p ucker's
er's r . Pic and
pract for if ofi-
cient ou'll p onally.
ally. picked a pick-
led peck of p d pep-
pers picked; r Piper
THREE MINUTES LATER....
It's okay to skip the panel.
Okay!
YOU CLEARED!
IT'S TRUE, THE TEST IS MADE EXCLUSIVELY FOR THE DRAMA CLUB.
Whaat?! The whole P section?!
3F CHECKPOINT② PANTOMIME.
Gotta act out what you get from the deck
Suspicious behavior of a boy who shoplifts
I'll nail it!
I WORKED REALLY HARD AT THE TRAINING.
I'M SURE I GOT BETTER.
Explode a volley-Ball
Falling-down drunk
A pathetic Bank robber
An alien creature

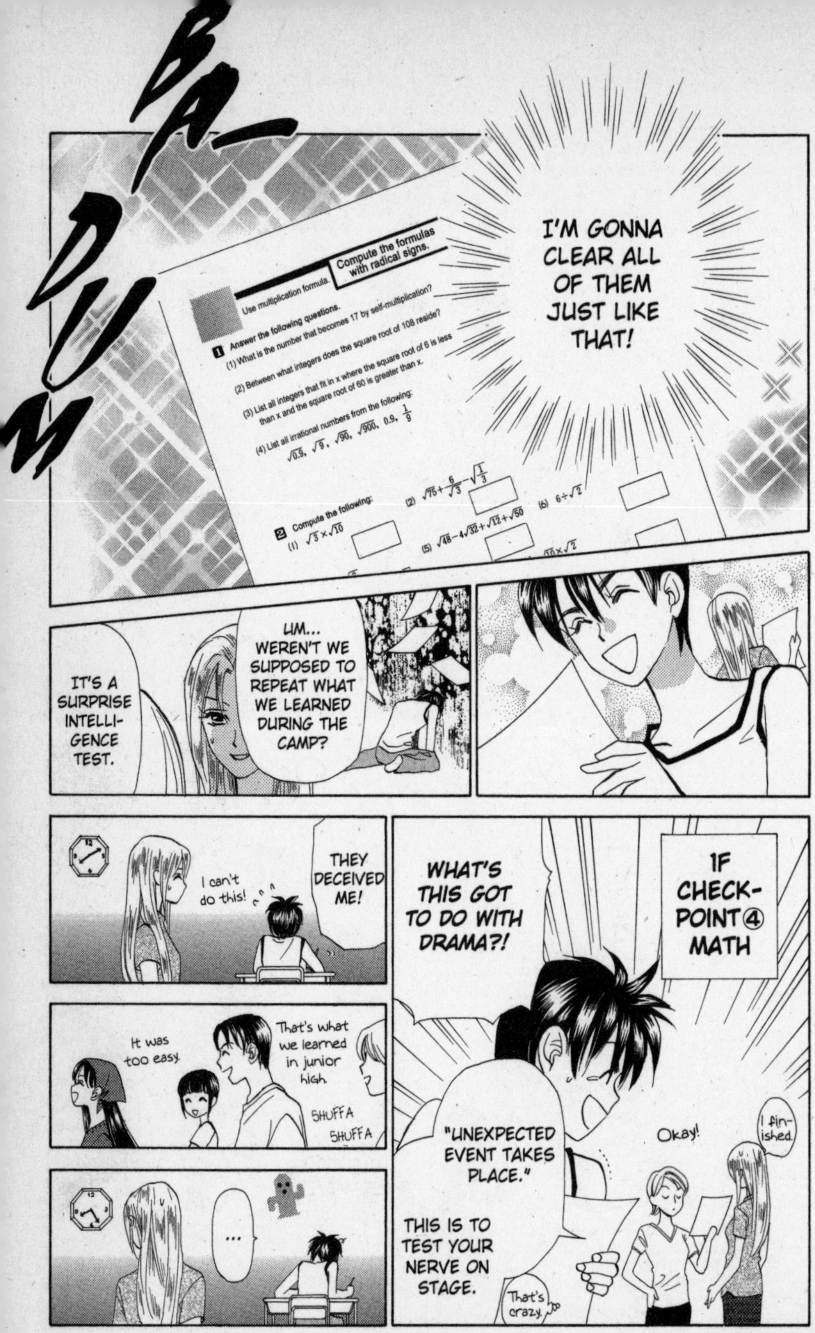
BA-DUM
Compute the formulas with radical signs.
Use multiplication formula.
1 Answer the following questions.
(1) What is the number that becomes 17 by self-multiplication?
(2) Between what integers does the square root of 108 reside?
(3) List all integers that fit in x where the square root of 6 is less than x and the square root of 60 is greater than x.
(4) List all irrational numbers from the following:
$\sqrt{0.9}$, $\sqrt{9}$, $\sqrt{90}$, $\sqrt{900}$, 0.9, $\frac{1}{9}$
2 Compute the following:
(1) $\sqrt{3}\times\sqrt{10}$
(2) $\sqrt{75}+\frac{6}{\sqrt{3}}-\sqrt{\frac{1}{3}}$
(5) $\sqrt{48}-4\sqrt{32}+\sqrt{12}+\sqrt{50}$
(6) $6\div\sqrt{2}$
I'M GONNA CLEAR ALL OF THEM JUST LIKE THAT!
UM... WEREN'T WE SUPPOSED TO REPEAT WHAT WE LEARNED DURING THE CAMP?
IT'S A SURPRISE INTELLIGENCE TEST.
1F CHECKPOINT ④ MATH
WHAT'S THIS GOT TO DO WITH DRAMA?!
I finished.
Okay!
"UNEXPECTED EVENT TAKES PLACE."
THIS IS TO TEST YOUR NERVE ON STAGE.
That's crazy.
THEY DECEIVED ME!
I can't do this!
That's what we learned in junior high.
It was too easy.
SHUFFA SHUFFA
...

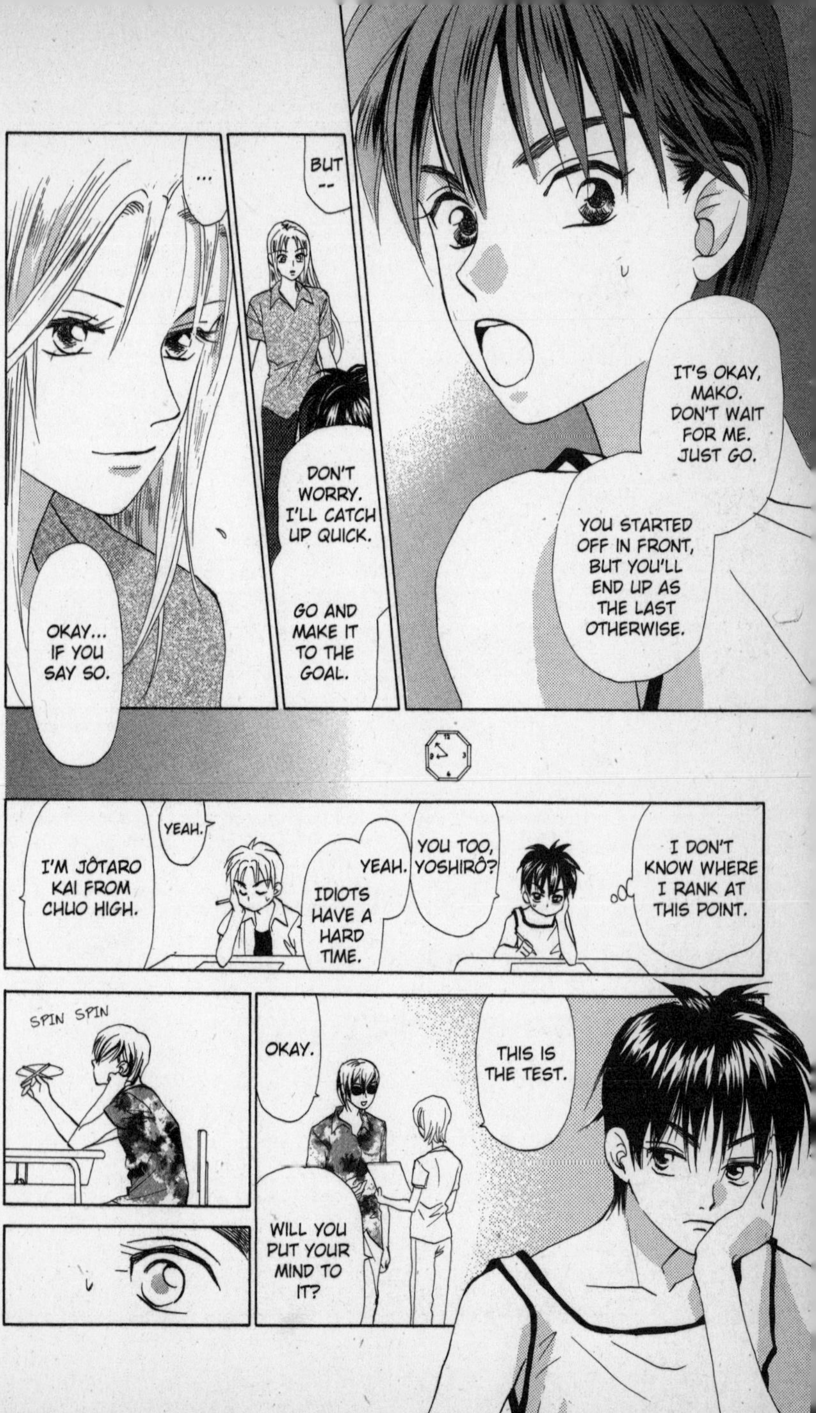

IT'S OKAY, MAKO. DON'T WAIT FOR ME. JUST GO.
YOU STARTED OFF IN FRONT, BUT YOU'LL END UP AS THE LAST OTHERWISE.
BUT --
DON'T WORRY. I'LL CATCH UP QUICK.
GO AND MAKE IT TO THE GOAL.
...
OKAY... IF YOU SAY SO.
I DON'T KNOW WHERE I RANK AT THIS POINT.
YOU TOO, YOSHIRÔ?
YEAH.
IDIOTS HAVE A HARD TIME.
YEAH.
I'M JÔTARO KAI FROM CHUO HIGH.
THIS IS THE TEST.
OKAY.
WILL YOU PUT YOUR MIND TO IT?
SPIN SPIN

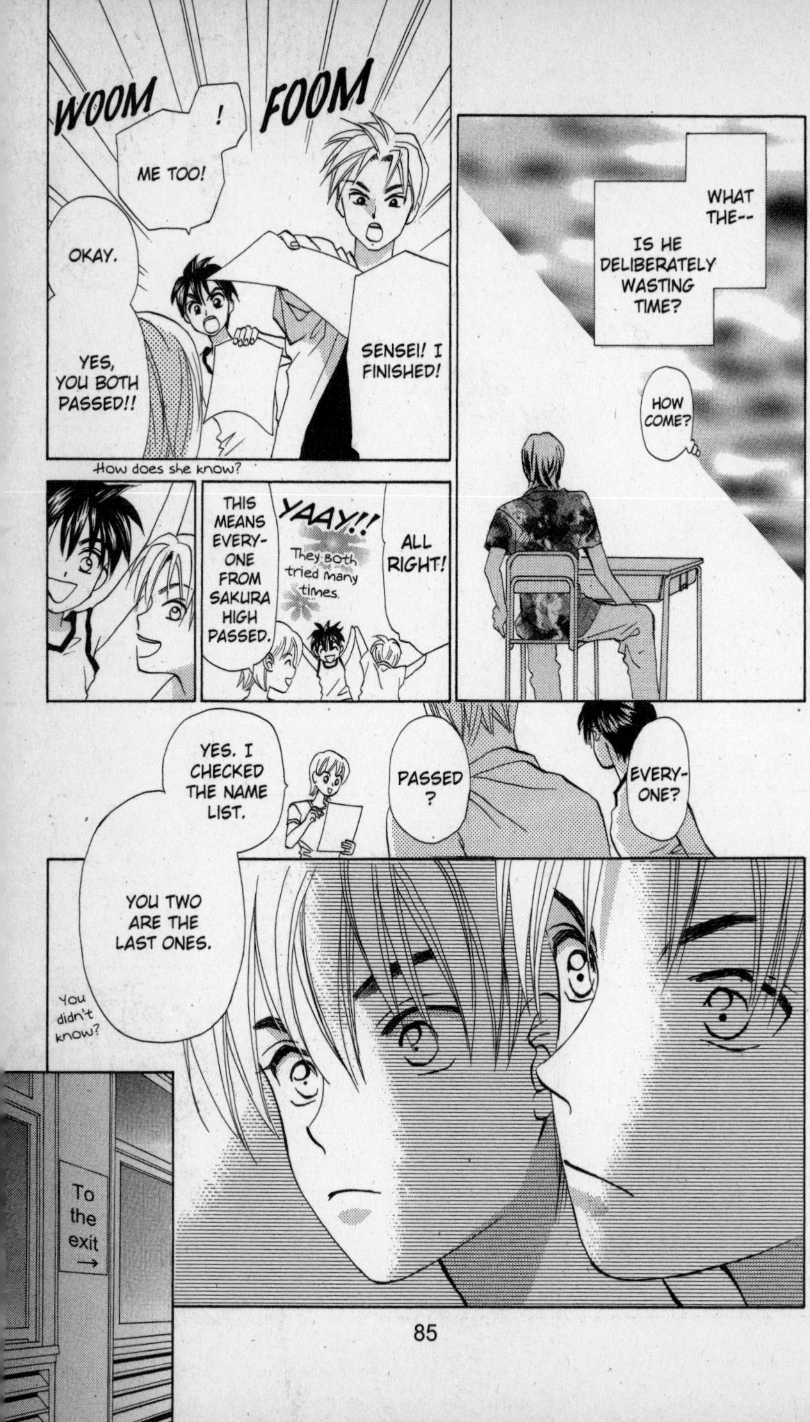

WHAT THE--
IS HE DELIBERATELY WASTING TIME?
HOW COME?
FOOM
SENSEI! I FINISHED!
!
WOOM
ME TOO!
OKAY.
YES, YOU BOTH PASSED!!
How does she know?
ALL RIGHT!
YAAY!!
They both tried many times.
THIS MEANS EVERY-ONE FROM SAKURA HIGH PASSED.
EVERY-ONE?
PASSED?
YES. I CHECKED THE NAME LIST.
YOU TWO ARE THE LAST ONES.
You didn't know?
To the exit →

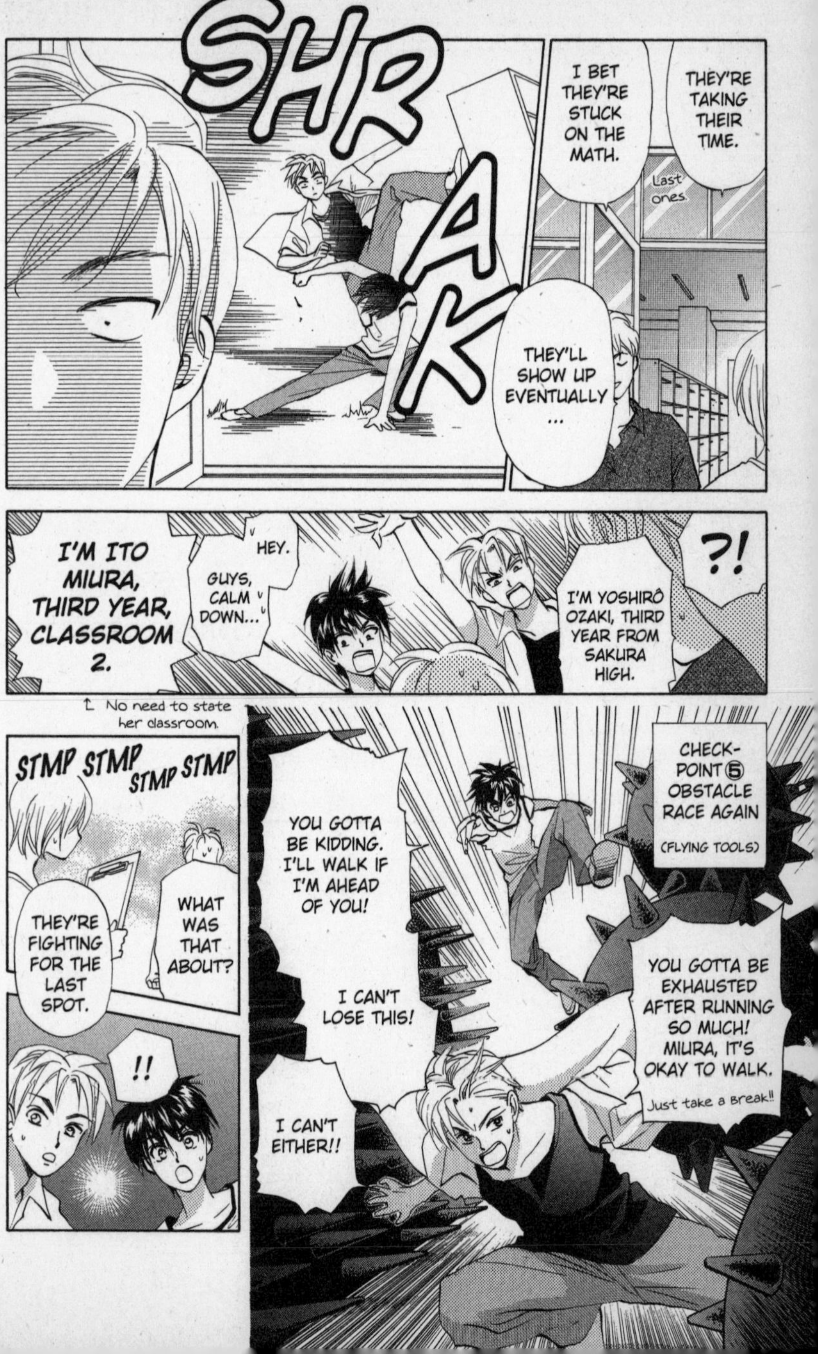
THEY'RE TAKING THEIR TIME.
I BET THEY'RE STUCK ON THE MATH.
Last ones.
THEY'LL SHOW UP EVENTUALLY ...
SHRAK
?!
I'M YOSHIRÔ OZAKI, THIRD YEAR FROM SAKURA HIGH.
HEY.
GUYS, CALM DOWN...
I'M ITO MIURA, THIRD YEAR, CLASSROOM 2.
↑ No need to state her classroom.
CHECK-POINT ⑤ OBSTACLE RACE AGAIN
(FLYING TOOLS)
YOU GOTTA BE EXHAUSTED AFTER RUNNING SO MUCH! MIURA, IT'S OKAY TO WALK.
Just take a Break!!
YOU GOTTA BE KIDDING. I'LL WALK IF I'M AHEAD OF YOU!
I CAN'T LOSE THIS!
I CAN'T EITHER!!
STMP STMP STMP STMP
WHAT WAS THAT ABOUT?
THEY'RE FIGHTING FOR THE LAST SPOT.
!!

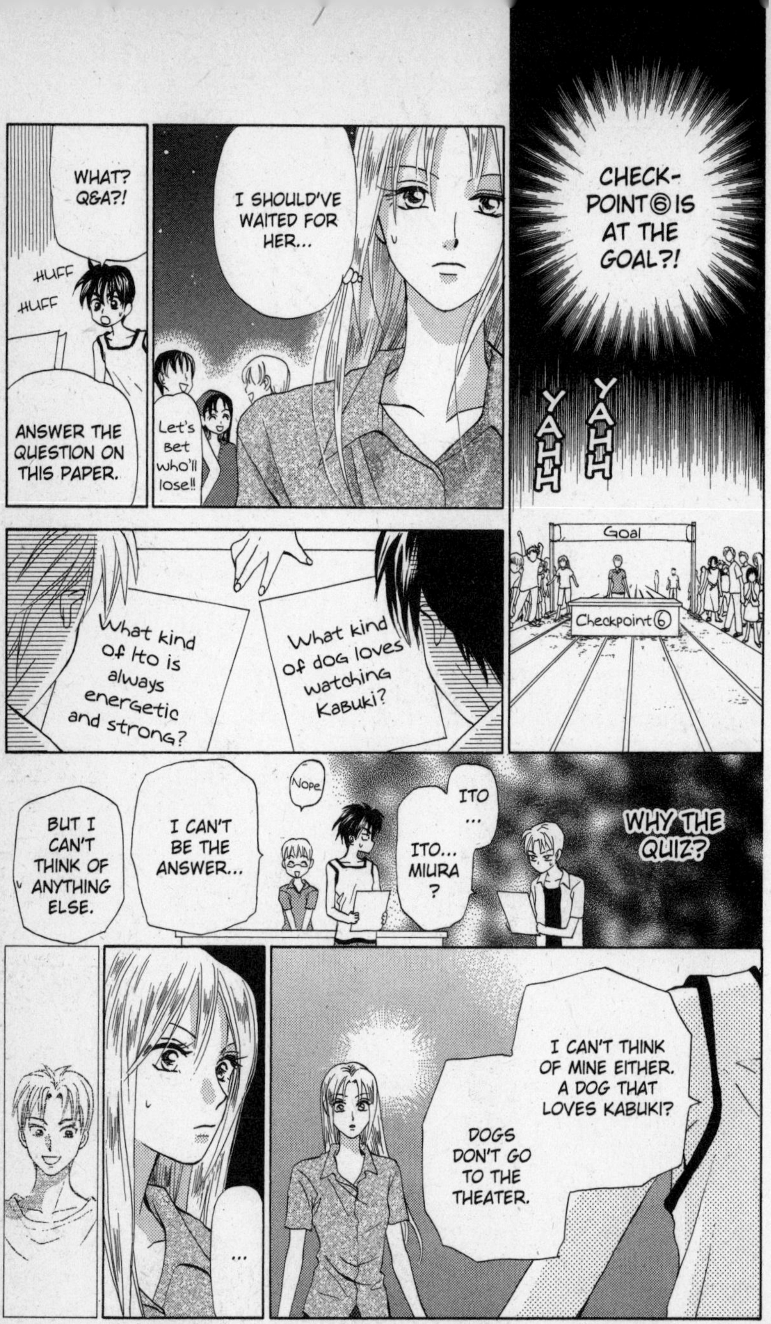
CHECK-POINT ⑥ IS AT THE GOAL?!
YAHH
YAHH
I SHOULD'VE WAITED FOR HER...
Let's Bet who'll lose!!
WHAT? Q&A?!
HUFF
HUFF
ANSWER THE QUESTION ON THIS PAPER.
Goal
Checkpoint ⑥
What kind of dog loves watching Kabuki?
What kind of Ito is always energetic and strong?
WHY THE QUIZ?
ITO...
ITO... MIURA?
Nope
I CAN'T BE THE ANSWER...
BUT I CAN'T THINK OF ANYTHING ELSE.
I CAN'T THINK OF MINE EITHER. A DOG THAT LOVES KABUKI?
DOGS DON'T GO TO THE THEATER.
...

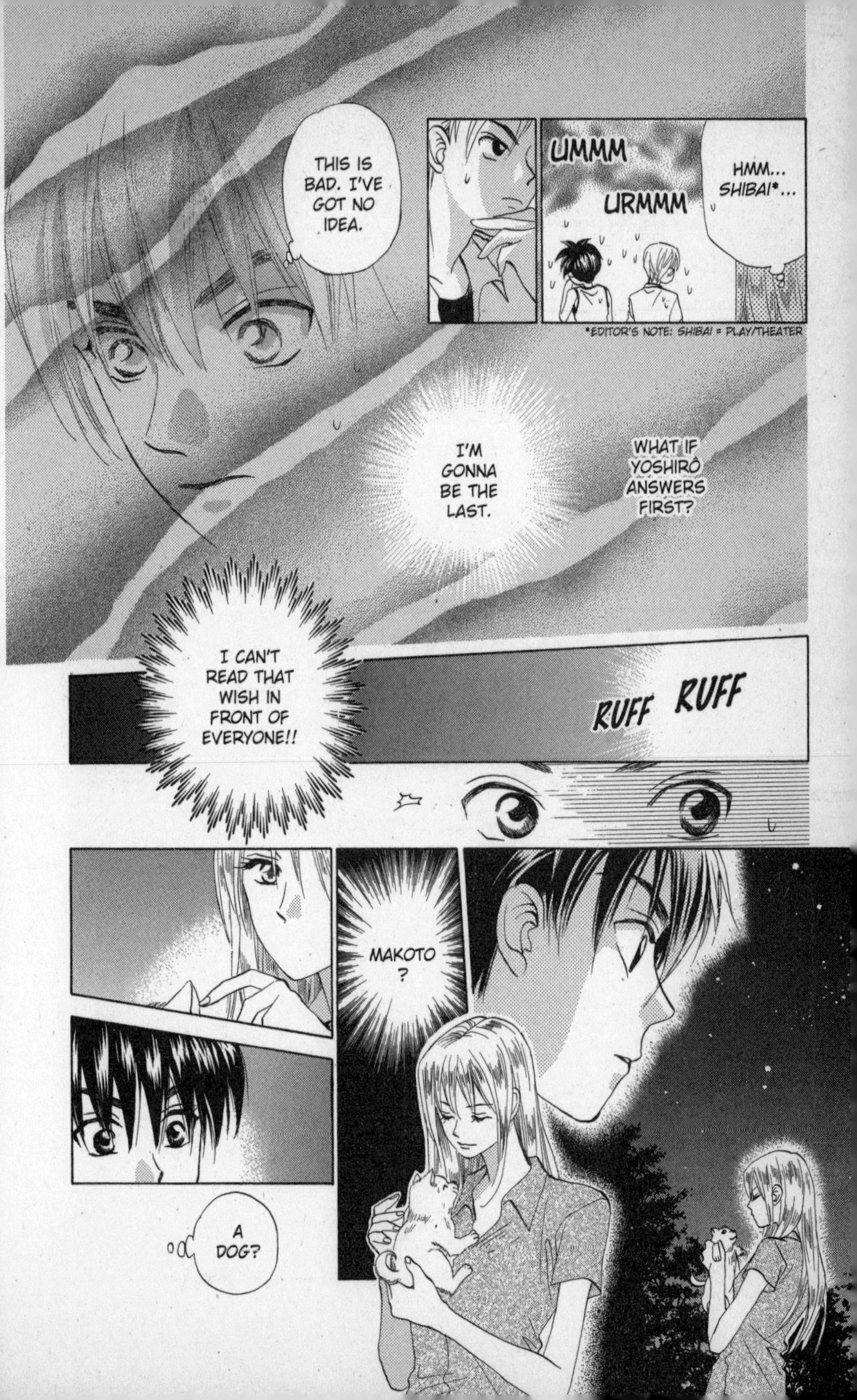
HMM... SHIBAI*...
UMMM
URMMM
THIS IS BAD. I'VE GOT NO IDEA.
*EDITOR'S NOTE: SHIBAI = PLAY/THEATER
WHAT IF YOSHIRÔ ANSWERS FIRST?
I'M GONNA BE THE LAST.
RUFF RUFF
I CAN'T READ THAT WISH IN FRONT OF EVERYONE!!
MAKOTO?
A DOG?

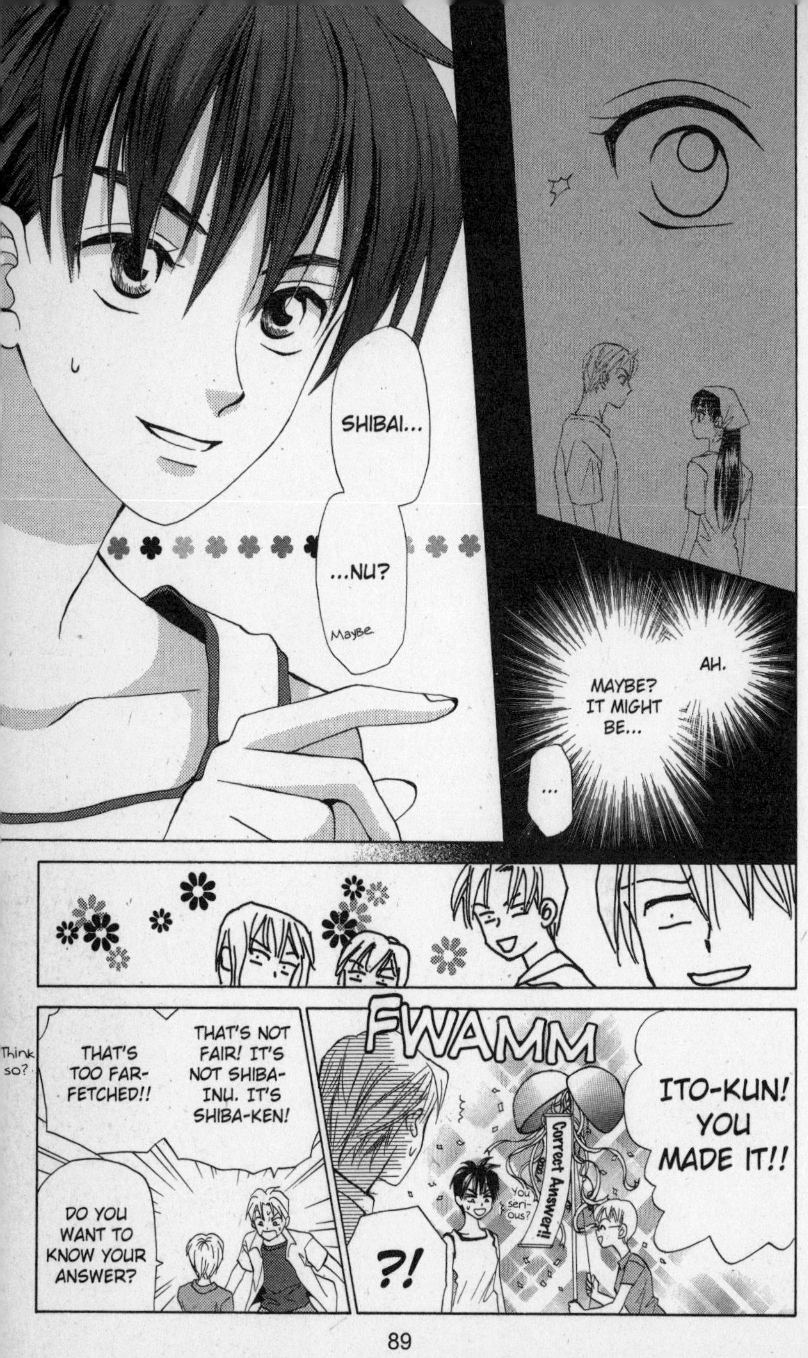
SHIBAI...
...NU?
Maybe.
AH.
MAYBE? IT MIGHT BE...
...
FWAMM
ITO-KUN! YOU MADE IT!!
Correct Answer!!
You seri-ous?
?!
THAT'S NOT FAIR! IT'S NOT SHIBA-INU. IT'S SHIBA-KEN!
THAT'S TOO FAR-FETCHED!!
Think so?
DO YOU WANT TO KNOW YOUR ANSWER?

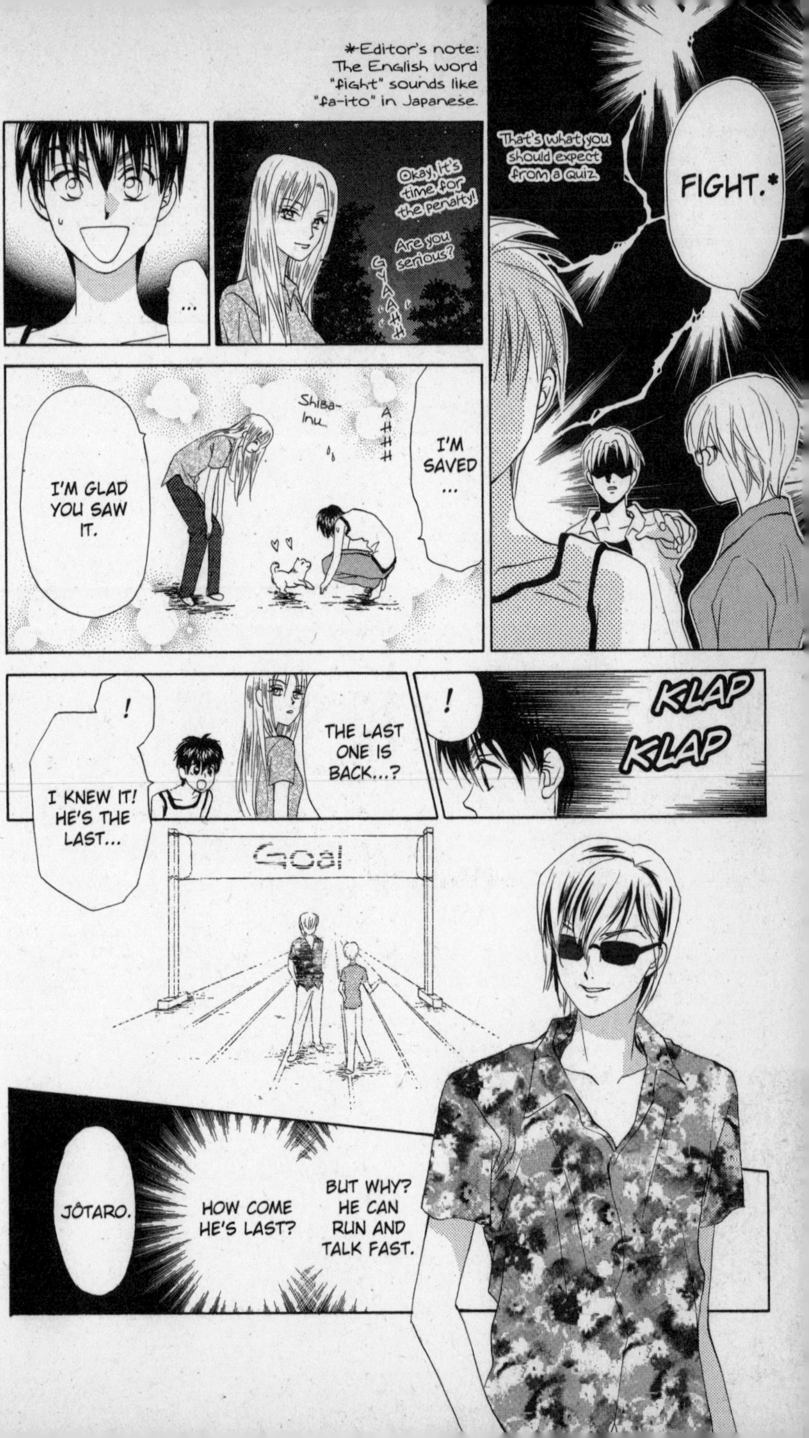
FIGHT.*
That's what you should expect from a quiz.
Okay, it's time for the penalty!
Are you serious?
GYAAAHH
...
I'M SAVED...
AHHH
Shiba-Inu..
I'M GLAD YOU SAW IT.
KLAP
KLAP
!
THE LAST ONE IS BACK...?
!
I KNEW IT! HE'S THE LAST...
Goal
BUT WHY? HE CAN RUN AND TALK FAST.
HOW COME HE'S LAST?
JÔTARO.

*Editor's note: The English word "fight" sounds like "fa-ito" in Japanese.

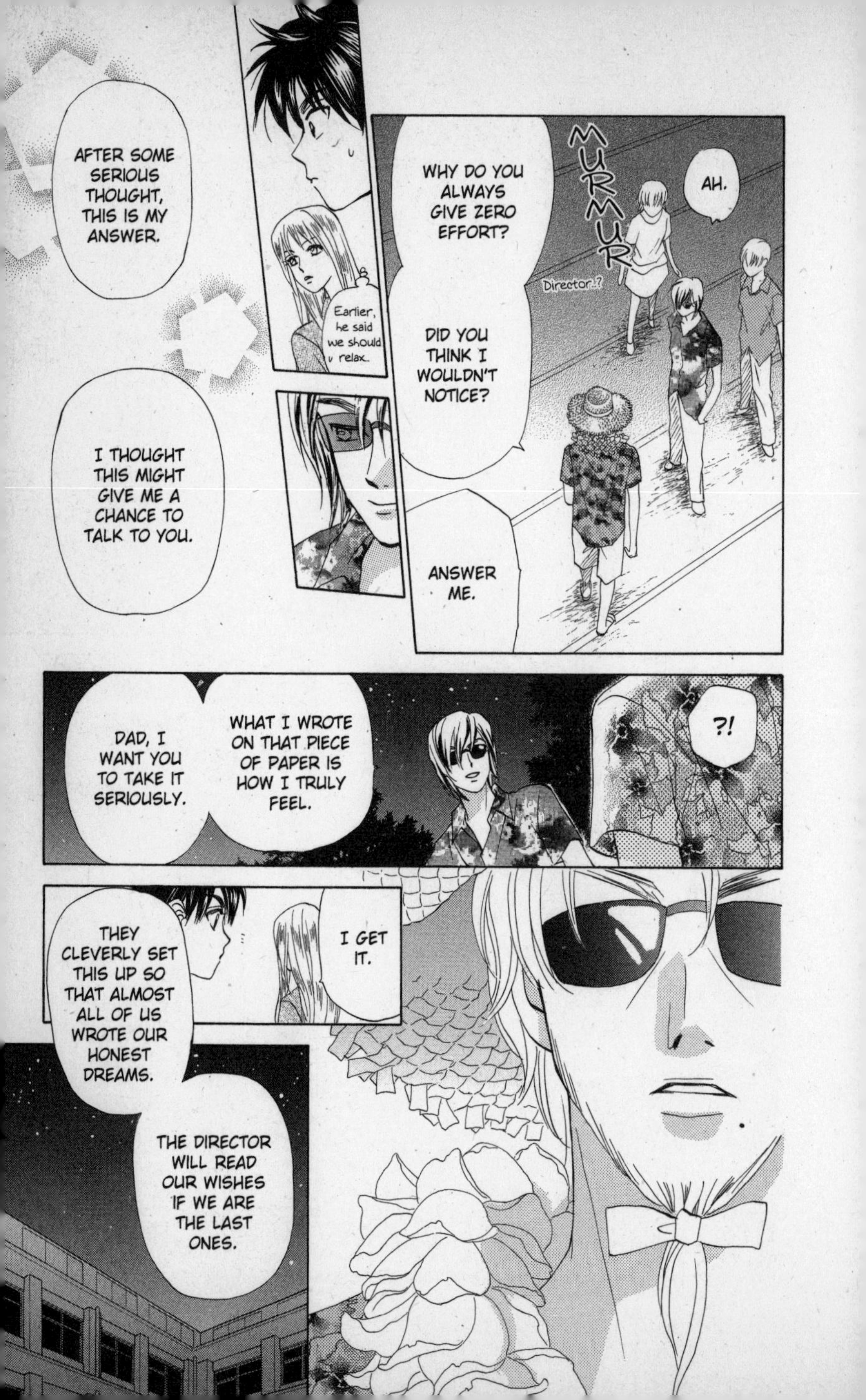
AH.
MURMUR
Director..?
WHY DO YOU ALWAYS GIVE ZERO EFFORT?
DID YOU THINK I WOULDN'T NOTICE?
ANSWER ME.
Earlier, he said we should relax..
AFTER SOME SERIOUS THOUGHT, THIS IS MY ANSWER.
I THOUGHT THIS MIGHT GIVE ME A CHANCE TO TALK TO YOU.
?!
WHAT I WROTE ON THAT PIECE OF PAPER IS HOW I TRULY FEEL.
DAD, I WANT YOU TO TAKE IT SERIOUSLY.
I GET IT.
THEY CLEVERLY SET THIS UP SO THAT ALMOST ALL OF US WROTE OUR HONEST DREAMS.
THE DIRECTOR WILL READ OUR WISHES IF WE ARE THE LAST ONES.

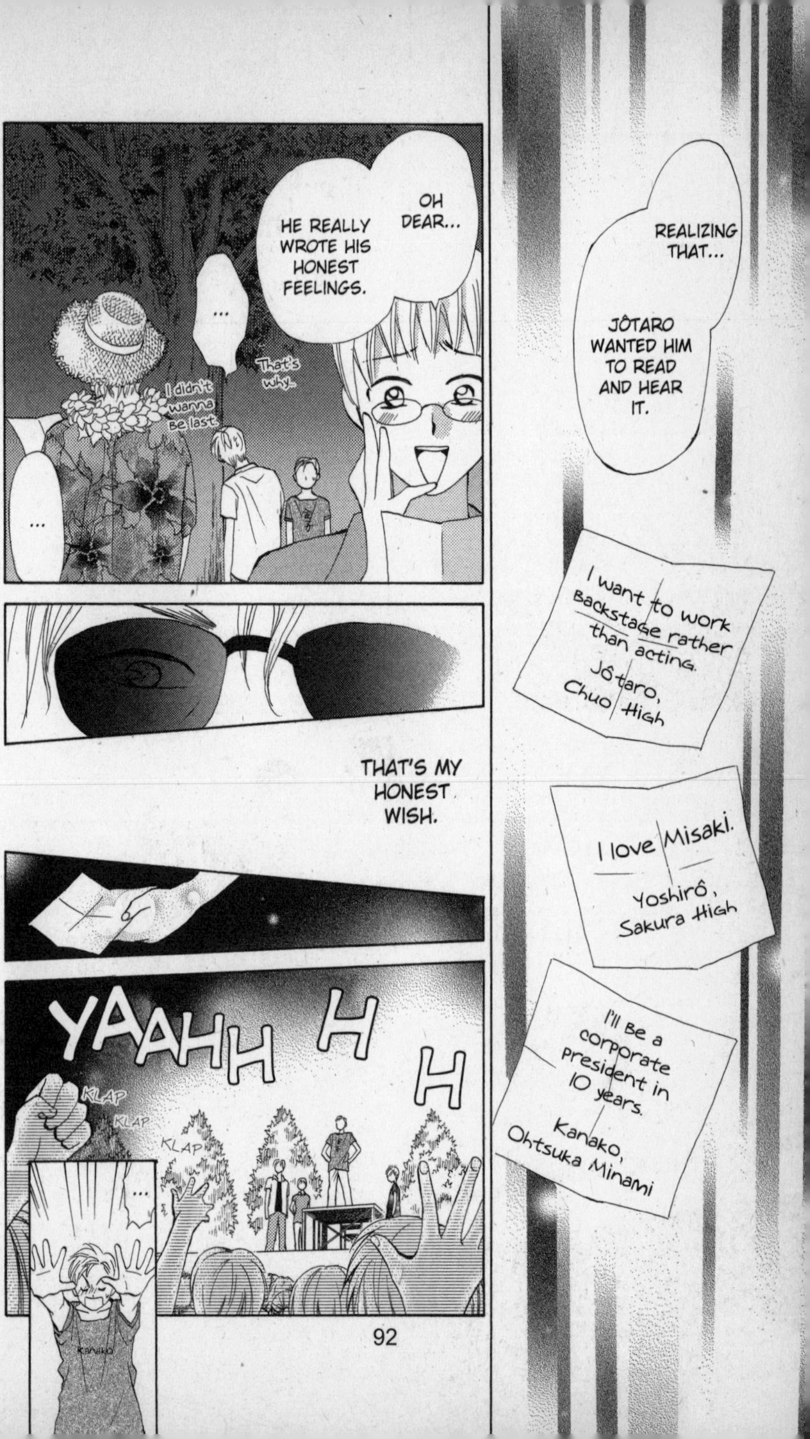
REALIZING THAT...
JÔTARO WANTED HIM TO READ AND HEAR IT.
I want to work Backstage rather than acting.
Jôtaro, Chuo High
I love Misaki.
Yoshirô, Sakura High
I'll Be a corporate president in 10 years.
Kanako, Ohtsuka Minami
OH DEAR...
HE REALLY WROTE HIS HONEST FEELINGS.
...
That's why...
I didn't wanna be last.
...
THAT'S MY HONEST WISH.
YAAHH H H
KLAP
KLAP
KLAP
...
Kanako

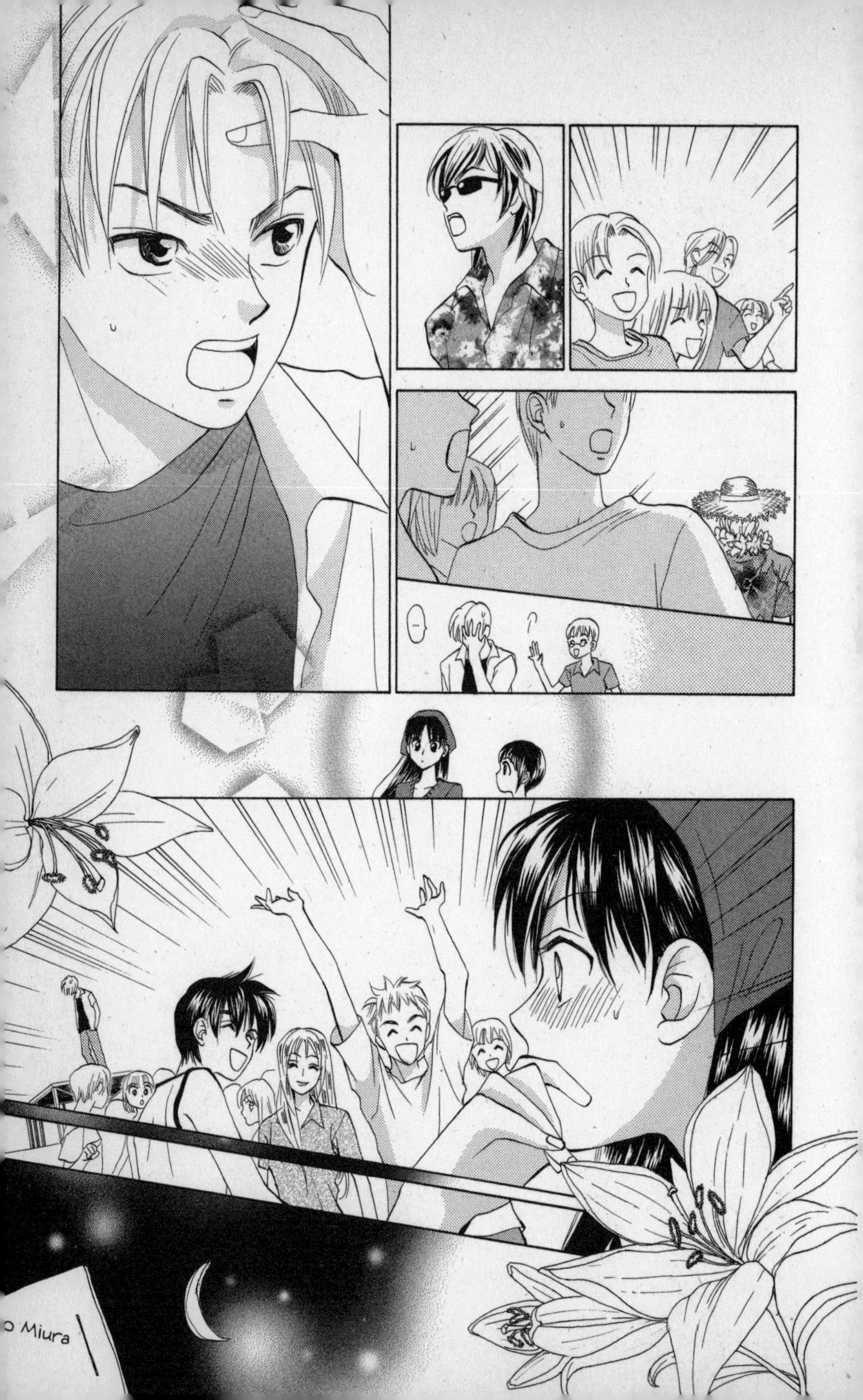
?
...
Miura

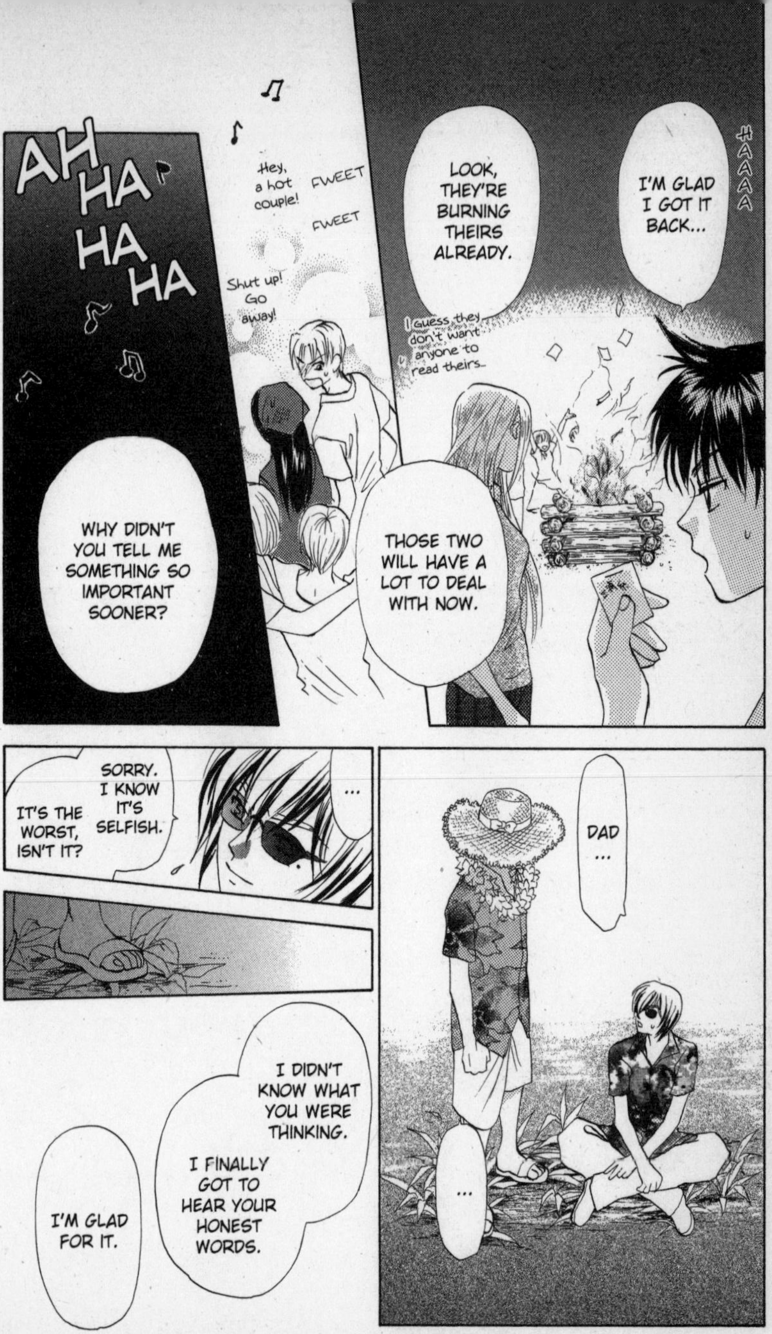
HAAAAA
I'M GLAD I GOT IT BACK...
LOOK, THEY'RE BURNING THEIRS ALREADY.
I guess they don't want anyone to read theirs...
THOSE TWO WILL HAVE A LOT TO DEAL WITH NOW.
Hey, a hot couple!
FWEET
FWEET
Shut up! Go away!
AH HA HA HA
WHY DIDN'T YOU TELL ME SOMETHING SO IMPORTANT SOONER?
DAD ...
...
...
SORRY. I KNOW IT'S SELFISH.
IT'S THE WORST, ISN'T IT?
I DIDN'T KNOW WHAT YOU WERE THINKING.
I FINALLY GOT TO HEAR YOUR HONEST WORDS.
I'M GLAD FOR IT.

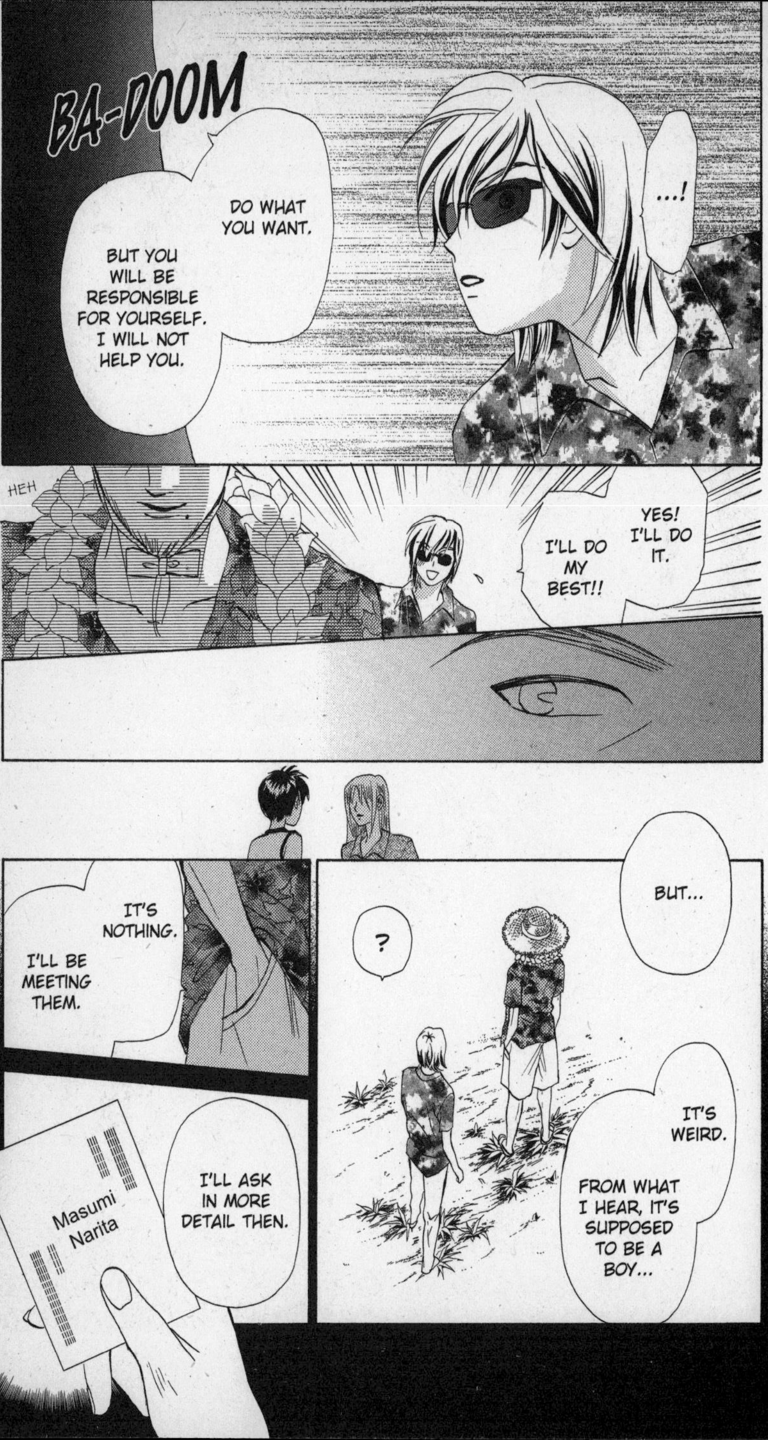
...!
BA-DOOM
DO WHAT YOU WANT.
BUT YOU WILL BE RESPONSIBLE FOR YOURSELF. I WILL NOT HELP YOU.
YES! I'LL DO IT.
I'LL DO MY BEST!!
HEH
BUT...
?
IT'S WEIRD.
FROM WHAT I HEAR, IT'S SUPPOSED TO BE A BOY...
IT'S NOTHING.
I'LL BE MEETING THEM.
I'LL ASK IN MORE DETAIL THEN.
Masumi Narita

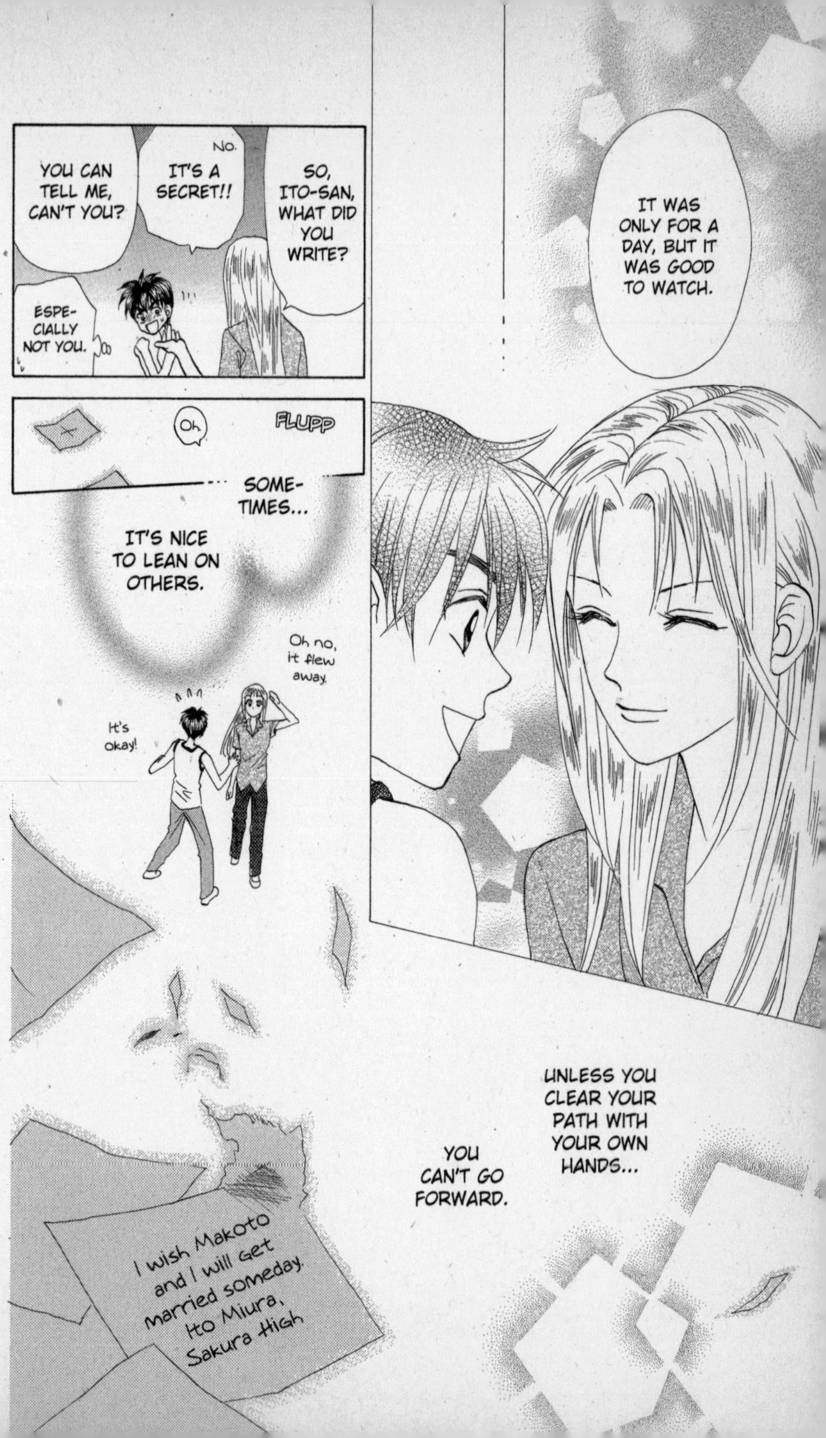
IT WAS ONLY FOR A DAY, BUT IT WAS GOOD TO WATCH.
SO, ITO-SAN, WHAT DID YOU WRITE?
No.
IT'S A SECRET!!
YOU CAN TELL ME, CAN'T YOU?
ESPE-CIALLY NOT YOU.
FLUPP
Oh.
... SOME-TIMES...
IT'S NICE TO LEAN ON OTHERS.
Oh no, it flew away.
It's okay!
UNLESS YOU CLEAR YOUR PATH WITH YOUR OWN HANDS...
YOU CAN'T GO FORWARD.
I wish Makoto and I will get married someday.
Ito Miura, Sakura High

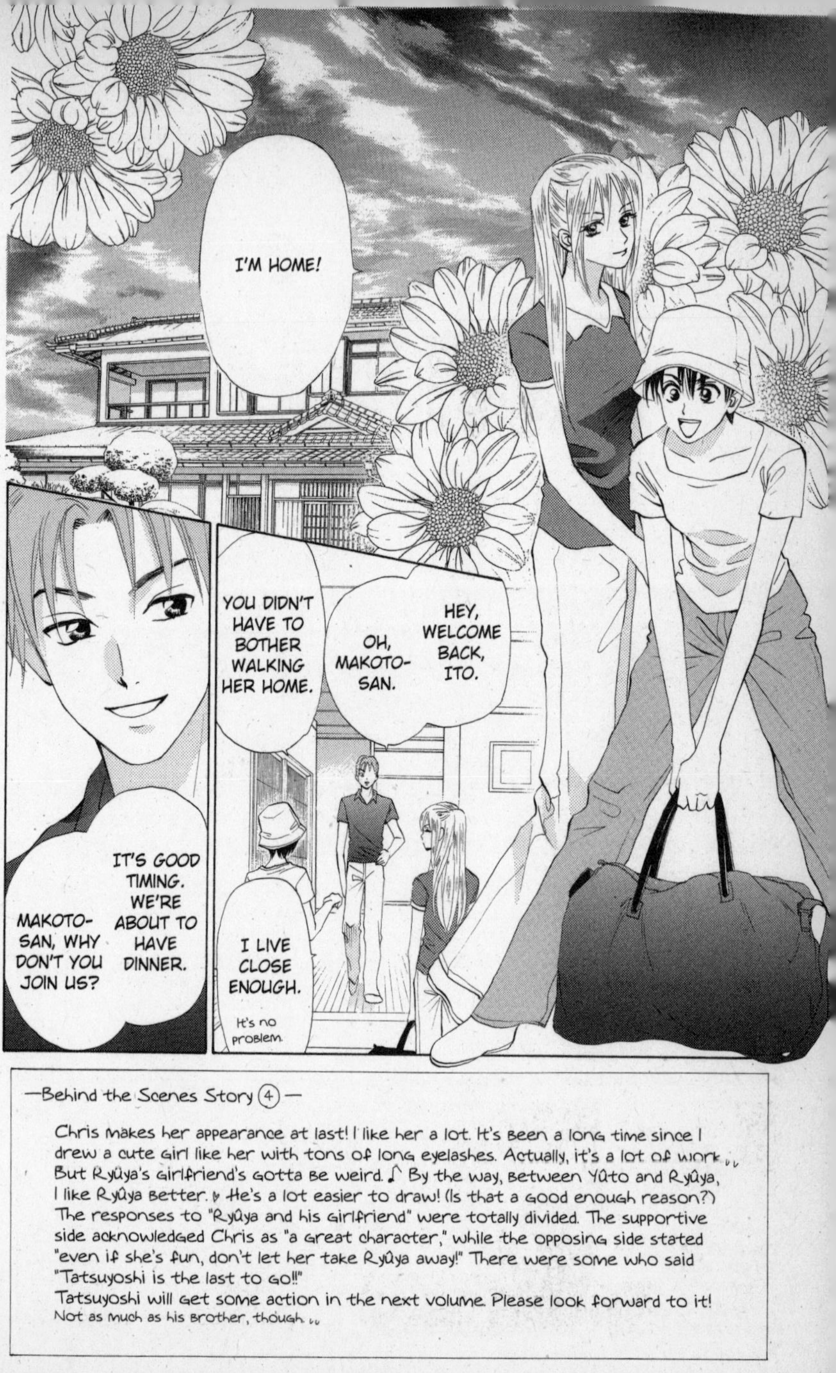
I'M HOME!
HEY, WELCOME BACK, ITO.
OH, MAKOTO-SAN.
YOU DIDN'T HAVE TO BOTHER WALKING HER HOME.
I LIVE CLOSE ENOUGH.
It's no problem.
IT'S GOOD TIMING. WE'RE ABOUT TO HAVE DINNER.
MAKOTO-SAN, WHY DON'T YOU JOIN US?

—Behind the Scenes Story ④—

Chris makes her appearance at last! I like her a lot. It's been a long time since I drew a cute girl like her with tons of long eyelashes. Actually, it's a lot of work... But Ryûya's girlfriend's gotta be weird.♪ By the way, between Yûto and Ryûya, I like Ryûya better.♥ He's a lot easier to draw! (Is that a good enough reason?) The responses to "Ryûya and his girlfriend" were totally divided. The supportive side acknowledged Chris as "a great character," while the opposing side stated "even if she's fun, don't let her take Ryûya away!" There were some who said "Tatsuyoshi is the last to go!!"
Tatsuyoshi will get some action in the next volume. Please look forward to it!
Not as much as his brother, though...

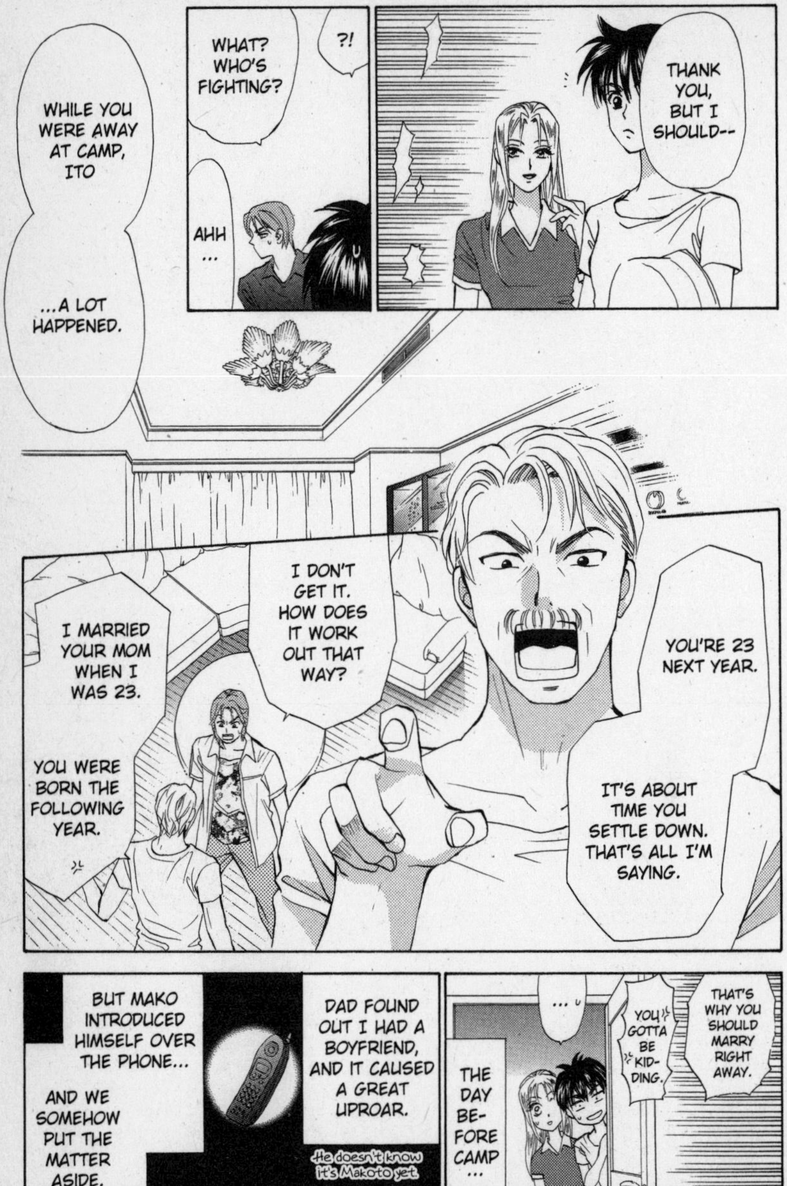
THANK YOU, BUT I SHOULD--
?!
WHAT? WHO'S FIGHTING?
AHH...
WHILE YOU WERE AWAY AT CAMP, ITO
...A LOT HAPPENED.
YOU'RE 23 NEXT YEAR.
IT'S ABOUT TIME YOU SETTLE DOWN. THAT'S ALL I'M SAYING.
I DON'T GET IT. HOW DOES IT WORK OUT THAT WAY?
I MARRIED YOUR MOM WHEN I WAS 23.
YOU WERE BORN THE FOLLOWING YEAR.
THAT'S WHY YOU SHOULD MARRY RIGHT AWAY.
YOU GOTTA BE KID-DING.
...
THE DAY BE-FORE CAMP...
DAD FOUND OUT I HAD A BOYFRIEND, AND IT CAUSED A GREAT UPROAR.
He doesn't know it's Makoto yet.
BUT MAKO INTRODUCED HIMSELF OVER THE PHONE...
AND WE SOMEHOW PUT THE MATTER ASIDE.

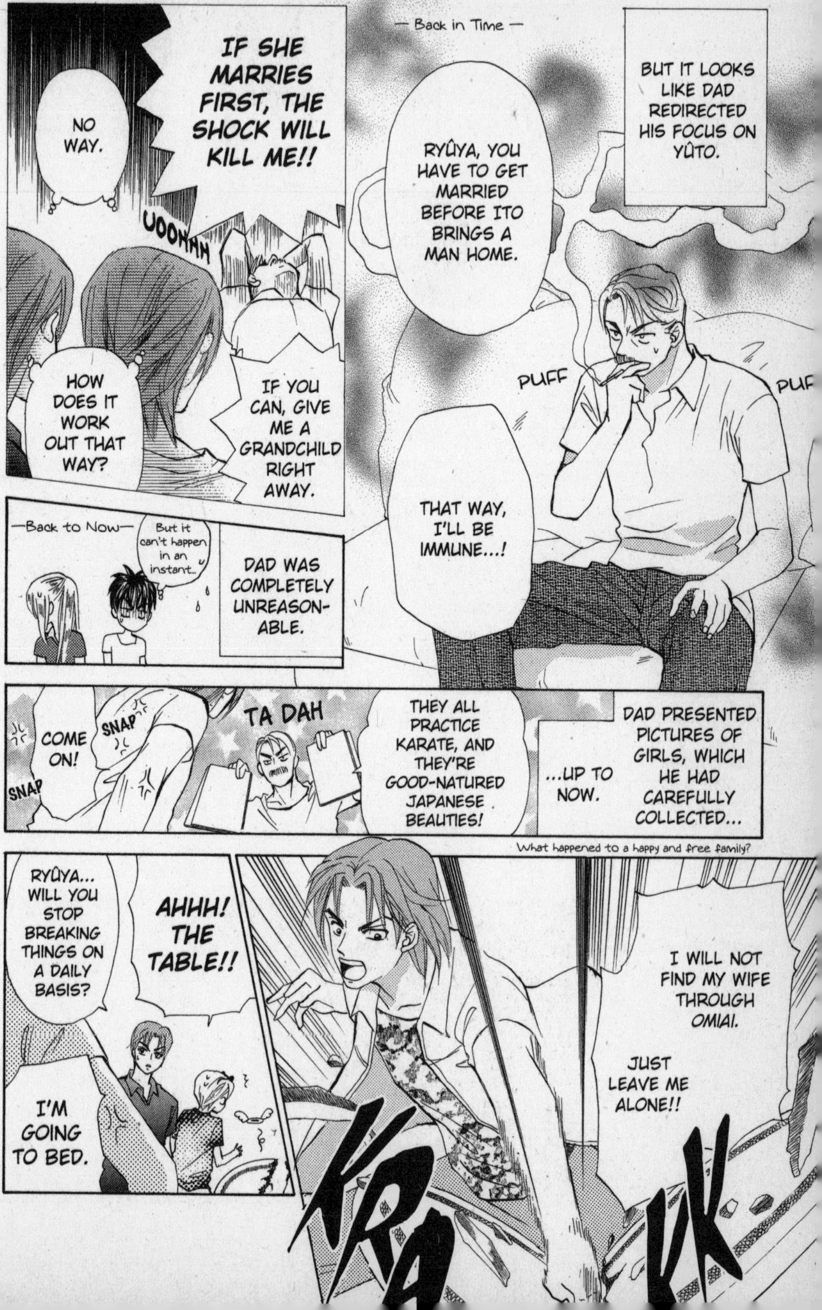
— Back in Time —
BUT IT LOOKS LIKE DAD REDIRECTED HIS FOCUS ON YÛTO.
RYÛYA, YOU HAVE TO GET MARRIED BEFORE ITO BRINGS A MAN HOME.
PUFF
PUFF
THAT WAY, I'LL BE IMMUNE...!
IF SHE MARRIES FIRST, THE SHOCK WILL KILL ME!!
NO WAY.
UOOHHH
IF YOU CAN, GIVE ME A GRANDCHILD RIGHT AWAY.
HOW DOES IT WORK OUT THAT WAY?
—Back to Now—
DAD WAS COMPLETELY UNREASON-ABLE.
But it can't happen in an instant...
DAD PRESENTED PICTURES OF GIRLS, WHICH HE HAD CAREFULLY COLLECTED...
...UP TO NOW.
THEY ALL PRACTICE KARATE, AND THEY'RE GOOD-NATURED JAPANESE BEAUTIES!
TA DAH
SNAP
COME ON!
SNAP
What happened to a happy and free family?
I WILL NOT FIND MY WIFE THROUGH OMIAI.
JUST LEAVE ME ALONE!!
KRAKK
AHHH! THE TABLE!!
RYÛYA... WILL YOU STOP BREAKING THINGS ON A DAILY BASIS?
I'M GOING TO BED.

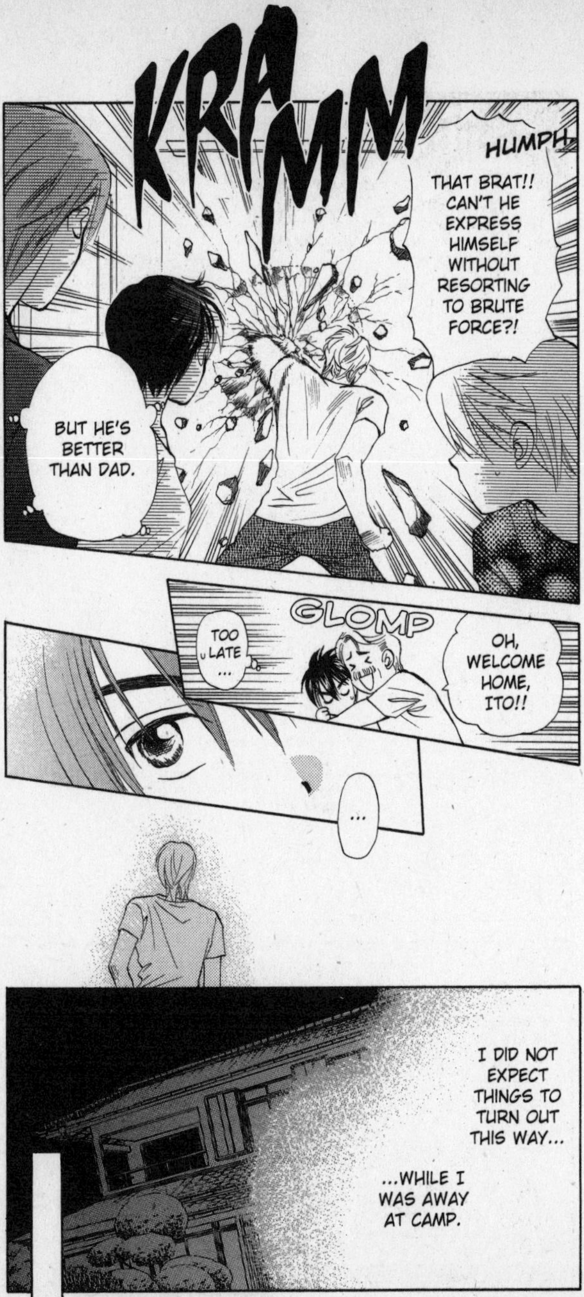
KRAMM
HUMPH
THAT BRAT!! CAN'T HE EXPRESS HIMSELF WITHOUT RESORTING TO BRUTE FORCE?!
BUT HE'S BETTER THAN DAD.
GLOMP
OH, WELCOME HOME, ITO!!
TOO LATE...
...
I DID NOT EXPECT THINGS TO TURN OUT THIS WAY...
...WHILE I WAS AWAY AT CAMP.

My sister handled both her day job and assisting me for a while, and she eventually realized she enjoyed assisting more. Instead of dreading the deadline, she'd get happier working on the assignments.

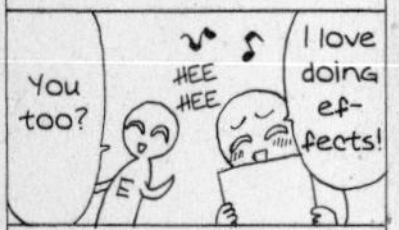
I love doing effects!
HEE HEE
You too?

We are so much alike. I love doing effects too!

And she made up her mind at last. She quit her day job and became my exclusive assistant. It was right around the time we were working on W Juliet volume 6. She was abusing her body to its limit by then. It wasn't easy (like dealing with our parents and all) to get to where we are today, but as I say, we somehow settled the matter okay...I think.

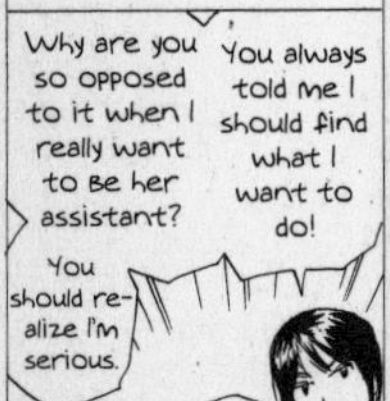
You always told me I should find what I want to do!
Why are you so opposed to it when I really want to be her assistant?
You should realize I'm serious.
You told me and our brother the same.

The Theme of the Siblings Conference "What the heck is wrong with parents?!"

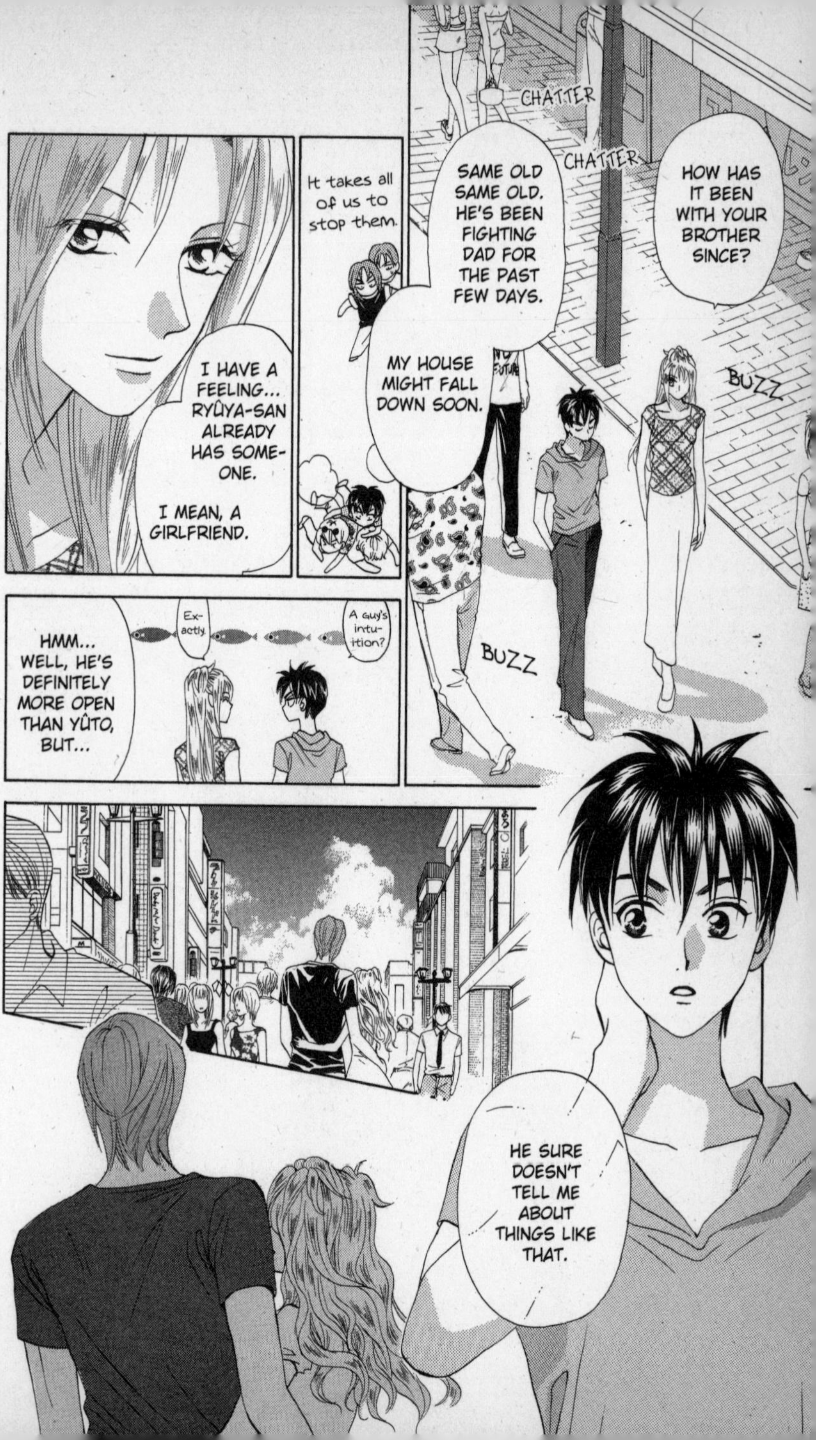
CHATTER
CHATTER
HOW HAS IT BEEN WITH YOUR BROTHER SINCE?
SAME OLD SAME OLD. HE'S BEEN FIGHTING DAD FOR THE PAST FEW DAYS.
MY HOUSE MIGHT FALL DOWN SOON.
BUZZ
BUZZ
It takes all of us to stop them.
I HAVE A FEELING... RYÛYA-SAN ALREADY HAS SOME-ONE.
I MEAN, A GIRLFRIEND.
A Guy's intu-ition?
Ex-actly.
HMM... WELL, HE'S DEFINITELY MORE OPEN THAN YÛTO, BUT...
HE SURE DOESN'T TELL ME ABOUT THINGS LIKE THAT.

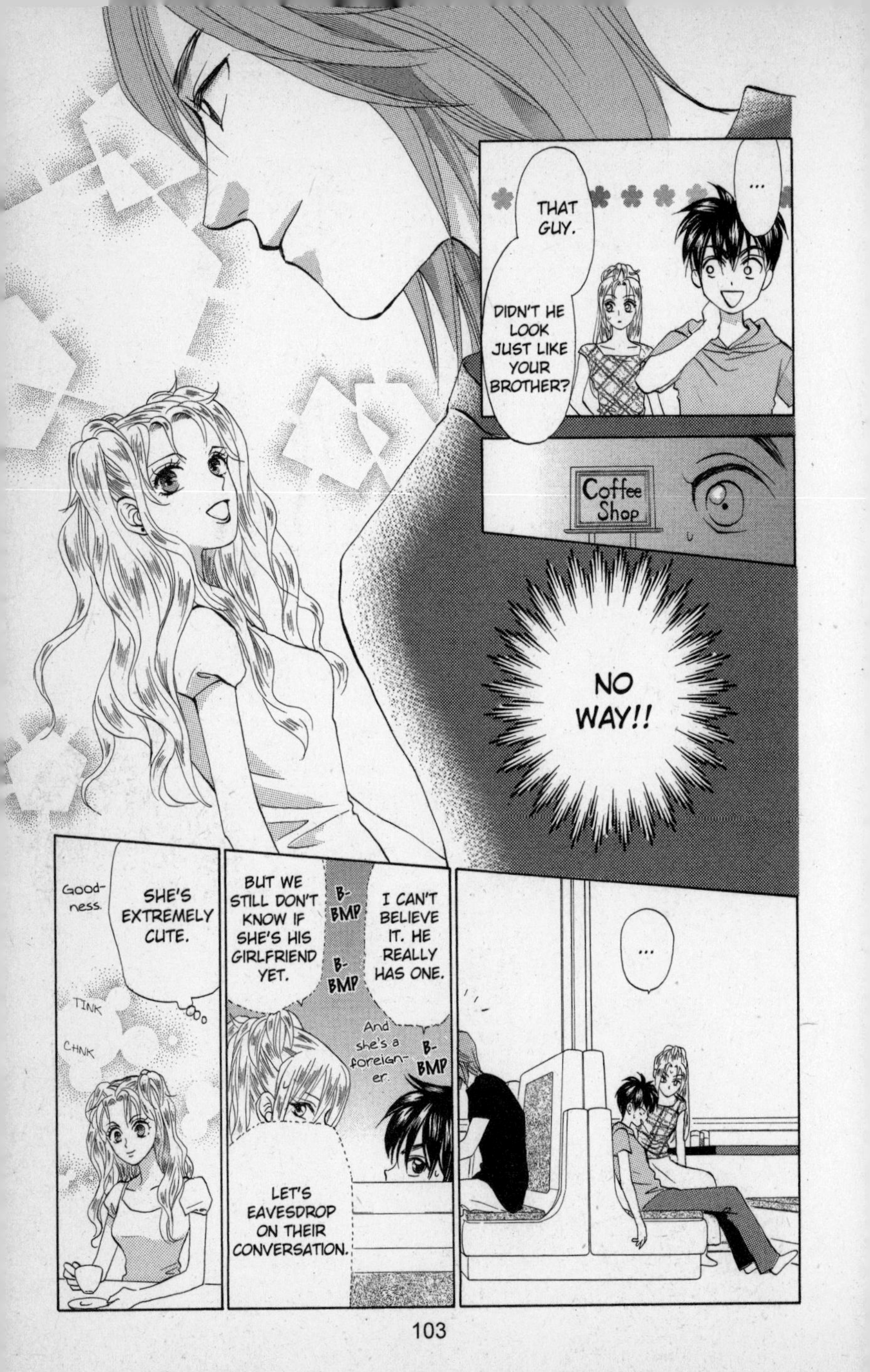
...
THAT GUY.
DIDN'T HE LOOK JUST LIKE YOUR BROTHER?
Coffee Shop
NO WAY!!
...
I CAN'T BELIEVE IT. HE REALLY HAS ONE.
B-BMP
BUT WE STILL DON'T KNOW IF SHE'S HIS GIRLFRIEND YET.
B-BMP
B-BMP
And she's a foreigner.
LET'S EAVESDROP ON THEIR CONVERSATION.
SHE'S EXTREMELY CUTE.
Goodness.
TINK
CHNK

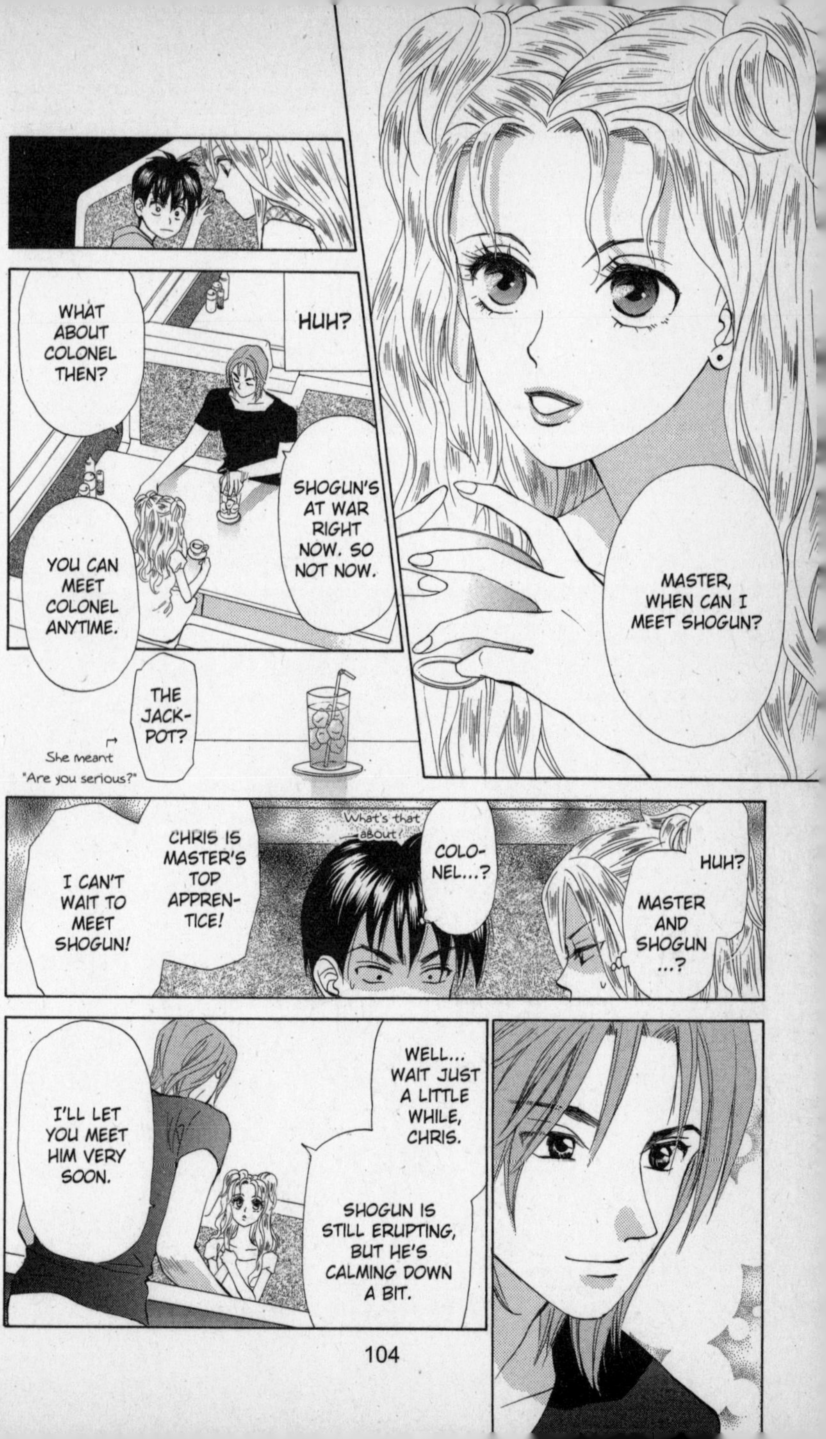
MASTER, WHEN CAN I MEET SHOGUN?
HUH?
SHOGUN'S AT WAR RIGHT NOW. SO NOT NOW.
WHAT ABOUT COLONEL THEN?
YOU CAN MEET COLONEL ANYTIME.
THE JACK-POT?
She meant "Are you serious?"
HUH?
MASTER AND SHOGUN ...?
COLO-NEL...?
What's that about!
CHRIS IS MASTER'S TOP APPREN-TICE!
I CAN'T WAIT TO MEET SHOGUN!
WELL... WAIT JUST A LITTLE WHILE, CHRIS.
SHOGUN IS STILL ERUPTING, BUT HE'S CALMING DOWN A BIT.
I'LL LET YOU MEET HIM VERY SOON.

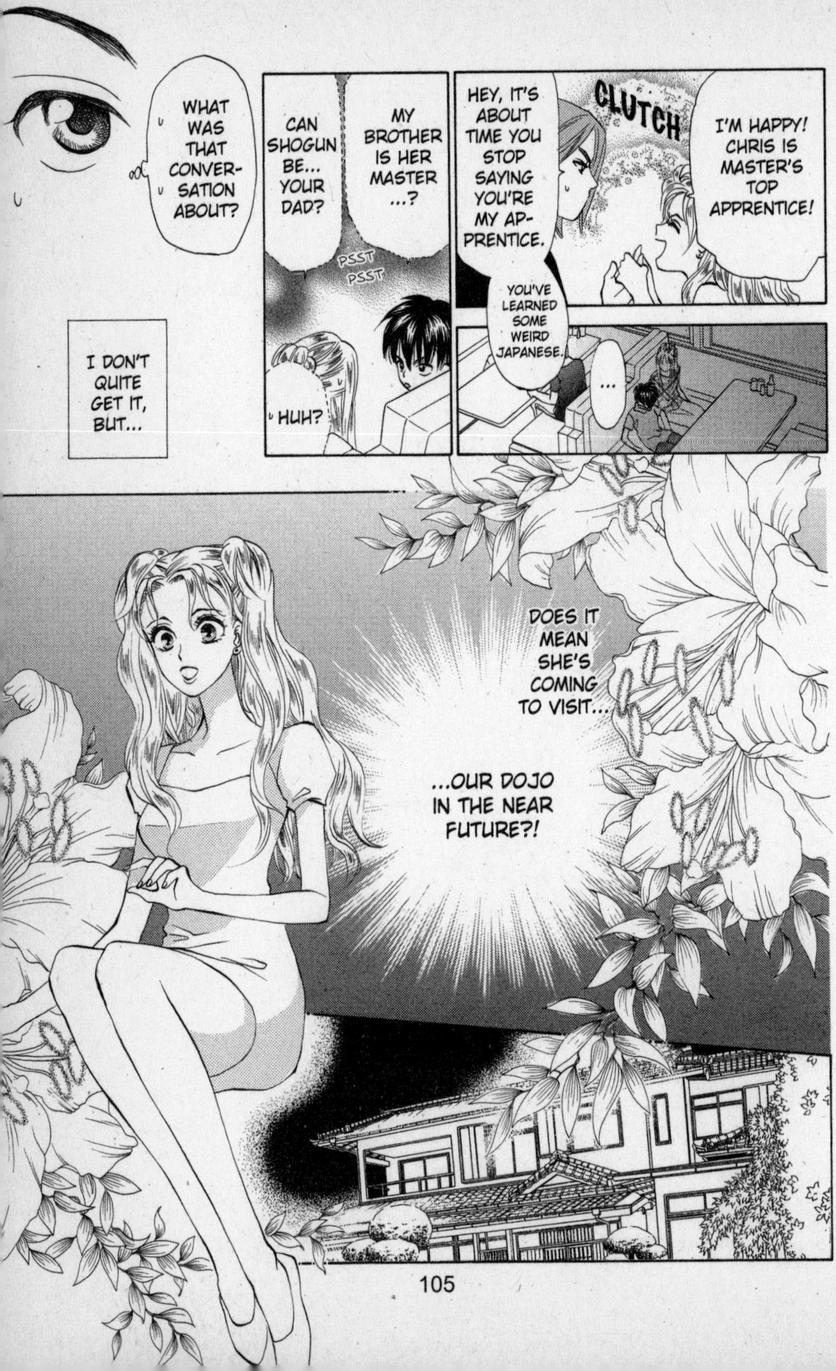
I'M HAPPY! CHRIS IS MASTER'S TOP APPRENTICE!
CLUTCH
HEY, IT'S ABOUT TIME YOU STOP SAYING YOU'RE MY APPRENTICE.
YOU'VE LEARNED SOME WEIRD JAPANESE.
...
MY BROTHER IS HER MASTER ...?
CAN SHOGUN BE... YOUR DAD?
PSST PSST
HUH?
WHAT WAS THAT CONVERSATION ABOUT?
I DON'T QUITE GET IT, BUT...
DOES IT MEAN SHE'S COMING TO VISIT...
...OUR DOJO IN THE NEAR FUTURE?!

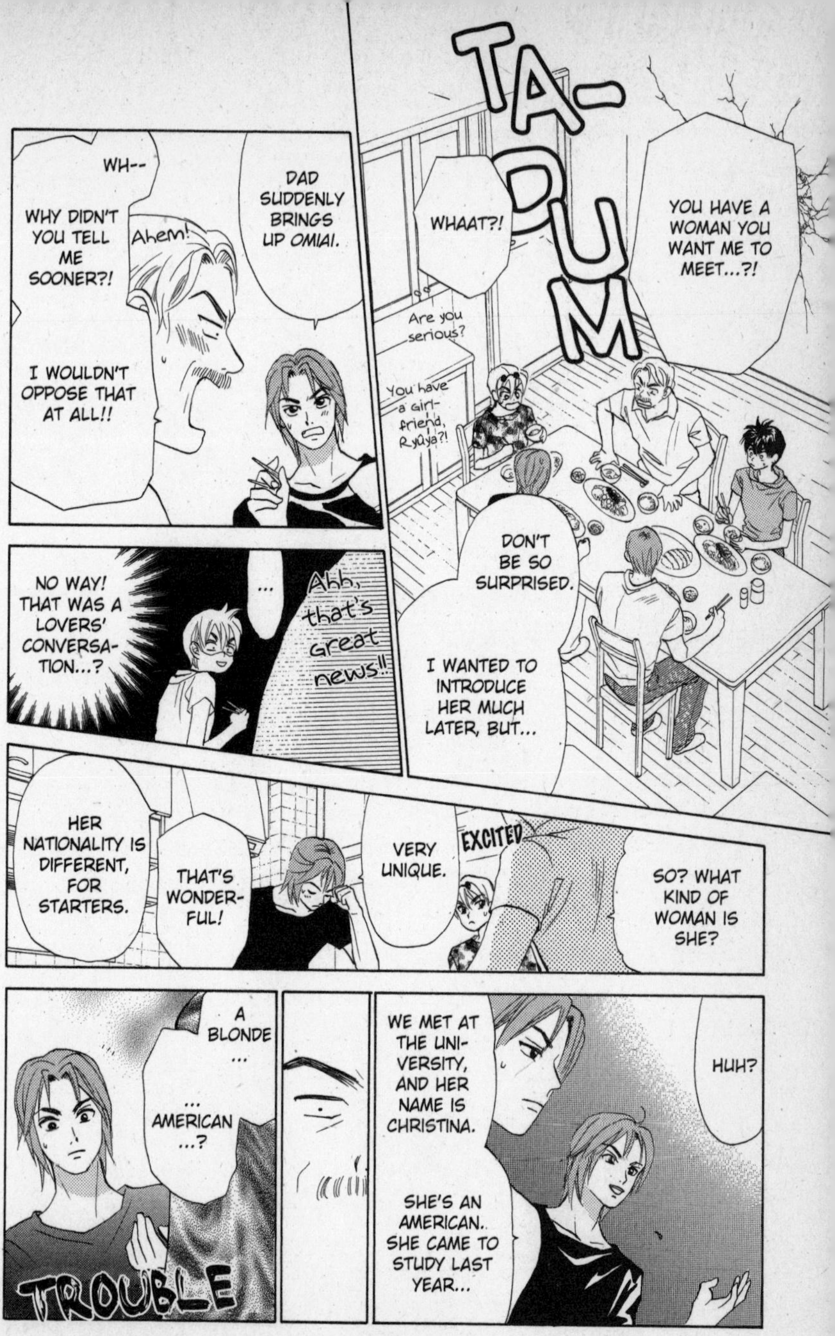
TA-DUM
YOU HAVE A WOMAN YOU WANT ME TO MEET...?!
WHAAT?!
Are you serious?
You have a girlfriend, Ryûya?!
DON'T BE SO SURPRISED.
I WANTED TO INTRODUCE HER MUCH LATER, BUT...
DAD SUDDENLY BRINGS UP OMIAI.
WH--
Ahem!
WHY DIDN'T YOU TELL ME SOONER?!
I WOULDN'T OPPOSE THAT AT ALL!!
Ahh, that's great news!!
...
NO WAY! THAT WAS A LOVERS' CONVERSATION...?
SO? WHAT KIND OF WOMAN IS SHE?
EXCITED
VERY UNIQUE.
THAT'S WONDERFUL!
HER NATIONALITY IS DIFFERENT, FOR STARTERS.
HUH?
WE MET AT THE UNIVERSITY, AND HER NAME IS CHRISTINA.
SHE'S AN AMERICAN. SHE CAME TO STUDY LAST YEAR...
A BLONDE ...
... AMERICAN ...?
TROUBLE

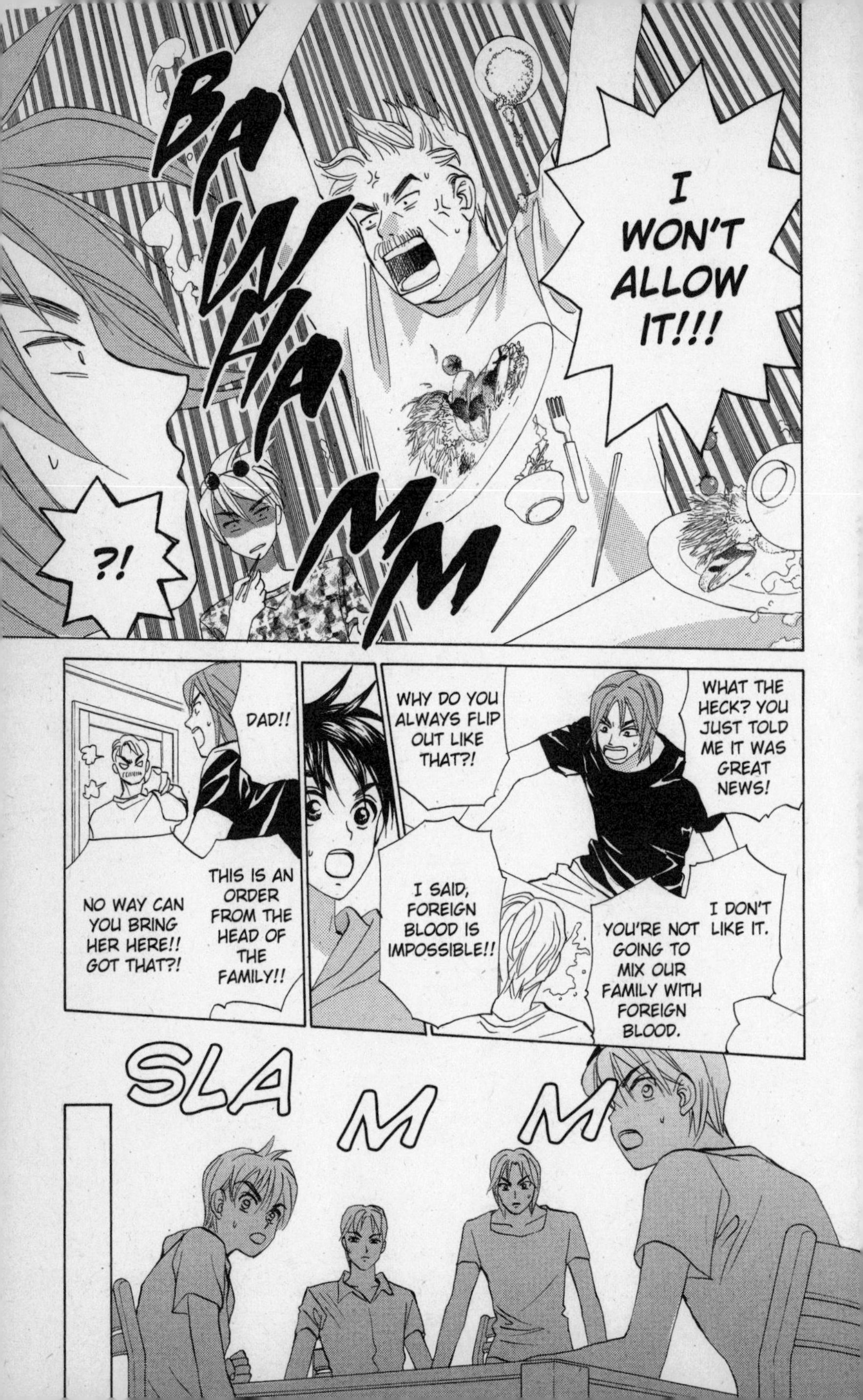
I WON'T ALLOW IT!!!
BAWHAMM
?!
WHAT THE HECK? YOU JUST TOLD ME IT WAS GREAT NEWS!
WHY DO YOU ALWAYS FLIP OUT LIKE THAT?!
I DON'T LIKE IT.
YOU'RE NOT GOING TO MIX OUR FAMILY WITH FOREIGN BLOOD.
I SAID, FOREIGN BLOOD IS IMPOSSIBLE!!
DAD!!
THIS IS AN ORDER FROM THE HEAD OF THE FAMILY!!
NO WAY CAN YOU BRING HER HERE!! GOT THAT?!
SLAMM

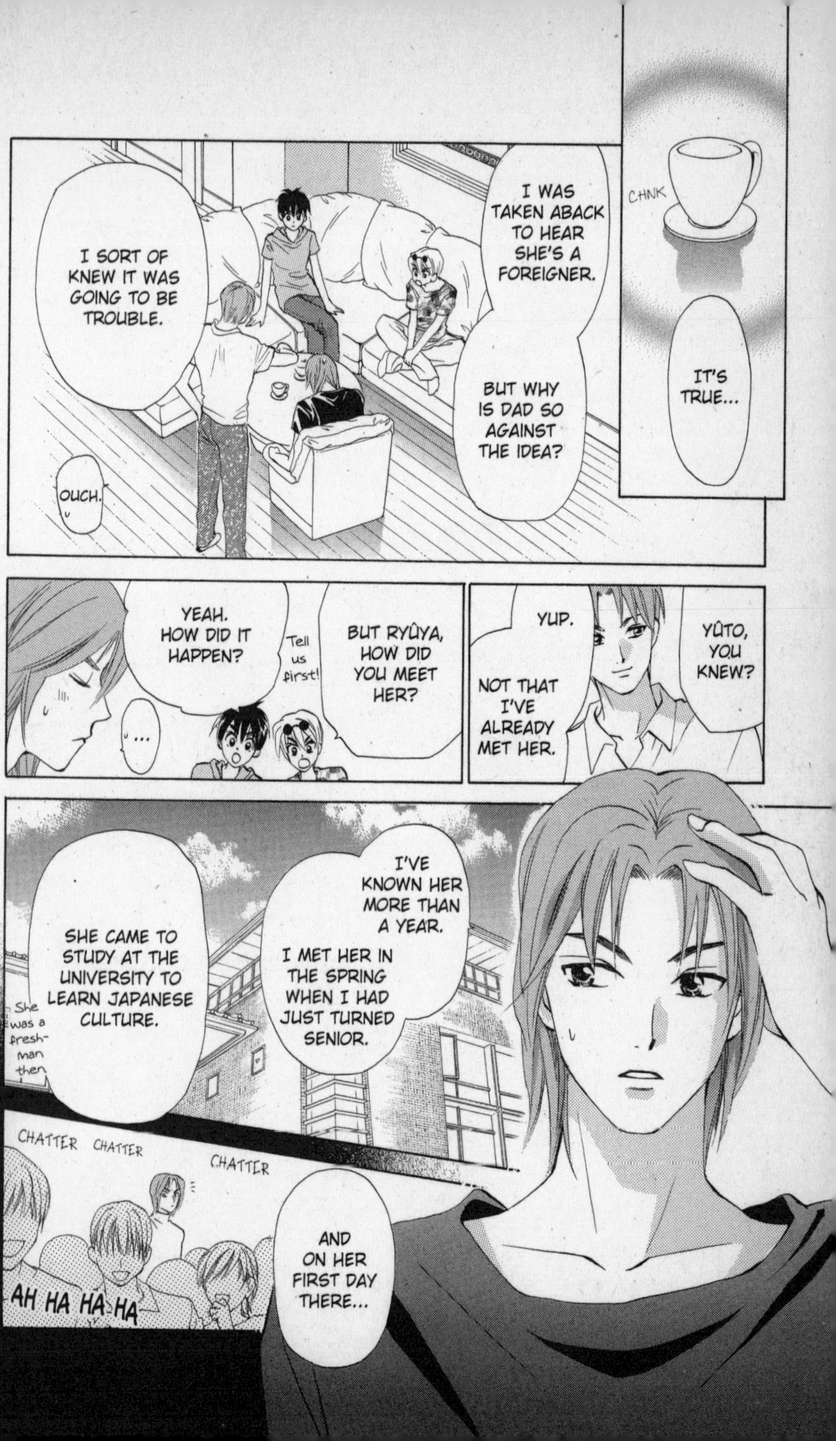
CHNK
IT'S TRUE...
I WAS TAKEN ABACK TO HEAR SHE'S A FOREIGNER.
BUT WHY IS DAD SO AGAINST THE IDEA?
I SORT OF KNEW IT WAS GOING TO BE TROUBLE.
OUCH.
YÛTO, YOU KNEW?
YUP.
NOT THAT I'VE ALREADY MET HER.
BUT RYÛYA, HOW DID YOU MEET HER?
Tell us first!
YEAH. HOW DID IT HAPPEN?
...
I'VE KNOWN HER MORE THAN A YEAR.
I MET HER IN THE SPRING WHEN I HAD JUST TURNED SENIOR.
SHE CAME TO STUDY AT THE UNIVERSITY TO LEARN JAPANESE CULTURE.
She was a fresh-man then
CHATTER CHATTER
CHATTER
AND ON HER FIRST DAY THERE...
AH HA HA HA

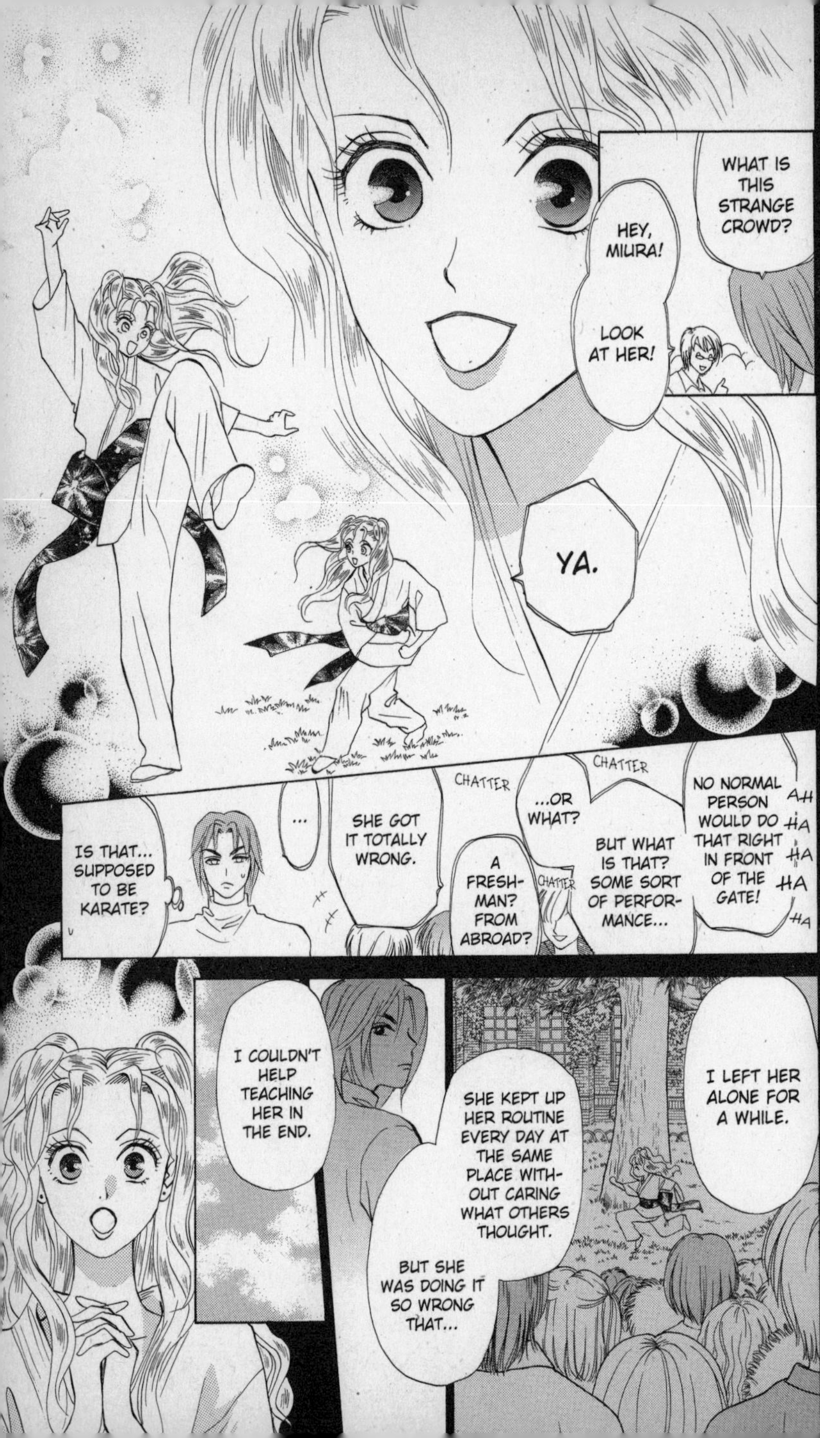
WHAT IS THIS STRANGE CROWD?
HEY, MIURA!
LOOK AT HER!
YA.
NO NORMAL PERSON WOULD DO THAT RIGHT IN FRONT OF THE GATE!
AH HA HA HA HA
CHATTER
BUT WHAT IS THAT? SOME SORT OF PERFORMANCE...
...OR WHAT?
CHATTER
A FRESHMAN? FROM ABROAD?
CHATTER
SHE GOT IT TOTALLY WRONG.
...
IS THAT... SUPPOSED TO BE KARATE?
I LEFT HER ALONE FOR A WHILE.
SHE KEPT UP HER ROUTINE EVERY DAY AT THE SAME PLACE WITHOUT CARING WHAT OTHERS THOUGHT.
BUT SHE WAS DOING IT SO WRONG THAT...
I COULDN'T HELP TEACHING HER IN THE END.

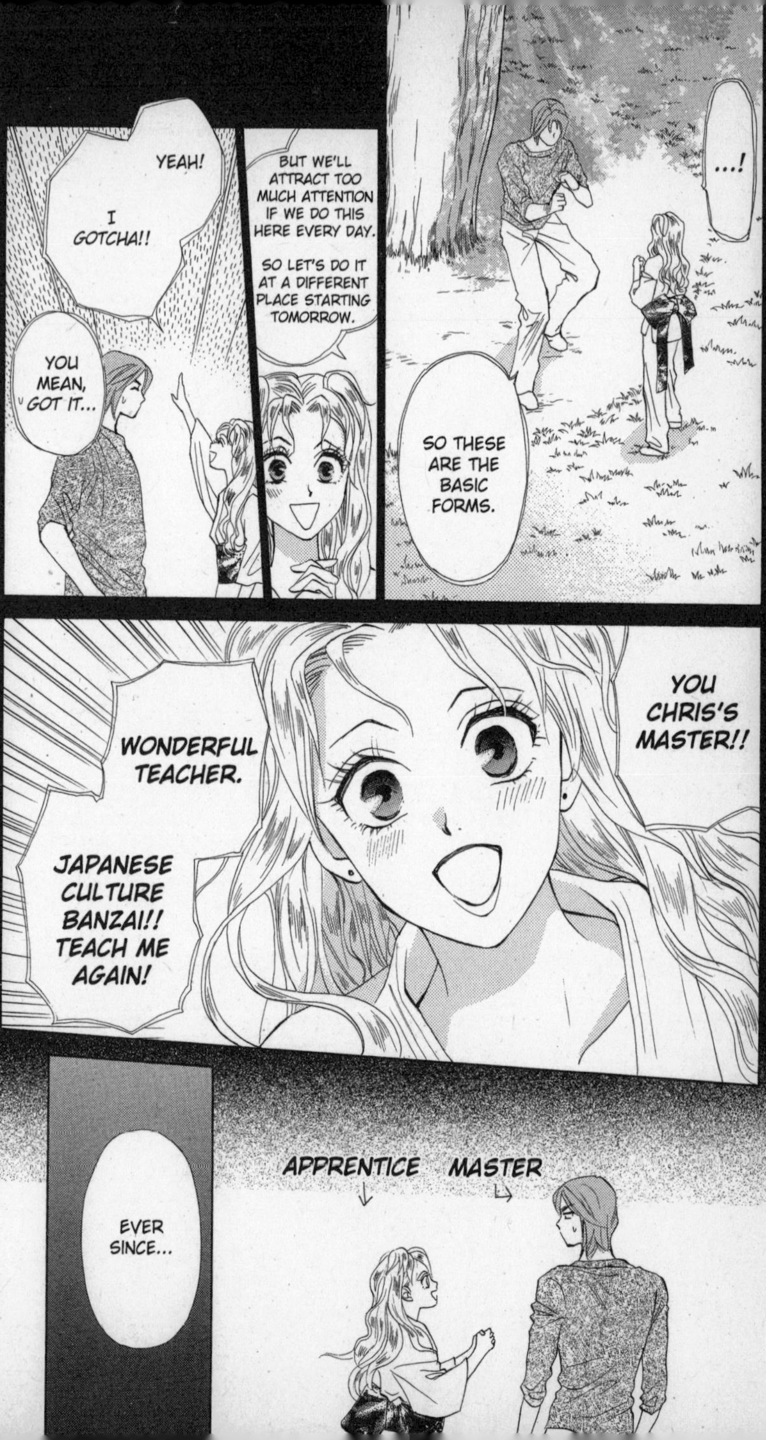
...!
SO THESE ARE THE BASIC FORMS.
BUT WE'LL ATTRACT TOO MUCH ATTENTION IF WE DO THIS HERE EVERY DAY.
SO LET'S DO IT AT A DIFFERENT PLACE STARTING TOMORROW.
YEAH!
I GOTCHA!!
YOU MEAN, GOT IT...
YOU CHRIS'S MASTER!!
WONDERFUL TEACHER.
JAPANESE CULTURE BANZAI!! TEACH ME AGAIN!
MASTER
APPRENTICE
EVER SINCE...

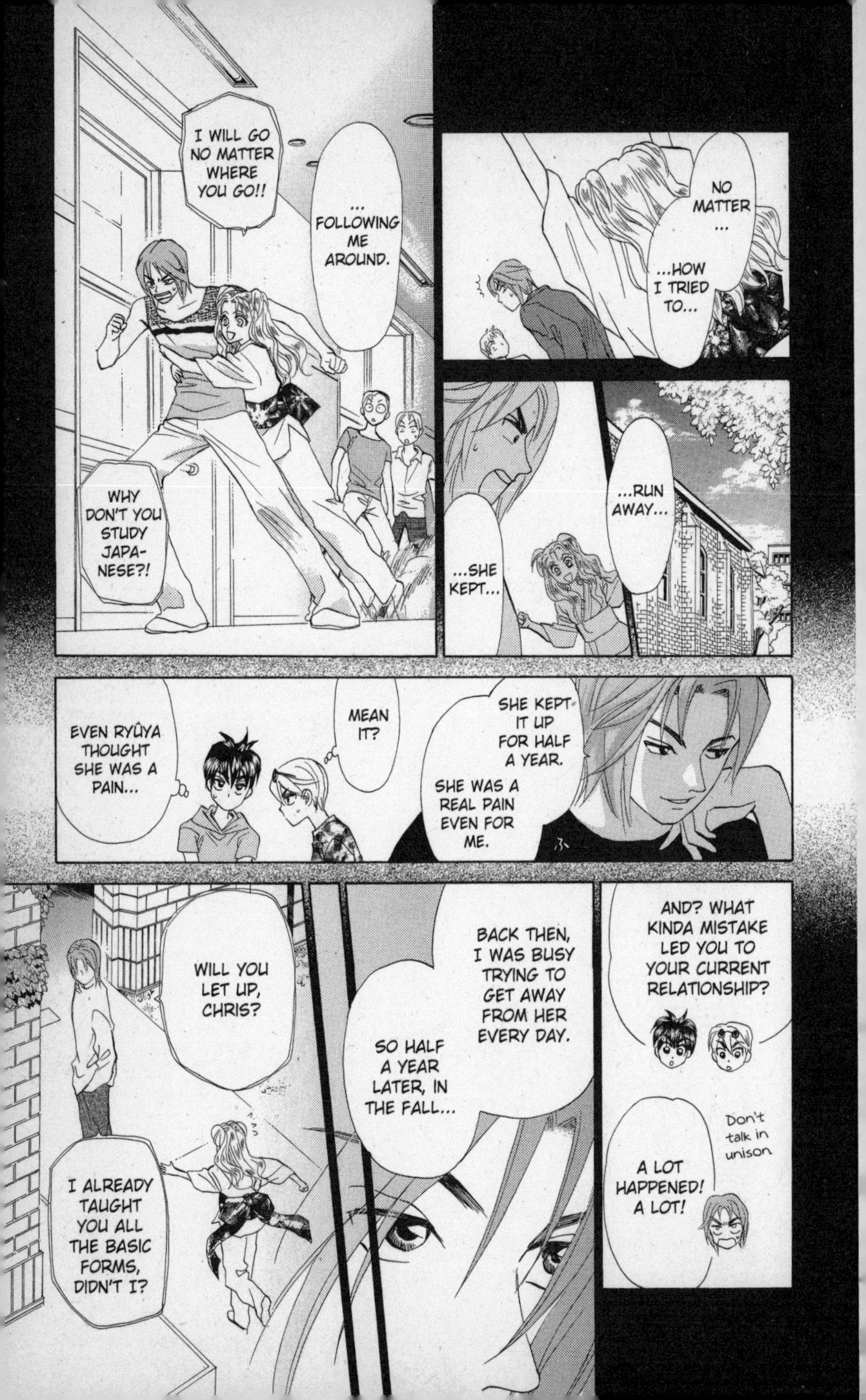
NO MATTER ...
...HOW I TRIED TO...
...RUN AWAY...
...SHE KEPT...
... FOLLOWING ME AROUND.
I WILL GO NO MATTER WHERE YOU GO!!
WHY DON'T YOU STUDY JAPA-NESE?!
SHE KEPT IT UP FOR HALF A YEAR.
SHE WAS A REAL PAIN EVEN FOR ME.
MEAN IT?
EVEN RYÛYA THOUGHT SHE WAS A PAIN...
AND? WHAT KINDA MISTAKE LED YOU TO YOUR CURRENT RELATIONSHIP?
Don't talk in unison
A LOT HAPPENED! A LOT!
BACK THEN, I WAS BUSY TRYING TO GET AWAY FROM HER EVERY DAY.
SO HALF A YEAR LATER, IN THE FALL...
WILL YOU LET UP, CHRIS?
I ALREADY TAUGHT YOU ALL THE BASIC FORMS, DIDN'T I?

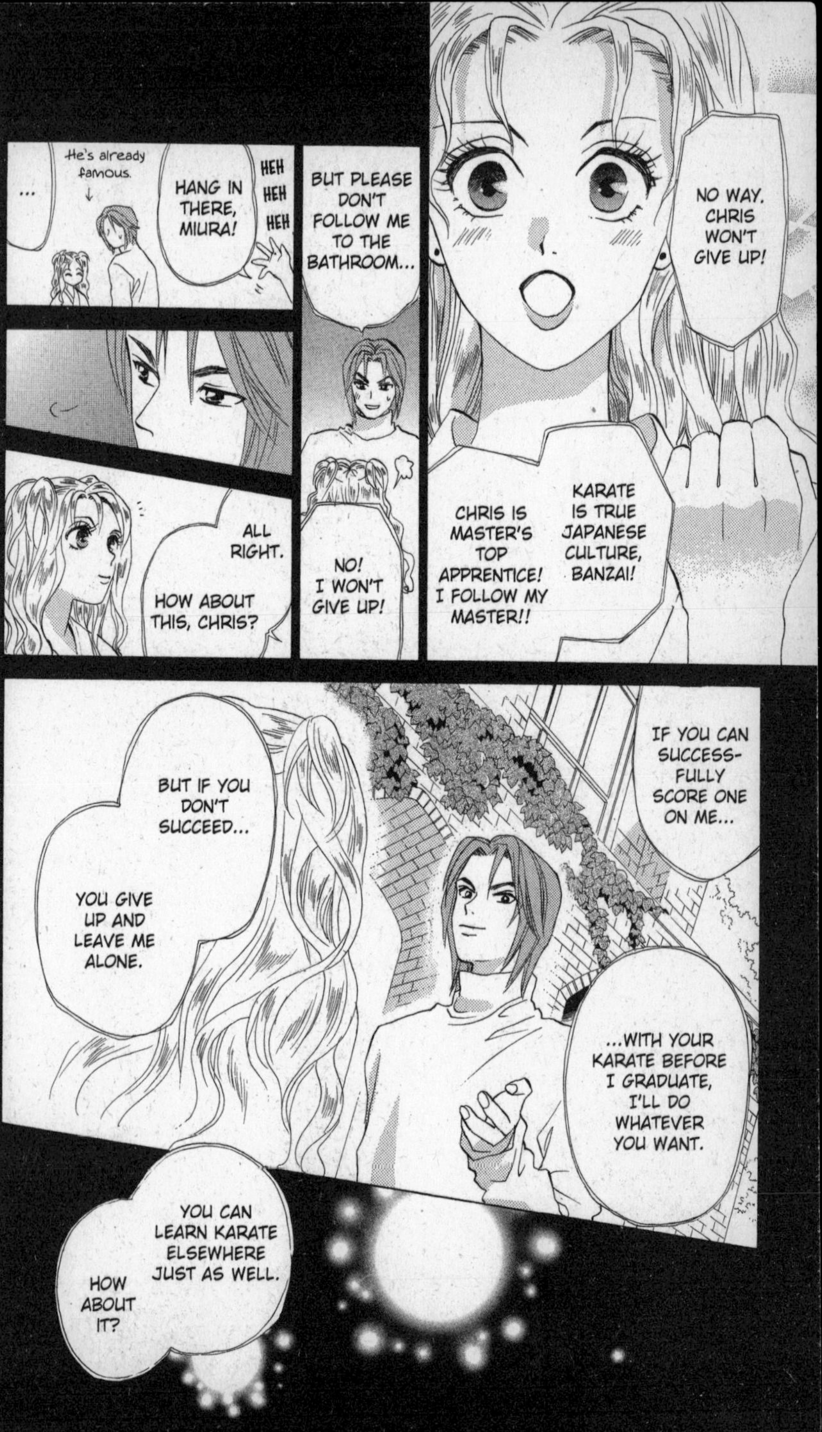
NO WAY. CHRIS WON'T GIVE UP!
KARATE IS TRUE JAPANESE CULTURE, BANZAI!
CHRIS IS MASTER'S TOP APPRENTICE! I FOLLOW MY MASTER!!
BUT PLEASE DON'T FOLLOW ME TO THE BATHROOM...
NO! I WON'T GIVE UP!
HEH HEH HEH
HANG IN THERE, MIURA!
He's already famous.
...
ALL RIGHT.
HOW ABOUT THIS, CHRIS?
IF YOU CAN SUCCESS-FULLY SCORE ONE ON ME...
...WITH YOUR KARATE BEFORE I GRADUATE, I'LL DO WHATEVER YOU WANT.
BUT IF YOU DON'T SUCCEED...
YOU GIVE UP AND LEAVE ME ALONE.
YOU CAN LEARN KARATE ELSEWHERE JUST AS WELL.
HOW ABOUT IT?

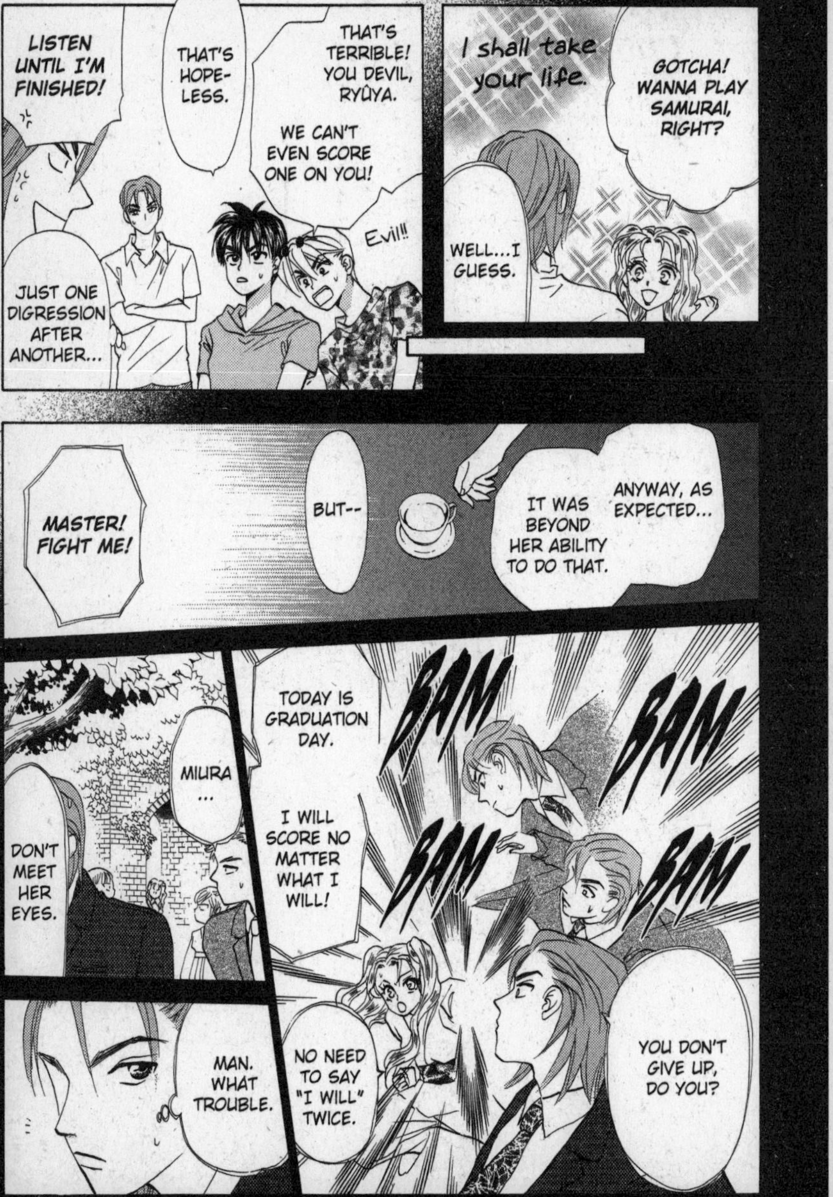
GOTCHA! WANNA PLAY SAMURAI, RIGHT?
I shall take your life.
WELL...I GUESS.
THAT'S TERRIBLE! YOU DEVIL, RYÛYA.
WE CAN'T EVEN SCORE ONE ON YOU!
Evil!!
THAT'S HOPE-LESS.
LISTEN UNTIL I'M FINISHED!
JUST ONE DIGRESSION AFTER ANOTHER...
ANYWAY, AS EXPECTED...
IT WAS BEYOND HER ABILITY TO DO THAT.
BUT--
MASTER! FIGHT ME!
BAM
BAM
BAM
BAM
TODAY IS GRADUATION DAY.
I WILL SCORE NO MATTER WHAT I WILL!
YOU DON'T GIVE UP, DO YOU?
NO NEED TO SAY "I WILL" TWICE.
MIURA...
DON'T MEET HER EYES.
MAN. WHAT TROUBLE.

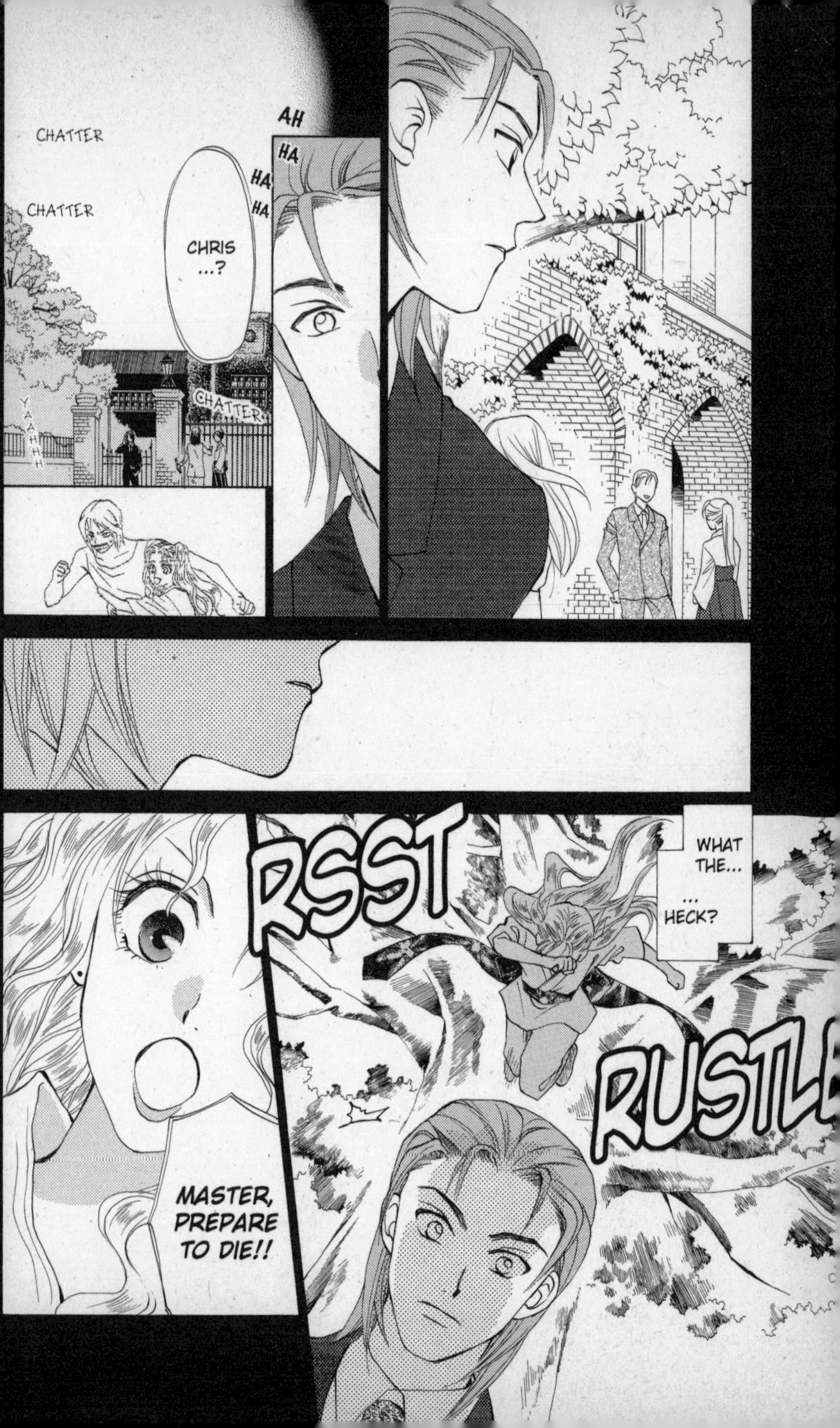
AH HA HA HA
CHATTER
CHATTER
CHRIS ...?
CHATTER
YAAHHH
WHAT THE... ...HECK?
RUSTL
RSST
MASTER, PREPARE TO DIE!!

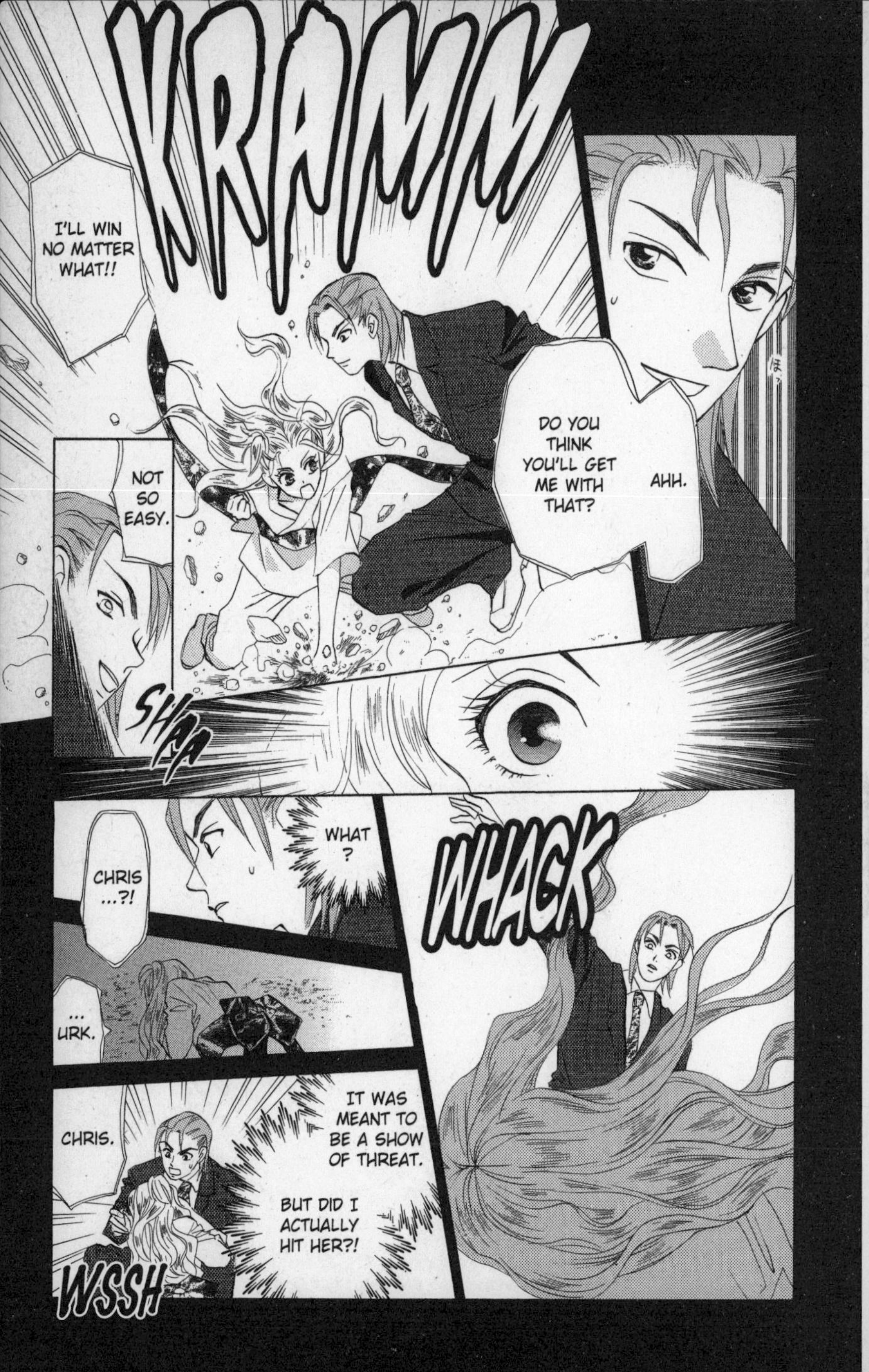
KRAMM
I'LL WIN NO MATTER WHAT!!
ほっ
AHH.
DO YOU THINK YOU'LL GET ME WITH THAT?
NOT SO EASY.
SHAPP
WHACK
WHAT ?
CHRIS ...?!
... URK.
IT WAS MEANT TO BE A SHOW OF THREAT.
BUT DID I ACTUALLY HIT HER?!
CHRIS.
WSSH

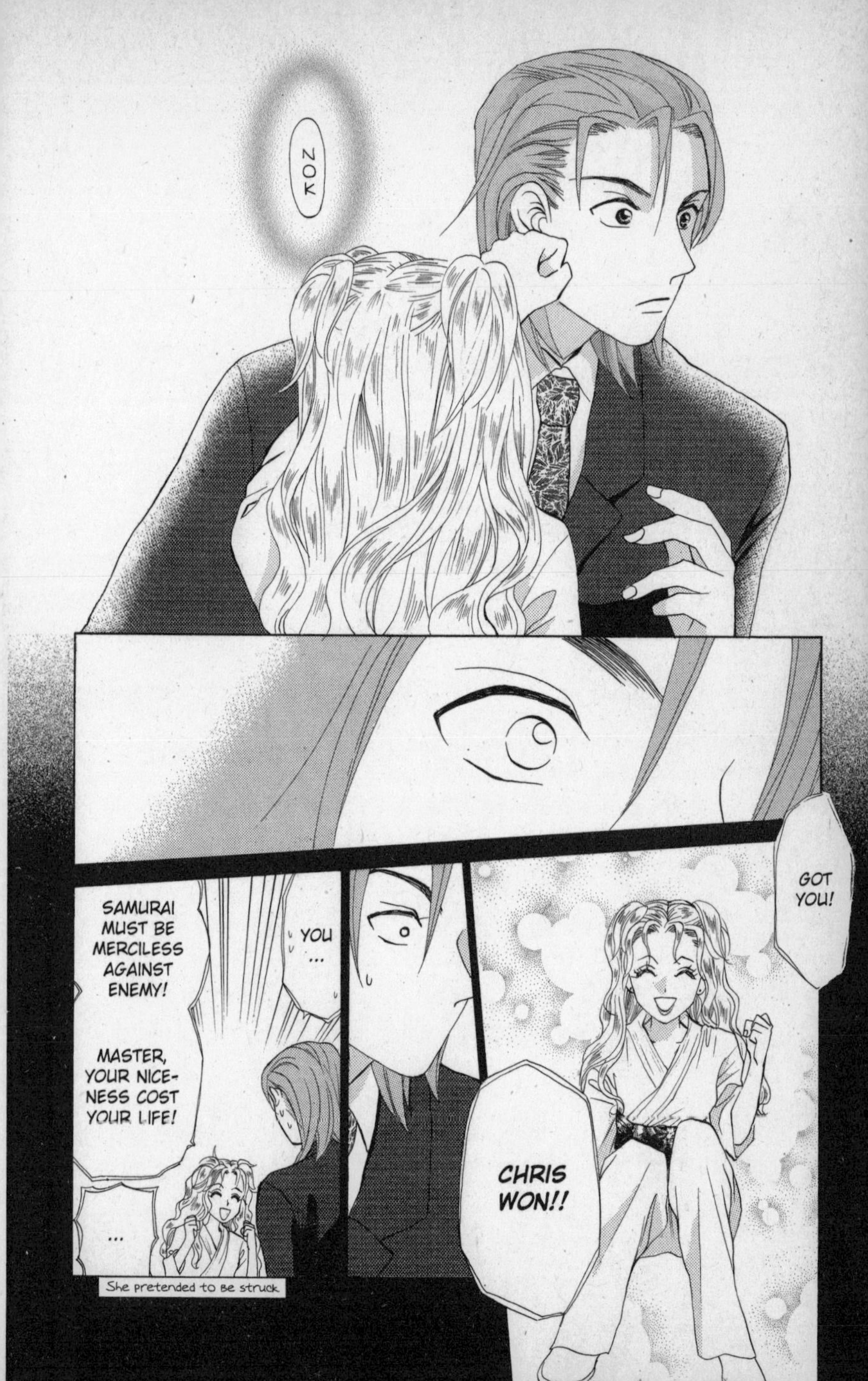
NOK
GOT YOU!
CHRIS WON!!
YOU ...
SAMURAI MUST BE MERCILESS AGAINST ENEMY!
MASTER, YOUR NICENESS COST YOUR LIFE!
...
She pretended to be struck

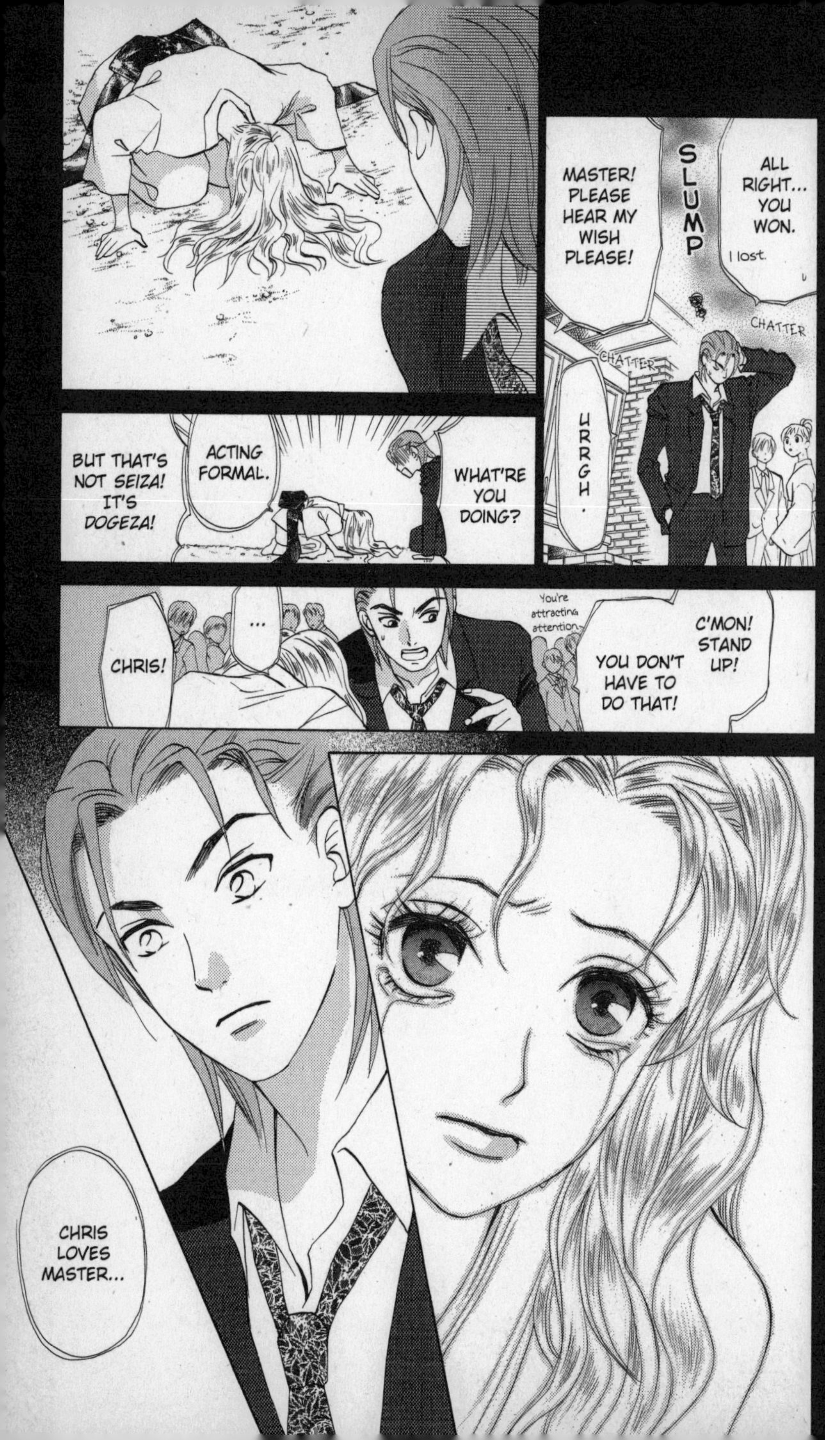
ALL RIGHT... YOU WON.
I lost.
SLUMP
MASTER! PLEASE HEAR MY WISH PLEASE!
CHATTER
CHATTER
URRGH.
WHAT'RE YOU DOING?
ACTING FORMAL.
BUT THAT'S NOT SEIZA! IT'S DOGEZA!
C'MON! STAND UP!
YOU DON'T HAVE TO DO THAT!
You're attracting attention~
...
CHRIS!
CHRIS LOVES MASTER...

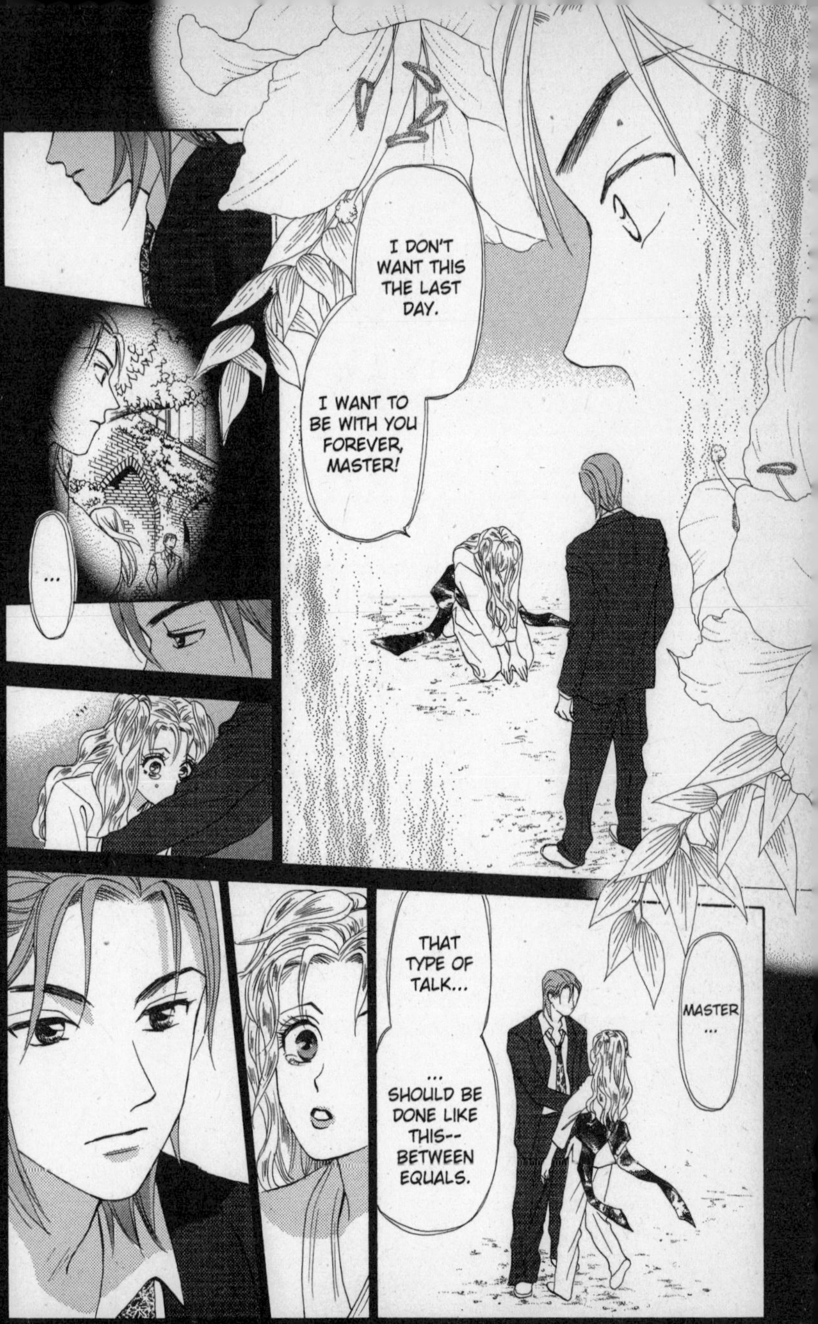
I DON'T WANT THIS THE LAST DAY.
I WANT TO BE WITH YOU FOREVER, MASTER!
...
...
MASTER ...
THAT TYPE OF TALK...
... SHOULD BE DONE LIKE THIS-- BETWEEN EQUALS.

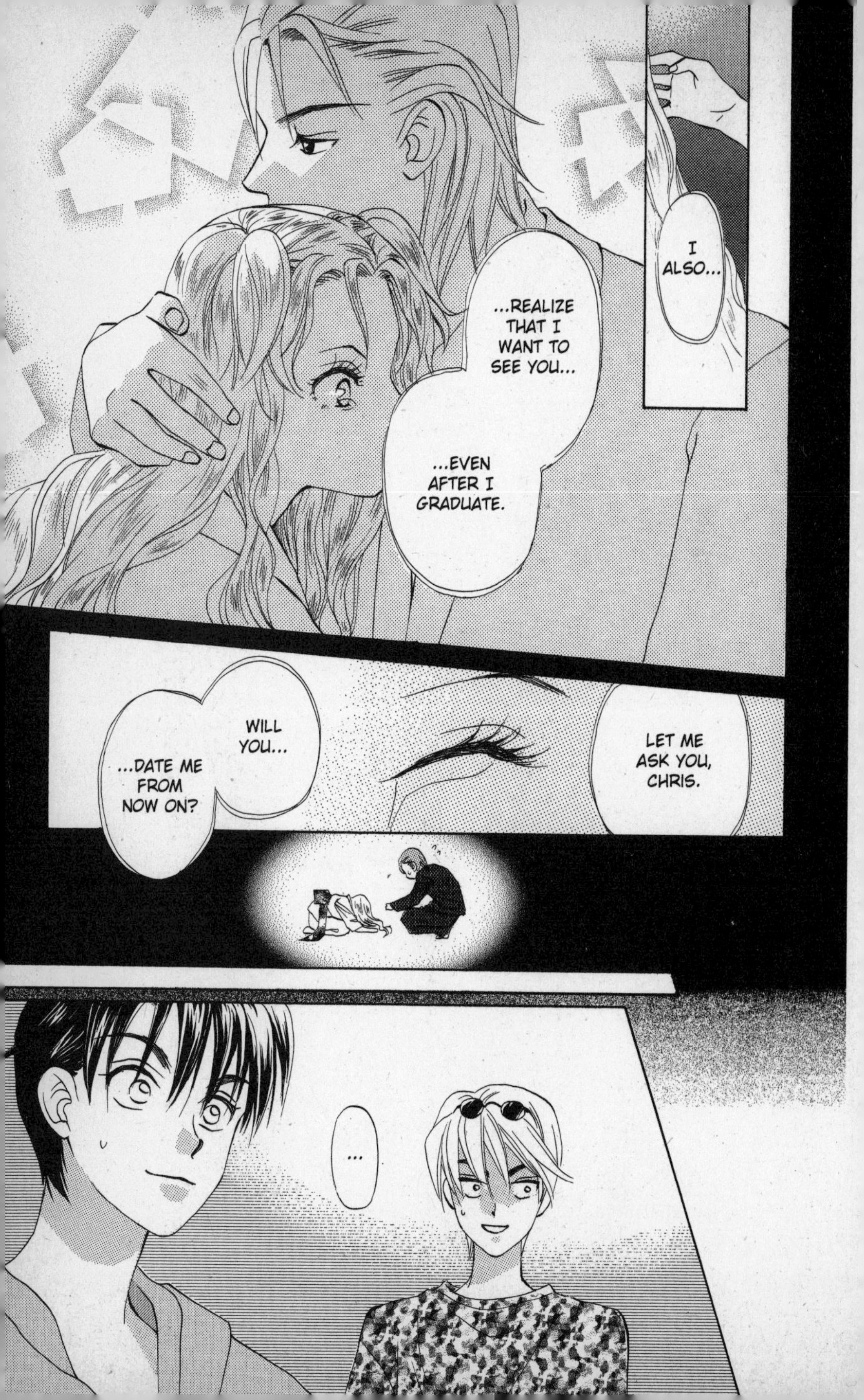
I ALSO...
...REALIZE THAT I WANT TO SEE YOU...
...EVEN AFTER I GRADUATE.
LET ME ASK YOU, CHRIS.
WILL YOU...
...DATE ME FROM NOW ON?
...

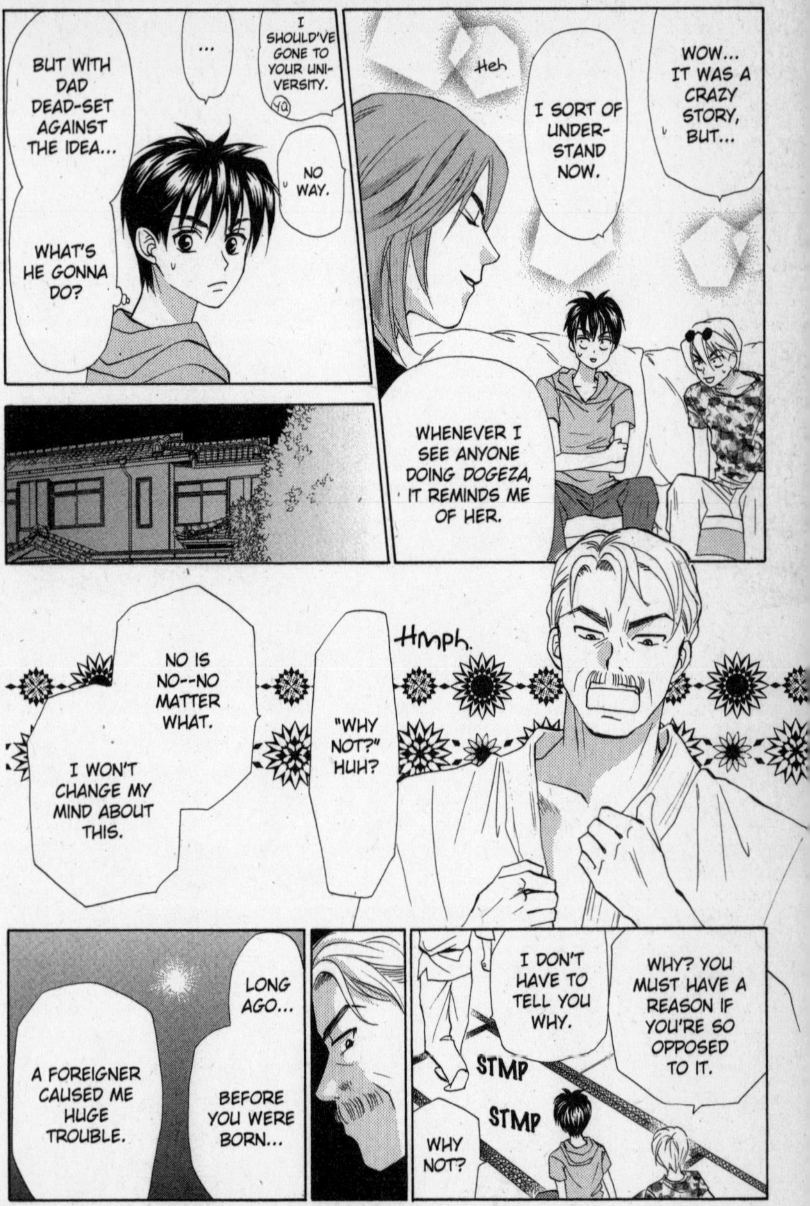
WOW... IT WAS A CRAZY STORY, BUT...
Heh
I SORT OF UNDER-STAND NOW.
WHENEVER I SEE ANYONE DOING DOGEZA, IT REMINDS ME OF HER.
I SHOULD'VE GONE TO YOUR UNI-VERSITY.
...
NO WAY.
BUT WITH DAD DEAD-SET AGAINST THE IDEA...
WHAT'S HE GONNA DO?
Hmph.
"WHY NOT?" HUH?
NO IS NO--NO MATTER WHAT.
I WON'T CHANGE MY MIND ABOUT THIS.
WHY? YOU MUST HAVE A REASON IF YOU'RE SO OPPOSED TO IT.
I DON'T HAVE TO TELL YOU WHY.
STMP
STMP
WHY NOT?
LONG AGO...
BEFORE YOU WERE BORN...
A FOREIGNER CAUSED ME HUGE TROUBLE.

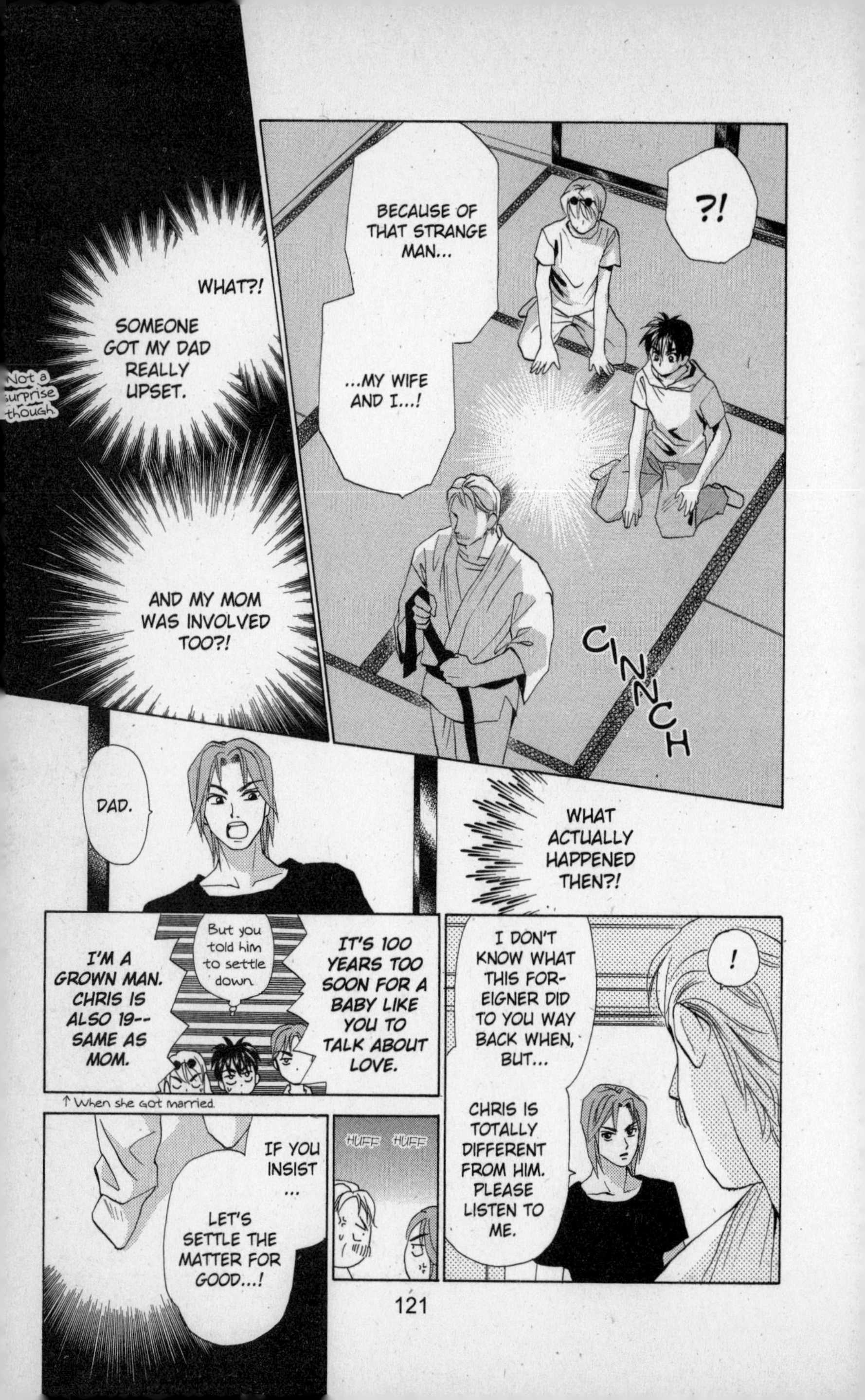
?!
BECAUSE OF THAT STRANGE MAN...
...MY WIFE AND I...!
CINNCH
WHAT?!
SOMEONE GOT MY DAD REALLY UPSET.
Not a surprise though.
AND MY MOM WAS INVOLVED TOO?!
WHAT ACTUALLY HAPPENED THEN?!
DAD.
!
I DON'T KNOW WHAT THIS FOR-EIGNER DID TO YOU WAY BACK WHEN, BUT...
CHRIS IS TOTALLY DIFFERENT FROM HIM. PLEASE LISTEN TO ME.
IT'S 100 YEARS TOO SOON FOR A BABY LIKE YOU TO TALK ABOUT LOVE.
But you told him to settle down.
I'M A GROWN MAN. CHRIS IS ALSO 19-- SAME AS MOM.
↑ When she got married.
HUFF HUFF
IF YOU INSIST...
LET'S SETTLE THE MATTER FOR GOOD...!

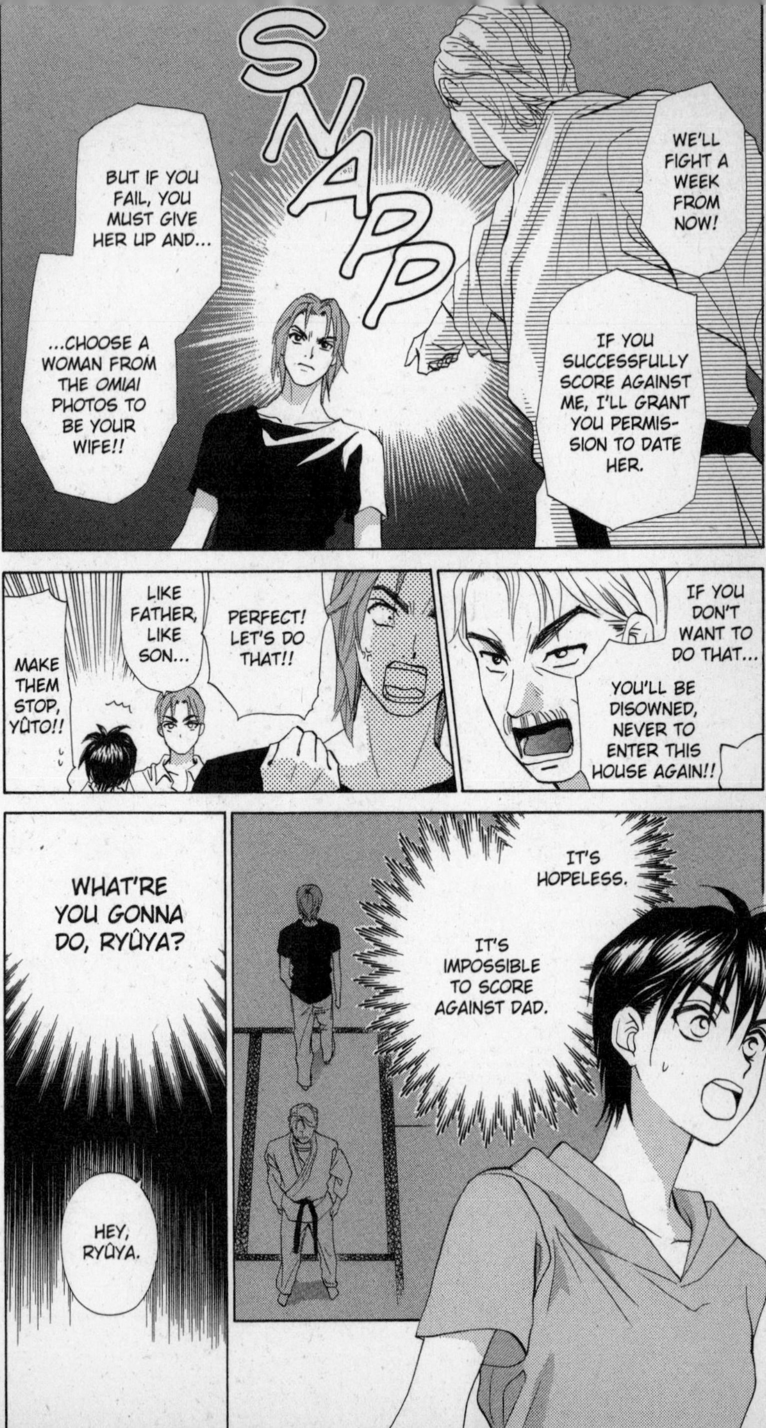
WE'LL FIGHT A WEEK FROM NOW!
SNAPP
IF YOU SUCCESSFULLY SCORE AGAINST ME, I'LL GRANT YOU PERMISSION TO DATE HER.
BUT IF YOU FAIL, YOU MUST GIVE HER UP AND...
...CHOOSE A WOMAN FROM THE *OMIAI* PHOTOS TO BE YOUR WIFE!!
IF YOU DON'T WANT TO DO THAT...
YOU'LL BE DISOWNED, NEVER TO ENTER THIS HOUSE AGAIN!!
PERFECT! LET'S DO THAT!!
LIKE FATHER, LIKE SON...
MAKE THEM STOP, YÛTO!!
IT'S HOPELESS.
IT'S IMPOSSIBLE TO SCORE AGAINST DAD.
WHAT'RE YOU GONNA DO, RYÛYA?
HEY, RYÛYA.

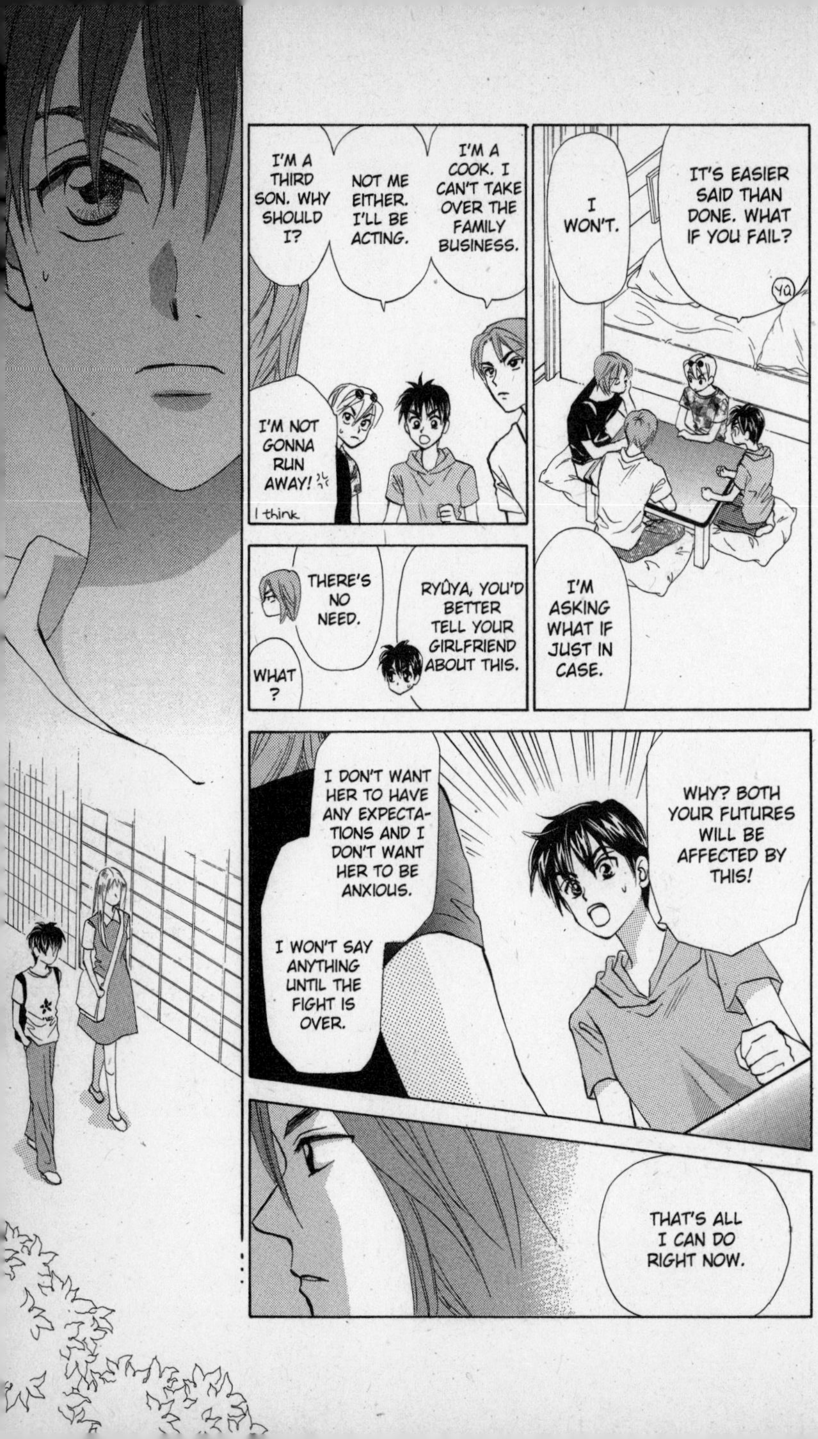
IT'S EASIER SAID THAN DONE. WHAT IF YOU FAIL?
YA
I WON'T.
I'M ASKING WHAT IF JUST IN CASE.
I'M A COOK. I CAN'T TAKE OVER THE FAMILY BUSINESS.
NOT ME EITHER. I'LL BE ACTING.
I'M A THIRD SON. WHY SHOULD I?
I'M NOT GONNA RUN AWAY!
I think
RYÛYA, YOU'D BETTER TELL YOUR GIRLFRIEND ABOUT THIS.
THERE'S NO NEED.
WHAT?
WHY? BOTH YOUR FUTURES WILL BE AFFECTED BY THIS!
I DON'T WANT HER TO HAVE ANY EXPECTATIONS AND I DON'T WANT HER TO BE ANXIOUS.
I WON'T SAY ANYTHING UNTIL THE FIGHT IS OVER.
THAT'S ALL I CAN DO RIGHT NOW.

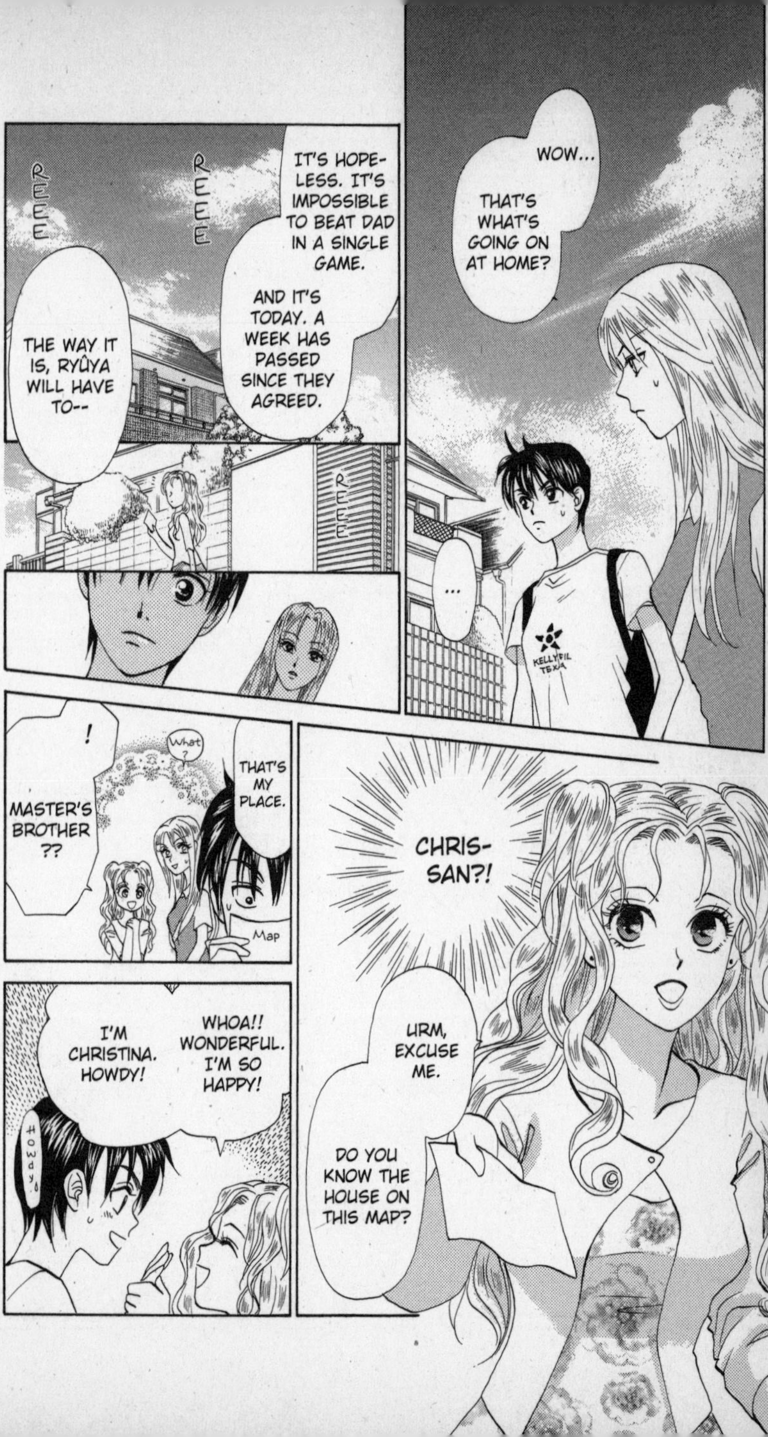
WOW...
THAT'S WHAT'S GOING ON AT HOME?
...
IT'S HOPE-LESS. IT'S IMPOSSIBLE TO BEAT DAD IN A SINGLE GAME.
REEE
AND IT'S TODAY. A WEEK HAS PASSED SINCE THEY AGREED.
REEE
THE WAY IT IS, RYÛYA WILL HAVE TO--
REEE
CHRIS-SAN?!
URM, EXCUSE ME.
DO YOU KNOW THE HOUSE ON THIS MAP?
THAT'S MY PLACE.
What?
!
MASTER'S BROTHER ??
Map
WHOA!! WONDERFUL. I'M SO HAPPY!
I'M CHRISTINA. HOWDY!
Howdy.

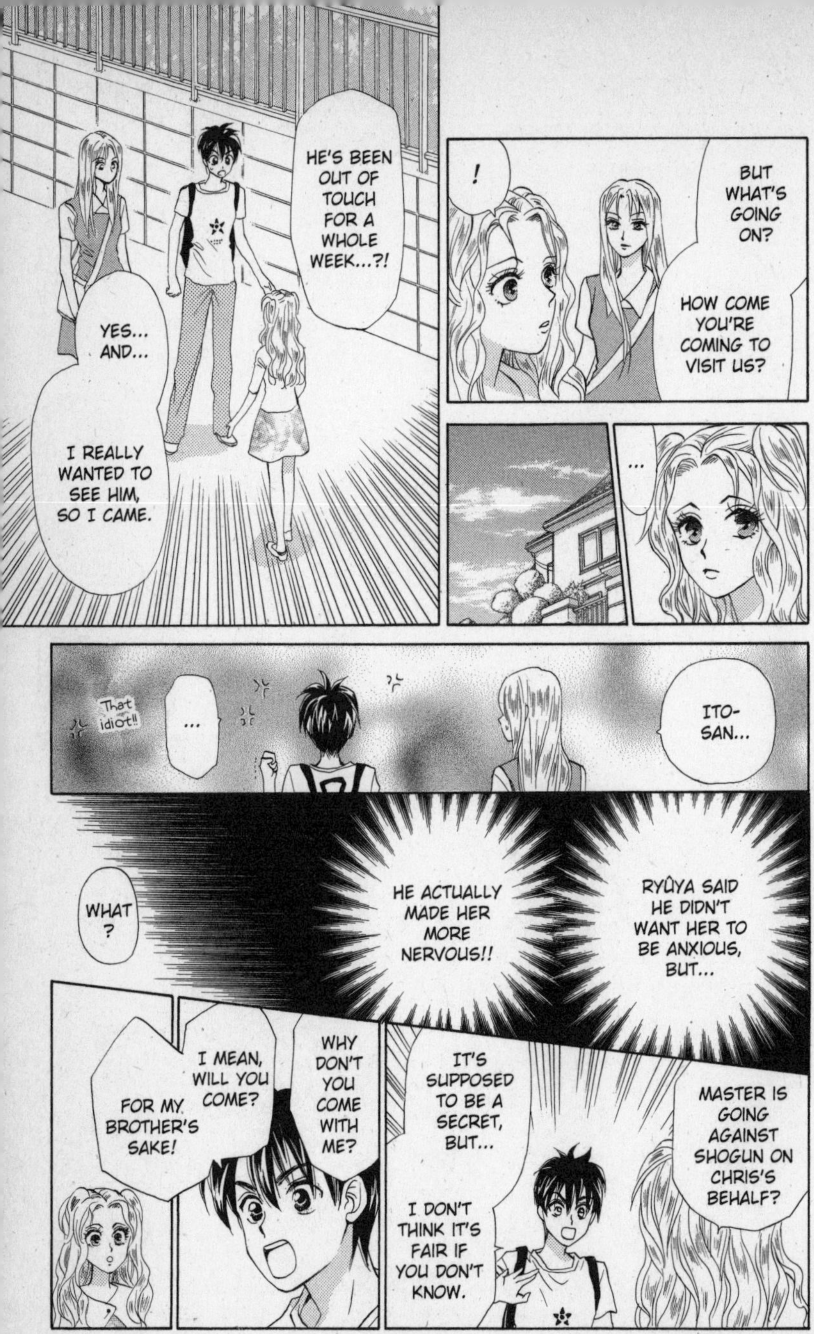
BUT WHAT'S GOING ON?
HOW COME YOU'RE COMING TO VISIT US?
!
...
HE'S BEEN OUT OF TOUCH FOR A WHOLE WEEK...?!
YES... AND...
I REALLY WANTED TO SEE HIM, SO I CAME.
ITO-SAN...
...
That idiot!!
RYÛYA SAID HE DIDN'T WANT HER TO BE ANXIOUS, BUT...
HE ACTUALLY MADE HER MORE NERVOUS!!
WHAT?
MASTER IS GOING AGAINST SHOGUN ON CHRIS'S BEHALF?
IT'S SUPPOSED TO BE A SECRET, BUT...
I DON'T THINK IT'S FAIR IF YOU DON'T KNOW.
WHY DON'T YOU COME WITH ME?
I MEAN, WILL YOU COME?
FOR MY BROTHER'S SAKE!

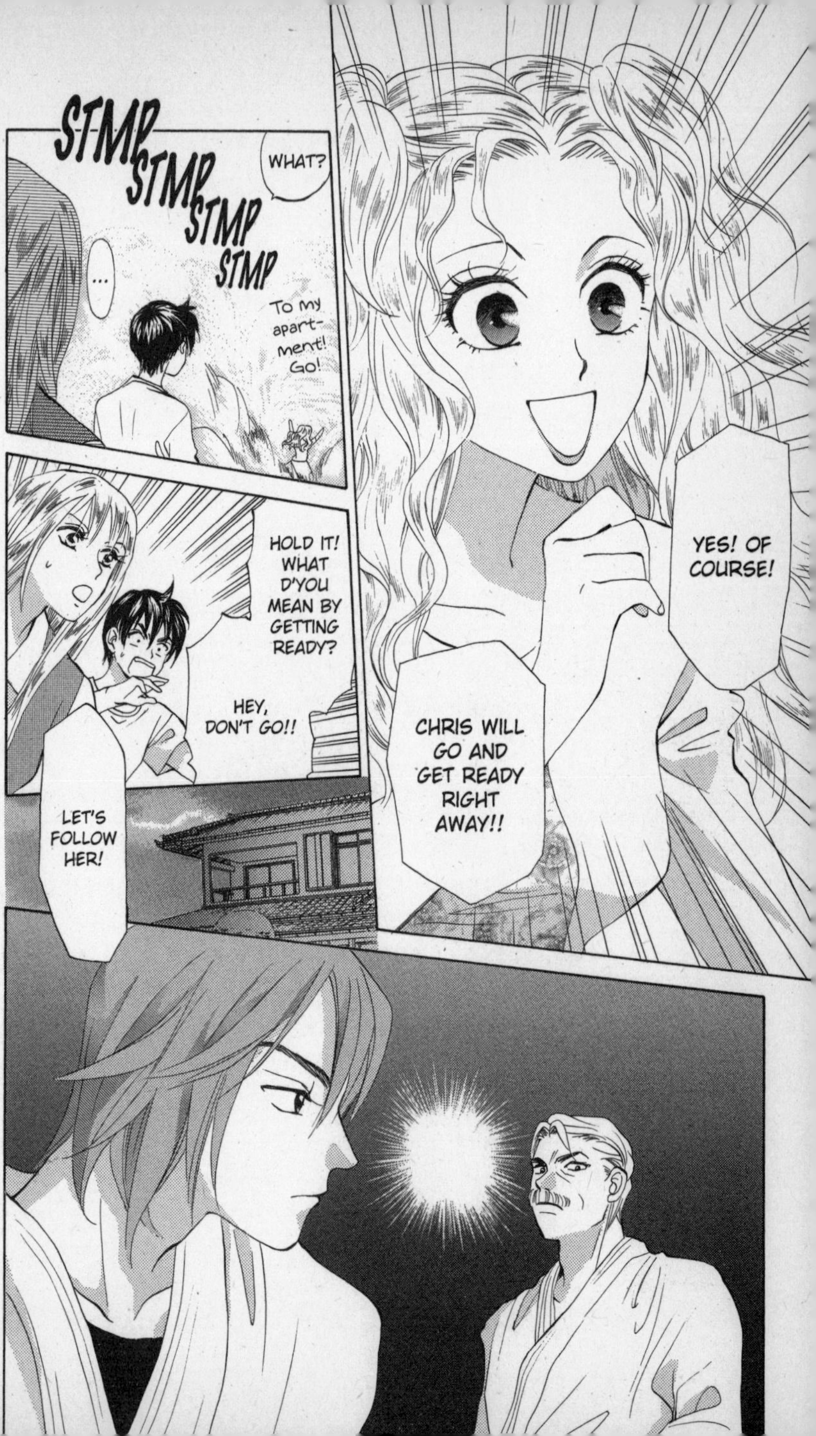
YES! OF COURSE!
CHRIS WILL GO AND GET READY RIGHT AWAY!!
WHAT?
STMP STMP STMP STMP
To my apartment! Go!
...
HOLD IT! WHAT D'YOU MEAN BY GETTING READY?
HEY, DON'T GO!!
LET'S FOLLOW HER!

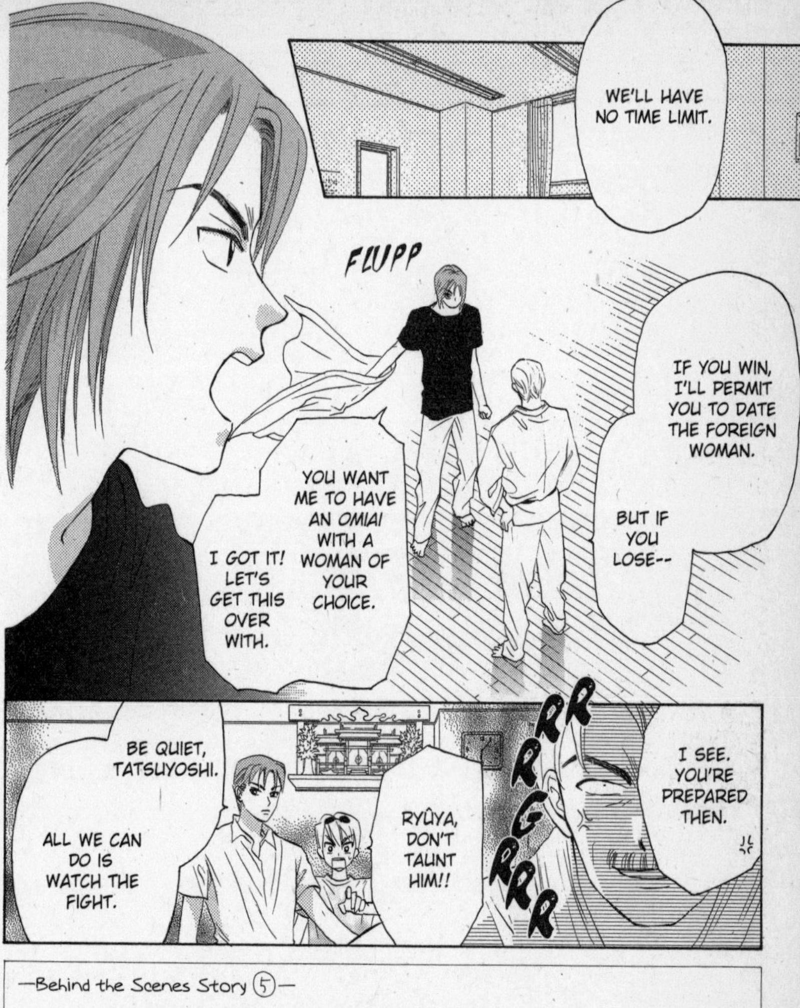
WE'LL HAVE NO TIME LIMIT.
IF YOU WIN, I'LL PERMIT YOU TO DATE THE FOREIGN WOMAN.
BUT IF YOU LOSE--
FLUPP
YOU WANT ME TO HAVE AN OMIAI WITH A WOMAN OF YOUR CHOICE.
I GOT IT! LET'S GET THIS OVER WITH.
I SEE. YOU'RE PREPARED THEN.
RRRRGRRRR
RYÛYA, DON'T TAUNT HIM!!
BE QUIET, TATSUYOSHI.
ALL WE CAN DO IS WATCH THE FIGHT.

—Behind the Scenes Story ⑤—

The Dad hardly had a chance to be in the spotlight—but as soon as he is, this is what happens. (Laugh) Well, what I really wanted to draw was the scene in which he's punched. As I drew it, I felt supremely good. Is this really Shôjo manga?

By the way, although I couldn't include it in this episode, Ryûya and Chris won't be sharing the same bedroom. What happened is that, thanks to Ito's persuasion, Chris moved to a spare room. But, well, I say it's just a matter of time for them to share a bed.

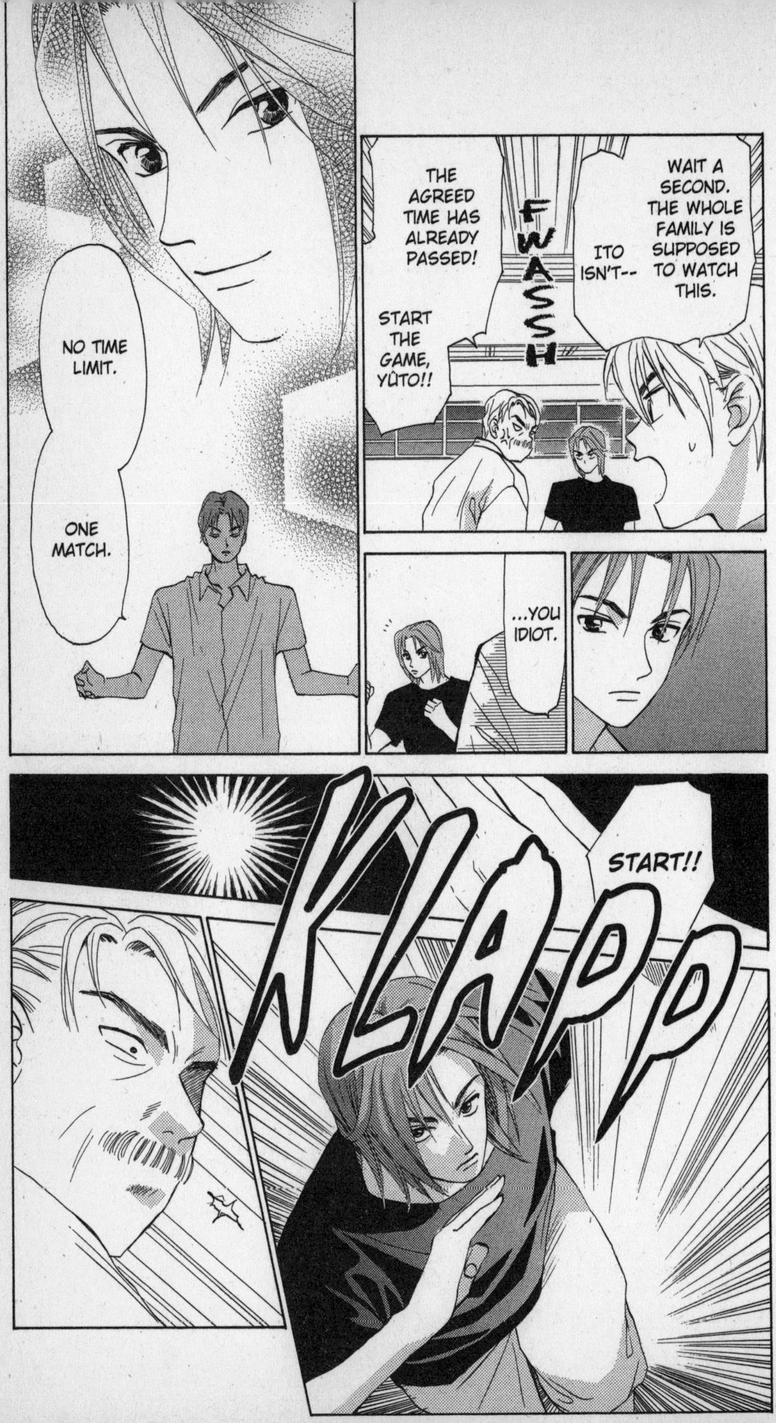
WAIT A SECOND. THE WHOLE FAMILY IS SUPPOSED TO WATCH THIS.
ITO ISN'T--
FWASSH
THE AGREED TIME HAS ALREADY PASSED!
START THE GAME, YÛTO!!
...YOU IDIOT.
NO TIME LIMIT.
ONE MATCH.
START!!
KLAPP

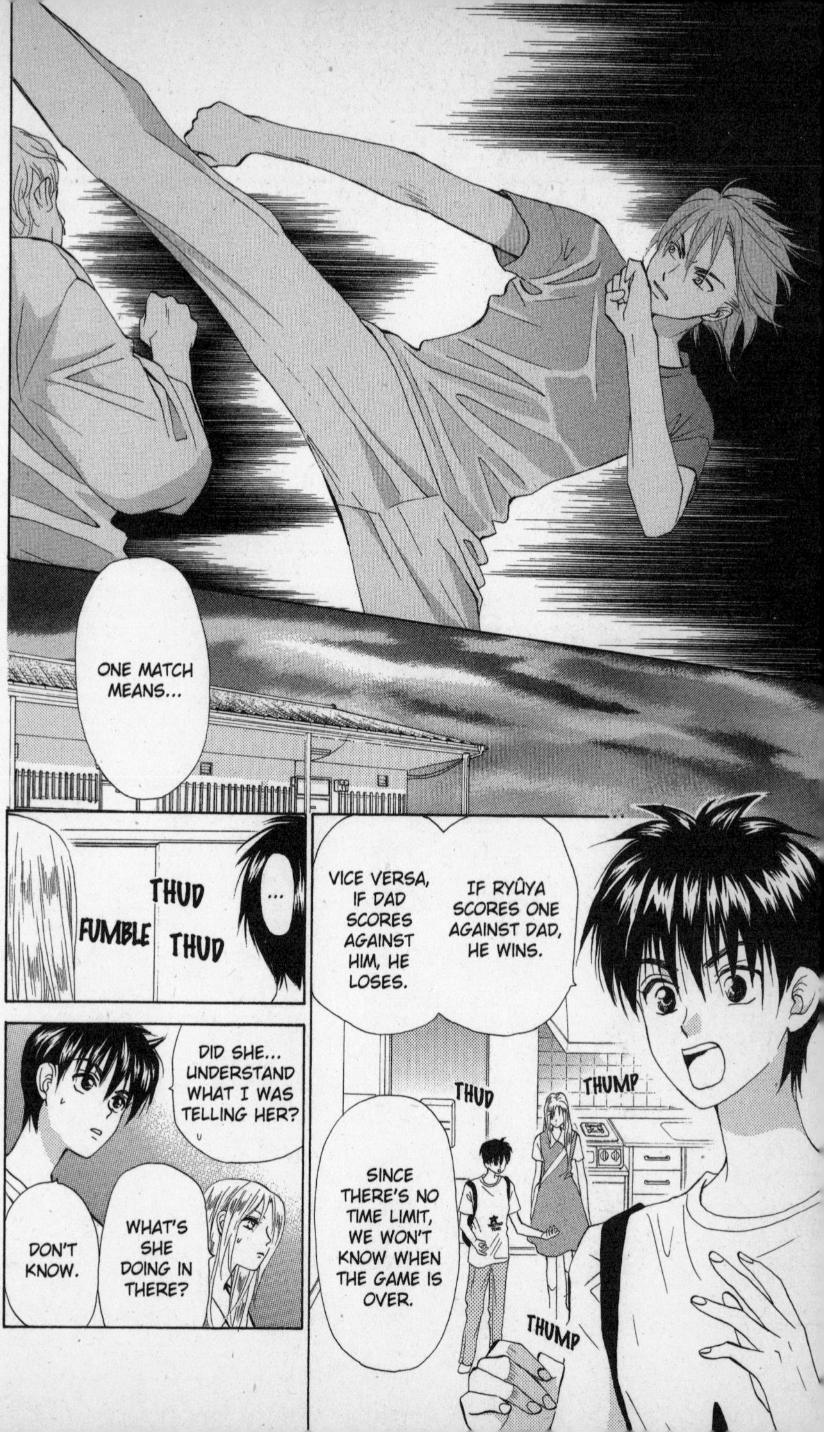
ONE MATCH MEANS...
IF RYÛYA SCORES ONE AGAINST DAD, HE WINS.
VICE VERSA, IF DAD SCORES AGAINST HIM, HE LOSES.
THUMP
THUD
SINCE THERE'S NO TIME LIMIT, WE WON'T KNOW WHEN THE GAME IS OVER.
THUMP
...
THUD
THUD
FUMBLE
DID SHE... UNDERSTAND WHAT I WAS TELLING HER?
WHAT'S SHE DOING IN THERE?
DON'T KNOW.

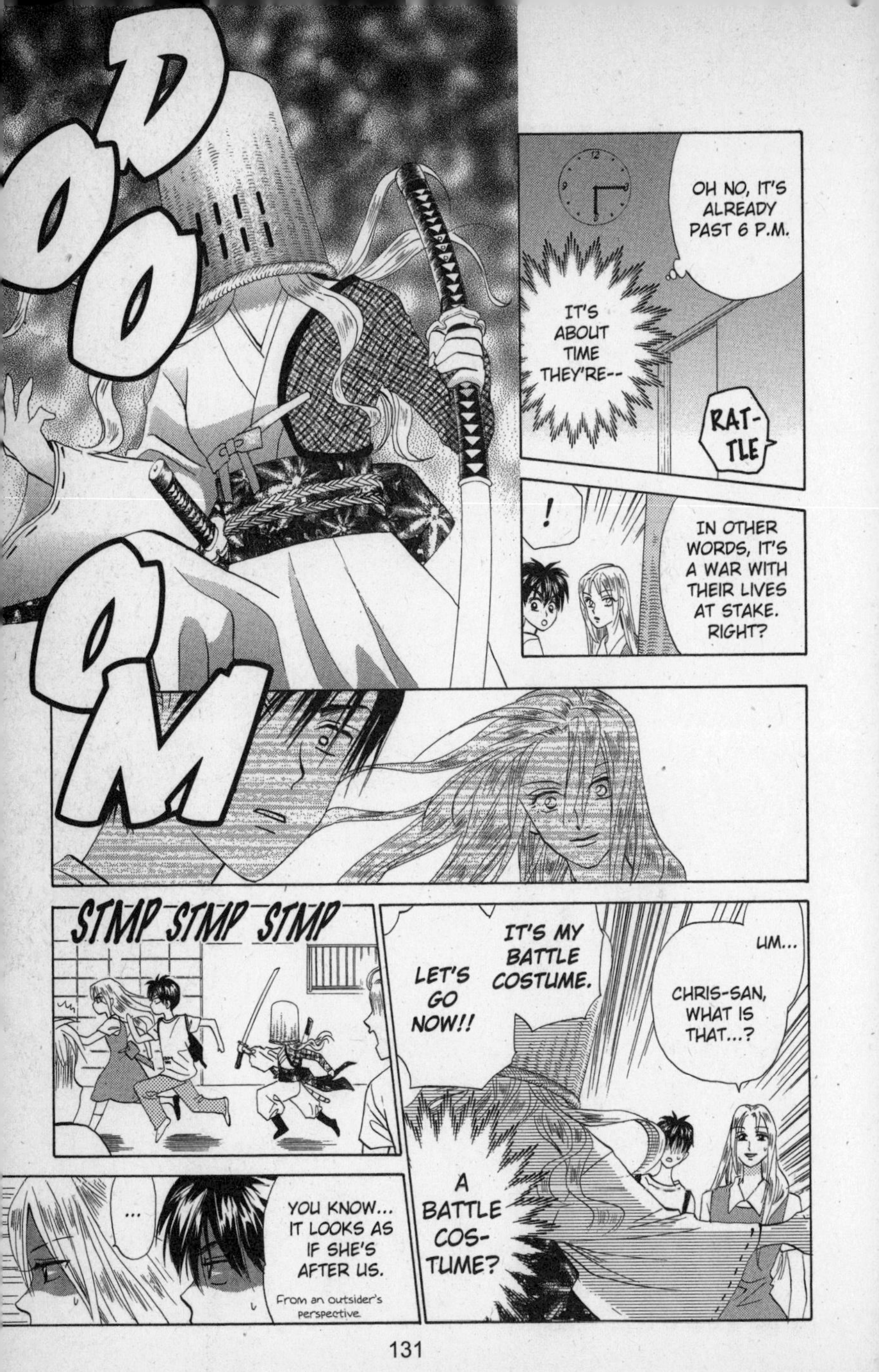
OH NO, IT'S ALREADY PAST 6 P.M.
IT'S ABOUT TIME THEY'RE--
RAT-TLE
!
IN OTHER WORDS, IT'S A WAR WITH THEIR LIVES AT STAKE. RIGHT?
DOOOOM
UM...
CHRIS-SAN, WHAT IS THAT...?
IT'S MY BATTLE COSTUME.
LET'S GO NOW!!
A BATTLE COS-TUME?
STMP STMP STMP
...
YOU KNOW... IT LOOKS AS IF SHE'S AFTER US.
From an outsider's perspective.

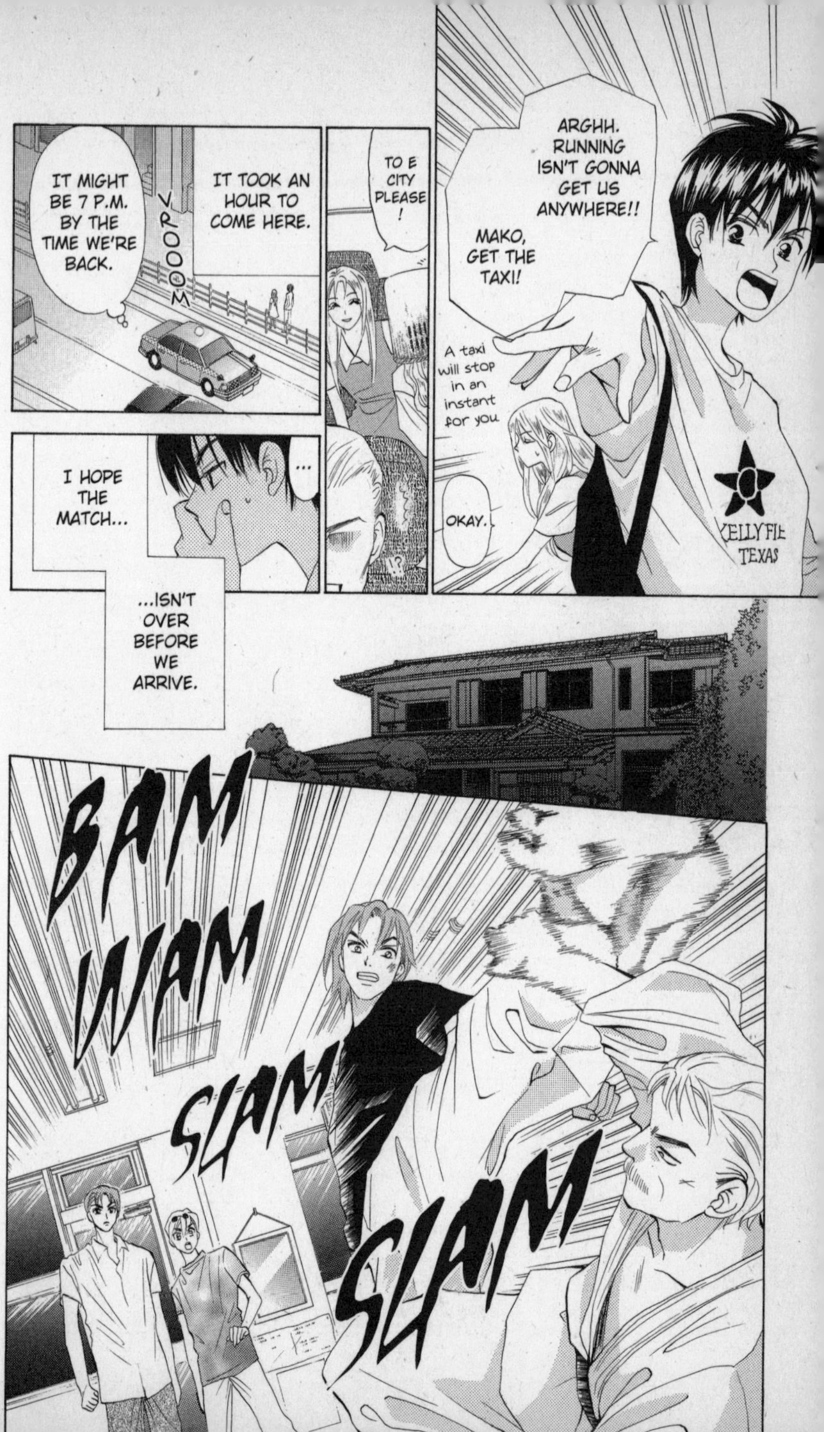
ARGHH. RUNNING ISN'T GONNA GET US ANYWHERE!!
MAKO, GET THE TAXI!
A taxi will stop in an instant for you.
OKAY.
KELLY FIE TEXAS
TO E CITY PLEASE!
IT TOOK AN HOUR TO COME HERE.
VROOOM
IT MIGHT BE 7 P.M. BY THE TIME WE'RE BACK.
!?
...
I HOPE THE MATCH...
...ISN'T OVER BEFORE WE ARRIVE.
BAM
WAM
SLAM
SLAM

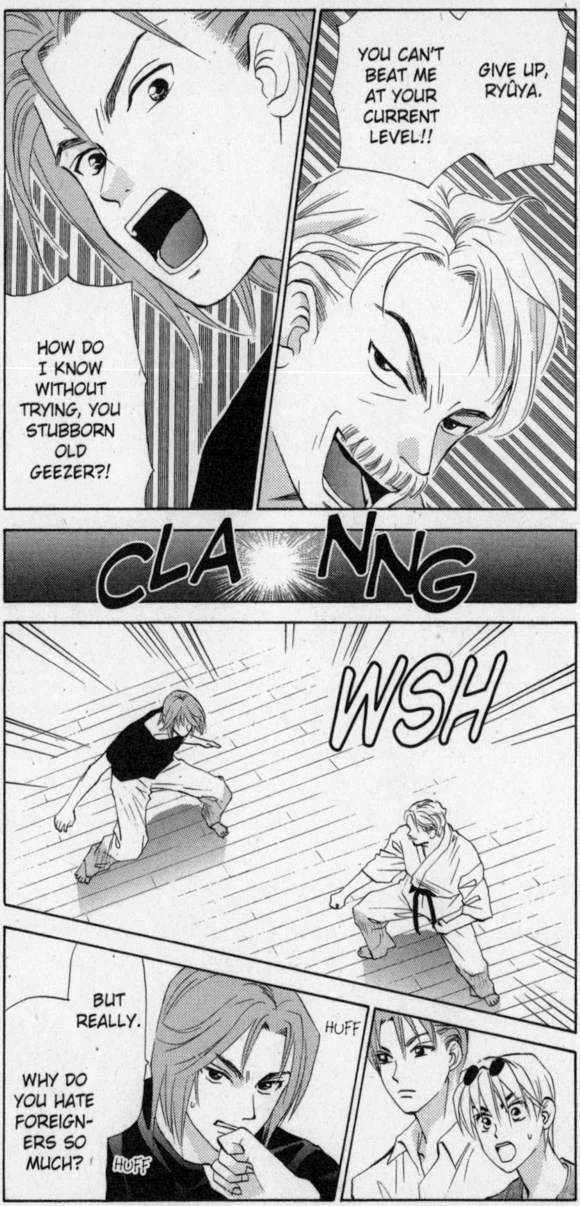
GIVE UP, RYÛYA.
YOU CAN'T BEAT ME AT YOUR CURRENT LEVEL!!
HOW DO I KNOW WITHOUT TRYING, YOU STUBBORN OLD GEEZER?!
CLANNG
WSH
HUFF
BUT REALLY.
WHY DO YOU HATE FOREIGNERS SO MUCH?
HUFF

Just as I described, a lot happened, but she's now actively involved as my right hand! Her special skill is in drawing lines for effects. She's best when it comes to drawing focus lines, painting flashes (be it solid, toned, or otherwise) and shading down!
And she's unbelievably fast in sticking.

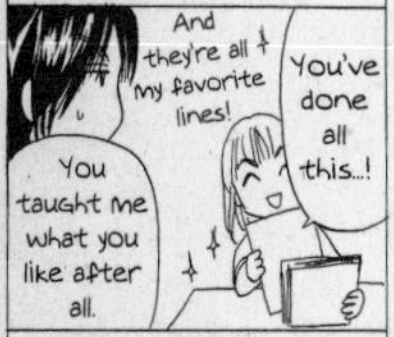
You've done all this...!
And they're all my favorite lines!
You taught me what you like after all.

At this point, she can easily handle more difficult backgrounds like looking-up or looking-down perspectives.
She's much better than I am.

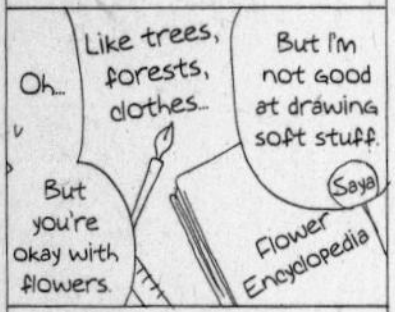
But I'm not good at drawing soft stuff.
Saya
Like trees, forests, clothes...
Flower Encyclopedia
Oh...
But you're okay with flowers.

Apparently, she's good at drawing hard stuff, like buildings and props.

And, I'm sure you're all wondering about this!
"Does my sister draw her own manga??"

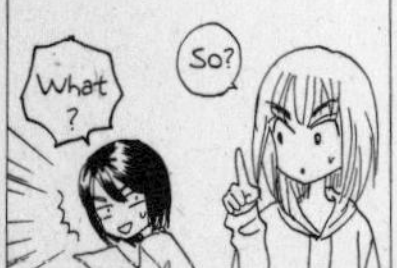
So?
What?

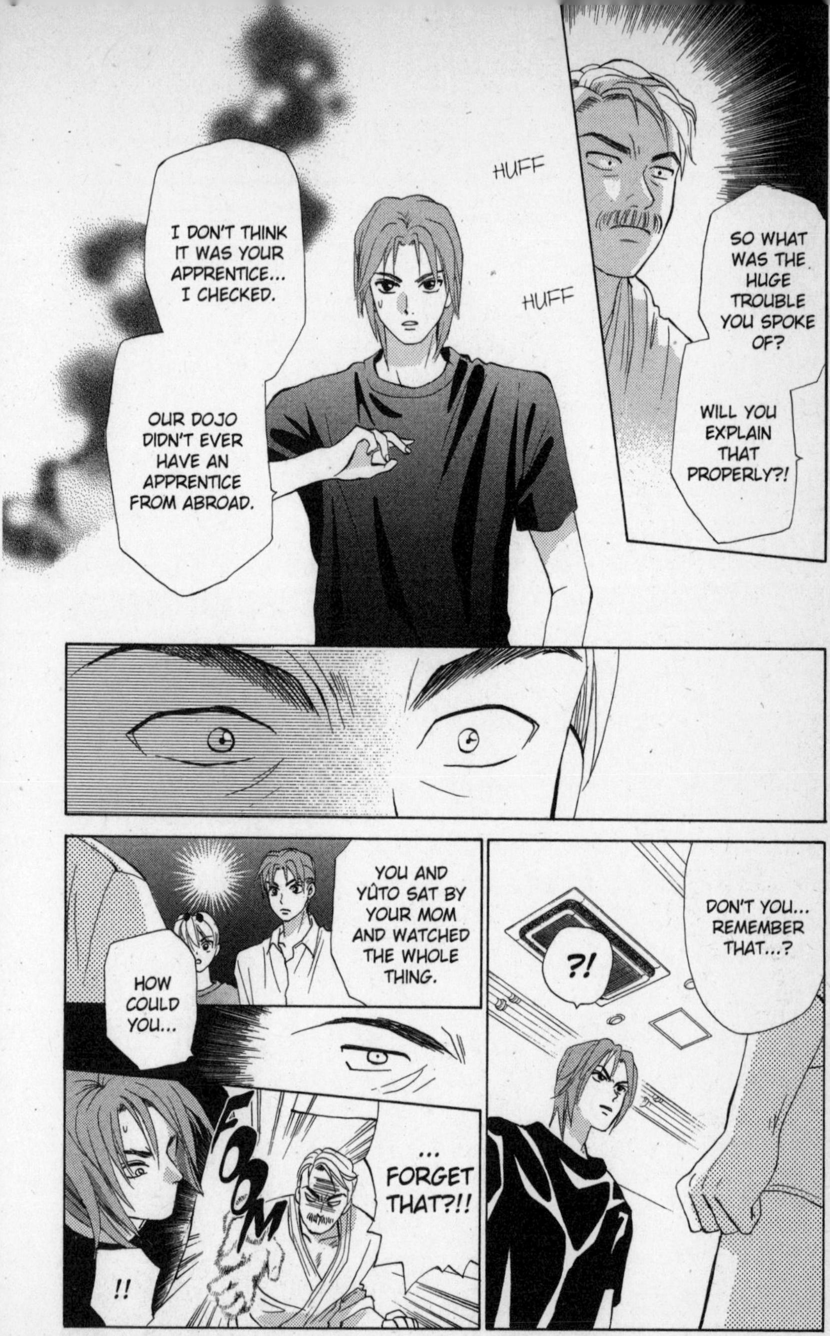
SO WHAT WAS THE HUGE TROUBLE YOU SPOKE OF?
WILL YOU EXPLAIN THAT PROPERLY?!
HUFF
HUFF
I DON'T THINK IT WAS YOUR APPRENTICE... I CHECKED.
OUR DOJO DIDN'T EVER HAVE AN APPRENTICE FROM ABROAD.
DON'T YOU... REMEMBER THAT...?
?!
YOU AND YÛTO SAT BY YOUR MOM AND WATCHED THE WHOLE THING.
HOW COULD YOU...
... FORGET THAT?!!
FOOM
!!

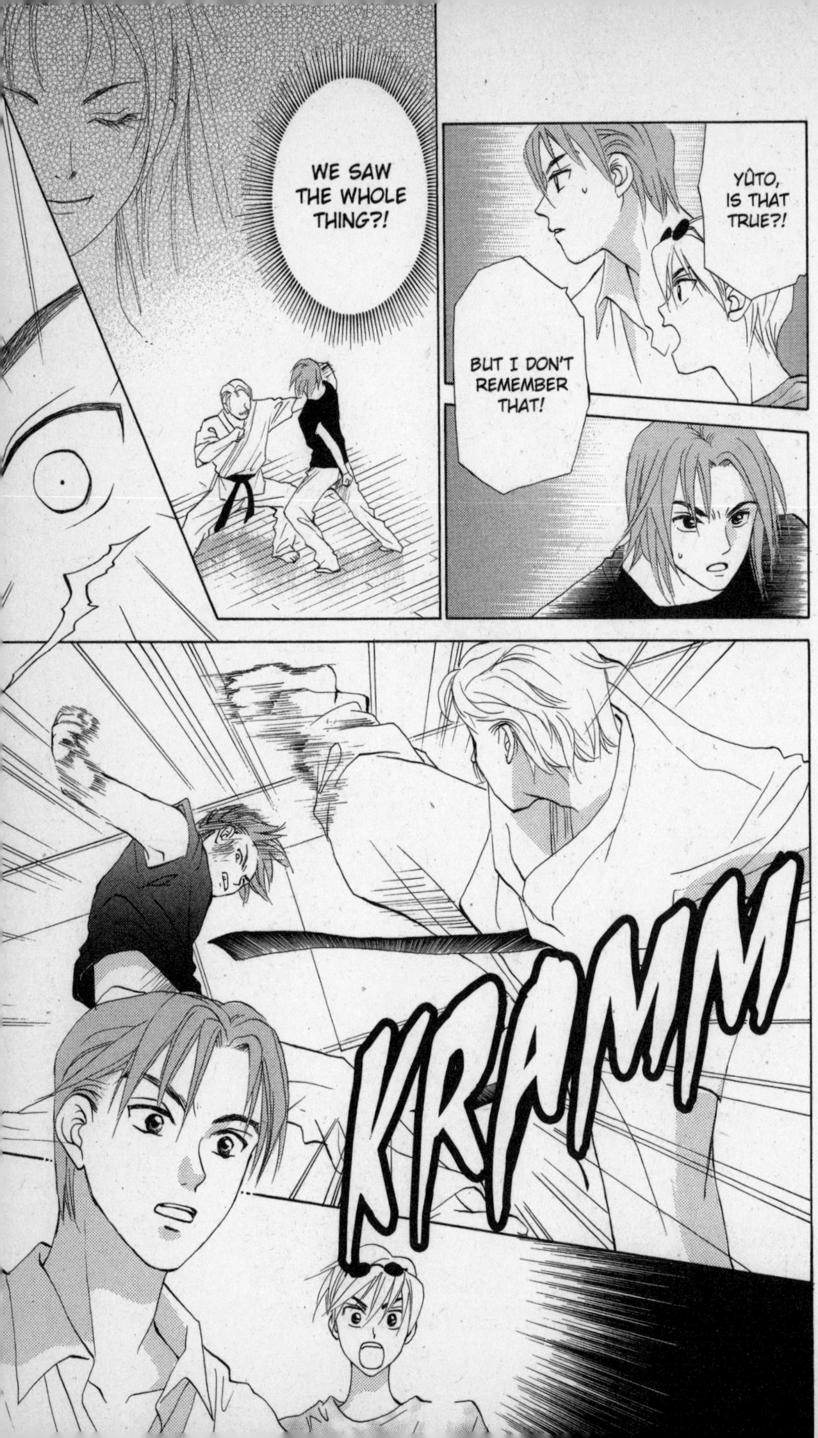
YÛTO, IS THAT TRUE?!
BUT I DON'T REMEMBER THAT!
WE SAW THE WHOLE THING?!
KRAMM

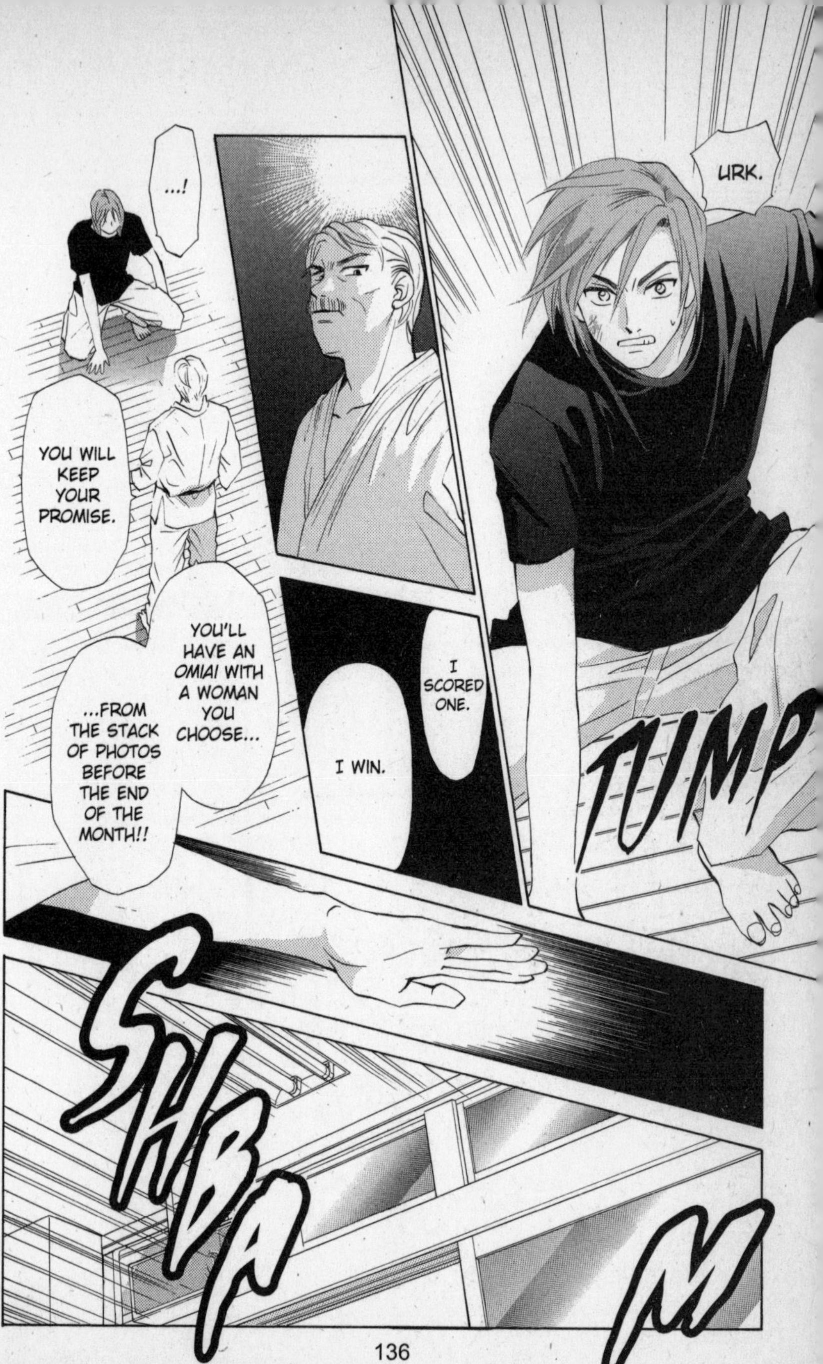
URK.
TUMP
I SCORED ONE.
I WIN.
...!
YOU WILL KEEP YOUR PROMISE.
YOU'LL HAVE AN OMIAI WITH A WOMAN YOU CHOOSE...
...FROM THE STACK OF PHOTOS BEFORE THE END OF THE MONTH!!
SHBAM

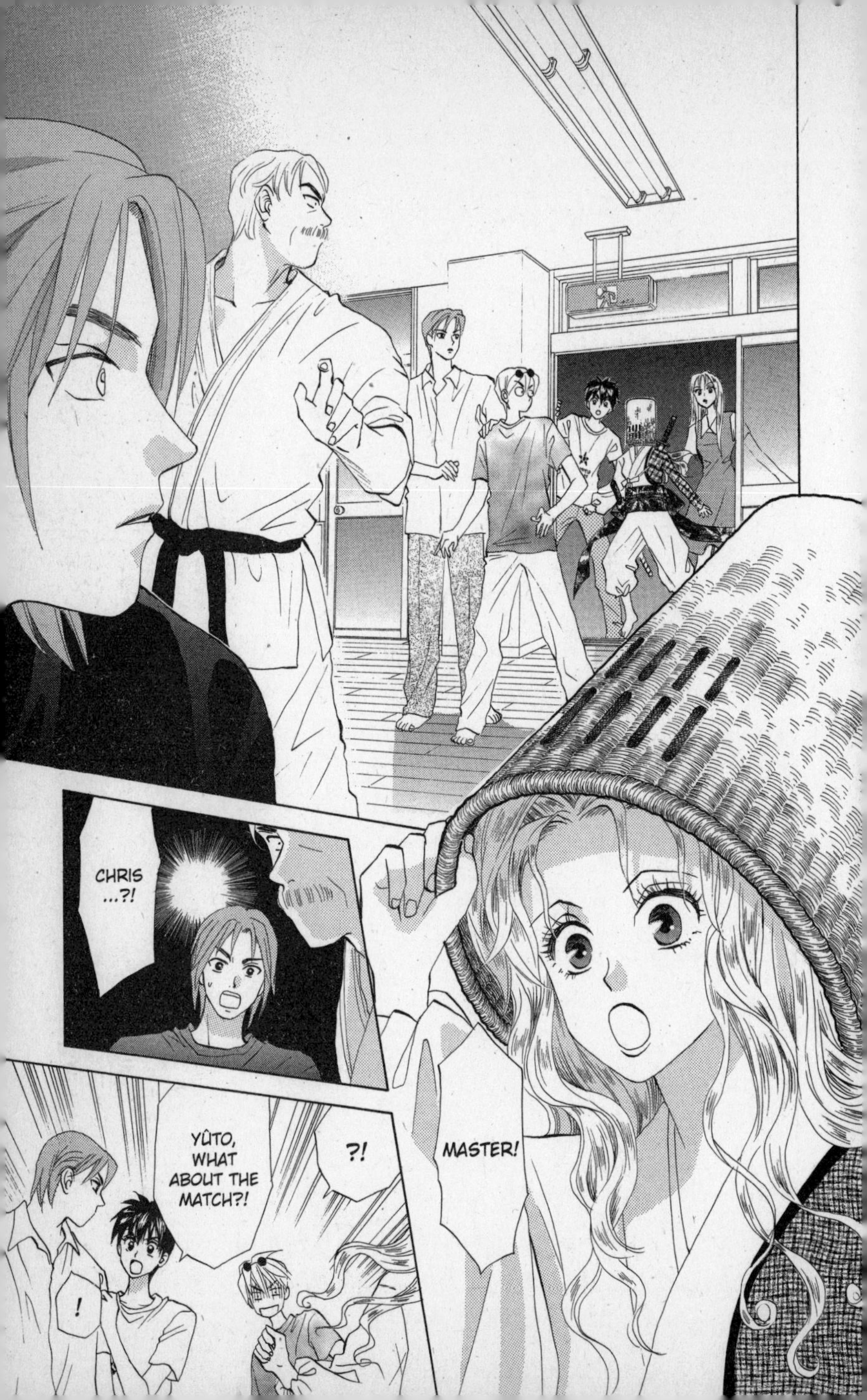
MASTER!
CHRIS ...?!
?!
YÛTO, WHAT ABOUT THE MATCH?!
!

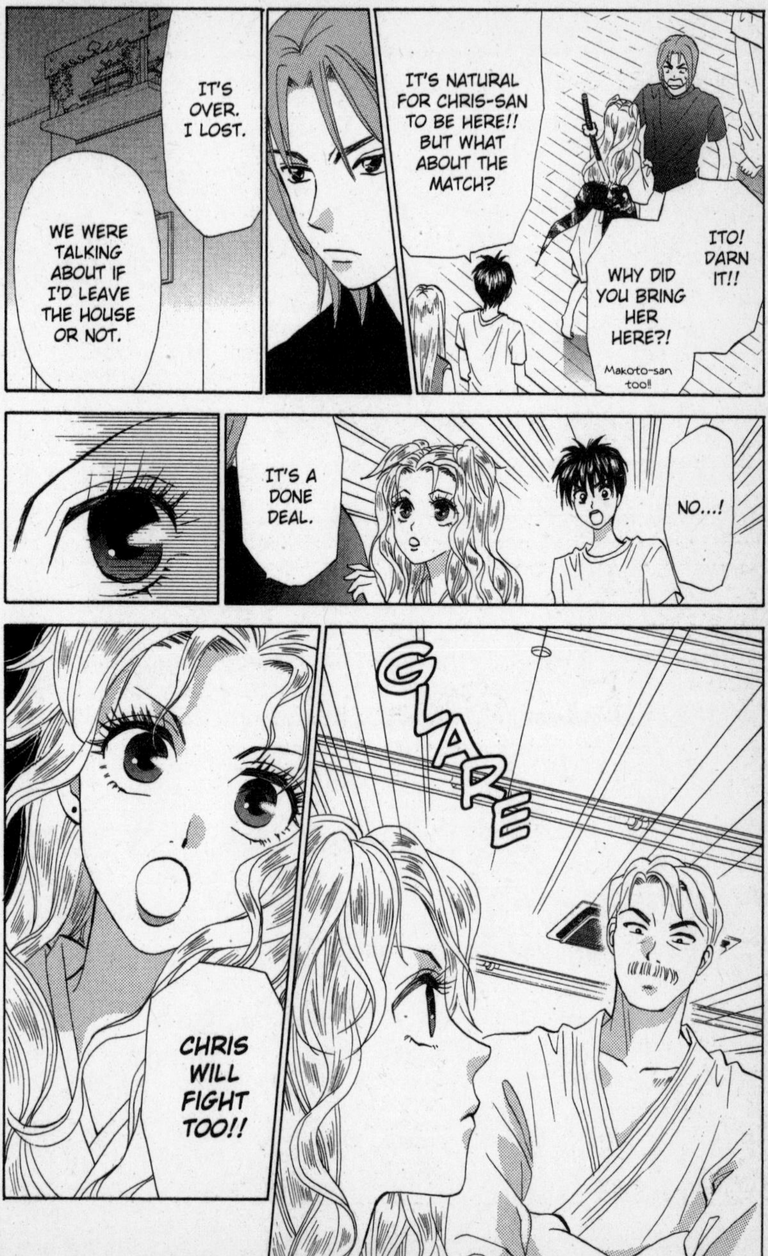
ITO! DARN IT!!
WHY DID YOU BRING HER HERE?!
Makoto-san too!!
IT'S NATURAL FOR CHRIS-SAN TO BE HERE!! BUT WHAT ABOUT THE MATCH?
IT'S OVER. I LOST.
WE WERE TALKING ABOUT IF I'D LEAVE THE HOUSE OR NOT.
NO...!
IT'S A DONE DEAL.
GLARE
CHRIS WILL FIGHT TOO!!

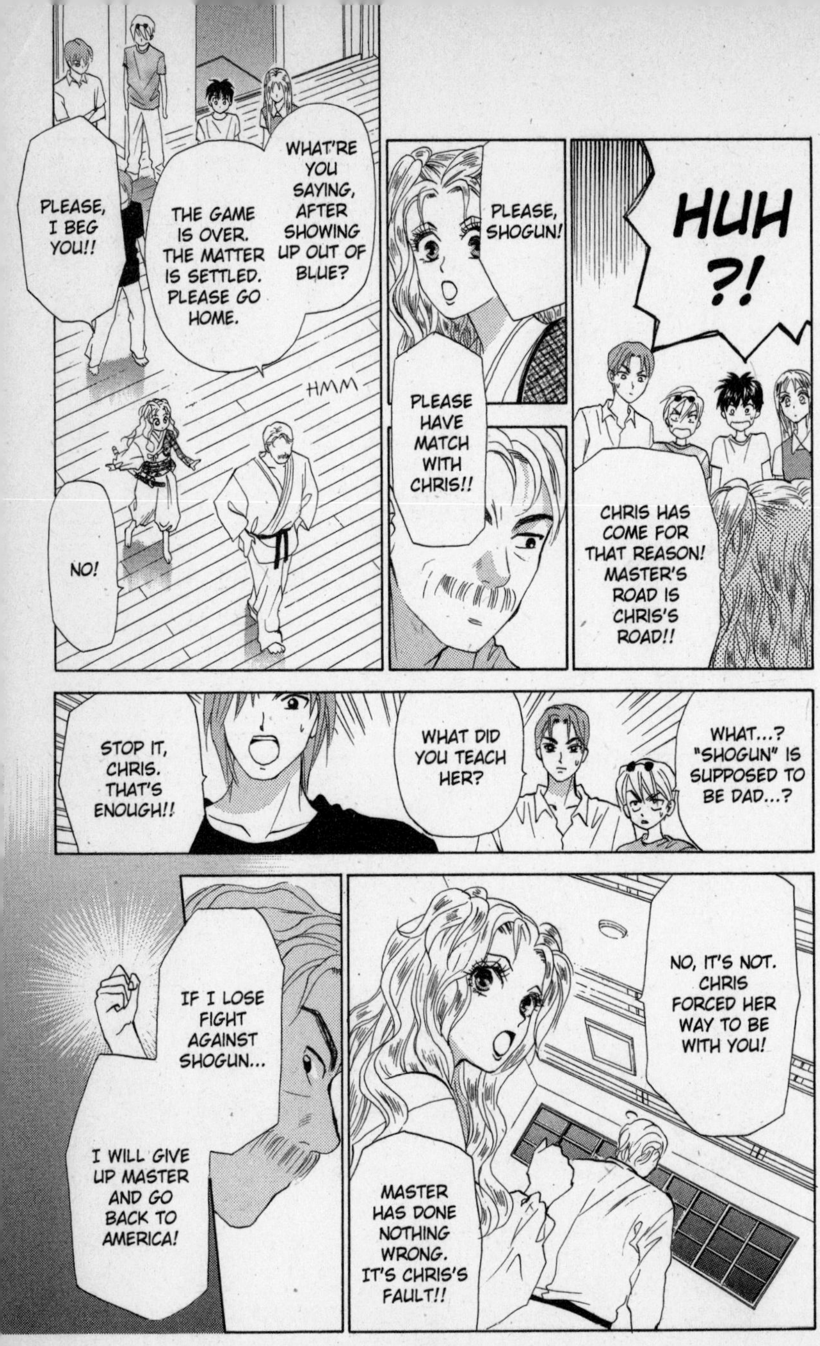
HUH ?!
CHRIS HAS COME FOR THAT REASON! MASTER'S ROAD IS CHRIS'S ROAD!!
PLEASE, SHOGUN!
PLEASE HAVE MATCH WITH CHRIS!!
WHAT'RE YOU SAYING, AFTER SHOWING UP OUT OF BLUE?
THE GAME IS OVER. THE MATTER IS SETTLED. PLEASE GO HOME.
PLEASE, I BEG YOU!!
HMM
NO!
WHAT...? "SHOGUN" IS SUPPOSED TO BE DAD...?
WHAT DID YOU TEACH HER?
STOP IT, CHRIS. THAT'S ENOUGH!!
NO, IT'S NOT. CHRIS FORCED HER WAY TO BE WITH YOU!
MASTER HAS DONE NOTHING WRONG. IT'S CHRIS'S FAULT!!
IF I LOSE FIGHT AGAINST SHOGUN...
I WILL GIVE UP MASTER AND GO BACK TO AMERICA!

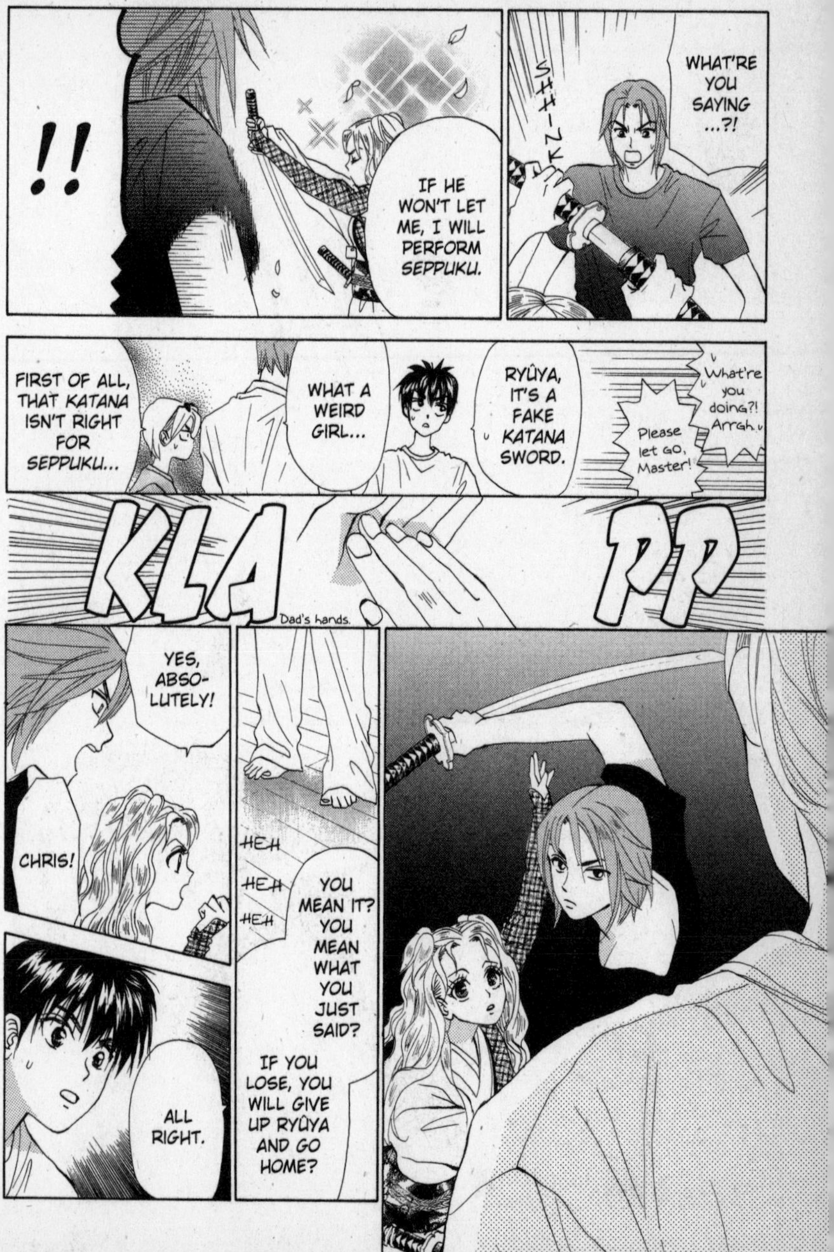
WHAT'RE YOU SAYING ...?!
SHHINK
IF HE WON'T LET ME, I WILL PERFORM SEPPUKU.
!!
What're you doing?! Arrgh.
Please let GO, Master!
RYÛYA, IT'S A FAKE KATANA SWORD.
WHAT A WEIRD GIRL...
FIRST OF ALL, THAT KATANA ISN'T RIGHT FOR SEPPUKU...
KLAPP
Dad's hands.
HEH
HEH
HEH
YOU MEAN IT? YOU MEAN WHAT YOU JUST SAID?
IF YOU LOSE, YOU WILL GIVE UP RYÛYA AND GO HOME?
YES, ABSOLUTELY!
CHRIS!
ALL RIGHT.

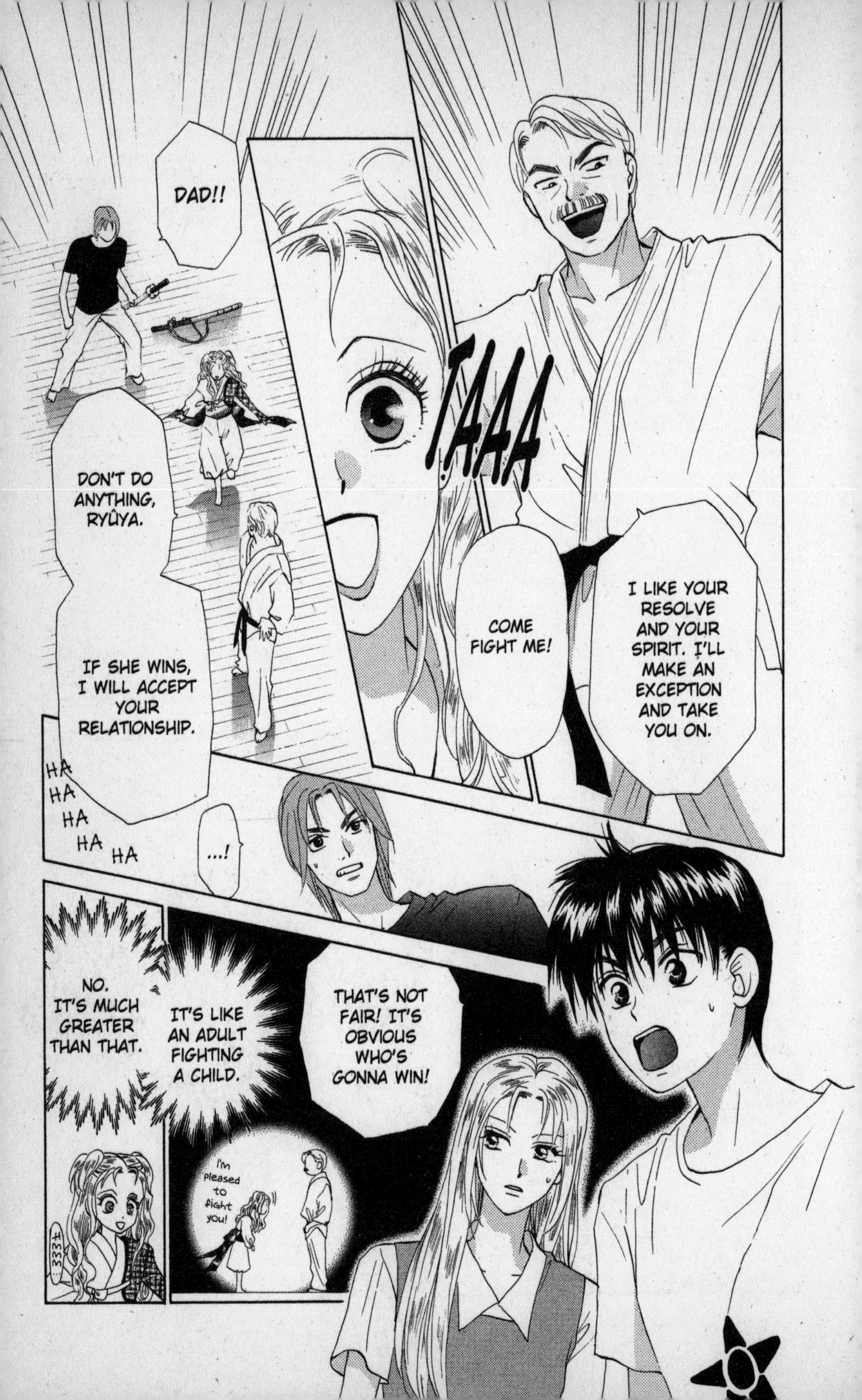
I LIKE YOUR RESOLVE AND YOUR SPIRIT. I'LL MAKE AN EXCEPTION AND TAKE YOU ON.
COME FIGHT ME!
TAAA
DAD!!
DON'T DO ANYTHING, RYÛYA.
IF SHE WINS, I WILL ACCEPT YOUR RELATIONSHIP.
HA HA HA HA HA
...!
THAT'S NOT FAIR! IT'S OBVIOUS WHO'S GONNA WIN!
IT'S LIKE AN ADULT FIGHTING A CHILD.
NO. IT'S MUCH GREATER THAN THAT.
I'm pleased to fight you!

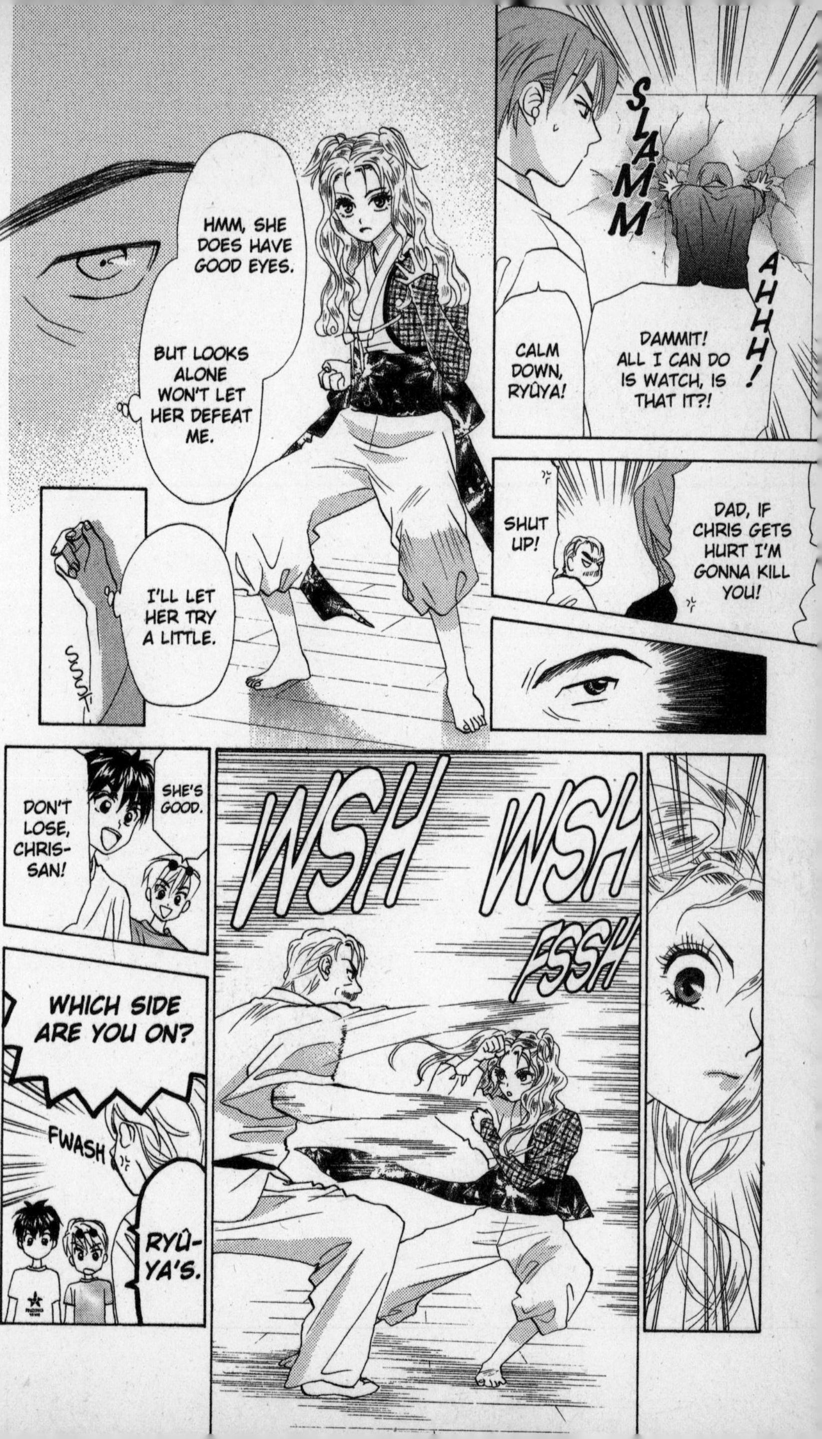
SLAMM
AHHH!
DAMMIT! ALL I CAN DO IS WATCH, IS THAT IT?!
CALM DOWN, RYÛYA!
DAD, IF CHRIS GETS HURT I'M GONNA KILL YOU!
SHUT UP!
HMM, SHE DOES HAVE GOOD EYES.
BUT LOOKS ALONE WON'T LET HER DEFEAT ME.
I'LL LET HER TRY A LITTLE.
WSH WSH
FSSH
SHE'S GOOD.
DON'T LOSE, CHRIS-SAN!
WHICH SIDE ARE YOU ON?
FWASH
RYÛ-YA'S.

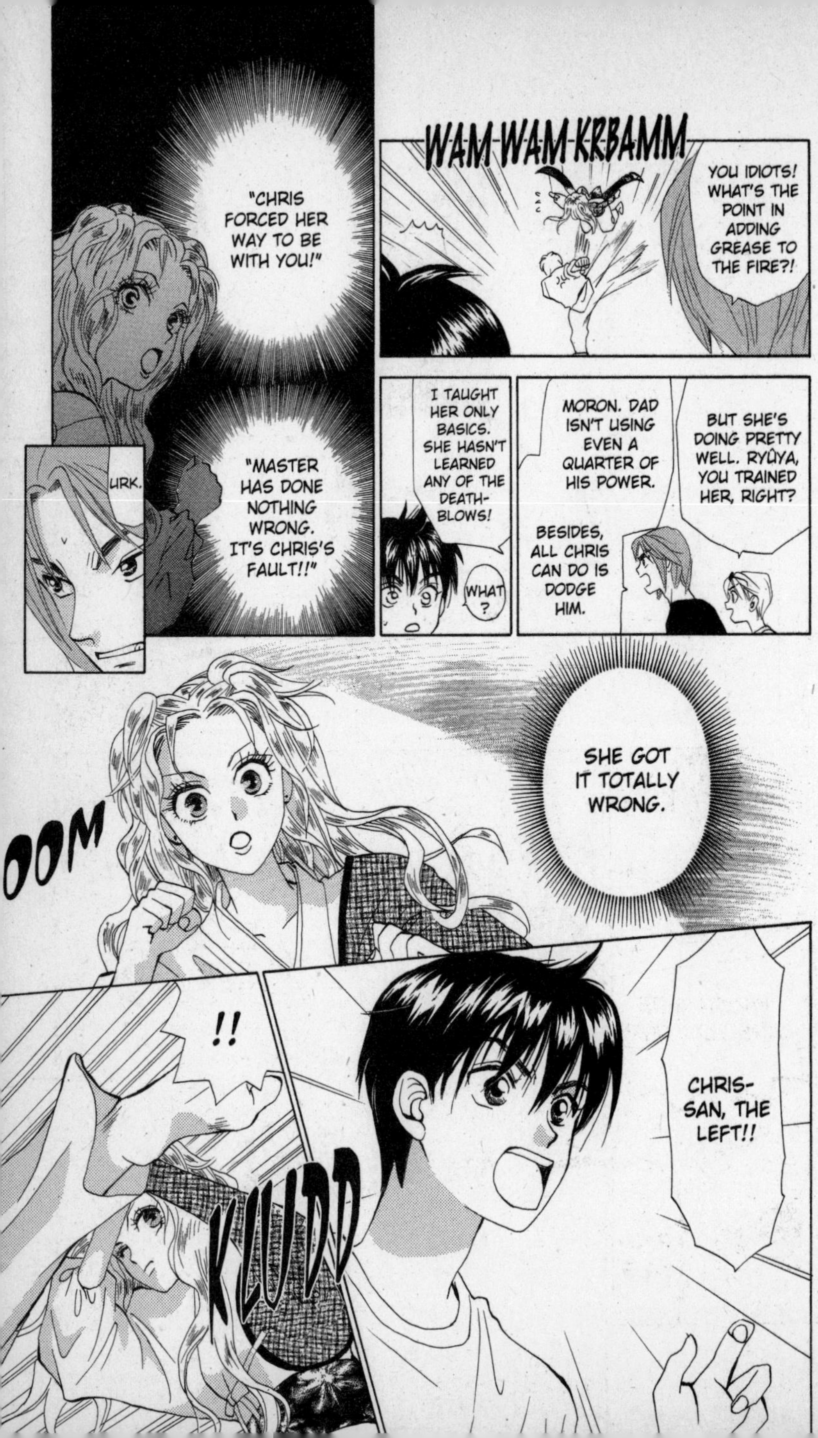
WAM WAM KRBAMM
YOU IDIOTS! WHAT'S THE POINT IN ADDING GREASE TO THE FIRE?!
BUT SHE'S DOING PRETTY WELL. RYÛYA, YOU TRAINED HER, RIGHT?
MORON. DAD ISN'T USING EVEN A QUARTER OF HIS POWER.
BESIDES, ALL CHRIS CAN DO IS DODGE HIM.
I TAUGHT HER ONLY BASICS. SHE HASN'T LEARNED ANY OF THE DEATH-BLOWS!
WHAT?
"CHRIS FORCED HER WAY TO BE WITH YOU!"
"MASTER HAS DONE NOTHING WRONG. IT'S CHRIS'S FAULT!!"
URK.
SHE GOT IT TOTALLY WRONG.
OOM
CHRIS-SAN, THE LEFT!!
!!
KLUDD

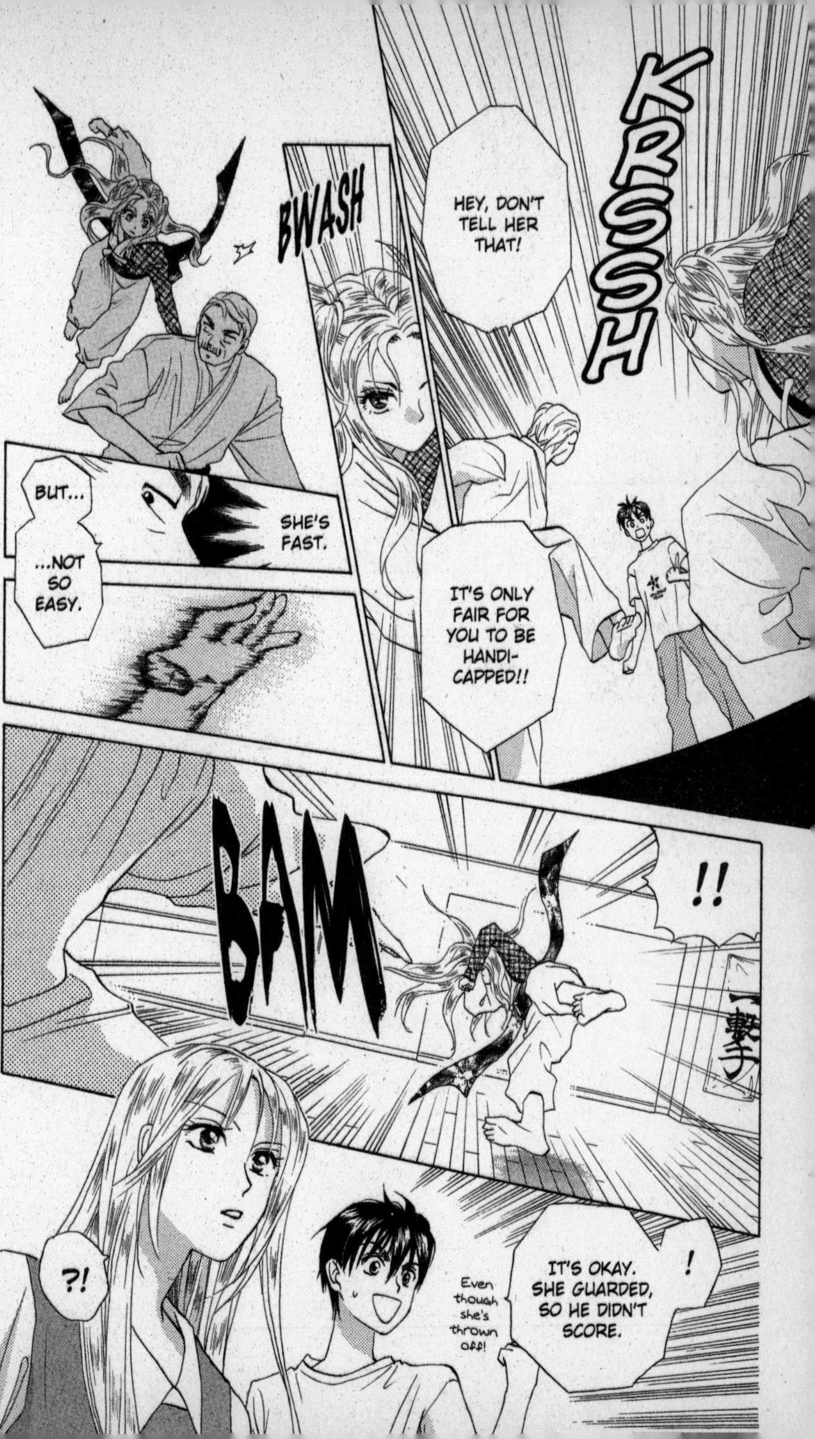
KRSSH
HEY, DON'T TELL HER THAT!
IT'S ONLY FAIR FOR YOU TO BE HANDI-CAPPED!!
BWASH
SHE'S FAST.
BUT... ...NOT SO EASY.
!!
BAM
!
IT'S OKAY. SHE GUARDED, SO HE DIDN'T SCORE.
Even though she's thrown off!
?!

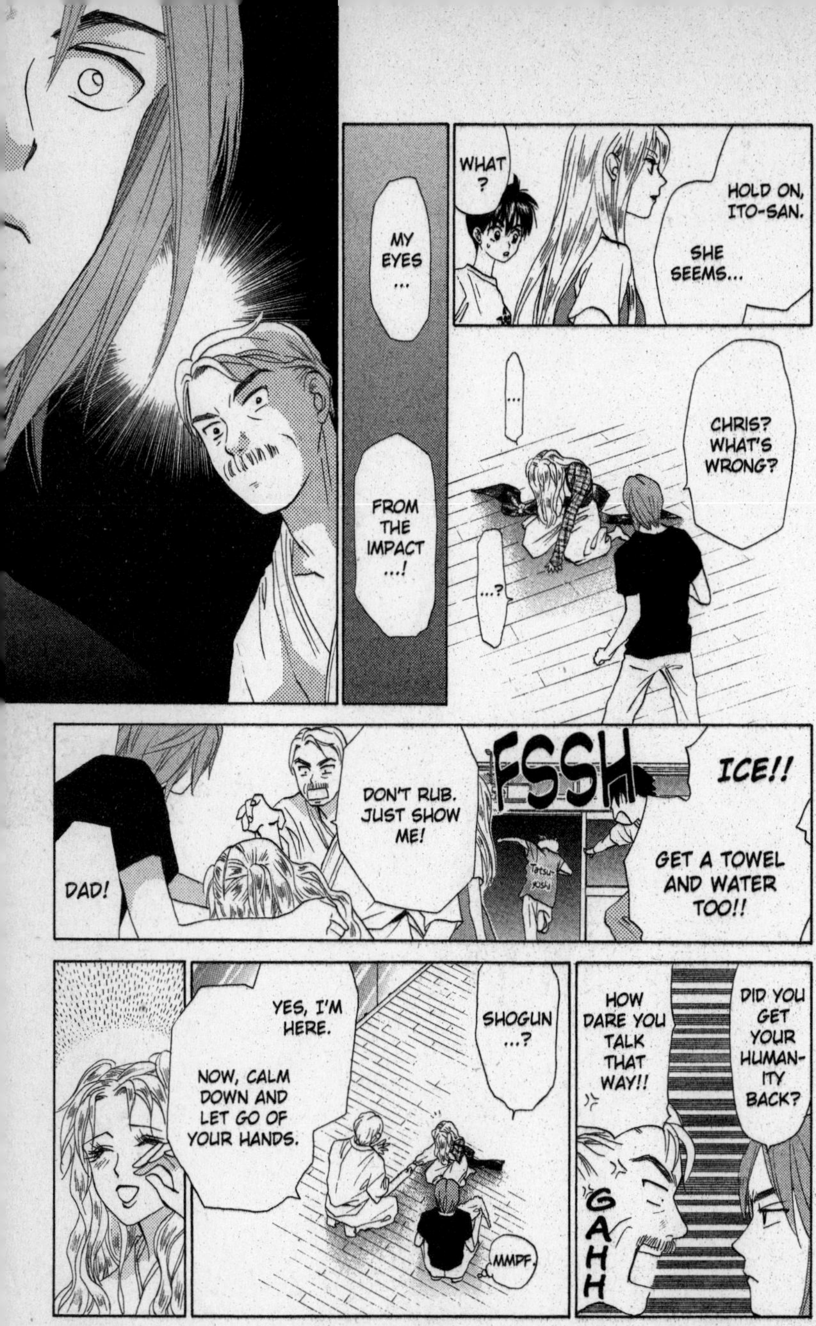
HOLD ON, ITO-SAN.
SHE SEEMS...
WHAT?
CHRIS? WHAT'S WRONG?
...
...?
MY EYES...
FROM THE IMPACT...!
ICE!!
GET A TOWEL AND WATER TOO!!
FSSH
Tatsu-yoshi
DON'T RUB. JUST SHOW ME!
DAD!
DID YOU GET YOUR HUMAN-ITY BACK?
HOW DARE YOU TALK THAT WAY!!
GAHH
SHOGUN...?
YES, I'M HERE.
NOW, CALM DOWN AND LET GO OF YOUR HANDS.
MMPF.

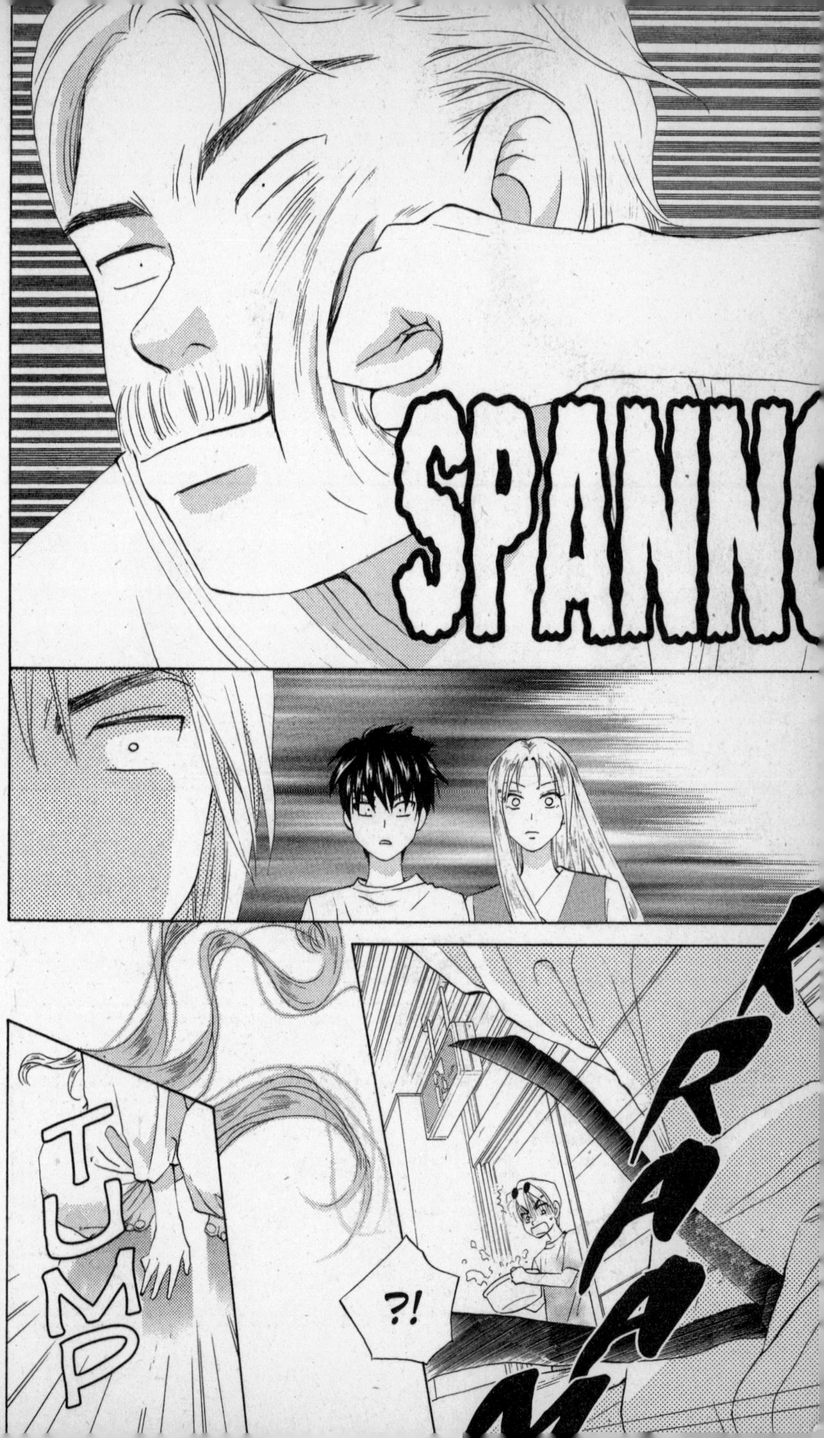
SPANN
KRAAAM
?!
TUMP

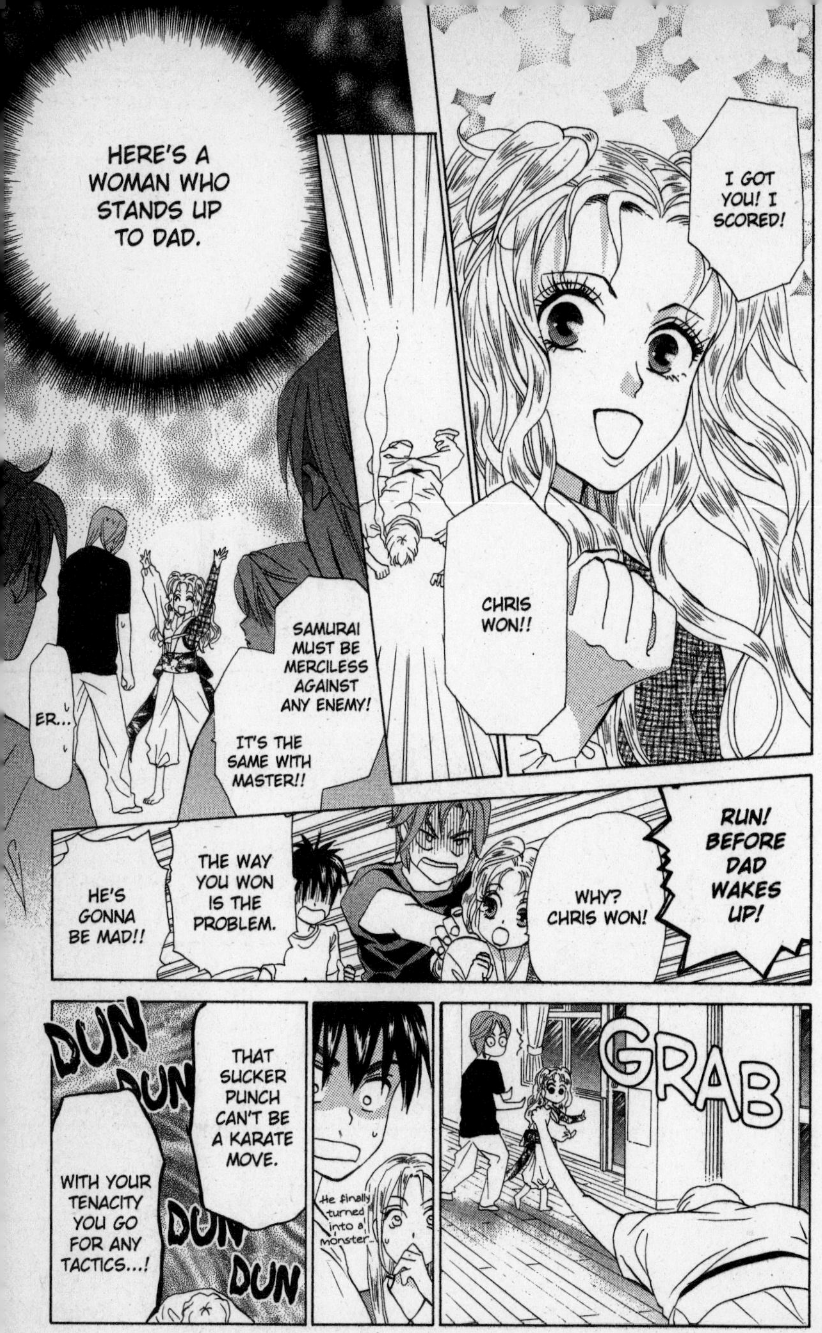
I GOT YOU! I SCORED!
CHRIS WON!!
SAMURAI MUST BE MERCILESS AGAINST ANY ENEMY!
IT'S THE SAME WITH MASTER!!
HERE'S A WOMAN WHO STANDS UP TO DAD.
ER...
RUN! BEFORE DAD WAKES UP!
WHY? CHRIS WON!
THE WAY YOU WON IS THE PROBLEM.
HE'S GONNA BE MAD!!
GRAB
He finally turned into a monster...
DUN DUN
THAT SUCKER PUNCH CAN'T BE A KARATE MOVE.
WITH YOUR TENACITY YOU GO FOR ANY TACTICS...!
DUN DUN

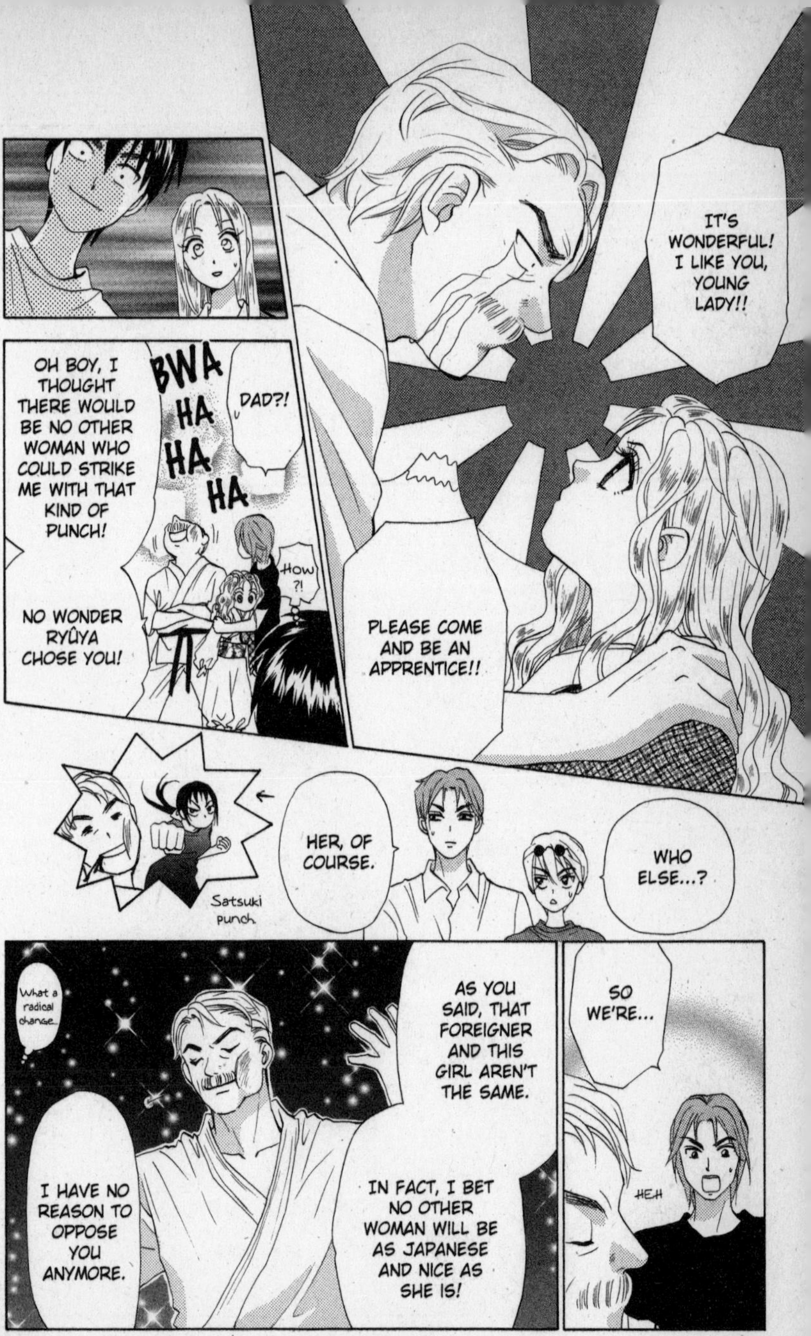
IT'S WONDERFUL! I LIKE YOU, YOUNG LADY!!
PLEASE COME AND BE AN APPRENTICE!!
DAD?!
BWA HA HA HA
OH BOY, I THOUGHT THERE WOULD BE NO OTHER WOMAN WHO COULD STRIKE ME WITH THAT KIND OF PUNCH!
HOW ?!
NO WONDER RYÛYA CHOSE YOU!
WHO ELSE...?
HER, OF COURSE.
Satsuki punch
SO WE'RE...
HEH
AS YOU SAID, THAT FOREIGNER AND THIS GIRL AREN'T THE SAME.
IN FACT, I BET NO OTHER WOMAN WILL BE AS JAPANESE AND NICE AS SHE IS!
I HAVE NO REASON TO OPPOSE YOU ANYMORE.
What a radical change...

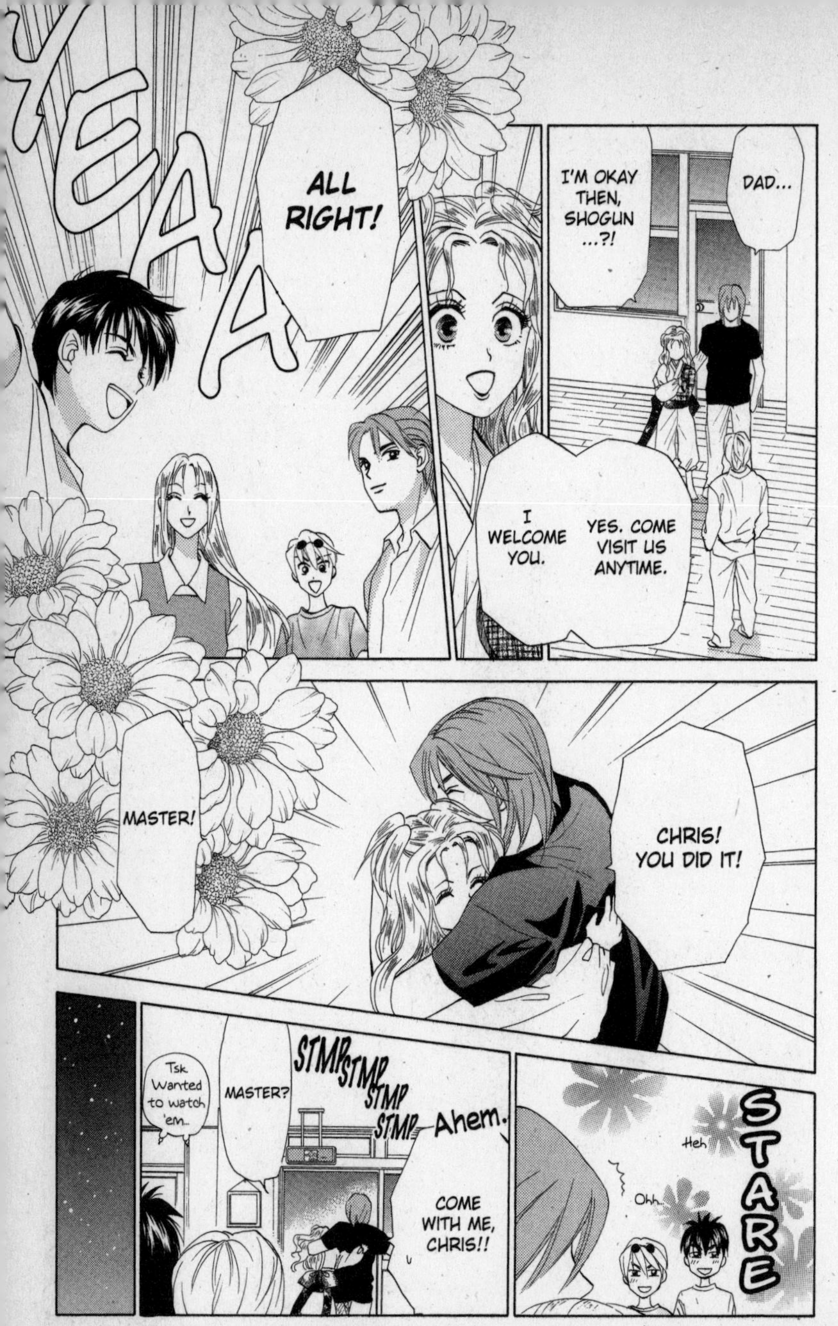
DAD...
I'M OKAY THEN, SHOGUN ...?!
YES. COME VISIT US ANYTIME.
I WELCOME YOU.
YEAAA
ALL RIGHT!
CHRIS! YOU DID IT!
MASTER!
STARE
Heh
Ohh...
Ahem.
COME WITH ME, CHRIS!!
STMP STMP STMP STMP
MASTER?
Tsk Wanted to watch 'em...

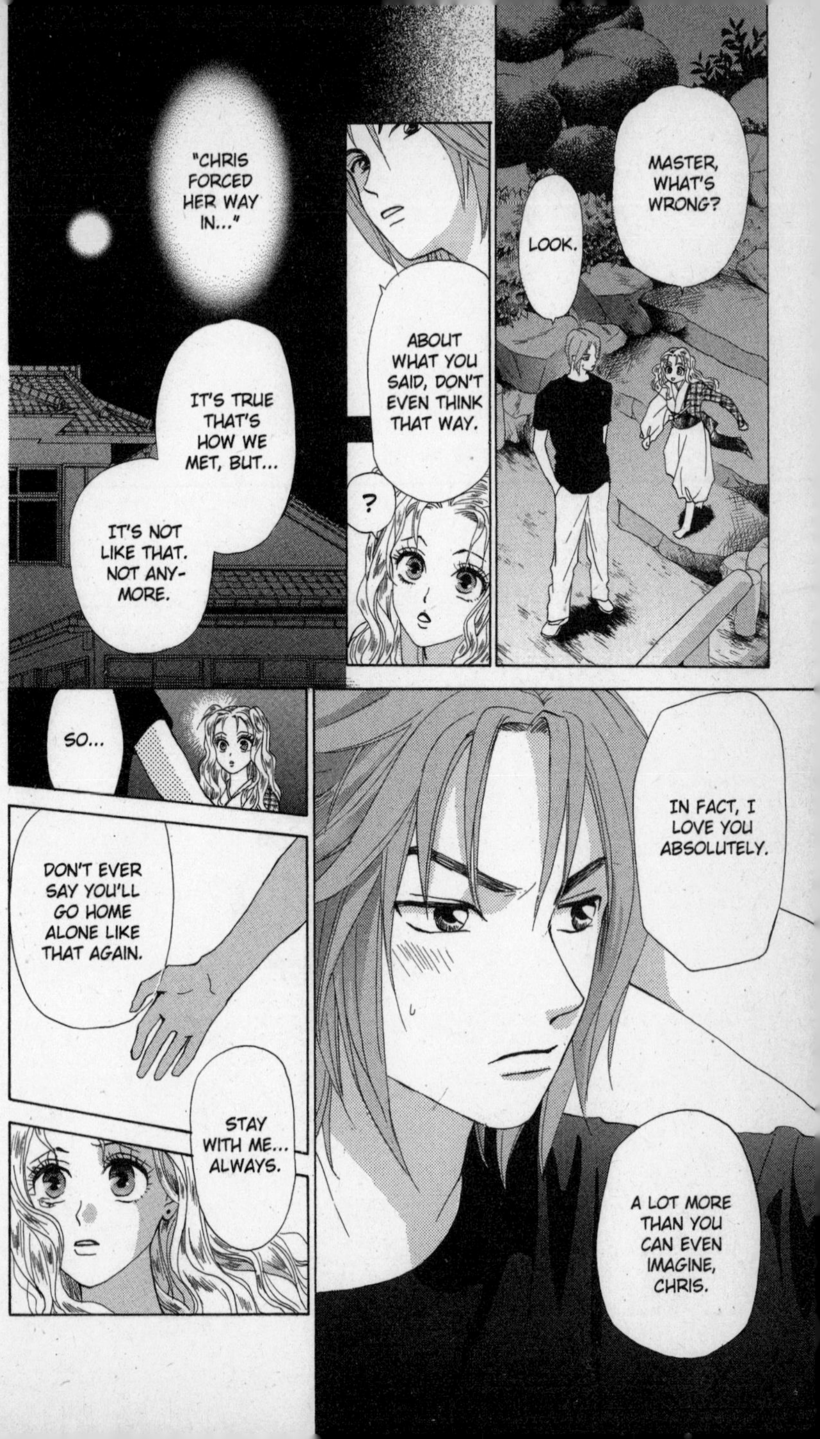
MASTER, WHAT'S WRONG?
LOOK.
ABOUT WHAT YOU SAID, DON'T EVEN THINK THAT WAY.
?
"CHRIS FORCED HER WAY IN..."
IT'S TRUE THAT'S HOW WE MET, BUT...
IT'S NOT LIKE THAT. NOT ANY-MORE.
IN FACT, I LOVE YOU ABSOLUTELY.
A LOT MORE THAN YOU CAN EVEN IMAGINE, CHRIS.
SO...
DON'T EVER SAY YOU'LL GO HOME ALONE LIKE THAT AGAIN.
STAY WITH ME... ALWAYS.

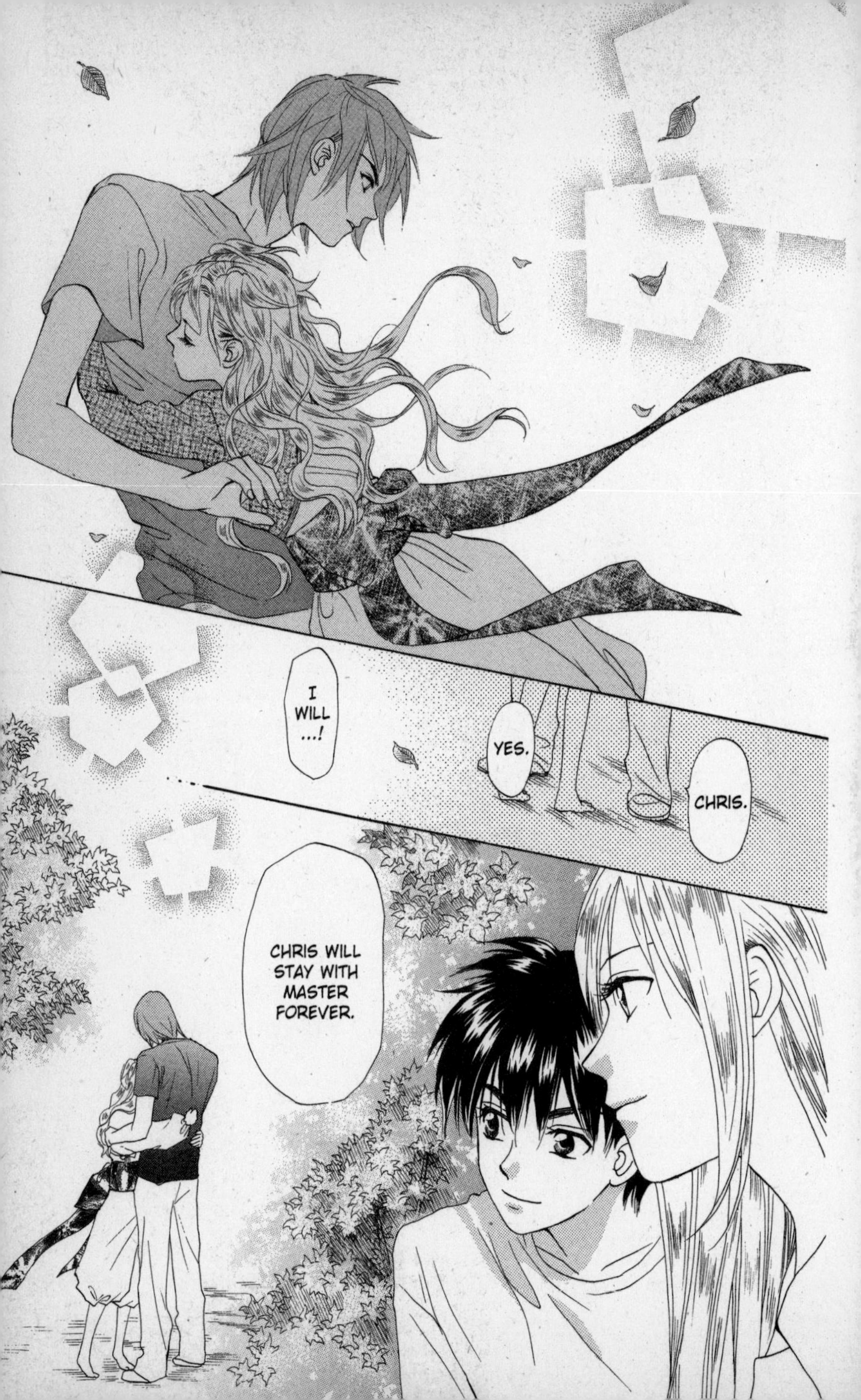
CHRIS.
YES.
I WILL ...!
CHRIS WILL STAY WITH MASTER FOREVER.

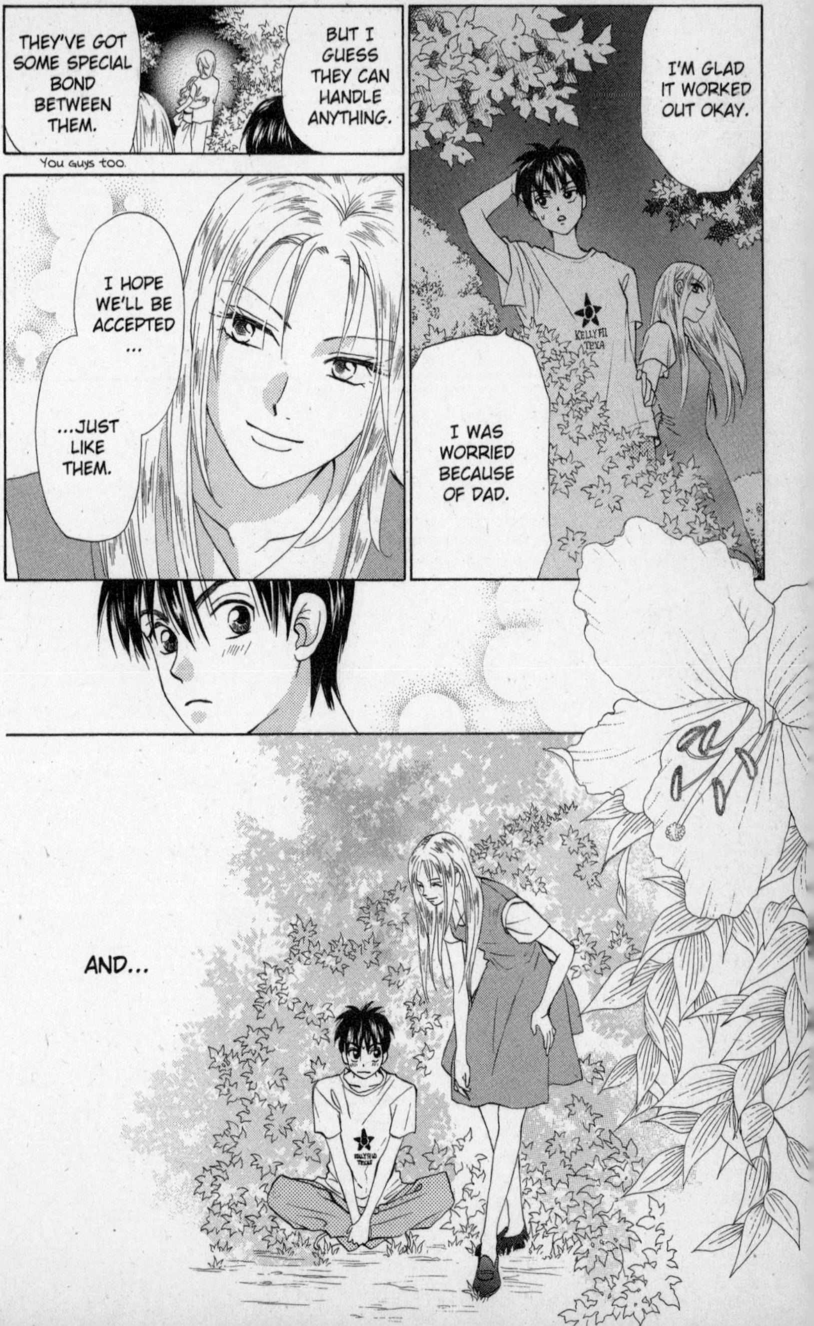
I'M GLAD IT WORKED OUT OKAY.
I WAS WORRIED BECAUSE OF DAD.
BUT I GUESS THEY CAN HANDLE ANYTHING.
THEY'VE GOT SOME SPECIAL BOND BETWEEN THEM.
You guys too.
I HOPE WE'LL BE ACCEPTED ...
...JUST LIKE THEM.
AND...

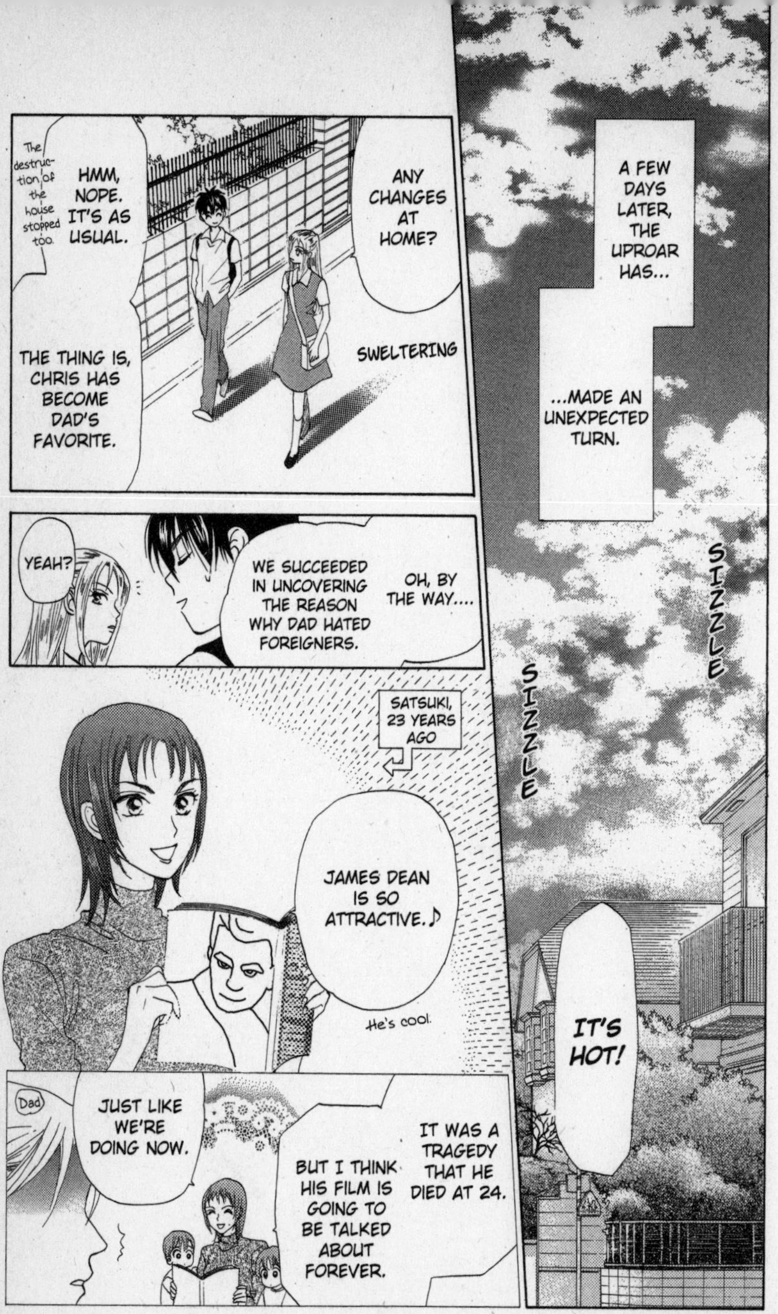
A FEW DAYS LATER, THE UPROAR HAS...
...MADE AN UNEXPECTED TURN.
SIZZLE
SIZZLE
IT'S HOT!
ANY CHANGES AT HOME?
SWELTERING
HMM, NOPE. IT'S AS USUAL.
The destruction of the house stopped too.
THE THING IS, CHRIS HAS BECOME DAD'S FAVORITE.
OH, BY THE WAY....
WE SUCCEEDED IN UNCOVERING THE REASON WHY DAD HATED FOREIGNERS.
YEAH?
SATSUKI, 23 YEARS AGO
JAMES DEAN IS SO ATTRACTIVE.♪
He's cool.
IT WAS A TRAGEDY THAT HE DIED AT 24.
BUT I THINK HIS FILM IS GOING TO BE TALKED ABOUT FOREVER.
JUST LIKE WE'RE DOING NOW.
Dad

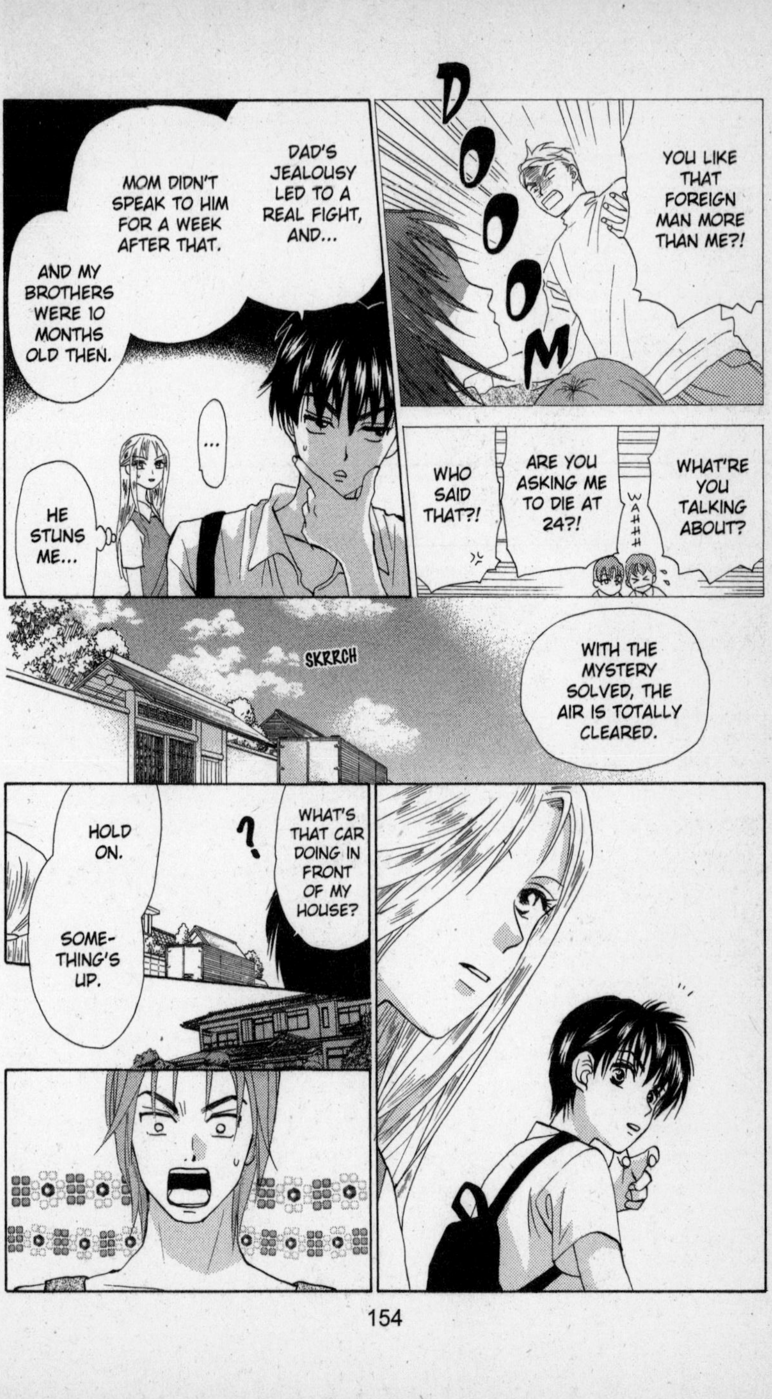
DOOOM
YOU LIKE THAT FOREIGN MAN MORE THAN ME?!
WHAT'RE YOU TALKING ABOUT?
WAHHH
ARE YOU ASKING ME TO DIE AT 24?!
WHO SAID THAT?!
DAD'S JEALOUSY LED TO A REAL FIGHT, AND...
MOM DIDN'T SPEAK TO HIM FOR A WEEK AFTER THAT.
AND MY BROTHERS WERE 10 MONTHS OLD THEN.
...
HE STUNS ME...
WITH THE MYSTERY SOLVED, THE AIR IS TOTALLY CLEARED.
SKRRCH
WHAT'S THAT CAR DOING IN FRONT OF MY HOUSE?
?
HOLD ON.
SOME-THING'S UP.

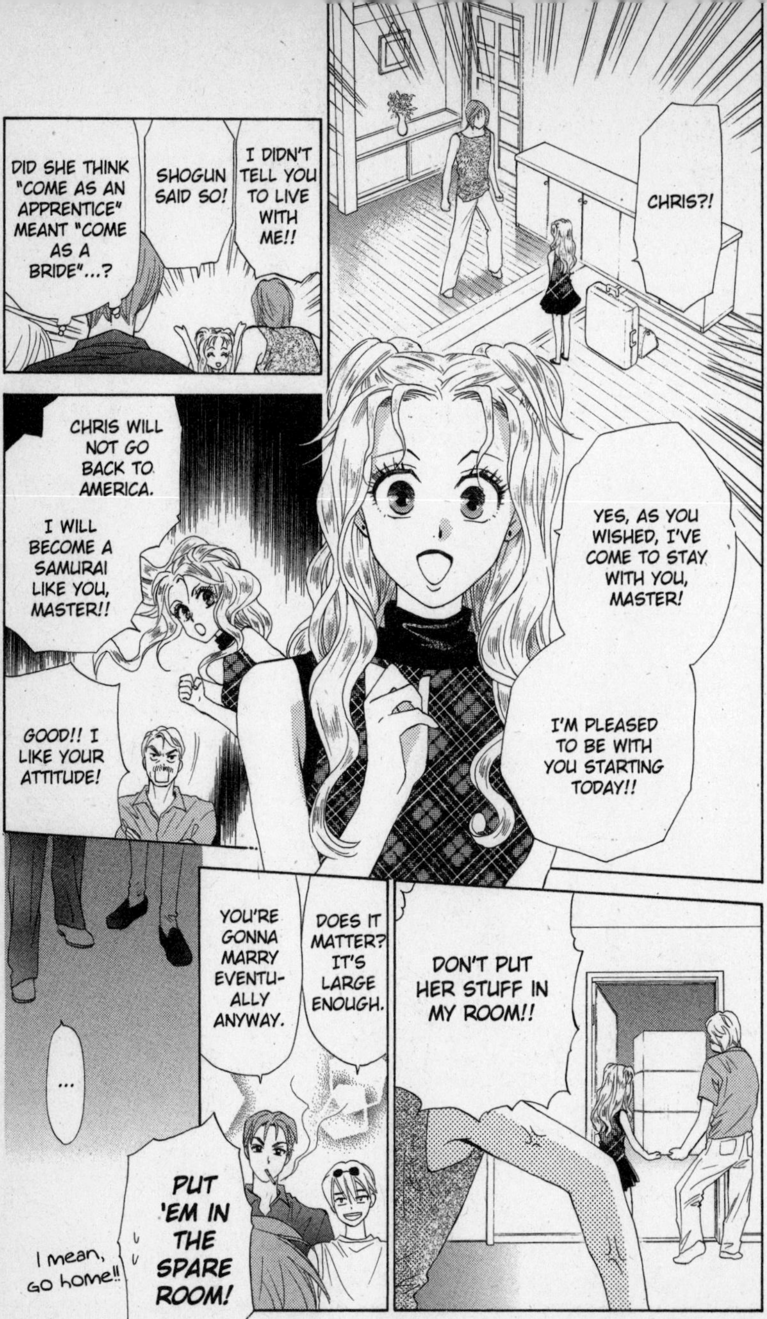
CHRIS?!
YES, AS YOU WISHED, I'VE COME TO STAY WITH YOU, MASTER!
I'M PLEASED TO BE WITH YOU STARTING TODAY!!
I DIDN'T TELL YOU TO LIVE WITH ME!!
SHOGUN SAID SO!
DID SHE THINK "COME AS AN APPRENTICE" MEANT "COME AS A BRIDE"...?
CHRIS WILL NOT GO BACK TO AMERICA.
I WILL BECOME A SAMURAI LIKE YOU, MASTER!!
GOOD!! I LIKE YOUR ATTITUDE!
DON'T PUT HER STUFF IN MY ROOM!!
DOES IT MATTER? IT'S LARGE ENOUGH.
YOU'RE GONNA MARRY EVENTU-ALLY ANYWAY.
PUT 'EM IN THE SPARE ROOM!
I mean, go home!!
...

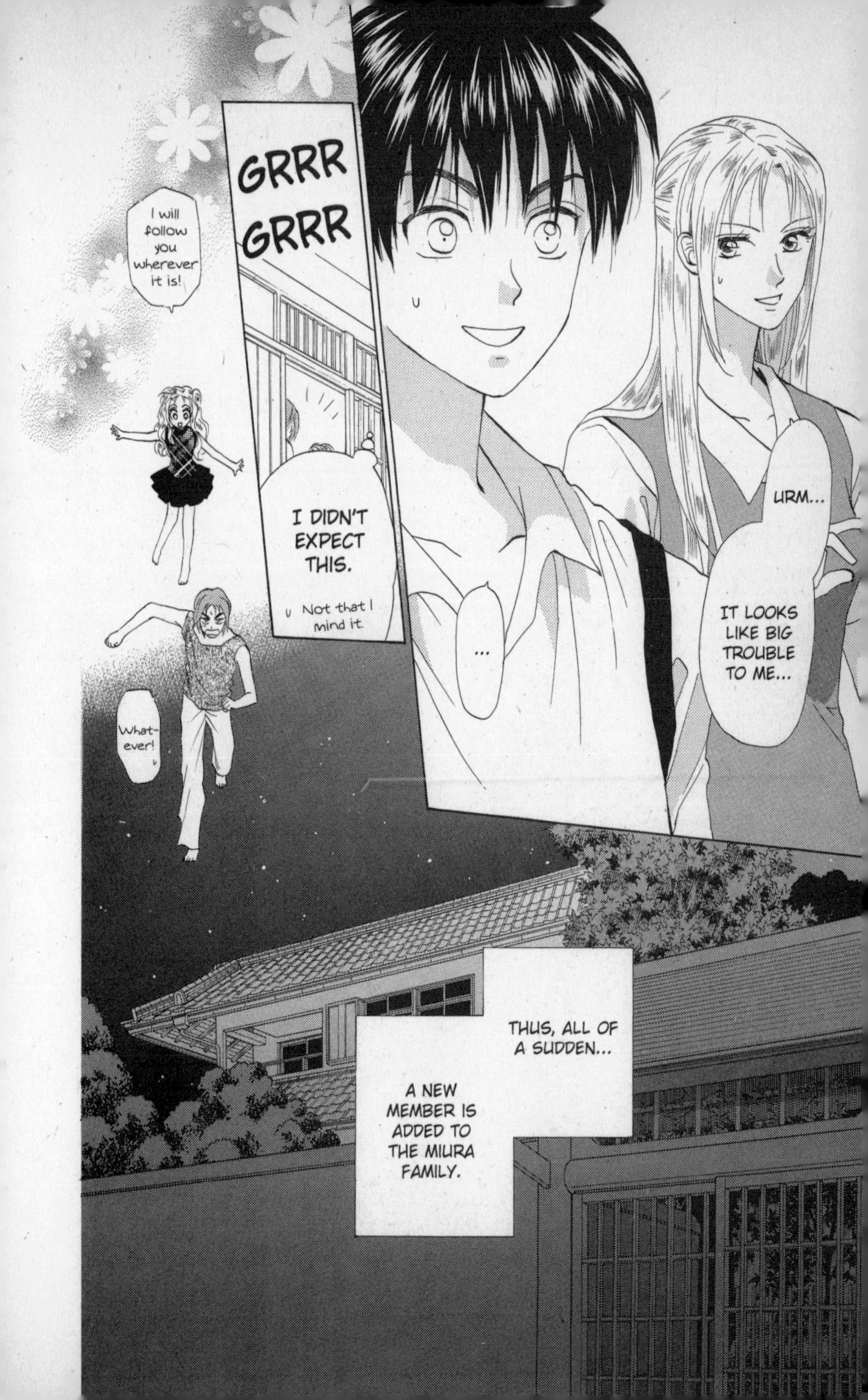
URM...
IT LOOKS LIKE BIG TROUBLE TO ME...
...
GRRR GRRR
I DIDN'T EXPECT THIS.
Not that I mind it.
I will follow you wherever it is!
What-ever!
THUS, ALL OF A SUDDEN...
A NEW MEMBER IS ADDED TO THE MIURA FAMILY.

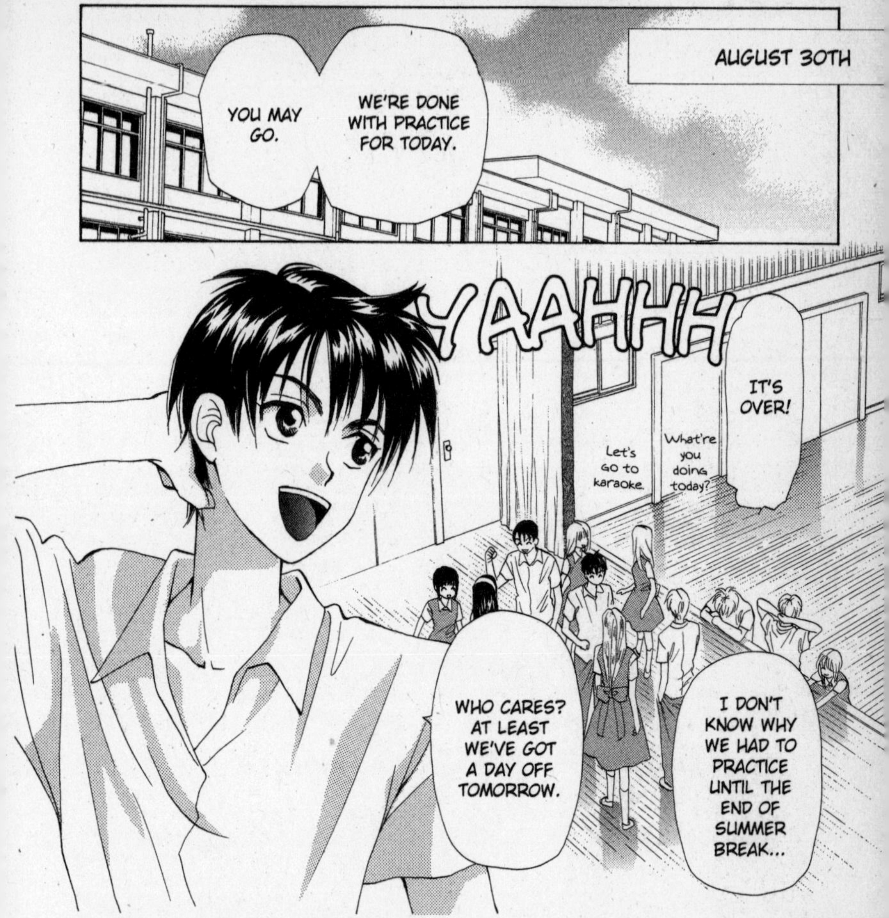
AUGUST 30TH
WE'RE DONE WITH PRACTICE FOR TODAY.
YOU MAY GO.
YAAHHH
IT'S OVER!
What're you doing today?
Let's go to karaoke.
I DON'T KNOW WHY WE HAD TO PRACTICE UNTIL THE END OF SUMMER BREAK...
WHO CARES? AT LEAST WE'VE GOT A DAY OFF TOMORROW.

—Behind the Scenes Story ⑥—

The trio reappears after their long absence. And I've also worked on finalizing—what I haven't done for a while. It's the one in which Ito says "Seven colors" (page 183) under the moonlight. I haven't blurred tones for so long that it made me despair a little.

I tried my best, but I wonder if it looks like a moon. And about the trio, as Tsugumi mentions at the end, they will show up at the Cultural Festival and wreak havoc. Please look forward to it!!

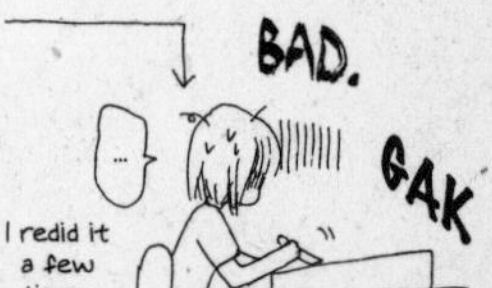
BAD.
...
GAK
I redid it a few times.

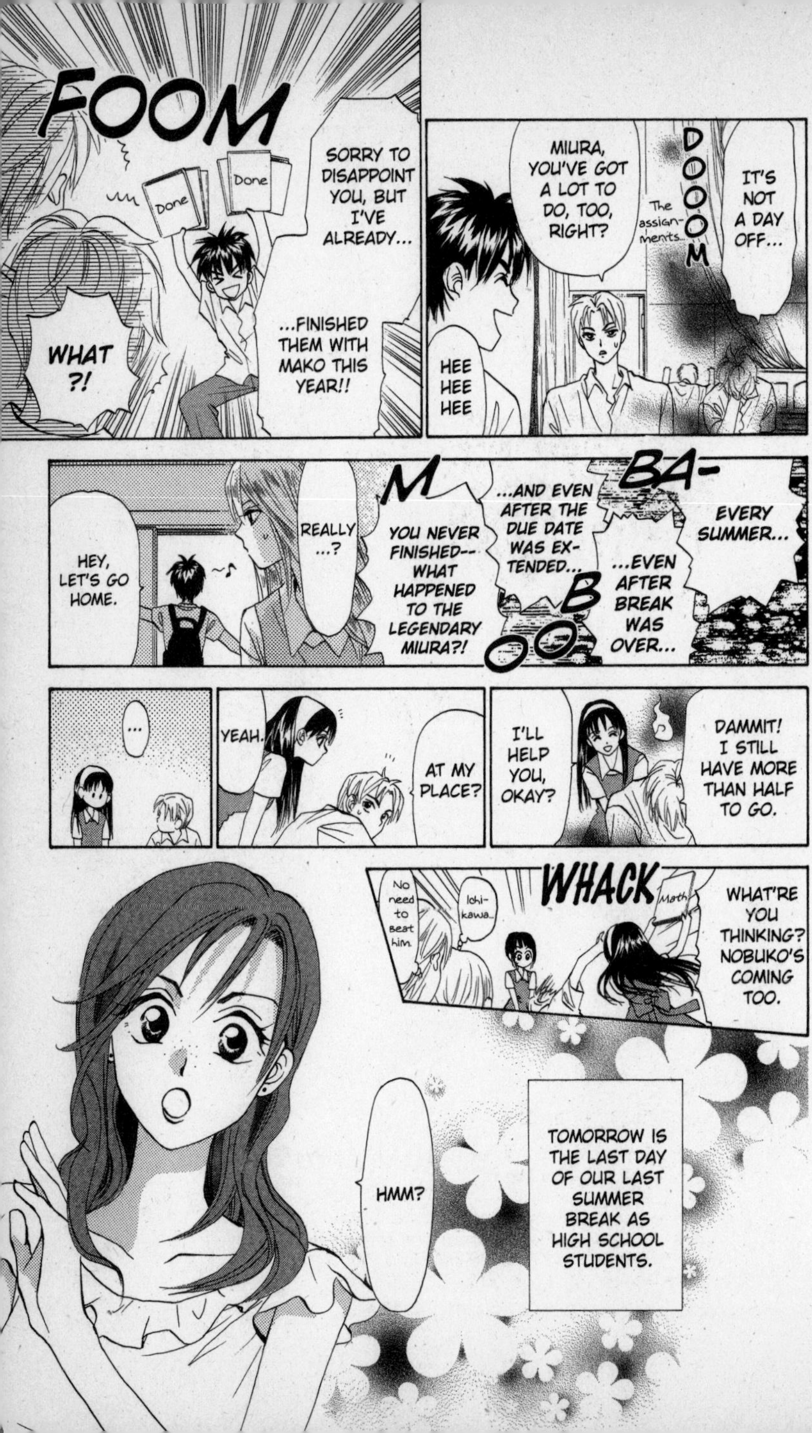
IT'S NOT A DAY OFF...
DOOOM
The assignments...
MIURA, YOU'VE GOT A LOT TO DO, TOO, RIGHT?
HEE HEE HEE
FOOM
SORRY TO DISAPPOINT YOU, BUT I'VE ALREADY...
Done
Done
...FINISHED THEM WITH MAKO THIS YEAR!!
WHAT ?!
EVERY SUMMER...
BA-
...EVEN AFTER BREAK WAS OVER...
...AND EVEN AFTER THE DUE DATE WAS EXTENDED...
M
B
O
O
YOU NEVER FINISHED--WHAT HAPPENED TO THE LEGENDARY MIURA?!
REALLY ...?
HEY, LET'S GO HOME.
DAMMIT! I STILL HAVE MORE THAN HALF TO GO.
I'LL HELP YOU, OKAY?
AT MY PLACE?
YEAH.
...
WHAT'RE YOU THINKING? NOBUKO'S COMING TOO.
Math
WHACK
Ichikawa...
No need to beat him.
TOMORROW IS THE LAST DAY OF OUR LAST SUMMER BREAK AS HIGH SCHOOL STUDENTS.
HMM?

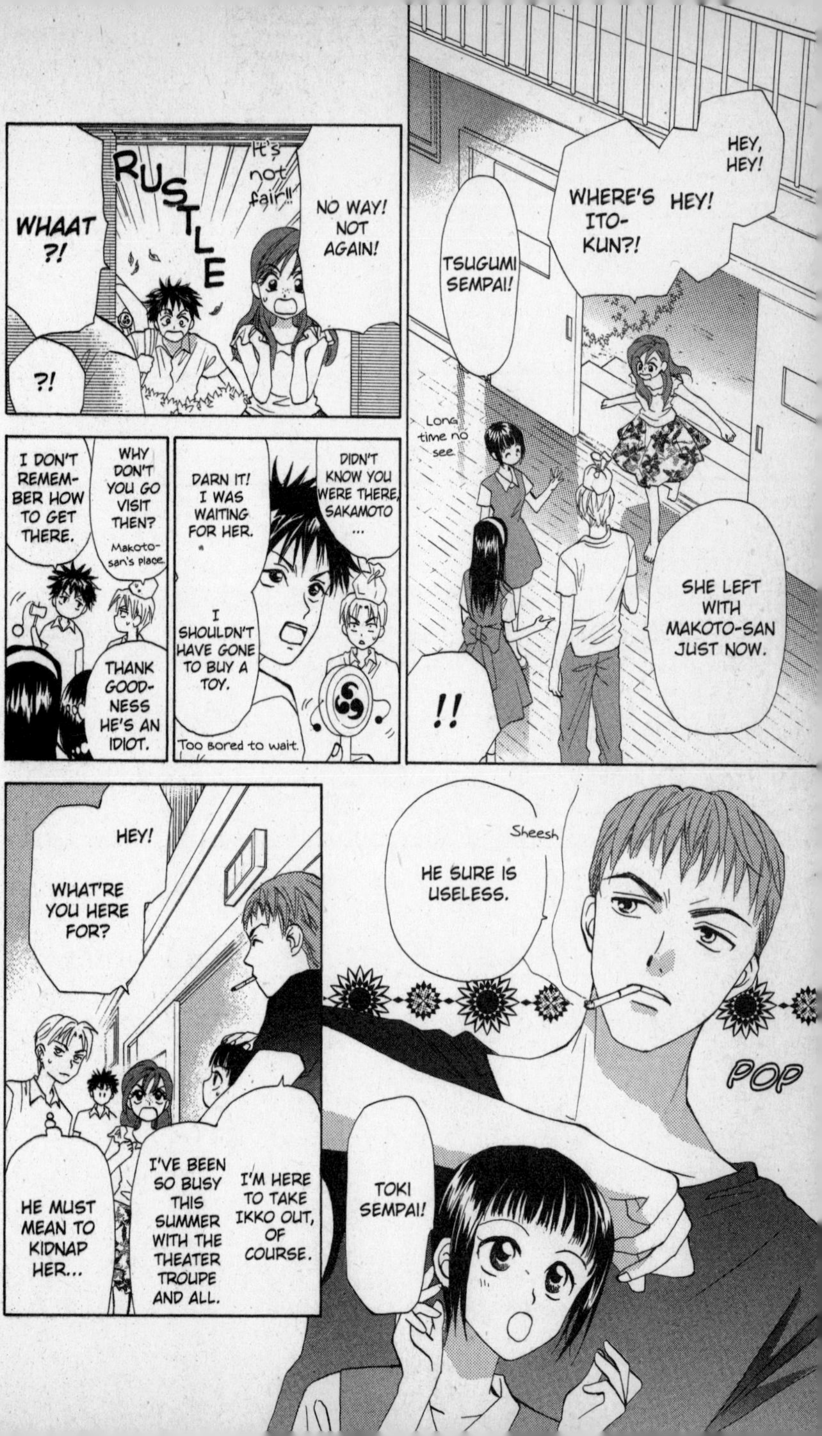
HEY, HEY!
HEY!
WHERE'S ITO-KUN?!
TSUGUMI SEMPAI!
Long time no see
SHE LEFT WITH MAKOTO-SAN JUST NOW.
!!
NO WAY! NOT AGAIN!
It's not fair!!
RUSTLE
WHAAT ?!
?!
DIDN'T KNOW YOU WERE THERE, SAKAMOTO ...
DARN IT! I WAS WAITING FOR HER.
I SHOULDN'T HAVE GONE TO BUY A TOY.
Too bored to wait.
WHY DON'T YOU GO VISIT THEN?
Makoto-san's place.
I DON'T REMEMBER HOW TO GET THERE.
THANK GOODNESS HE'S AN IDIOT.
Sheesh
HE SURE IS USELESS.
POP
TOKI SEMPAI!
HEY!
WHAT'RE YOU HERE FOR?
I'M HERE TO TAKE IKKO OUT, OF COURSE.
I'VE BEEN SO BUSY THIS SUMMER WITH THE THEATER TROUPE AND ALL.
HE MUST MEAN TO KIDNAP HER...

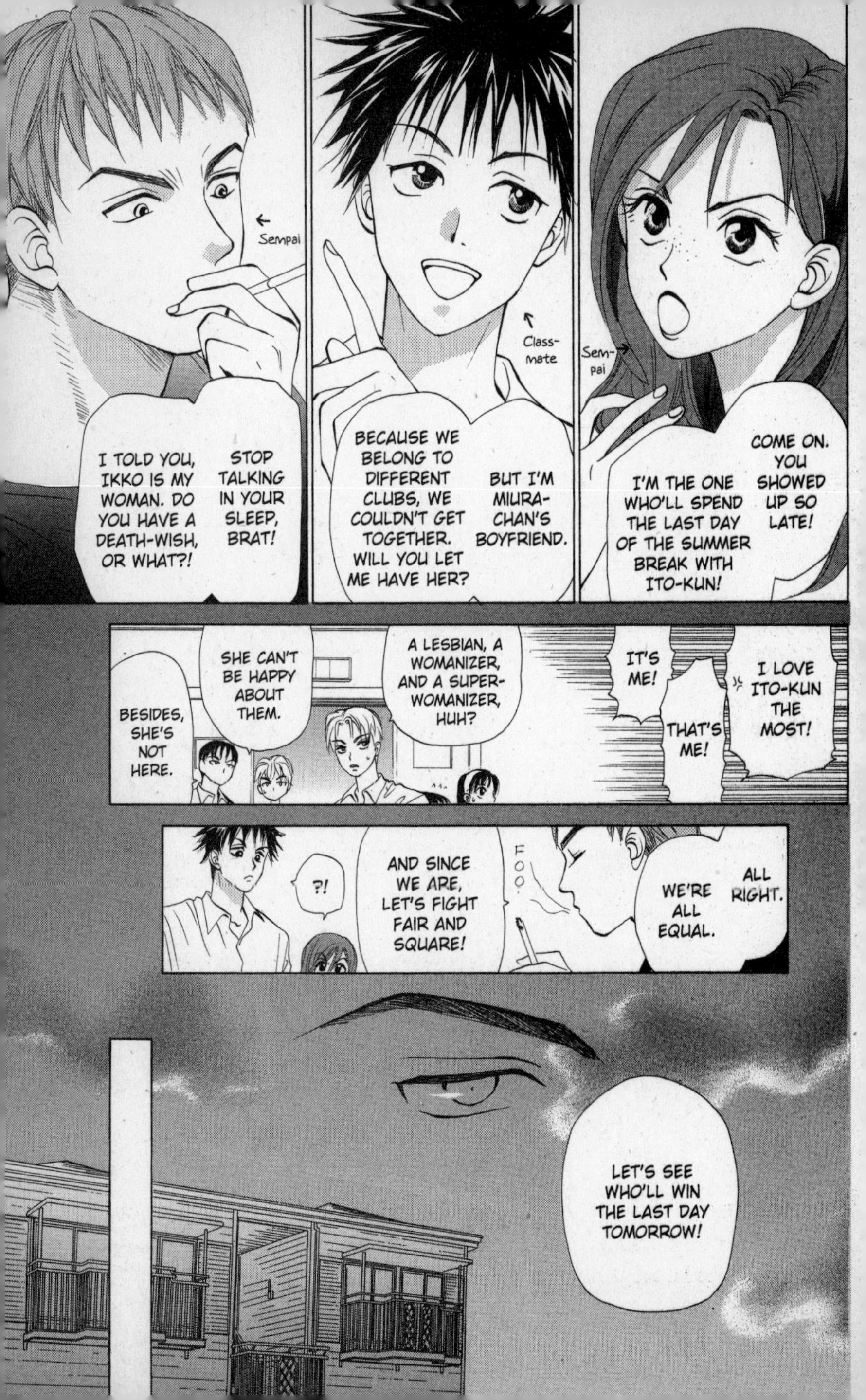
Sem-pai
COME ON. YOU SHOWED UP SO LATE!
I'M THE ONE WHO'LL SPEND THE LAST DAY OF THE SUMMER BREAK WITH ITO-KUN!
Class-mate
BUT I'M MIURA-CHAN'S BOYFRIEND.
BECAUSE WE BELONG TO DIFFERENT CLUBS, WE COULDN'T GET TOGETHER. WILL YOU LET ME HAVE HER?
Sempai
STOP TALKING IN YOUR SLEEP, BRAT!
I TOLD YOU, IKKO IS MY WOMAN. DO YOU HAVE A DEATH-WISH, OR WHAT?!
I LOVE ITO-KUN THE MOST!
IT'S ME!
THAT'S ME!
A LESBIAN, A WOMANIZER, AND A SUPER-WOMANIZER, HUH?
SHE CAN'T BE HAPPY ABOUT THEM.
BESIDES, SHE'S NOT HERE.
ALL RIGHT.
WE'RE ALL EQUAL.
FOO
AND SINCE WE ARE, LET'S FIGHT FAIR AND SQUARE!
?!
LET'S SEE WHO'LL WIN THE LAST DAY TOMORROW!

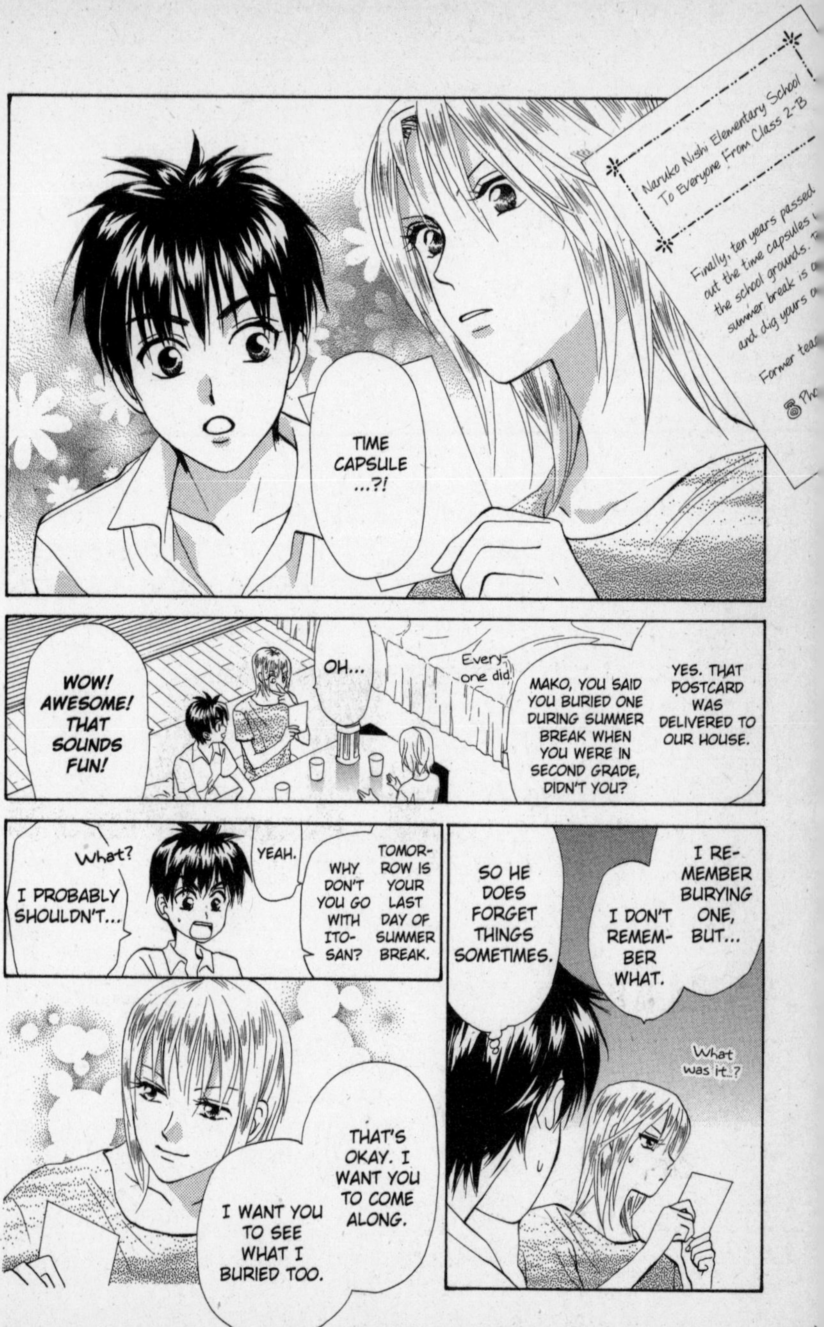
Naruko Nishi Elementary School
To Everyone From Class 2-B
Finally, ten years passed.
out the time capsules
the school grounds.
summer break is
and dig yours
TIME CAPSULE ...?!
YES. THAT POSTCARD WAS DELIVERED TO OUR HOUSE.
MAKO, YOU SAID YOU BURIED ONE DURING SUMMER BREAK WHEN YOU WERE IN SECOND GRADE, DIDN'T YOU?
Every-one did.
OH...
WOW! AWESOME! THAT SOUNDS FUN!
I RE-MEMBER BURYING ONE, BUT...
I DON'T REMEM-BER WHAT.
SO HE DOES FORGET THINGS SOMETIMES.
What was it..?
TOMOR-ROW IS YOUR LAST DAY OF SUMMER BREAK.
WHY DON'T YOU GO WITH ITO-SAN?
YEAH.
What?
I PROBABLY SHOULDN'T...
THAT'S OKAY. I WANT YOU TO COME ALONG.
I WANT YOU TO SEE WHAT I BURIED TOO.

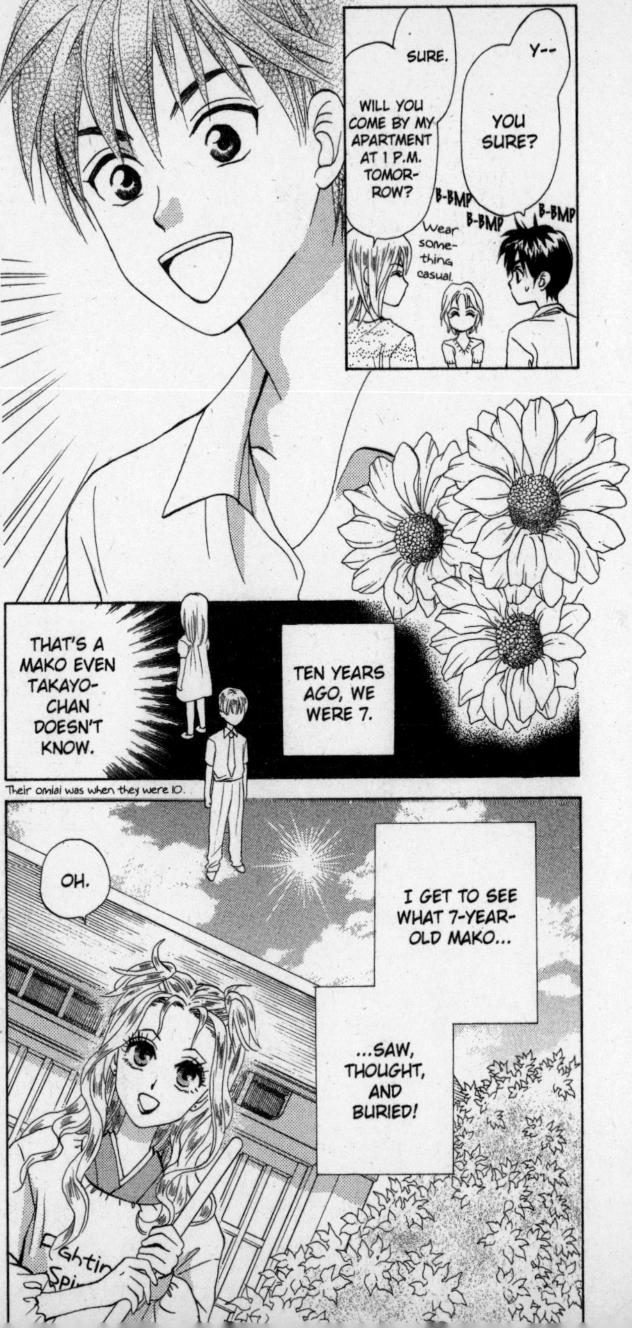
Y--
YOU SURE?
SURE.
WILL YOU COME BY MY APARTMENT AT 1 P.M. TOMOR-ROW?
B-BMP
B-BMP
B-BMP
Wear some-thing casual.
TEN YEARS AGO, WE WERE 7.
THAT'S A MAKO EVEN TAKAYO-CHAN DOESN'T KNOW.
I GET TO SEE WHAT 7-YEAR-OLD MAKO...
OH.
...SAW, THOUGHT, AND BURIED!
Their omiai was when they were 10.

Well, my sister has never drawn a manga since she was born. Not even an illustration. I mean, she says, it's not that "she doesn't draw" but that "she can't draw." She says she can copy, but it's impossible for her to draw original pictures and create stories on her own. But as an assistant, she's excellent.
(I think so anyway)

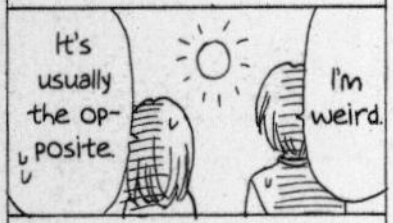
I'm weird.
It's usually the op-posite.

So I asked her to copy Ito for me. What do you think?

Special presentation (Laugh)

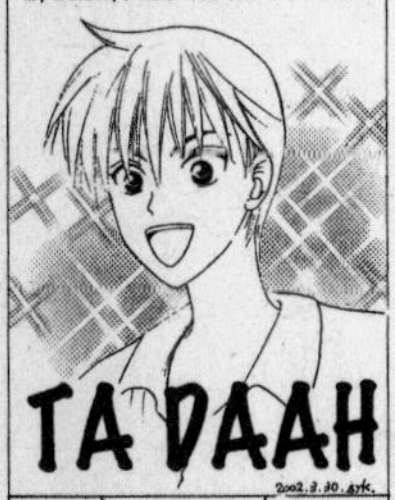
TA DAAH

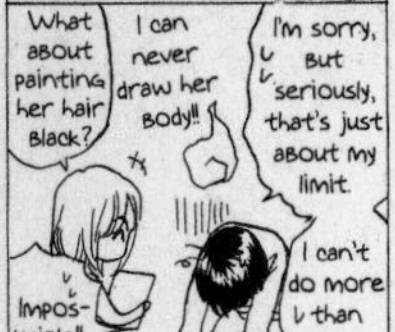
I'm sorry, but seriously, that's just about my limit.
I can never draw her body!!
What about painting her hair black?
I can't do more than this.
Impos-sible!!

Anyhow, I count on you, Sis.

Hey, she's done a good job drawing!

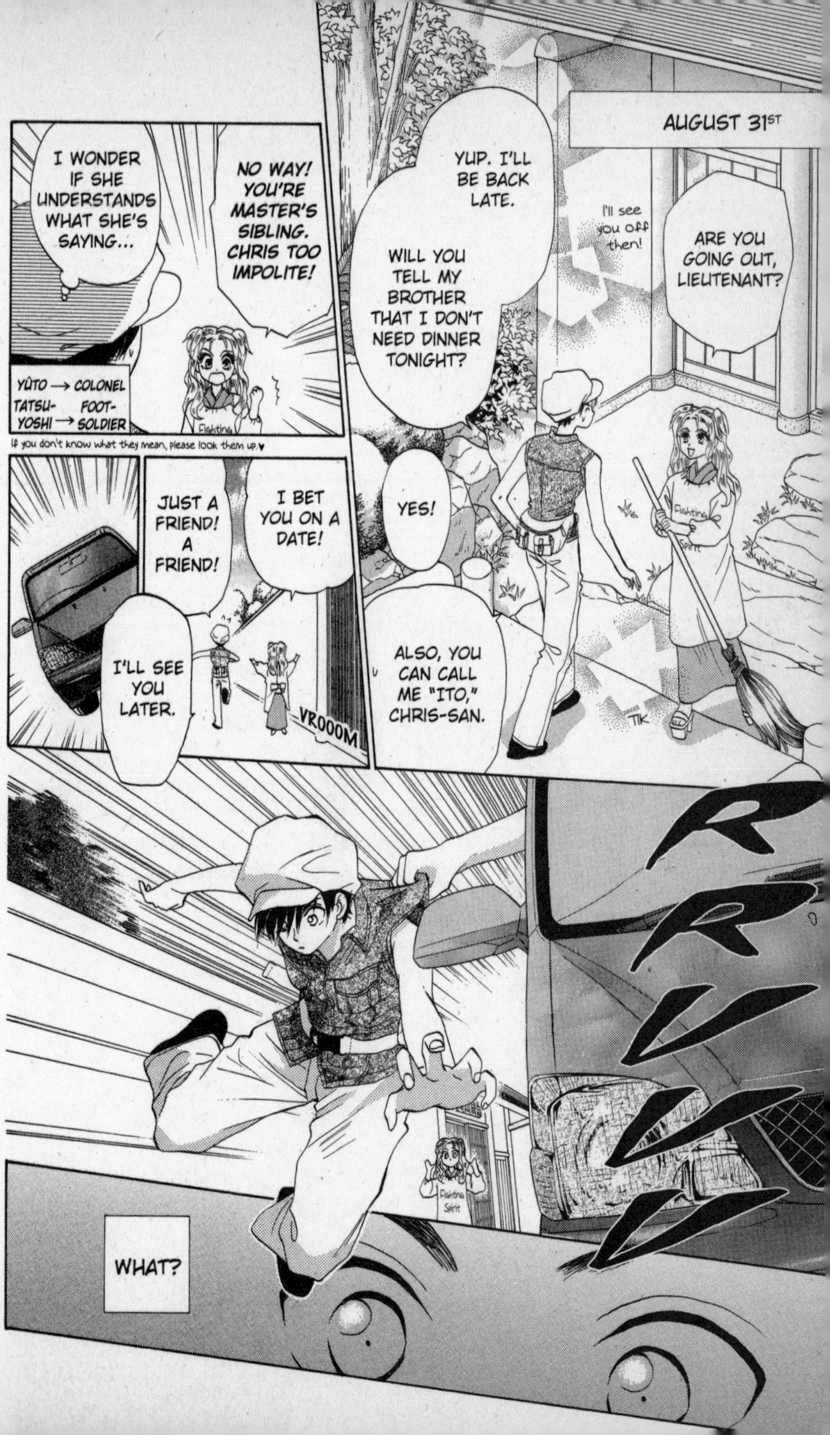
AUGUST 31ST
ARE YOU GOING OUT, LIEUTENANT?
I'll see you off then!
YUP. I'LL BE BACK LATE.
WILL YOU TELL MY BROTHER THAT I DON'T NEED DINNER TONIGHT?
YES!
ALSO, YOU CAN CALL ME "ITO," CHRIS-SAN.
TIK
Fighting Spirit
NO WAY! YOU'RE MASTER'S SIBLING. CHRIS TOO IMPOLITE!
I WONDER IF SHE UNDERSTANDS WHAT SHE'S SAYING...
YÛTO → COLONEL
TATSUYOSHI → FOOT-SOLDIER
Fighting
If you don't know what they mean, please look them up.♥
I BET YOU ON A DATE!
JUST A FRIEND! A FRIEND!
I'LL SEE YOU LATER.
VROOOM
WHAT?
Fighting Spirit

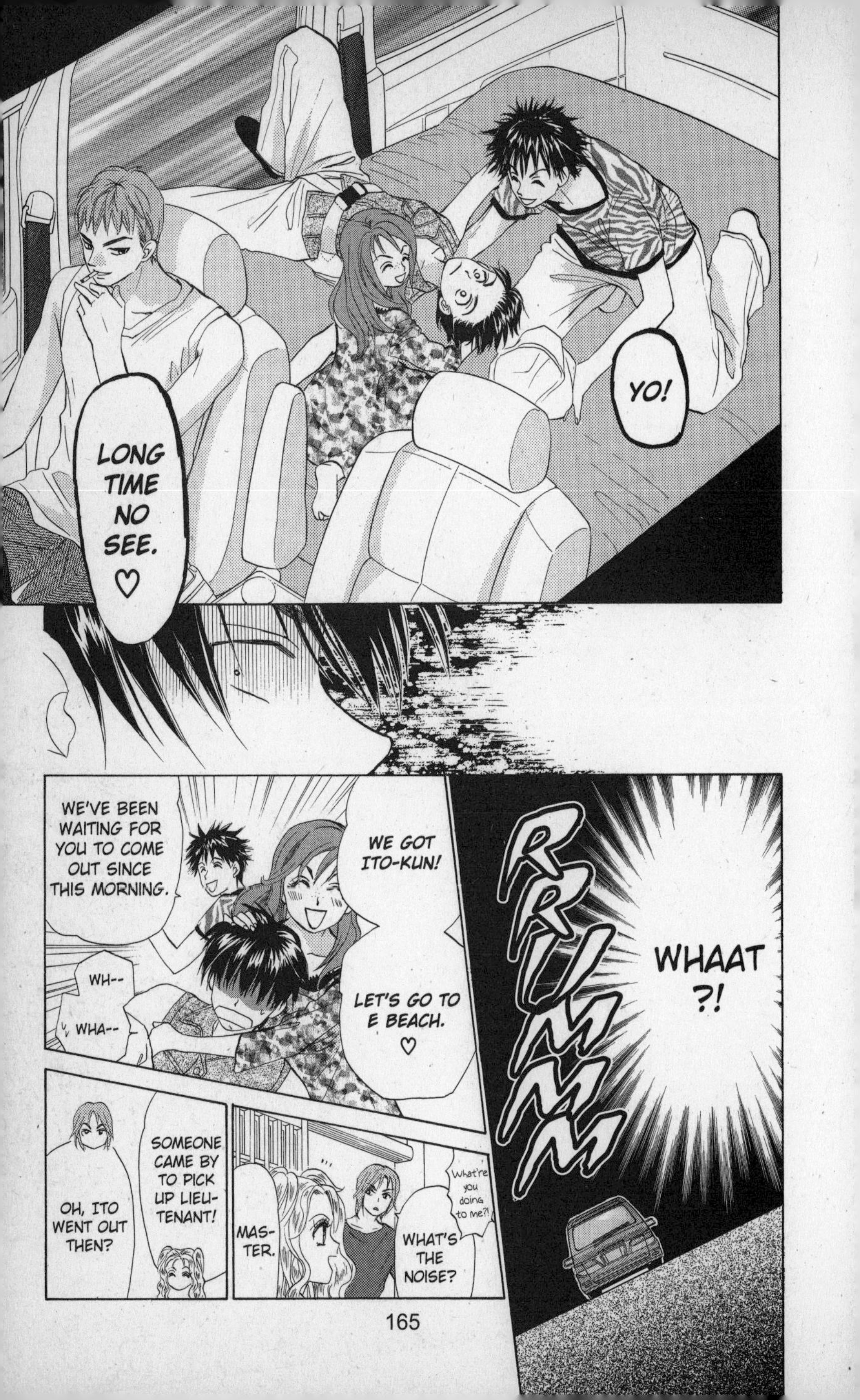
YO!
LONG TIME NO SEE. ♡
RRUMMM
WHAAT ?!
WE GOT ITO-KUN!
WE'VE BEEN WAITING FOR YOU TO COME OUT SINCE THIS MORNING.
LET'S GO TO E BEACH. ♡
WH--
WHA--
What're you doing to me?!
WHAT'S THE NOISE?
MASTER.
SOMEONE CAME BY TO PICK UP LIEUTENANT!
OH, ITO WENT OUT THEN?

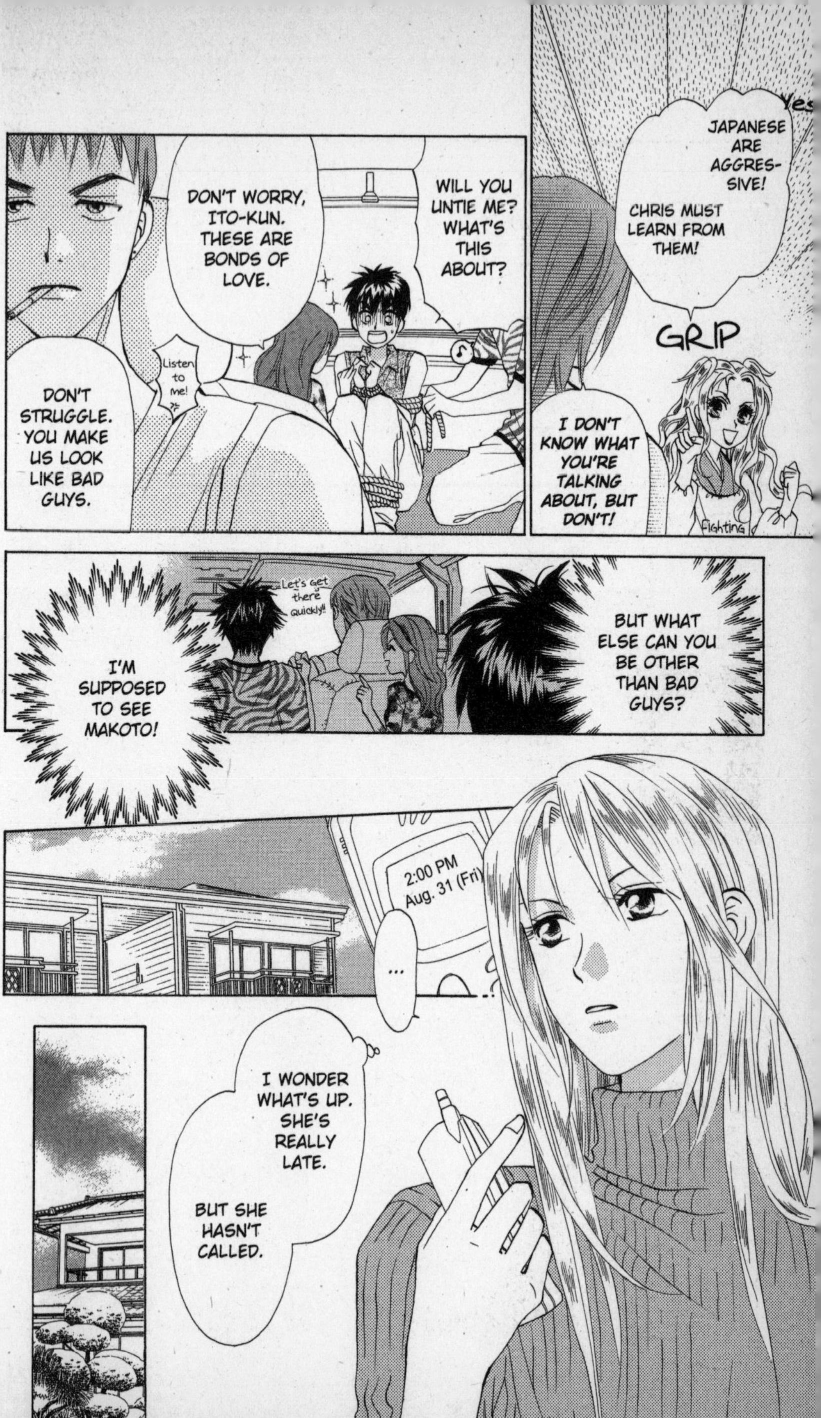
Yes
JAPANESE ARE AGGRES-SIVE!
CHRIS MUST LEARN FROM THEM!
GRIP
I DON'T KNOW WHAT YOU'RE TALKING ABOUT, BUT DON'T!
Fighting
WILL YOU UNTIE ME? WHAT'S THIS ABOUT?
DON'T WORRY, ITO-KUN. THESE ARE BONDS OF LOVE.
Listen to me!
DON'T STRUGGLE. YOU MAKE US LOOK LIKE BAD GUYS.
BUT WHAT ELSE CAN YOU BE OTHER THAN BAD GUYS?
Let's Get there Quickly!!
I'M SUPPOSED TO SEE MAKOTO!
2:00 PM
Aug. 31 (Fri)
...
I WONDER WHAT'S UP. SHE'S REALLY LATE.
BUT SHE HASN'T CALLED.

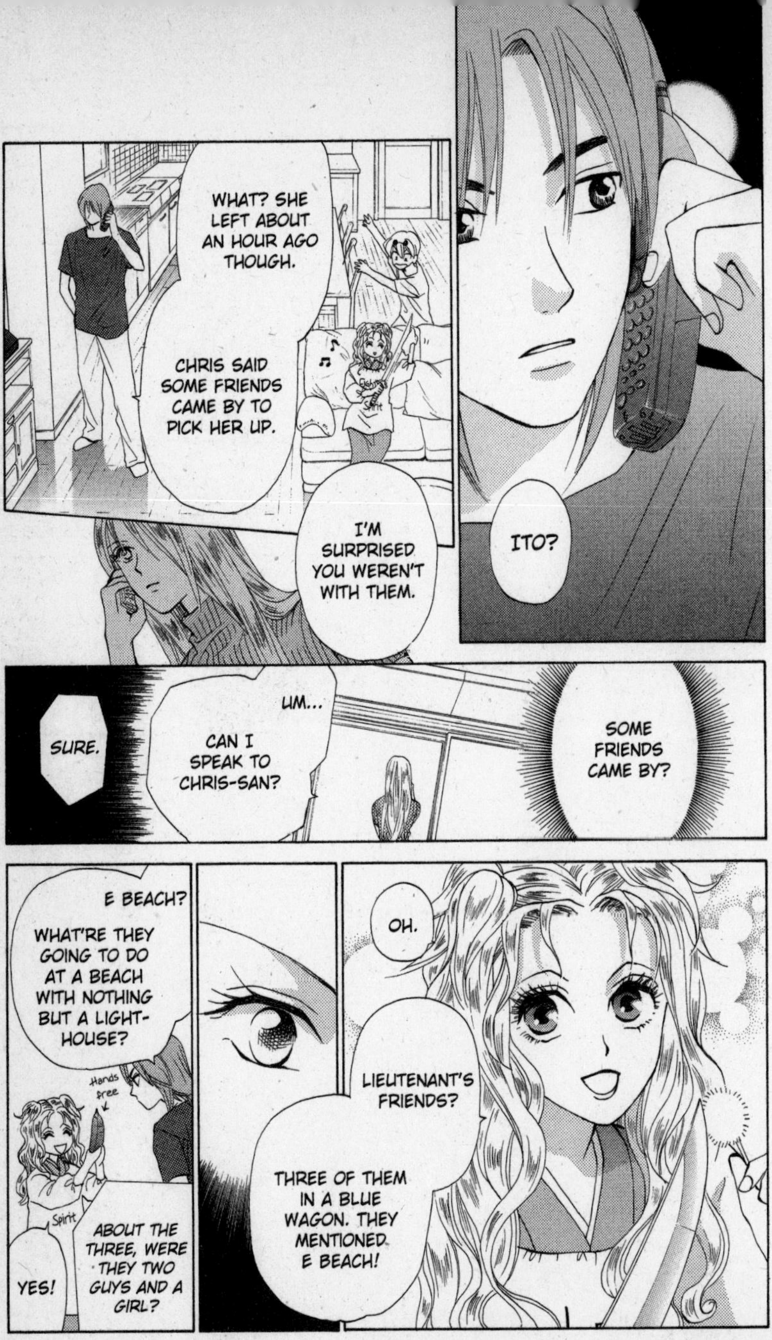
ITO?
WHAT? SHE LEFT ABOUT AN HOUR AGO THOUGH.
CHRIS SAID SOME FRIENDS CAME BY TO PICK HER UP.
I'M SURPRISED YOU WEREN'T WITH THEM.
SOME FRIENDS CAME BY?
UM... CAN I SPEAK TO CHRIS-SAN?
SURE.
OH.
LIEUTENANT'S FRIENDS?
THREE OF THEM IN A BLUE WAGON. THEY MENTIONED E BEACH!
E BEACH? WHAT'RE THEY GOING TO DO AT A BEACH WITH NOTHING BUT A LIGHT-HOUSE?
Hands free
Spirit
ABOUT THE THREE, WERE THEY TWO GUYS AND A GIRL?
YES!

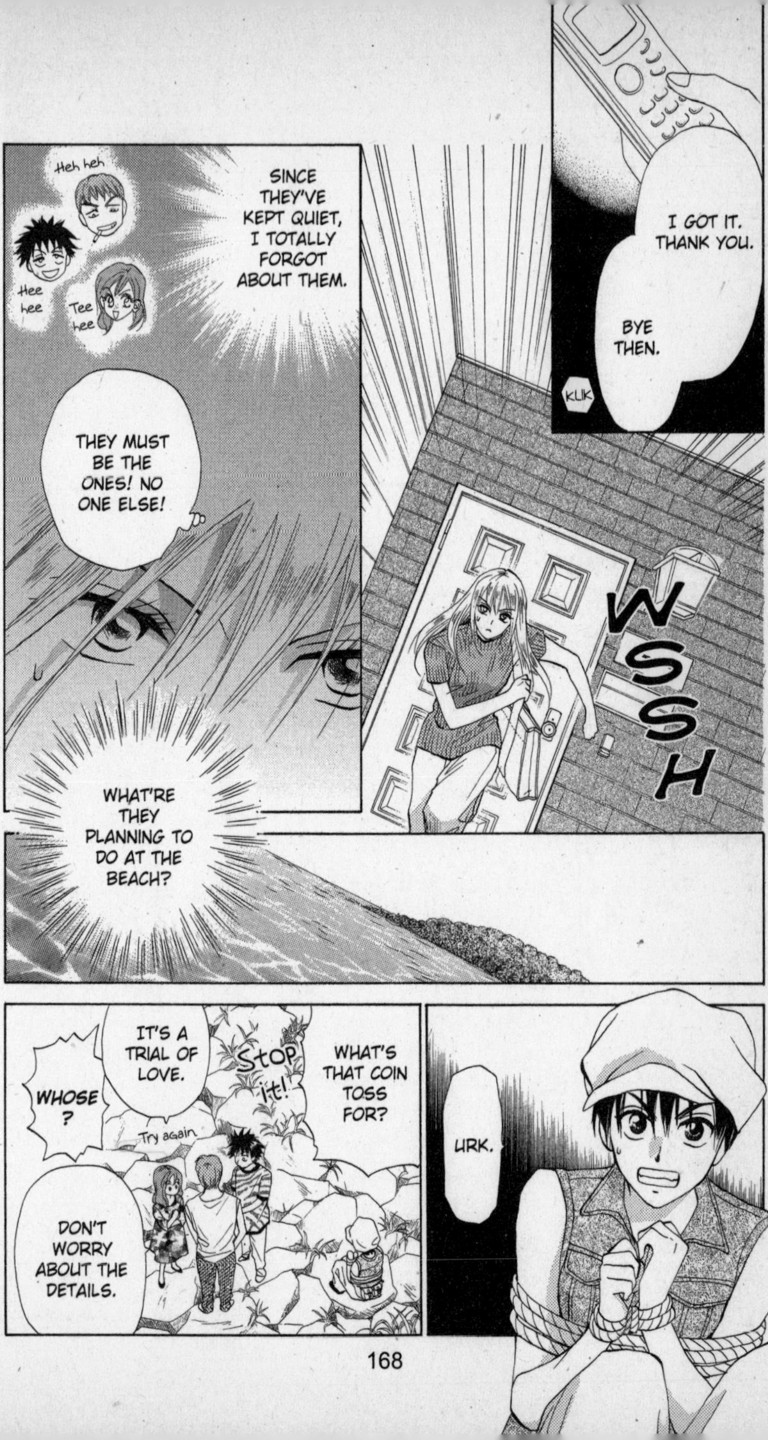
I GOT IT. THANK YOU.
BYE THEN.
KLIK
WSSH
SINCE THEY'VE KEPT QUIET, I TOTALLY FORGOT ABOUT THEM.
Heh heh
Hee hee
Tee hee
THEY MUST BE THE ONES! NO ONE ELSE!
WHAT'RE THEY PLANNING TO DO AT THE BEACH?
URK.
WHAT'S THAT COIN TOSS FOR?
Stop it!
IT'S A TRIAL OF LOVE.
WHOSE?
Try again.
DON'T WORRY ABOUT THE DETAILS.

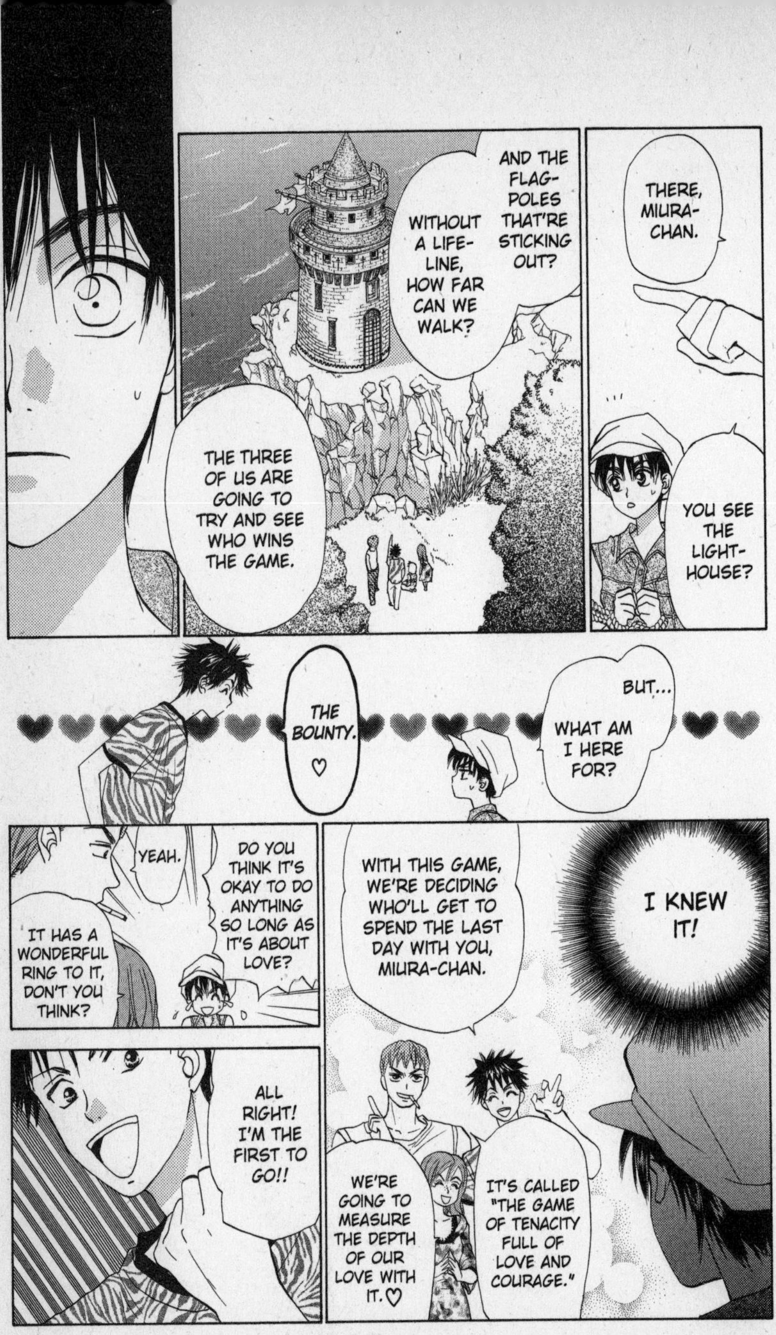
THERE, MIURA-CHAN.
YOU SEE THE LIGHT-HOUSE?
WITHOUT A LIFE-LINE, HOW FAR CAN WE WALK?
AND THE FLAG-POLES THAT'RE STICKING OUT?
THE THREE OF US ARE GOING TO TRY AND SEE WHO WINS THE GAME.
BUT...
WHAT AM I HERE FOR?
THE BOUNTY. ♡
I KNEW IT!
WITH THIS GAME, WE'RE DECIDING WHO'LL GET TO SPEND THE LAST DAY WITH YOU, MIURA-CHAN.
IT'S CALLED "THE GAME OF TENACITY FULL OF LOVE AND COURAGE."
WE'RE GOING TO MEASURE THE DEPTH OF OUR LOVE WITH IT. ♡
DO YOU THINK IT'S OKAY TO DO ANYTHING SO LONG AS IT'S ABOUT LOVE?
YEAH.
IT HAS A WONDERFUL RING TO IT, DON'T YOU THINK?
ALL RIGHT! I'M THE FIRST TO GO!!

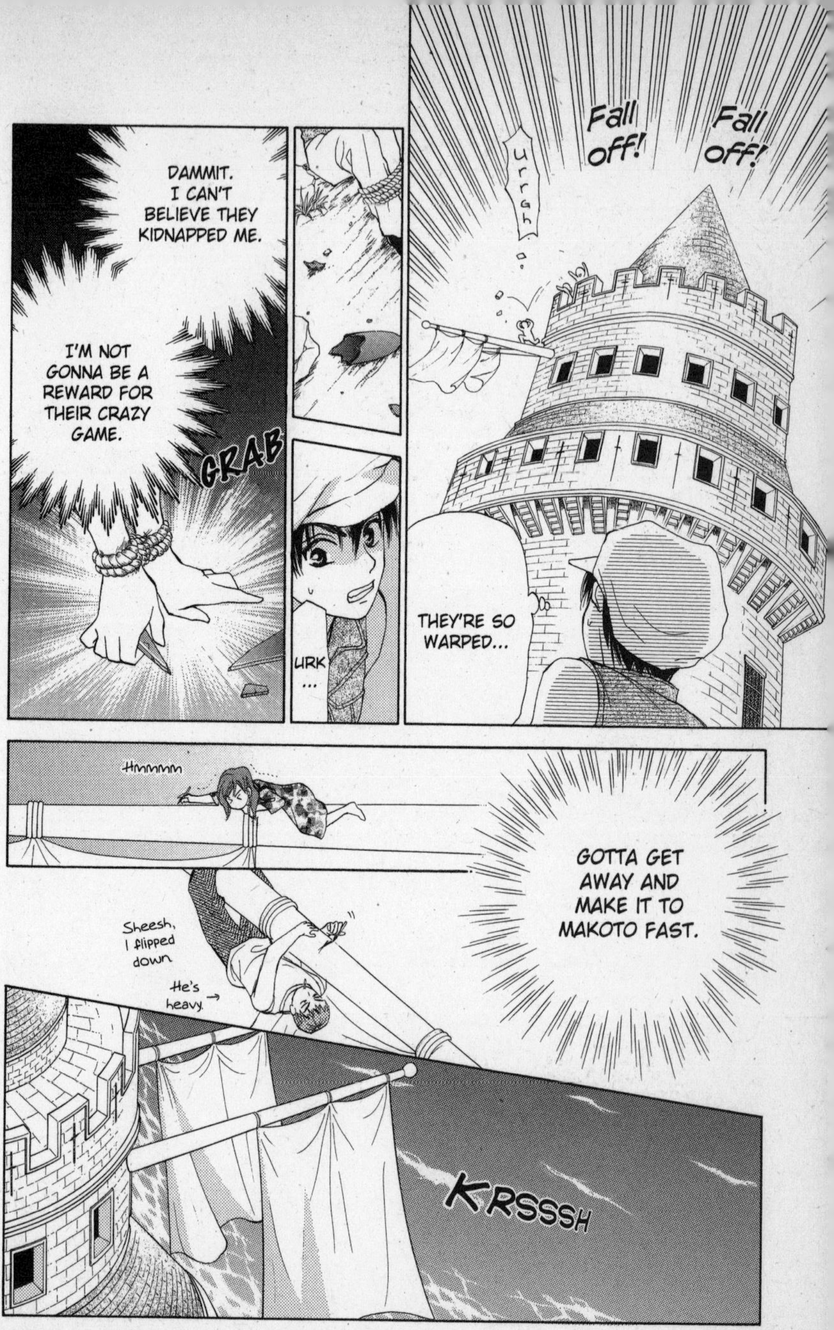
Urrgh
Fall off!
Fall off!
THEY'RE SO WARPED...
URK ...
DAMMIT. I CAN'T BELIEVE THEY KIDNAPPED ME.
I'M NOT GONNA BE A REWARD FOR THEIR CRAZY GAME.
GRAB
GOTTA GET AWAY AND MAKE IT TO MAKOTO FAST.
Hmmmm
Sheesh, I flipped down
He's heavy.
KRSSSH

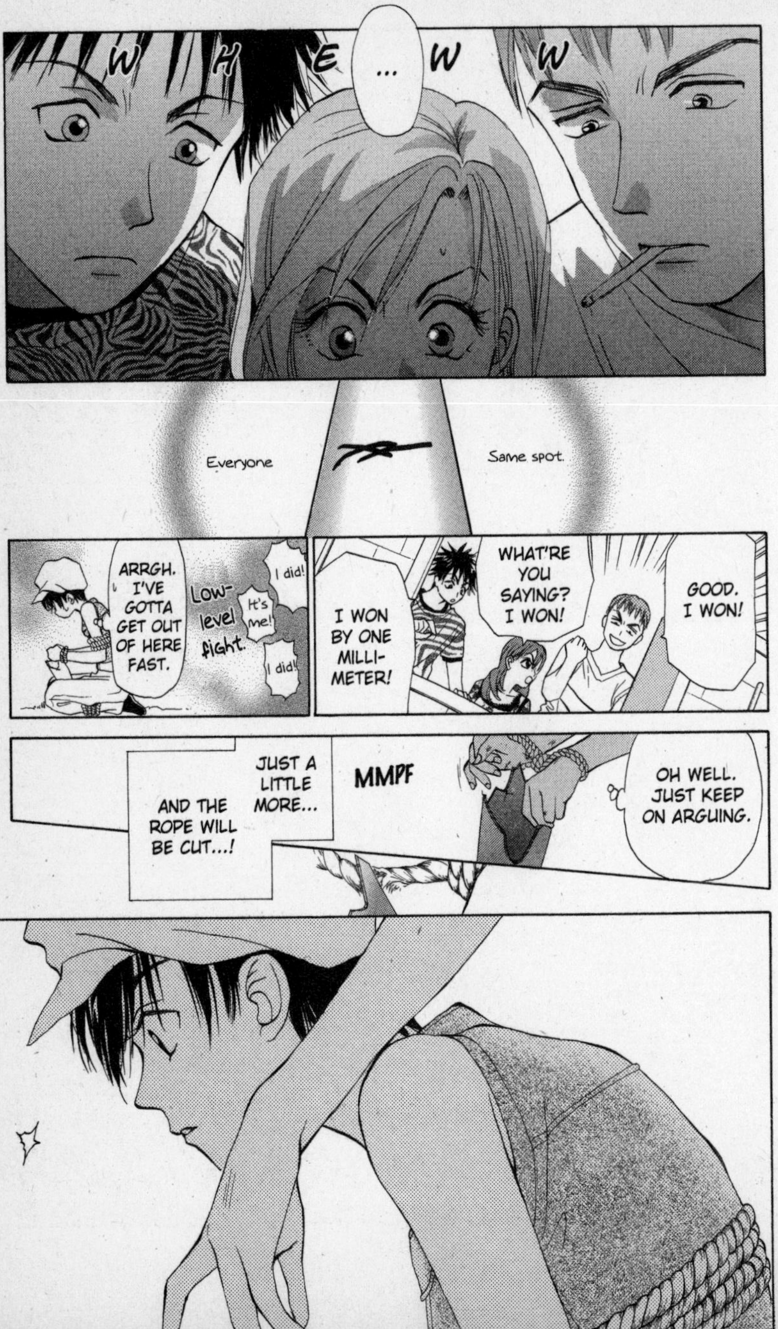
W H E W W
...
Same spot.
Everyone
GOOD. I WON!
WHAT'RE YOU SAYING? I WON!
I WON BY ONE MILLI-METER!
I did!
It's me!
I did!
Low-level fight.
ARRGH. I'VE GOTTA GET OUT OF HERE FAST.
OH WELL. JUST KEEP ON ARGUING.
MMPF
JUST A LITTLE MORE...
AND THE ROPE WILL BE CUT...!

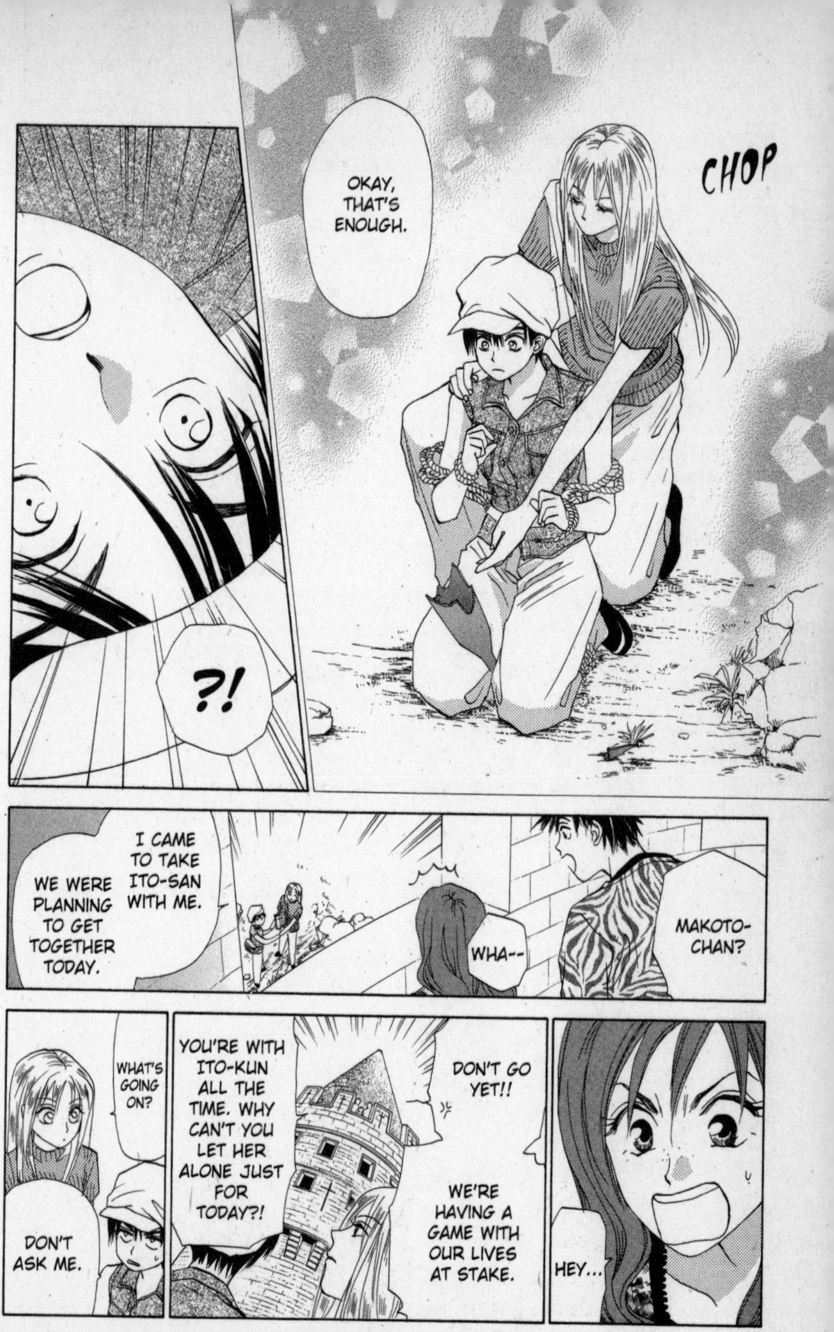

CHOP
OKAY, THAT'S ENOUGH.
?!
MAKOTO-CHAN?
WHA--
I CAME TO TAKE ITO-SAN WITH ME.
WE WERE PLANNING TO GET TOGETHER TODAY.
HEY...
DON'T GO YET!!
WE'RE HAVING A GAME WITH OUR LIVES AT STAKE.
YOU'RE WITH ITO-KUN ALL THE TIME. WHY CAN'T YOU LET HER ALONE JUST FOR TODAY?!
WHAT'S GOING ON?
DON'T ASK ME.

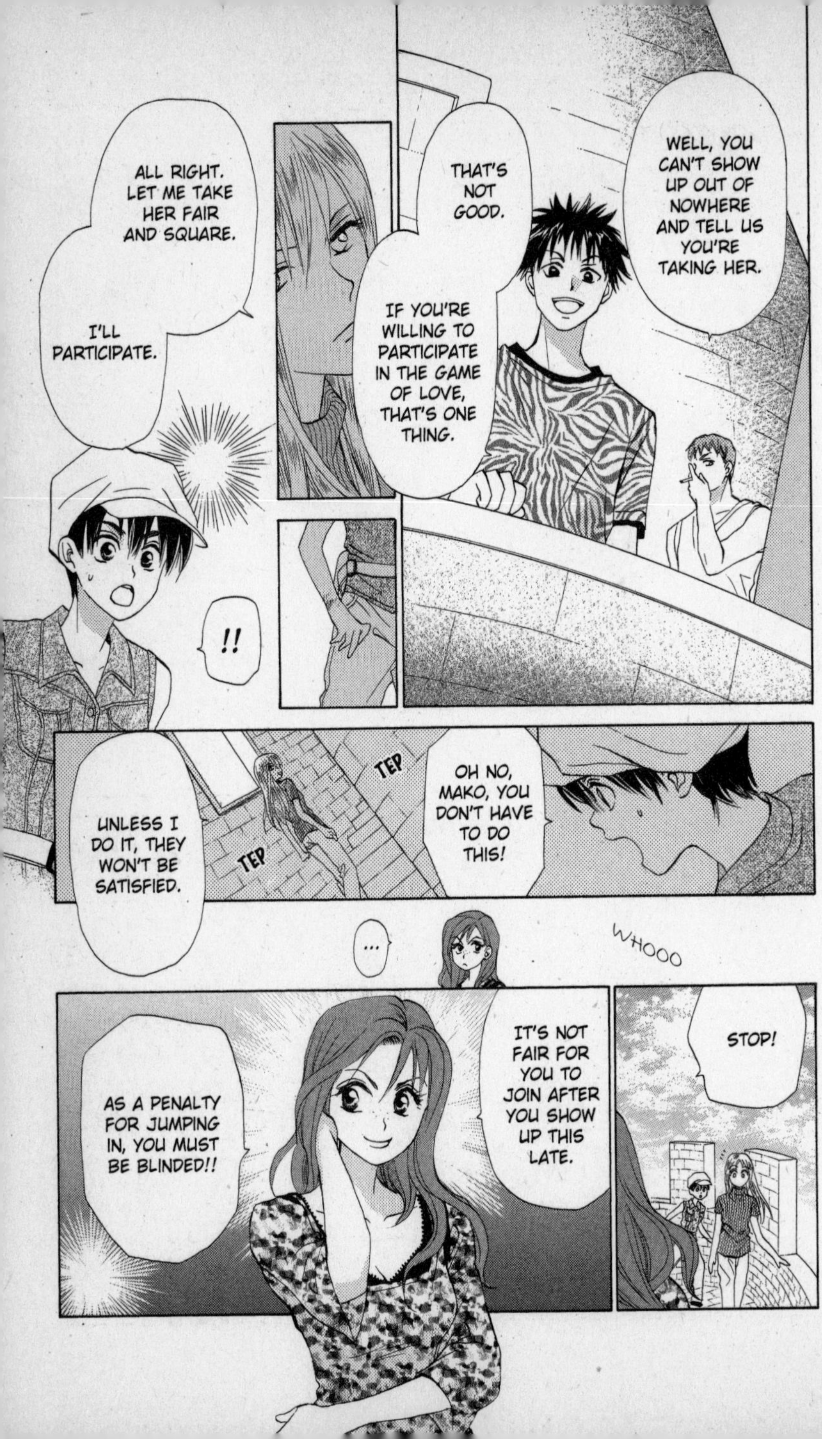
WELL, YOU CAN'T SHOW UP OUT OF NOWHERE AND TELL US YOU'RE TAKING HER.
THAT'S NOT GOOD.
IF YOU'RE WILLING TO PARTICIPATE IN THE GAME OF LOVE, THAT'S ONE THING.
ALL RIGHT. LET ME TAKE HER FAIR AND SQUARE.
I'LL PARTICIPATE.
!!
OH NO, MAKO, YOU DON'T HAVE TO DO THIS!
TEP
TEP
UNLESS I DO IT, THEY WON'T BE SATISFIED.
WHOOO
...
STOP!
IT'S NOT FAIR FOR YOU TO JOIN AFTER YOU SHOW UP THIS LATE.
AS A PENALTY FOR JUMPING IN, YOU MUST BE BLINDED!!

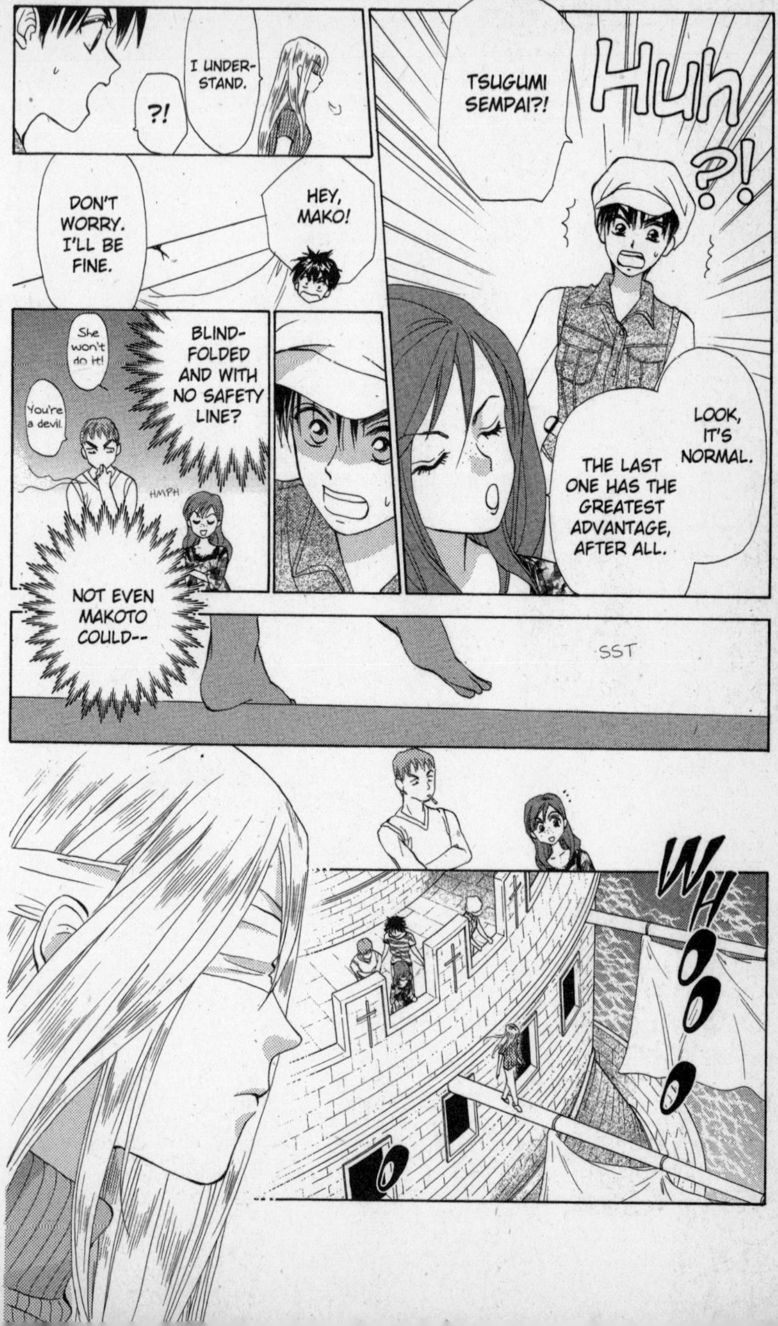
TSUGUMI SEMPAI?!
Huh ?!
LOOK, IT'S NORMAL.
THE LAST ONE HAS THE GREATEST ADVANTAGE, AFTER ALL.
I UNDER-STAND.
?!
HEY, MAKO!
DON'T WORRY. I'LL BE FINE.
BLIND-FOLDED AND WITH NO SAFETY LINE?
She won't do it!
You're a devil.
HMPH
NOT EVEN MAKOTO COULD--
SST
WHOOOO

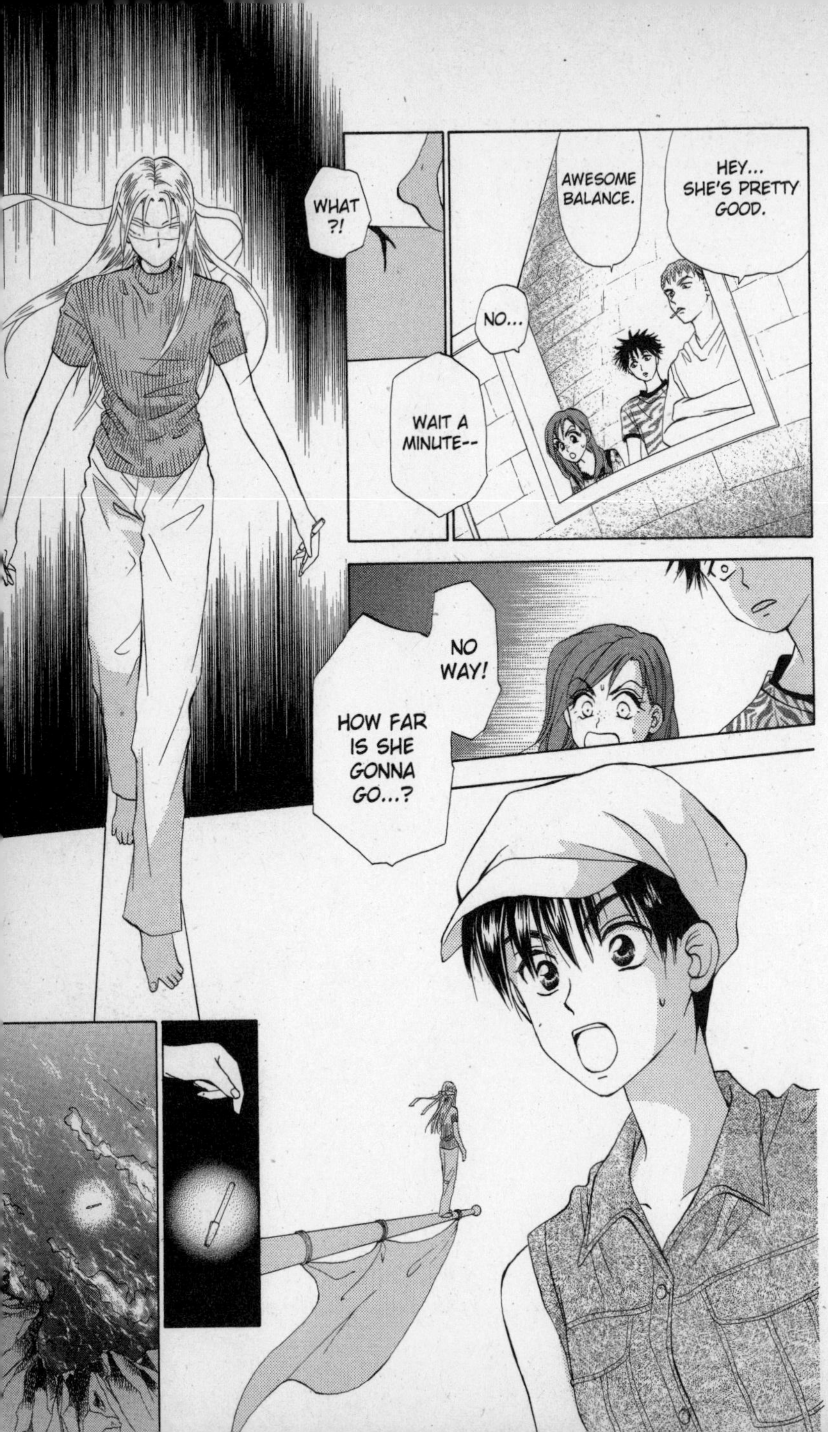
HEY... SHE'S PRETTY GOOD.
AWESOME BALANCE.
NO...
WAIT A MINUTE--
WHAT ?!
NO WAY!
HOW FAR IS SHE GONNA GO...?

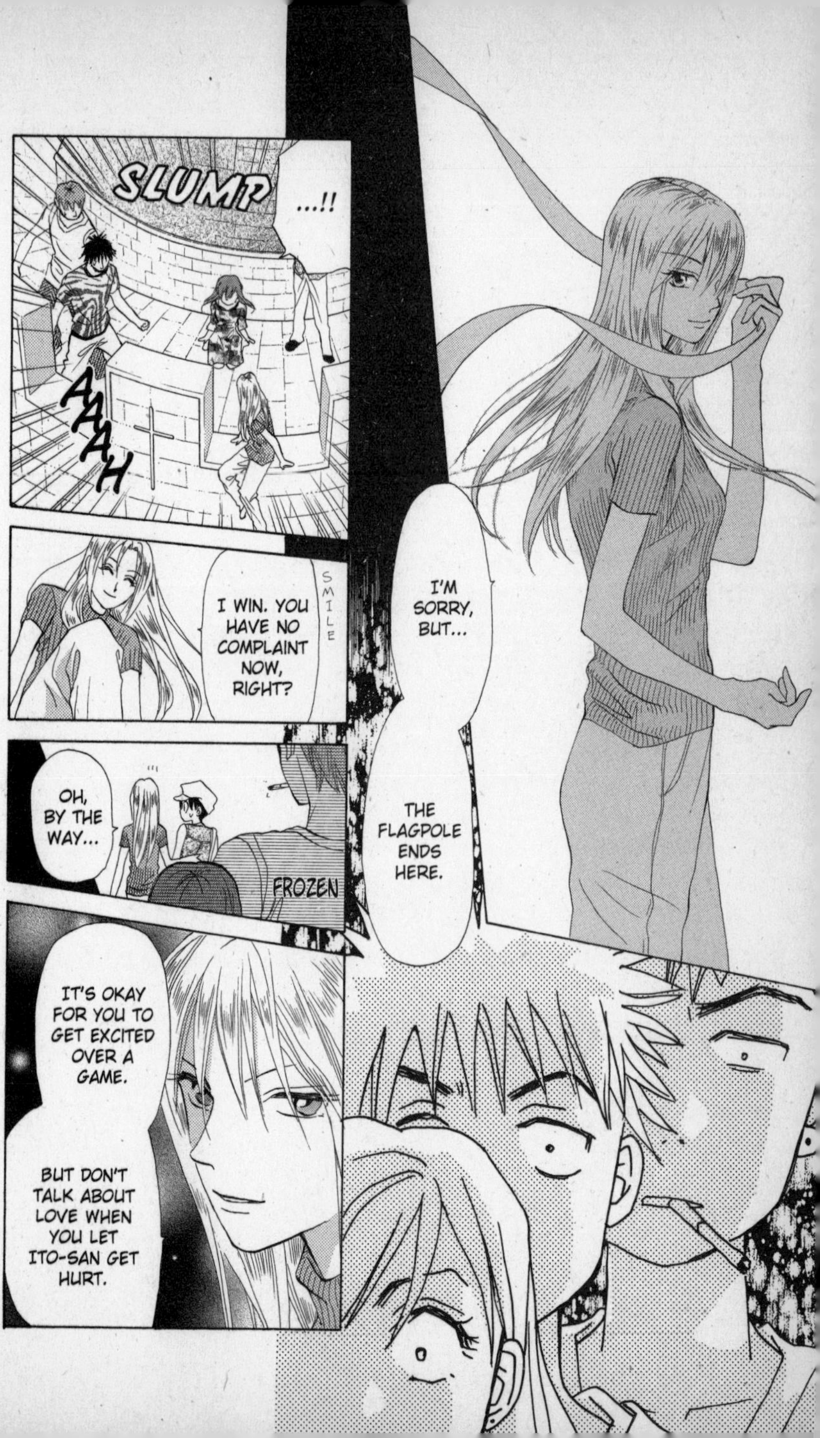
I'M SORRY, BUT...
THE FLAGPOLE ENDS HERE.
...!!
SLUMP
AAAH
SMILE
I WIN. YOU HAVE NO COMPLAINT NOW, RIGHT?
FROZEN
OH, BY THE WAY...
IT'S OKAY FOR YOU TO GET EXCITED OVER A GAME.
BUT DON'T TALK ABOUT LOVE WHEN YOU LET ITO-SAN GET HURT.

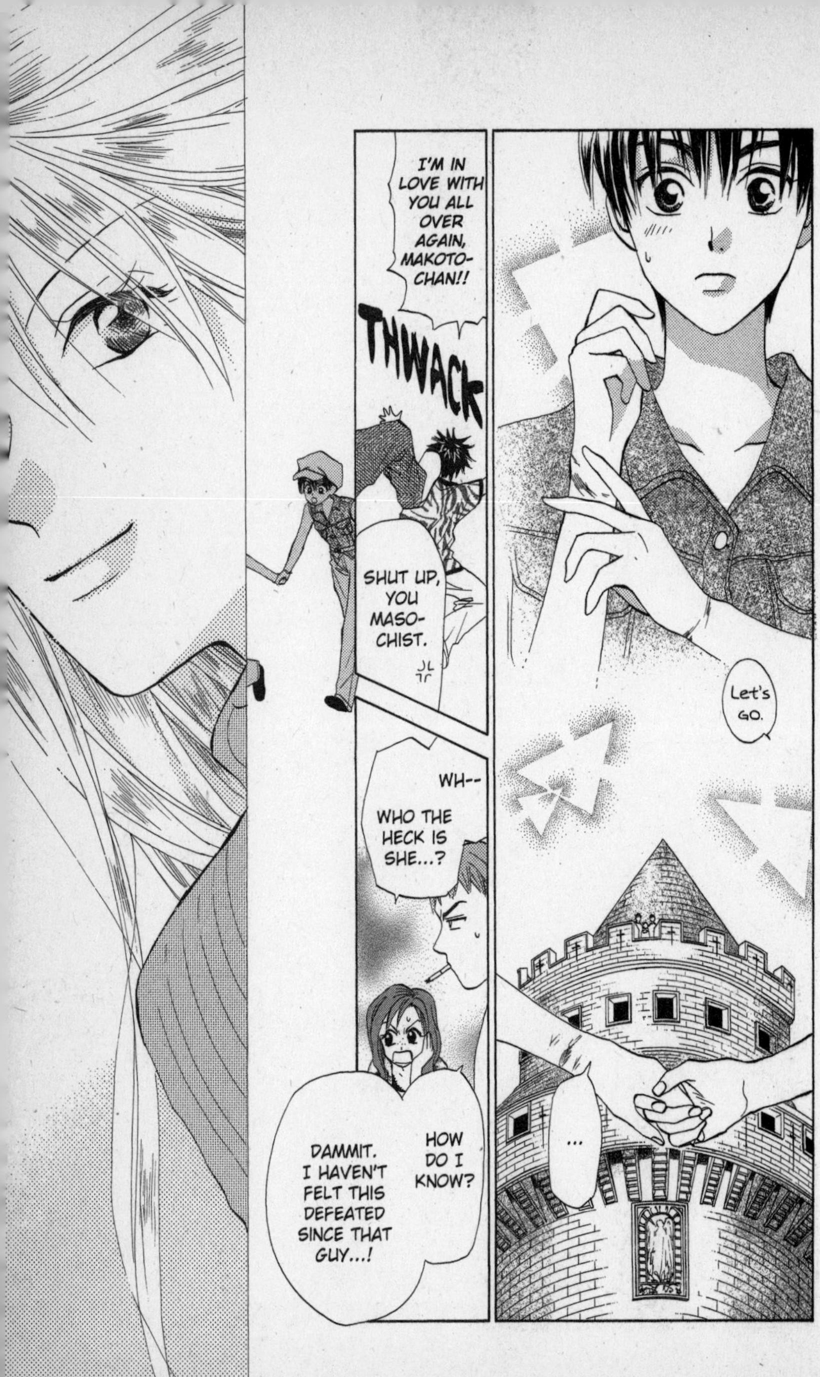
Let's GO.
...
I'M IN LOVE WITH YOU ALL OVER AGAIN, MAKOTO-CHAN!!
THWACK
SHUT UP, YOU MASO-CHIST.
WH--
WHO THE HECK IS SHE...?
HOW DO I KNOW?
DAMMIT. I HAVEN'T FELT THIS DEFEATED SINCE THAT GUY...!

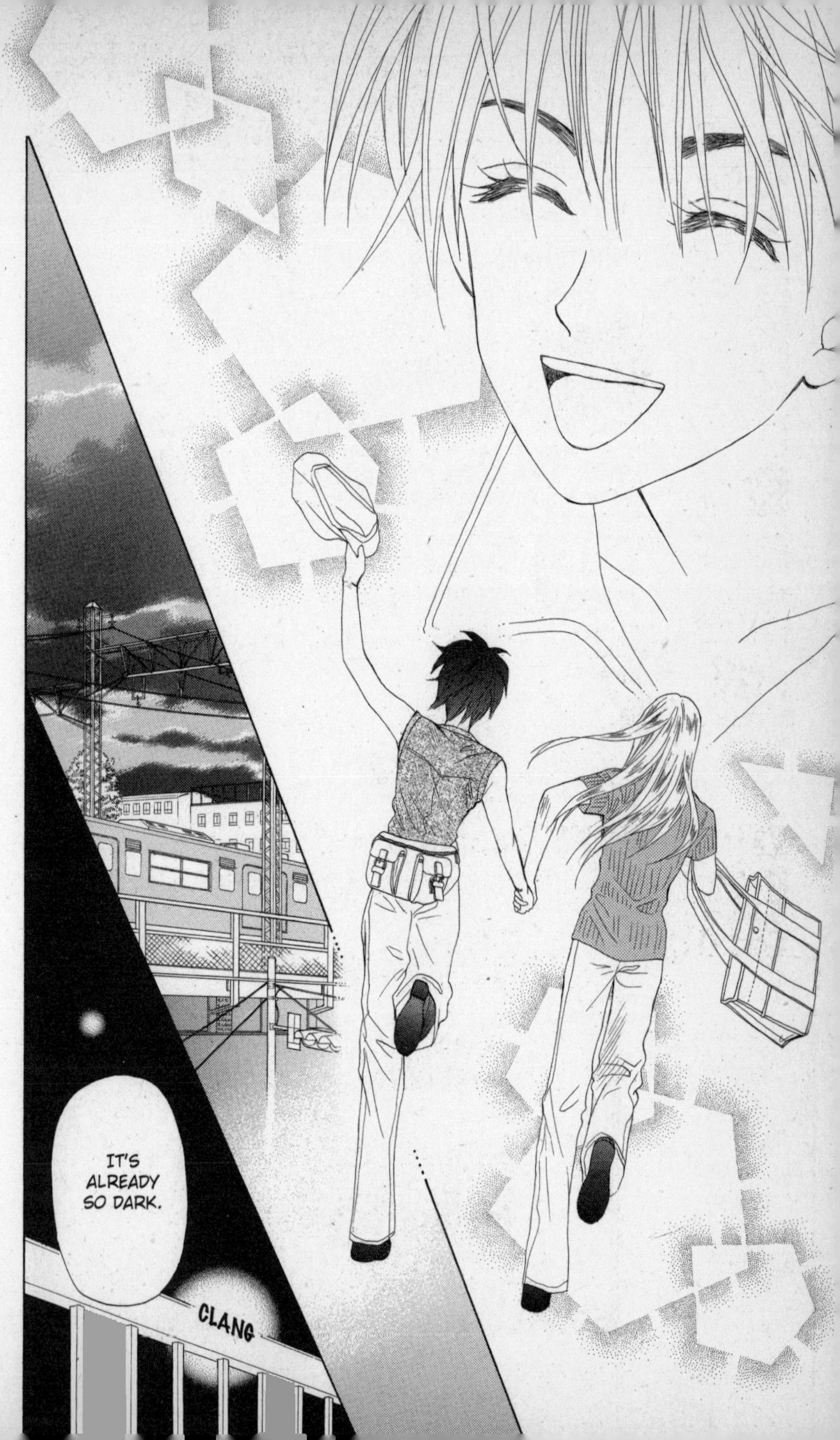
IT'S ALREADY SO DARK.
CLANG

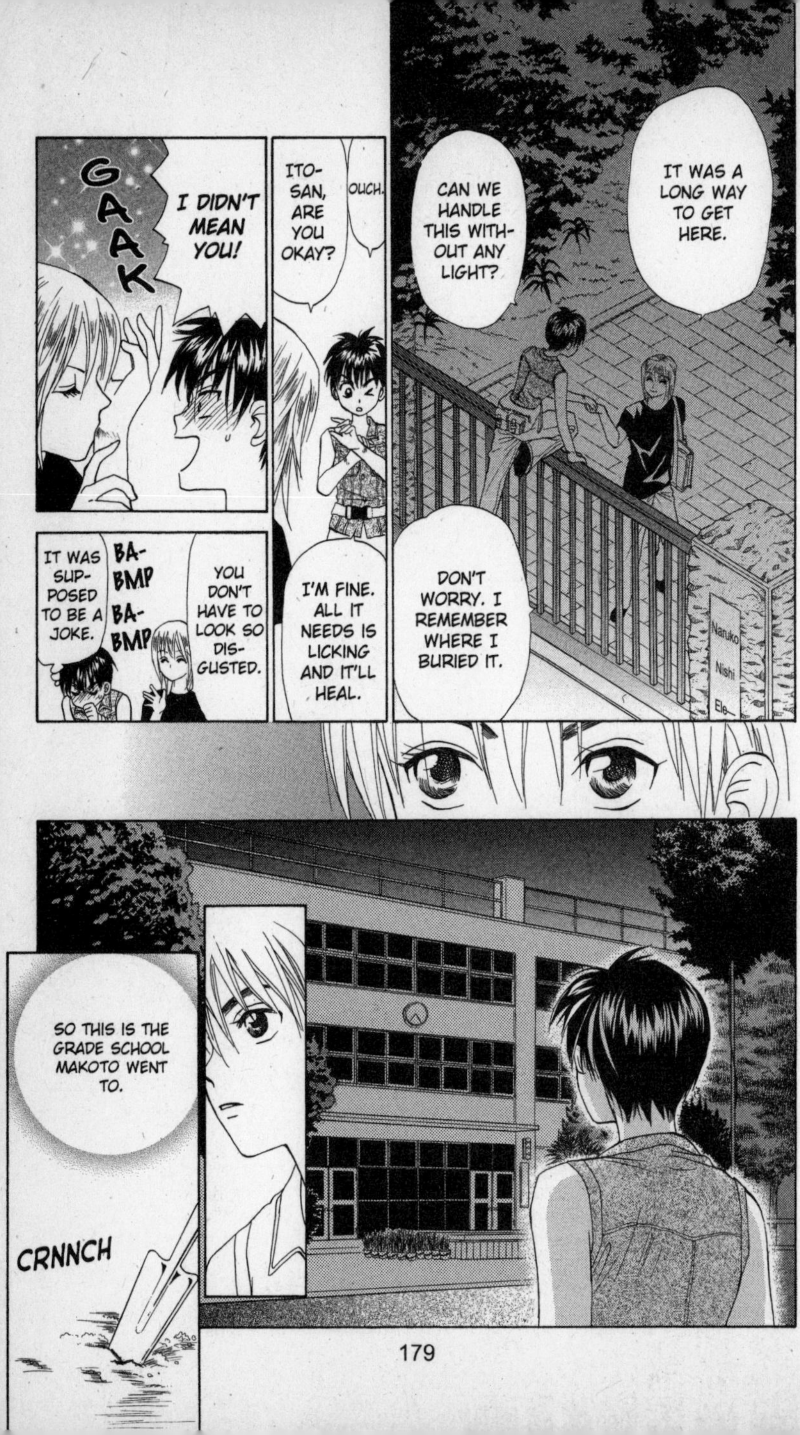
IT WAS A LONG WAY TO GET HERE.
CAN WE HANDLE THIS WITH-OUT ANY LIGHT?
DON'T WORRY. I REMEMBER WHERE I BURIED IT.
Naruko Nishi Ele—
OUCH.
ITO-SAN, ARE YOU OKAY?
I'M FINE. ALL IT NEEDS IS LICKING AND IT'LL HEAL.
I DIDN'T MEAN YOU!
GAAK
YOU DON'T HAVE TO LOOK SO DIS-GUSTED.
BA-BMP BA-BMP
IT WAS SUP-POSED TO BE A JOKE.
SO THIS IS THE GRADE SCHOOL MAKOTO WENT TO.
CRNNCH

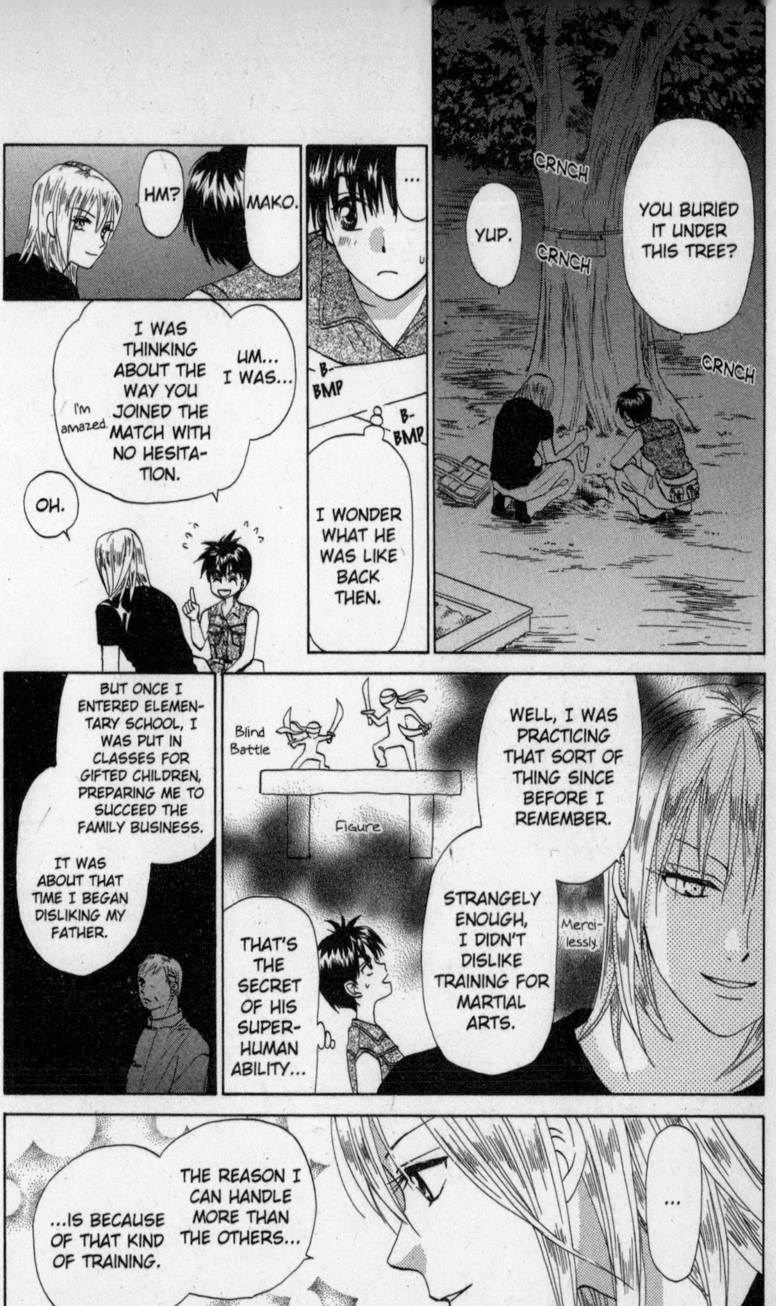
CRNCH
CRNCH
YOU BURIED IT UNDER THIS TREE?
YUP.
CRNCH
...
MAKO.
HM?
UM... I WAS...
B-BMP
B-BMP
I WAS THINKING ABOUT THE WAY YOU JOINED THE MATCH WITH NO HESITATION.
I'm amazed.
OH.
I WONDER WHAT HE WAS LIKE BACK THEN.
WELL, I WAS PRACTICING THAT SORT OF THING SINCE BEFORE I REMEMBER.
Blind Battle
Figure
STRANGELY ENOUGH, I DIDN'T DISLIKE TRAINING FOR MARTIAL ARTS.
Merci-lessly.
THAT'S THE SECRET OF HIS SUPER-HUMAN ABILITY...
BUT ONCE I ENTERED ELEMENTARY SCHOOL, I WAS PUT IN CLASSES FOR GIFTED CHILDREN, PREPARING ME TO SUCCEED THE FAMILY BUSINESS.
IT WAS ABOUT THAT TIME I BEGAN DISLIKING MY FATHER.
...
THE REASON I CAN HANDLE MORE THAN THE OTHERS...
...IS BECAUSE OF THAT KIND OF TRAINING.

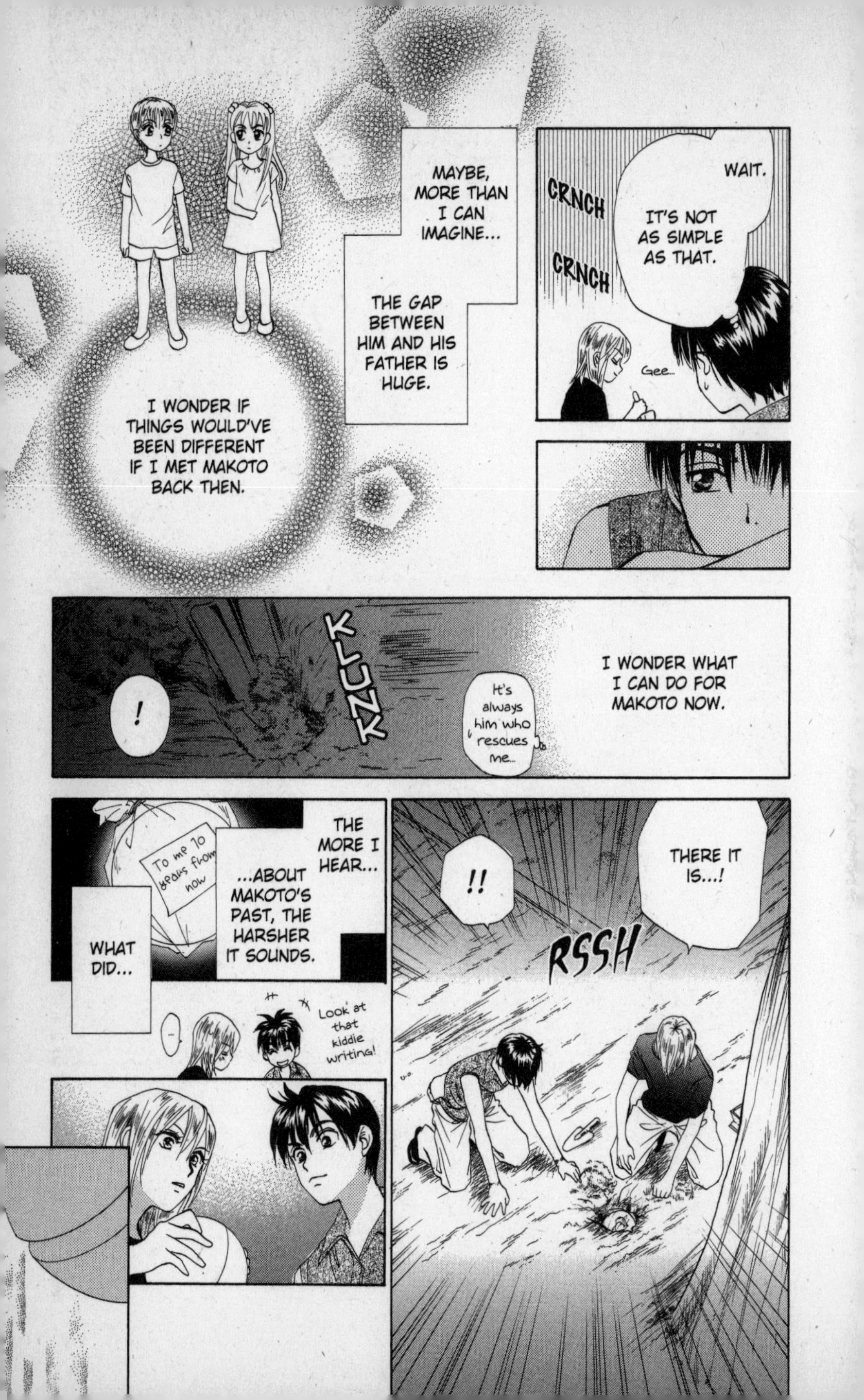
WAIT.
IT'S NOT AS SIMPLE AS THAT.
CRNCH
CRNCH
Gee...
MAYBE, MORE THAN I CAN IMAGINE...
THE GAP BETWEEN HIM AND HIS FATHER IS HUGE.
I WONDER IF THINGS WOULD'VE BEEN DIFFERENT IF I MET MAKOTO BACK THEN.
I WONDER WHAT I CAN DO FOR MAKOTO NOW.
It's always him who rescues me...
KLUNK
!
THERE IT IS...!
!!
RSSH
THE MORE I HEAR...
...ABOUT MAKOTO'S PAST, THE HARSHER IT SOUNDS.
To me 10 years from now
WHAT DID...
Look at that kiddie writing!
...

...MAKOTO LEAVE FOR HIS FUTURE SELF?

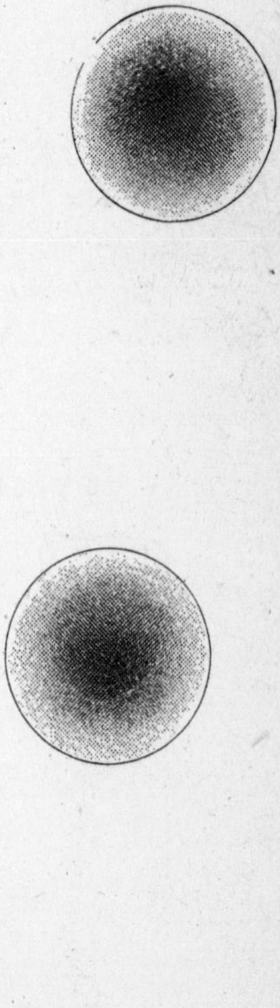

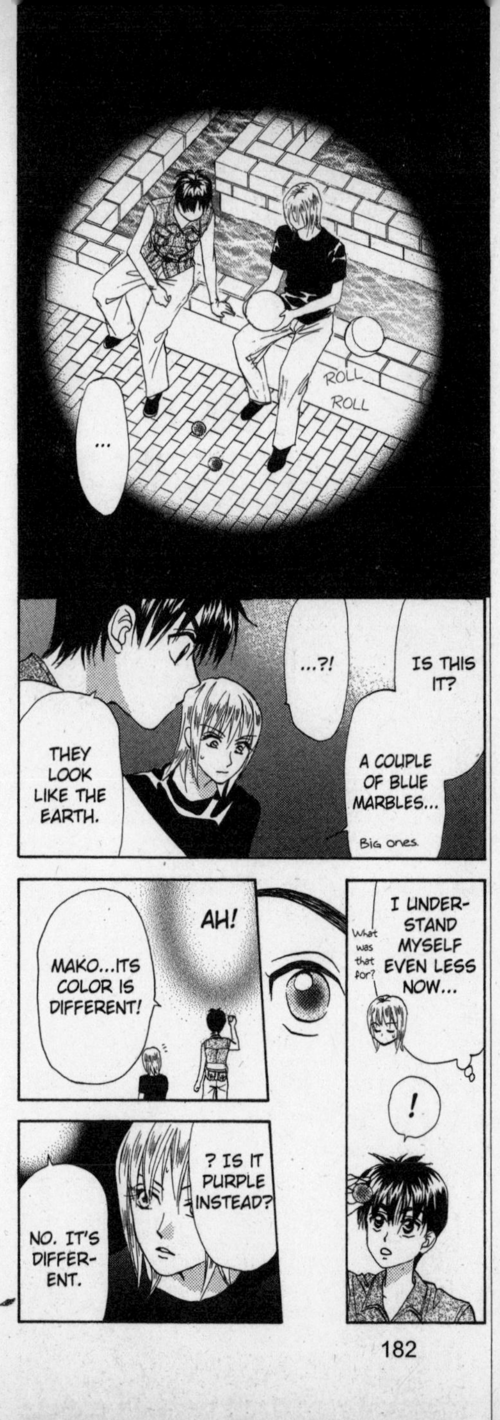
...
ROLL
ROLL
IS THIS IT?
...?!
A COUPLE OF BLUE MARBLES...
Big ones.
THEY LOOK LIKE THE EARTH.
I UNDERSTAND MYSELF EVEN LESS NOW...
What was that for?
!
AH!
MAKO...ITS COLOR IS DIFFERENT!
? IS IT PURPLE INSTEAD?
NO. IT'S DIFFERENT.

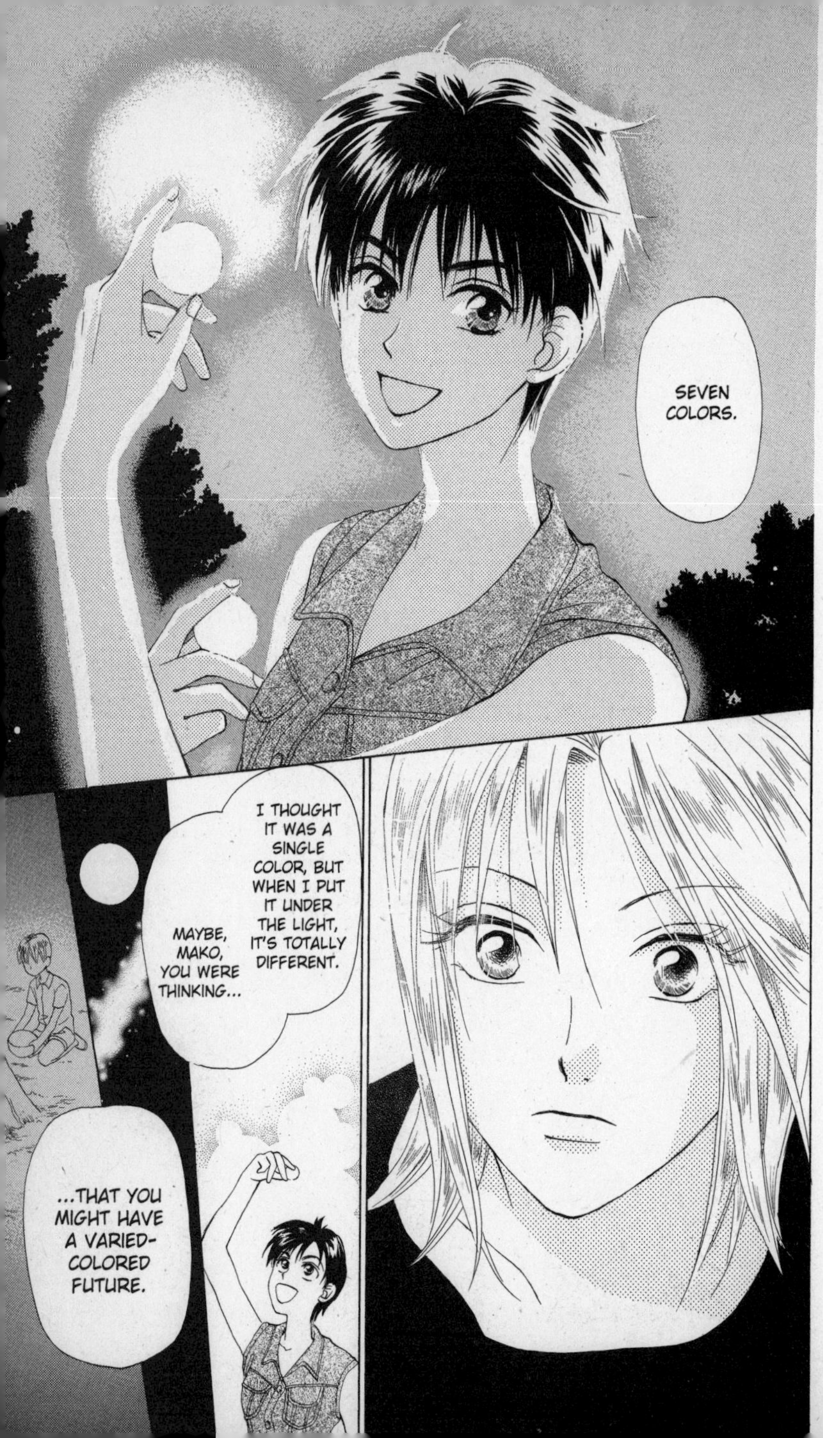
SEVEN COLORS.
I THOUGHT IT WAS A SINGLE COLOR, BUT WHEN I PUT IT UNDER THE LIGHT, IT'S TOTALLY DIFFERENT.
MAYBE, MAKO, YOU WERE THINKING...
...THAT YOU MIGHT HAVE A VARIED-COLORED FUTURE.

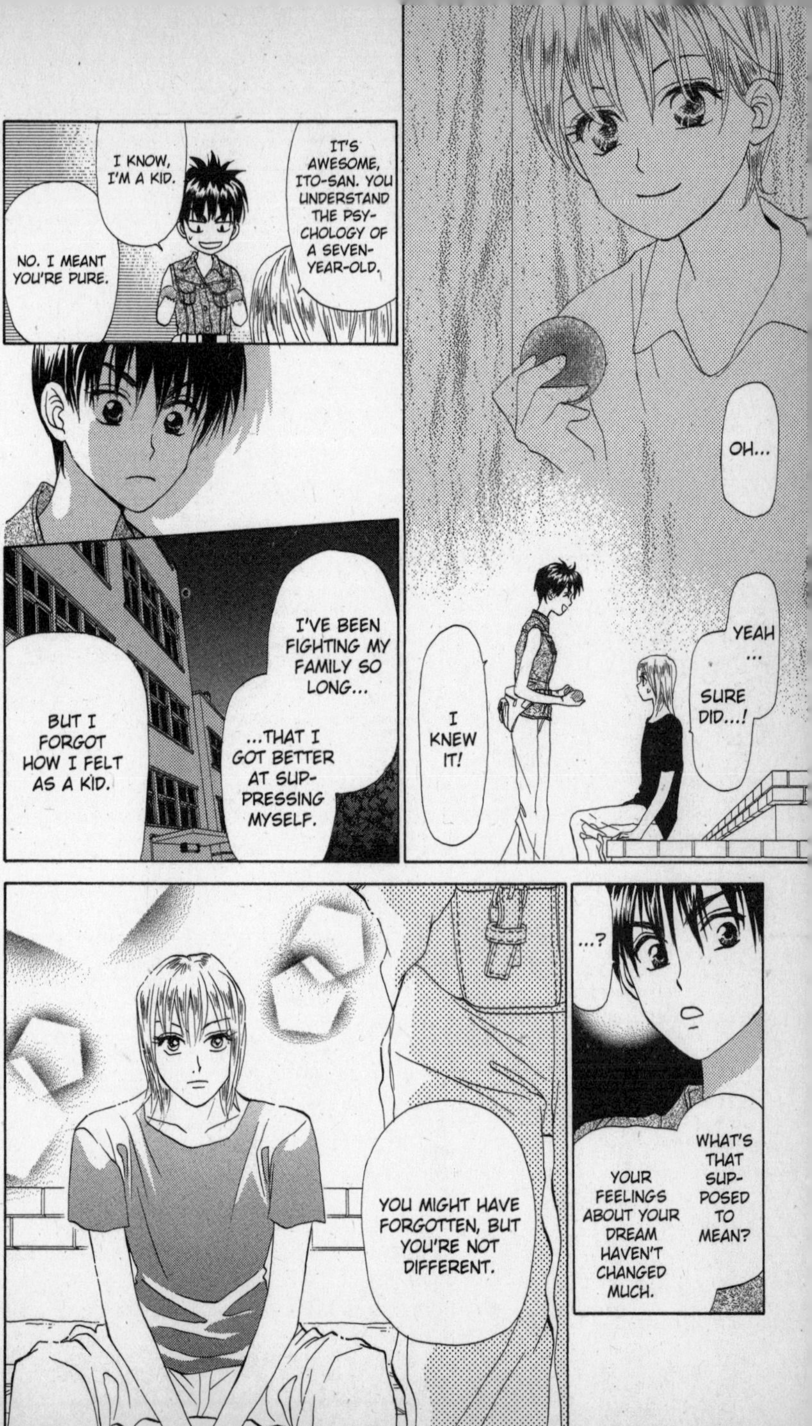
OH...
YEAH... SURE DID...!
I KNEW IT!
IT'S AWESOME, ITO-SAN. YOU UNDERSTAND THE PSY-CHOLOGY OF A SEVEN-YEAR-OLD.
I KNOW, I'M A KID.
NO. I MEANT YOU'RE PURE.
I'VE BEEN FIGHTING MY FAMILY SO LONG...
...THAT I GOT BETTER AT SUP-PRESSING MYSELF.
BUT I FORGOT HOW I FELT AS A KID.
...?
WHAT'S THAT SUP-POSED TO MEAN?
YOUR FEELINGS ABOUT YOUR DREAM HAVEN'T CHANGED MUCH.
YOU MIGHT HAVE FORGOTTEN, BUT YOU'RE NOT DIFFERENT.

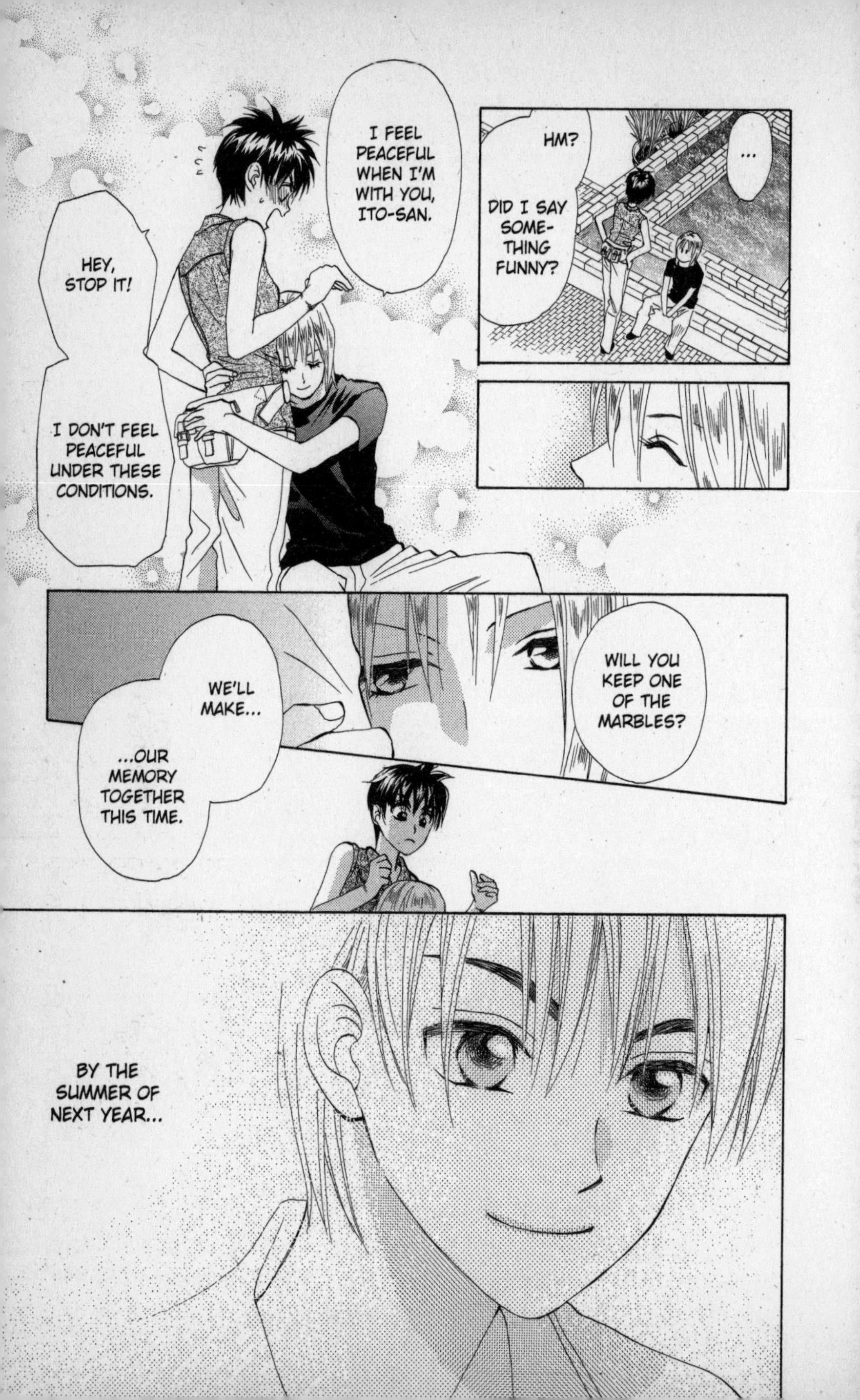
...
HM?
DID I SAY SOME-THING FUNNY?
I FEEL PEACEFUL WHEN I'M WITH YOU, ITO-SAN.
HEY, STOP IT!
I DON'T FEEL PEACEFUL UNDER THESE CONDITIONS.
WILL YOU KEEP ONE OF THE MARBLES?
WE'LL MAKE...
...OUR MEMORY TOGETHER THIS TIME.
BY THE SUMMER OF NEXT YEAR...

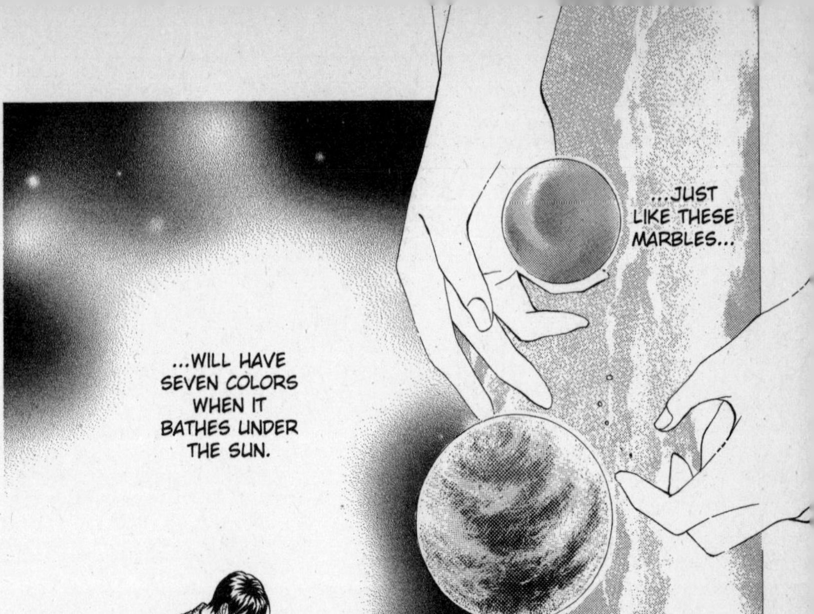
...JUST LIKE THESE MARBLES...
...I WONDER IF MAKOTO'S WORLD...
...WILL HAVE SEVEN COLORS WHEN IT BATHES UNDER THE SUN.

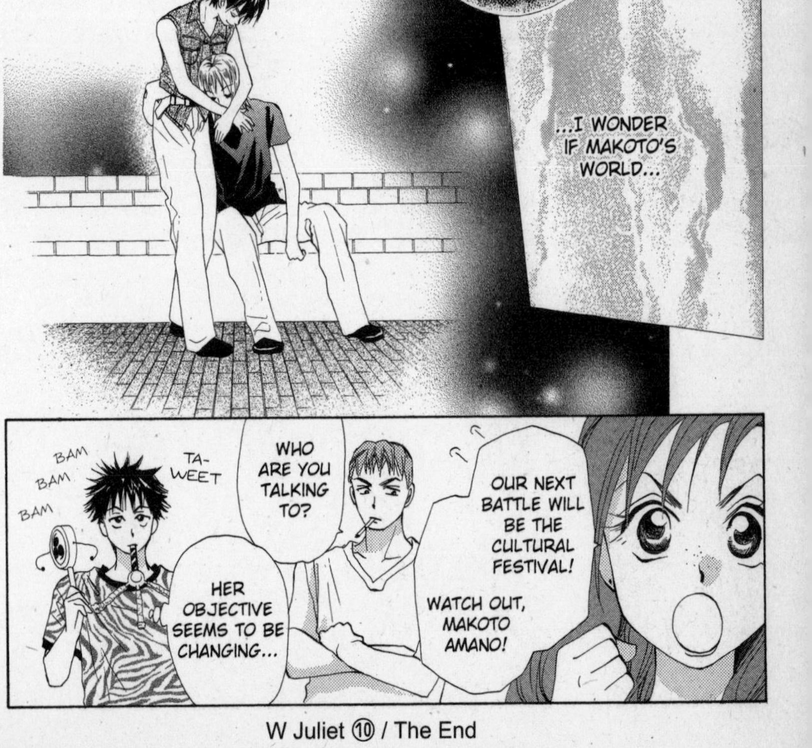
OUR NEXT BATTLE WILL BE THE CULTURAL FESTIVAL!
WATCH OUT, MAKOTO AMANO!
WHO ARE YOU TALKING TO?
HER OBJECTIVE SEEMS TO BE CHANGING...
TA-WEET
BAM
BAM
BAM

W Juliet ⑩ / The End

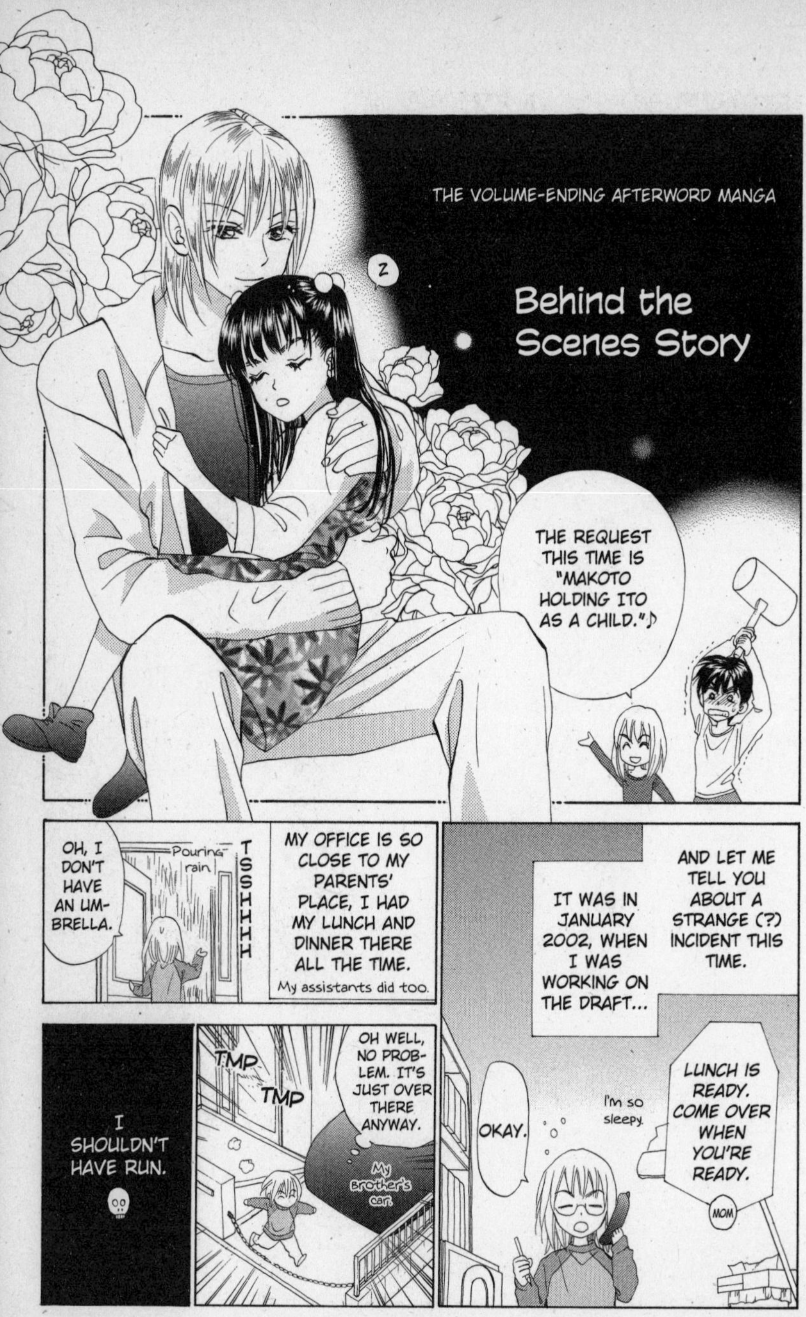
THE VOLUME-ENDING AFTERWORD MANGA
Behind the Scenes Story
Z
THE REQUEST THIS TIME IS "MAKOTO HOLDING ITO AS A CHILD."♪
AND LET ME TELL YOU ABOUT A STRANGE (?) INCIDENT THIS TIME.
IT WAS IN JANUARY 2002, WHEN I WAS WORKING ON THE DRAFT...
LUNCH IS READY. COME OVER WHEN YOU'RE READY.
MOM
I'm so sleepy.
OKAY.
MY OFFICE IS SO CLOSE TO MY PARENTS' PLACE, I HAD MY LUNCH AND DINNER THERE ALL THE TIME.
My assistants did too.
TSSHHHH
Pouring rain
OH, I DON'T HAVE AN UM-BRELLA.
OH WELL, NO PROB-LEM. IT'S JUST OVER THERE ANYWAY.
TMP
TMP
My brother's car.
I SHOULDN'T HAVE RUN.

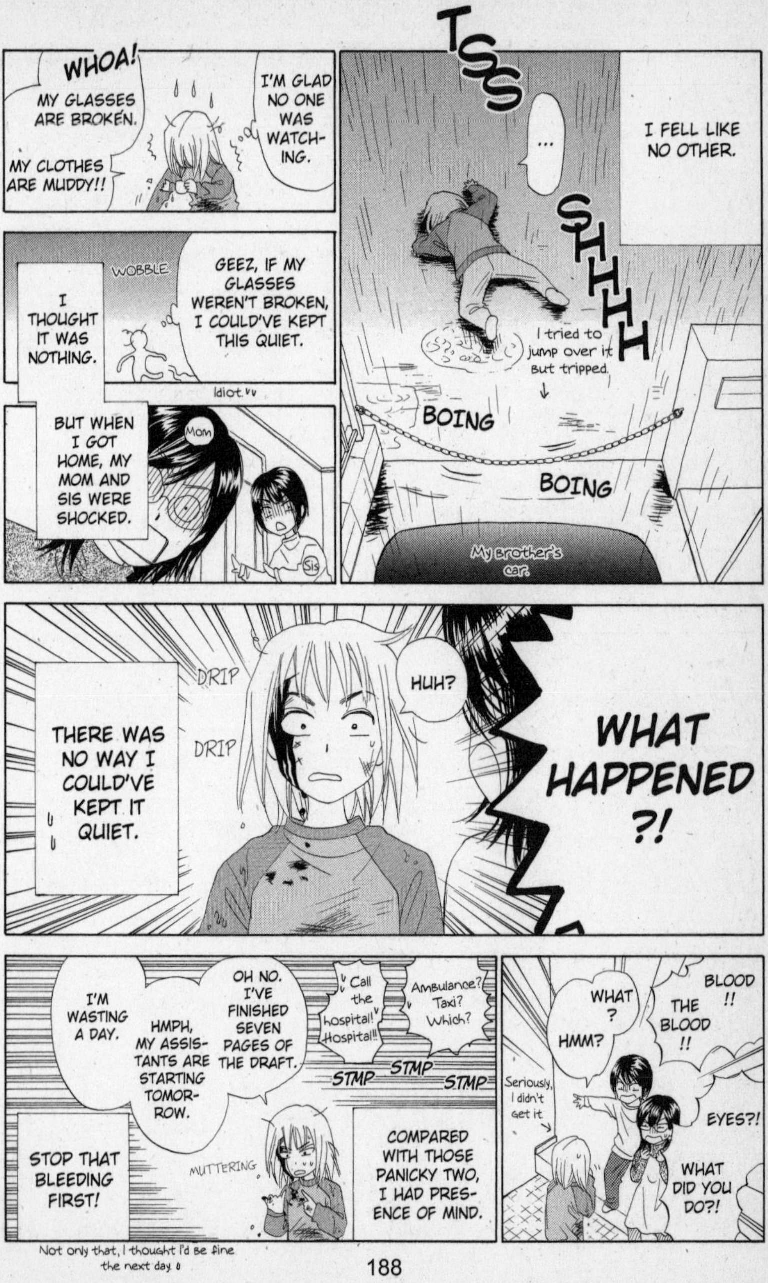
TSSS
...
I FELL LIKE NO OTHER.
SHHHH
I tried to jump over it but tripped.
BOING
BOING
My brother's car.
I'M GLAD NO ONE WAS WATCHING.
WHOA!
MY GLASSES ARE BROKEN.
MY CLOTHES ARE MUDDY!!
GEEZ, IF MY GLASSES WEREN'T BROKEN, I COULD'VE KEPT THIS QUIET.
WOBBLE
I THOUGHT IT WAS NOTHING.
Idiot.
BUT WHEN I GOT HOME, MY MOM AND SIS WERE SHOCKED.
Mom
Sis
WHAT HAPPENED ?!
HUH?
DRIP
DRIP
THERE WAS NO WAY I COULD'VE KEPT IT QUIET.
BLOOD !!
THE BLOOD !!
WHAT ?
HMM?
EYES?!
WHAT DID YOU DO?!
Seriously, I didn't get it
Ambulance? Taxi? Which?
Call the hospital! Hospital!!
OH NO. I'VE FINISHED SEVEN PAGES OF THE DRAFT.
HMPH, MY ASSISTANTS ARE STARTING TOMORROW.
I'M WASTING A DAY.
STMP
STMP
STMP
COMPARED WITH THOSE PANICKY TWO, I HAD PRESENCE OF MIND.
MUTTERING
STOP THAT BLEEDING FIRST!
Not only that, I thought I'd be fine the next day.

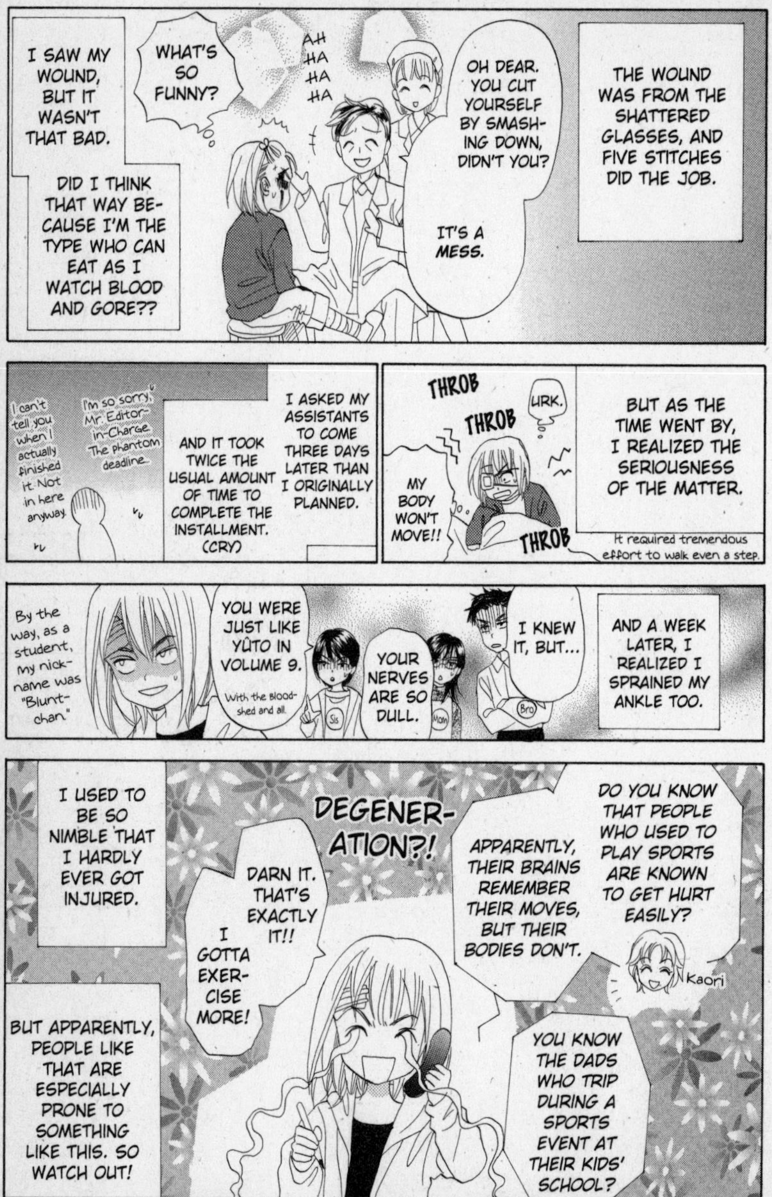
THE WOUND WAS FROM THE SHATTERED GLASSES, AND FIVE STITCHES DID THE JOB.
OH DEAR. YOU CUT YOURSELF BY SMASHING DOWN, DIDN'T YOU?
IT'S A MESS.
AH HA HA HA
WHAT'S SO FUNNY?
I SAW MY WOUND, BUT IT WASN'T THAT BAD.
DID I THINK THAT WAY BECAUSE I'M THE TYPE WHO CAN EAT AS I WATCH BLOOD AND GORE??
BUT AS THE TIME WENT BY, I REALIZED THE SERIOUSNESS OF THE MATTER.
It required tremendous effort to walk even a step.
URK.
THROB
THROB
MY BODY WON'T MOVE!!
THROB
I ASKED MY ASSISTANTS TO COME THREE DAYS LATER THAN I ORIGINALLY PLANNED.
AND IT TOOK TWICE THE USUAL AMOUNT OF TIME TO COMPLETE THE INSTALLMENT. (CRY)
I'm so sorry, Mr. Editor-in-Charge. The phantom deadline.
I can't tell you when I actually finished it. Not in here anyway.
AND A WEEK LATER, I REALIZED I SPRAINED MY ANKLE TOO.
I KNEW IT, BUT...
Bro
YOUR NERVES ARE SO DULL.
Mom
YOU WERE JUST LIKE YÛTO IN VOLUME 9.
With the bloodshed and all.
Sis
By the way, as a student, my nickname was "Blunt-chan."
DO YOU KNOW THAT PEOPLE WHO USED TO PLAY SPORTS ARE KNOWN TO GET HURT EASILY?
APPARENTLY, THEIR BRAINS REMEMBER THEIR MOVES, BUT THEIR BODIES DON'T.
Kaori
DEGENERATION?!
I USED TO BE SO NIMBLE THAT I HARDLY EVER GOT INJURED.
DARN IT. THAT'S EXACTLY IT!!
I GOTTA EXERCISE MORE!
YOU KNOW THE DADS WHO TRIP DURING A SPORTS EVENT AT THEIR KIDS' SCHOOL?
BUT APPARENTLY, PEOPLE LIKE THAT ARE ESPECIALLY PRONE TO SOMETHING LIKE THIS. SO WATCH OUT!

2002. 3. 30. 絵夢羅。 Emura. I've recovered completely. I'm up and running now!

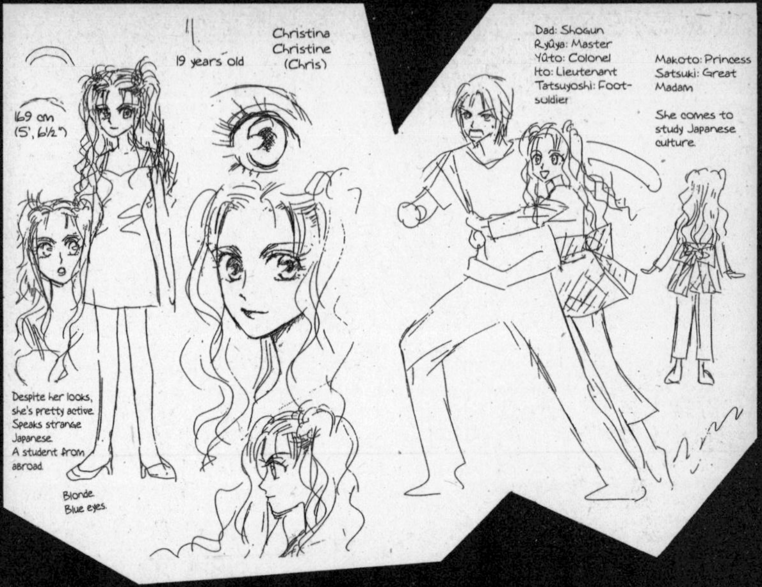
19 years old
Christina
Christine
(Chris)
169 cm
(5', 6½")
Despite her looks, she's pretty active.
Speaks strange Japanese.
A student from abroad.
Blonde.
Blue eyes.
Dad: Shogun
Ryûya: Master
Yûto: Colonel
Ito: Lieutenant
Tatsuyoshi: Foot-soldier
Makoto: Princess
Satsuki: Great Madam
She comes to study Japanese culture.

## Set up & Doodle Time

Chris can't be as tall as 169 cm. I doodled on my sketchbook mostly during 1998. It's unbelievable, but I did none during 2000 and 2001! I must've been cornered by the deadlines.

And this one is the only one from 1999. I don't even know what they're doing.

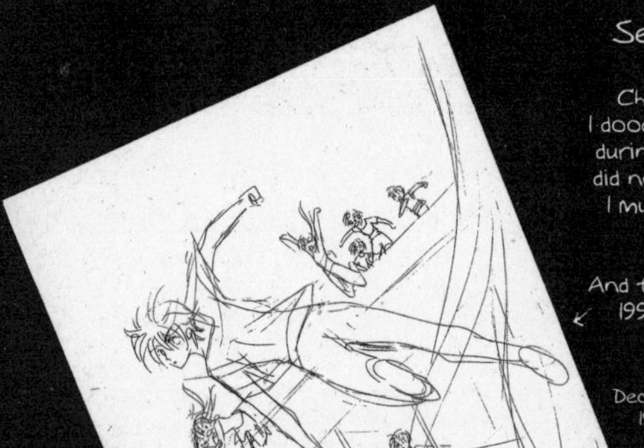
'99. 5. 27

December 1998

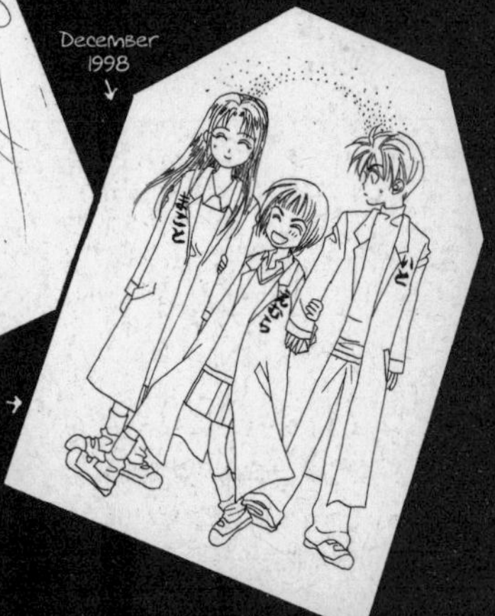

I presented this to Banri-san. I did this because I hear she loves people in white hospital frocks. I do too!

# Cultural Notes

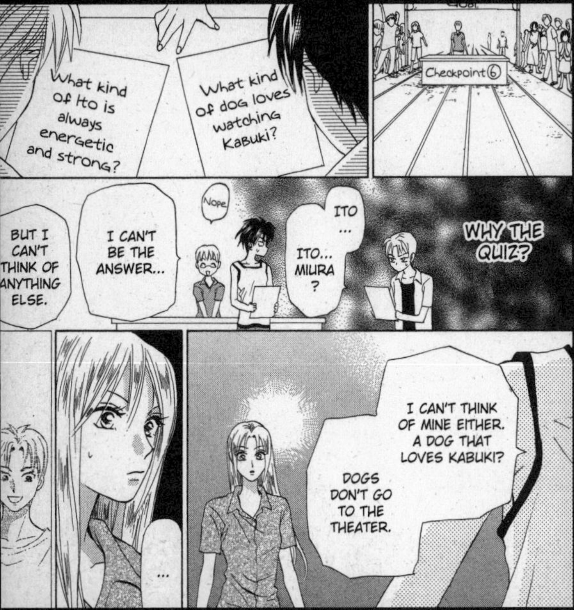
Checkpoint 6
What kind of dog loves watching Kabuki?
What kind of Ito is always energetic and strong?
WHY THE QUIZ?
ITO ...
ITO... MIURA ?
Nope
I CAN'T BE THE ANSWER...
BUT I CAN'T THINK OF ANYTHING ELSE.
I CAN'T THINK OF MINE EITHER. A DOG THAT LOVES KABUKI?
DOGS DON'T GO TO THE THEATER.
...

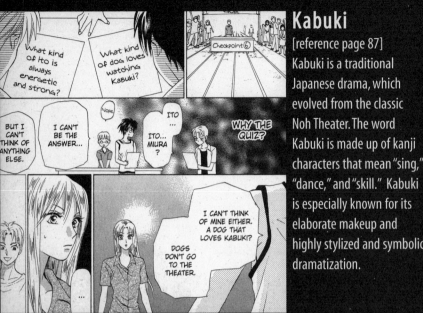

## Kabuki

[reference page 87]

Kabuki is a traditional Japanese drama, which evolved from the classic Noh Theater. The word Kabuki is made up of kanji characters that mean "sing," "dance," and "skill." Kabuki is especially known for its elaborate makeup and highly stylized and symbolic dramatization.

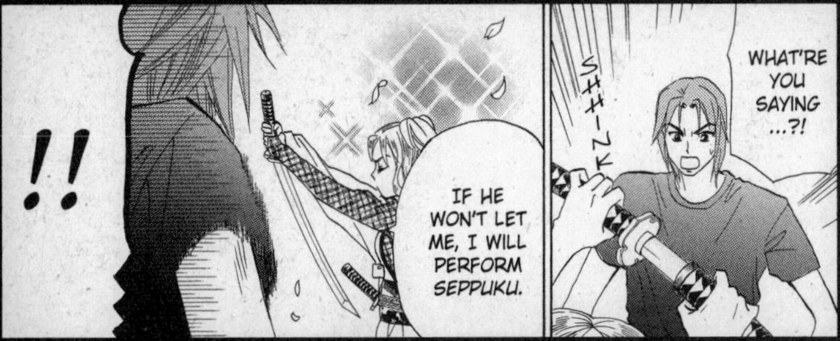
WHAT'RE YOU SAYING ...?!
SHHINK
IF HE WON'T LET ME, I WILL PERFORM SEPPUKU.
!!

## Seppuku

[reference page 140]

Seppuku is also known as "hara-kiri," which literally means cutting the belly. It is the traditional Japanese form of honorable suicide practiced by the feudal warrior class. If you watch samurai films, you're likely to see someone perform seppuku at some point, because it fits perfectly into the traditional code of the Japanese samurai, stressing honor, self-discipline, and bravery.

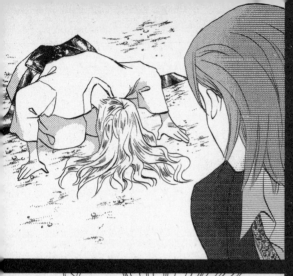

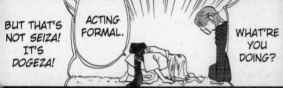

WHAT'RE YOU DOING?
ACTING FORMAL.
BUT THAT'S NOT SEIZA! IT'S DOGEZA!

## Seiza and Dogeza

[reference page 117]

Seiza is the traditional and formal way of sitting in Japan. It is quite polite to sit in seiza style, but it requires some getting used to. Try sitting by kneeling on the floor, resting your buttocks on your heels with the tops of your feet flat on the floor. It definitely is not comfortable. Seiza is also the traditional way of sitting for tea ceremonies, meditation (zazen), Japanese calligraphy (shodo), and flower arrangement (ikebana).

Dogeza dates back to when samurai served Japanese feudal lords, but it is still practiced today under extreme circumstances in which one begs for forgiveness or pleads for consent. The feet and legs are positioned as in seiza. However, unlike seiza, those performing dogeza bow deeply with their face down and hands to the side.

# In Dorm Life, Anything Goes!

When Kazuya's brother marries his love interest – and takes her home to live with them – he escapes to a prestigious all-boys' school. Little did he know that life at Ryokuto Academy's dorm (a.k.a. Greenwood) would be nuttier than his already chaotic existence!

**Only $9.99!**

*Here is Greenwood.*

Story and art by **Yukie Nasu** vol.1

# Here is Greenwood™

## Start your graphic novel collection today!

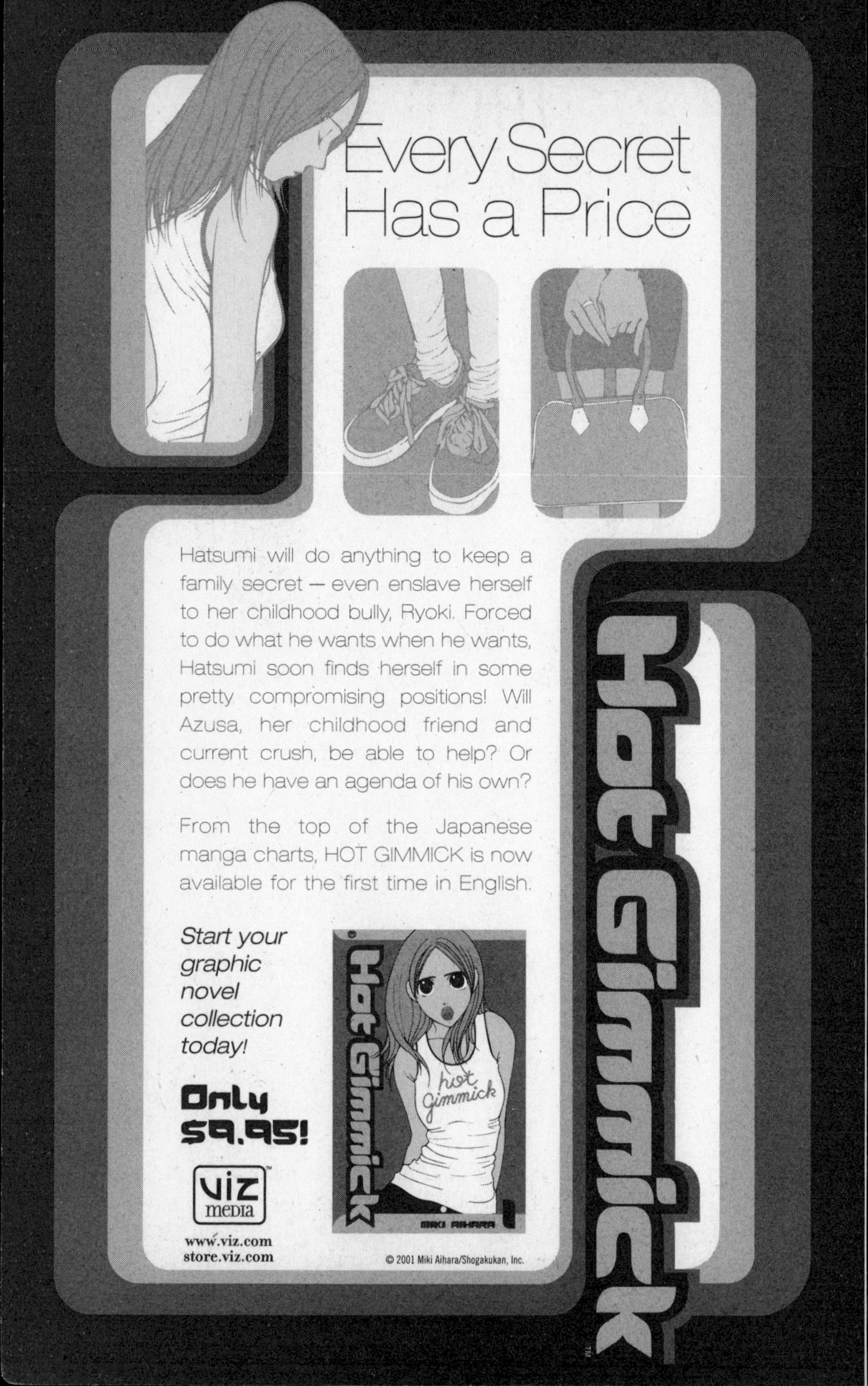
Every Secret Has a Price
Hatsumi will do anything to keep a family secret — even enslave herself to her childhood bully, Ryoki. Forced to do what he wants when he wants, Hatsumi soon finds herself in some pretty compromising positions! Will Azusa, her childhood friend and current crush, be able to help? Or does he have an agenda of his own?
From the top of the Japanese manga charts, HOT GIMMICK is now available for the first time in English.
Start your graphic novel collection today!
Only $9.95!
VIZ media
www.viz.com
store.viz.com
Hot Gimmick
hot gimmick
MIKI AIHARA
© 2001 Miki Aihara/Shogakukan, Inc.
Hot Gimmick

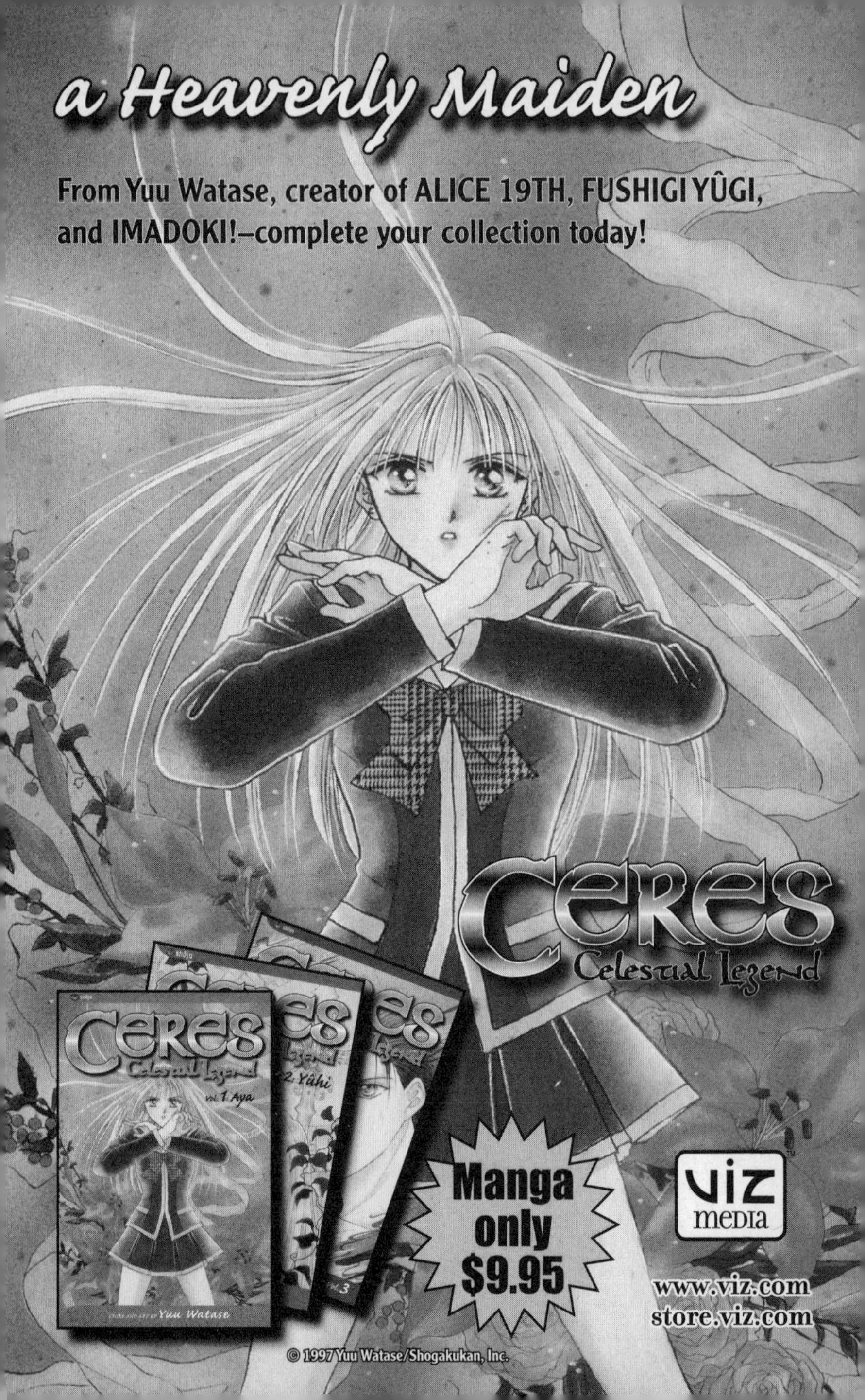
a Heavenly Maiden
From Yuu Watase, creator of ALICE 19TH, FUSHIGI YÛGI, and IMADOKI!–complete your collection today!
Ceres
Celestial Legend
Ceres
Celestial Legend
Vol. 1: Aya
Yuu Watase
Manga only $9.95
viz media
www.viz.com
store.viz.com
© 1997 Yuu Watase/Shogakukan, Inc.

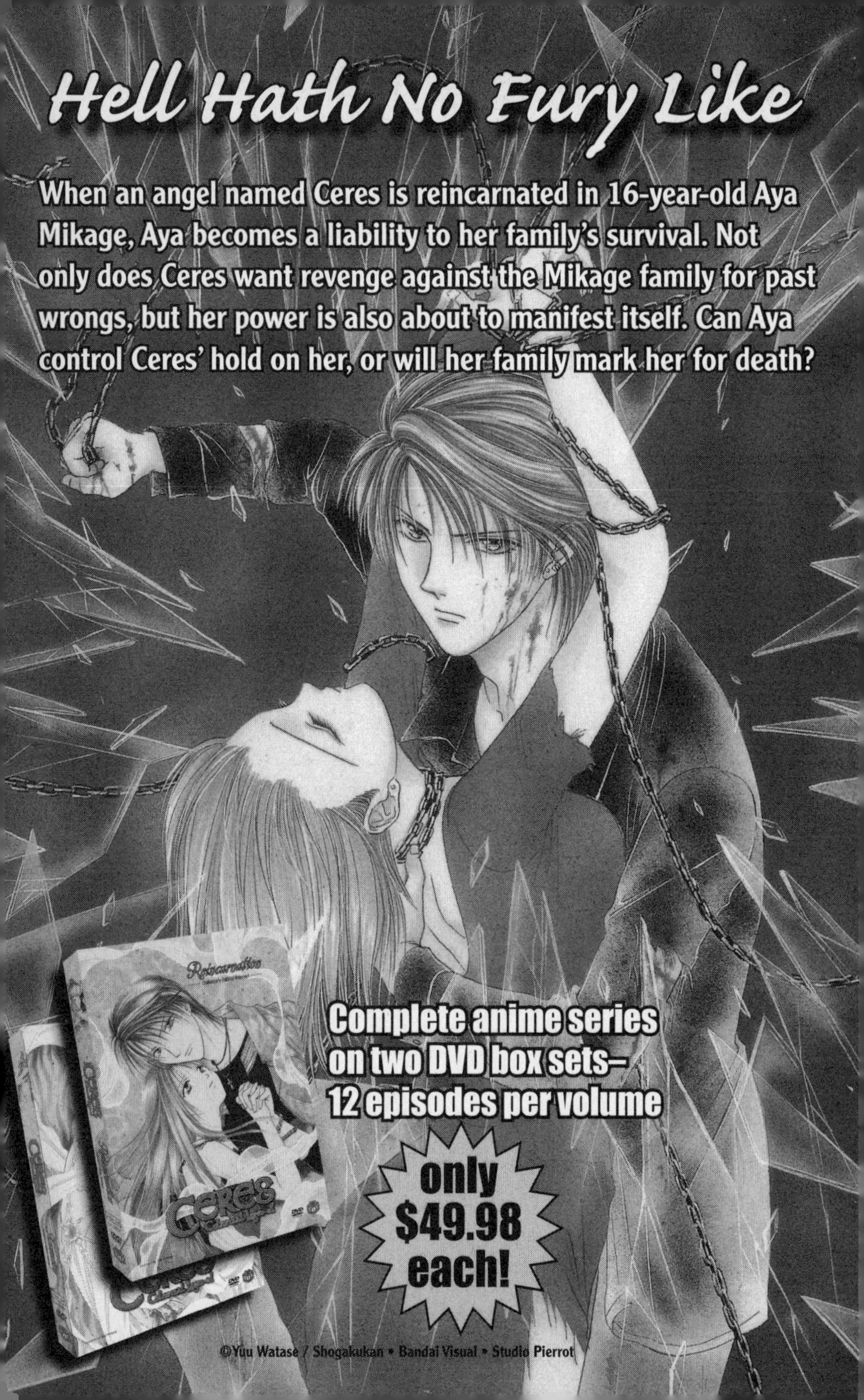
Hell Hath No Fury Like
When an angel named Ceres is reincarnated in 16-year-old Aya Mikage, Aya becomes a liability to her family's survival. Not only does Ceres want revenge against the Mikage family for past wrongs, but her power is also about to manifest itself. Can Aya control Ceres' hold on her, or will her family mark her for death?
Reincarnation
Ceres
Complete anime series on two DVD box sets–12 episodes per volume
only $49.98 each!
©Yuu Watase / Shogakukan • Bandai Visual • Studio Pierrot

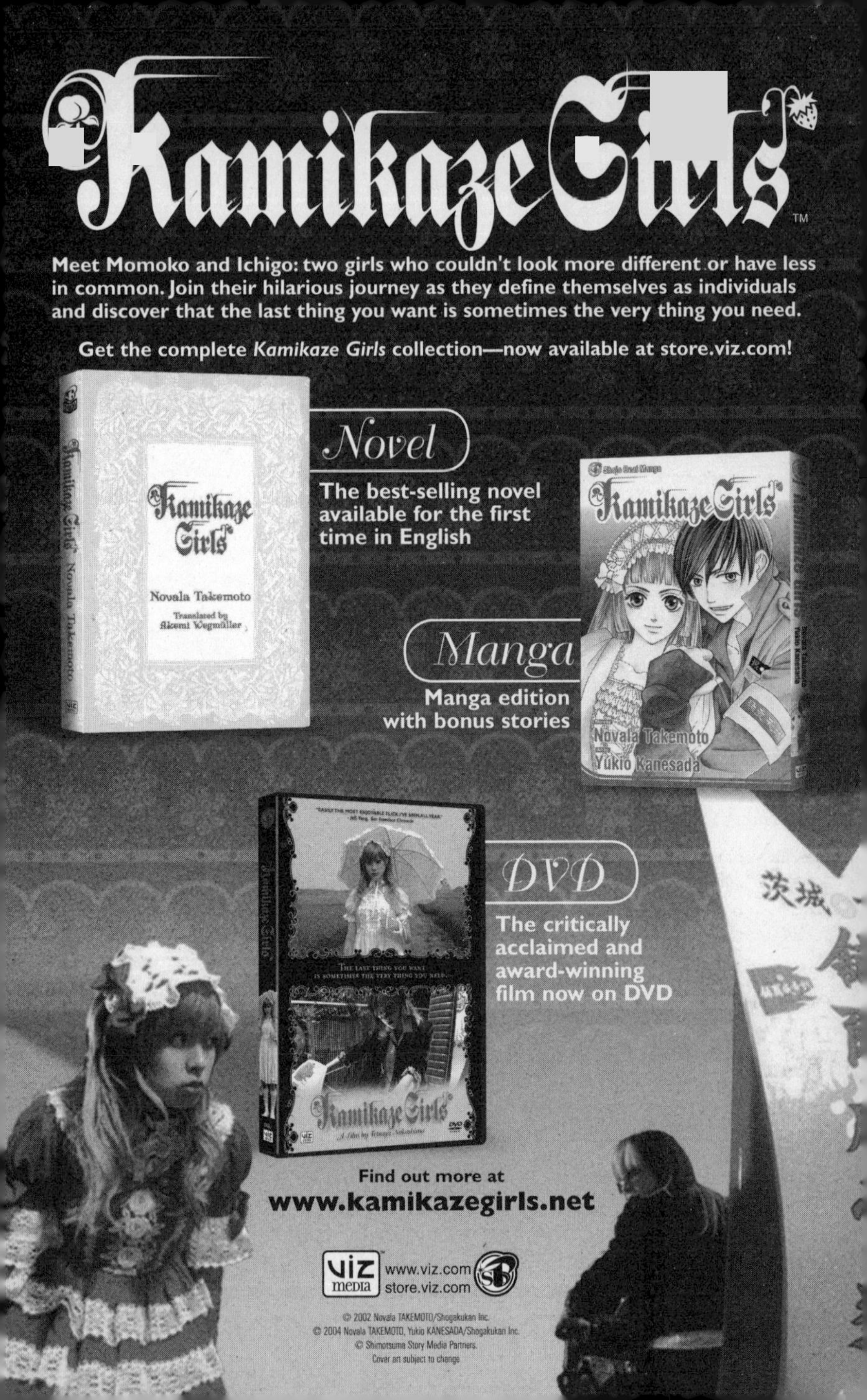
Kamikaze Girls™
Meet Momoko and Ichigo: two girls who couldn't look more different or have less in common. Join their hilarious journey as they define themselves as individuals and discover that the last thing you want is sometimes the very thing you need.
Get the complete Kamikaze Girls collection—now available at store.viz.com!
Novel
The best-selling novel available for the first time in English
Kamikaze Girls
Novala Takemoto
Translated by Akemi Wegmüller
Manga
Manga edition with bonus stories
Kamikaze Girls
Novala Takemoto
Yukio Kanesada
DVD
The critically acclaimed and award-winning film now on DVD
Kamikaze Girls
茨城
Find out more at
www.kamikazegirls.net
viz media
www.viz.com
store.viz.com
© 2002 Novala TAKEMOTO/Shogakukan Inc.
© 2004 Novala TAKEMOTO, Yukio KANESADA/Shogakukan Inc.
© Shimotsuma Story Media Partners.
Cover art subject to change

# LOVE SHOJO?  LET US KNOW!

☐ Please do NOT send me information about VIZ Media products, news and events, special offers, or other information.

☐ Please do NOT send me information from VIZ' trusted business partners.

**Name:** _____

**Address:** _____

**City:** _____ **State:** _____ **Zip:** _____

**E-mail:** _____

☐ **Male** ☐ **Female** **Date of Birth** (mm/dd/yyyy): ___ / ___ / ___ ( Under 13? Parental consent required )

**What race/ethnicity do you consider yourself?** (check all that apply)

☐ White/Caucasian ☐ Black/African American ☐ Hispanic/Latino

☐ Asian/Pacific Islander ☐ Native American/Alaskan Native ☐ Other: _____

**What VIZ shojo title(s) did you purchase?** (indicate title(s) purchased)

_____

**What other shojo titles from other publishers do you own?** _____

_____

**Reason for purchase:** (check all that apply)

☐ Special offer ☐ Favorite title / author / artist / genre

☐ Gift ☐ Recommendation ☐ Collection

☐ Read excerpt in VIZ manga sampler ☐ Other _____

**Where did you make your purchase?** (please check one)

☐ Comic store ☐ Bookstore ☐ Mass/Grocery Store

☐ Newsstand ☐ Video/Video Game Store

☐ Online (site:_____) ☐ Other _____

**How many shojo titles have you purchased in the last year? How many were VIZ shojo titles?**
(please check one from each column)

SHOJO MANGA

☐ None
☐ 1 – 4
☐ 5 – 10
☐ 11+

VIZ SHOJO MANGA

☐ None
☐ 1 – 4
☐ 5 – 10
☐ 11+

**What do you like most about shojo graphic novels?** (check all that apply)

☐ Romance
☐ Comedy
☐ Other _____

☐ Drama / conflict
☐ Real-life storylines

☐ Fantasy
☐ Relatable characters

**Do you purchase every volume of your favorite shojo series?**

☐ Yes! Gotta have 'em as my own
☐ No. Please explain: _____

**Who are your favorite shojo authors / artists?** _____

_____

**What shojo titles would like you translated and sold in English?** _____

_____

**THANK YOU! Please send the completed form to:**

**NJW Research**
ATTN: VIZ Media Shojo Survey
42 Catharine Street
Poughkeepsie, NY 12601